# Dedication

This is dedicated to my Vietnam Band of Brothers.

It is in memory of good friends who didn't come home. They will live in my memory as smiling, fun loving men, forever young, cut down too soon. They have been in my heart, my thoughts and my prayers, my entire life.

It is for the airmen, who never returned to their carriers or bases.

It is in memory of more than 58,000 Americans who risked and lost their lives in the rice paddies, mud, rivers, streams, canals, highlands, skies and jungles of Southeast Asia.

It is for the 153,303 with visible wounds, and hundreds of thousands with wounds no one can see.

It is in honor of veterans who have lived out their lives in hospitals, never to have married or had the blessing of raising children.

It is for homeless veterans.

It is for every day, working veterans who have never been able to put the nightmares of Vietnam behind them, and those who quietly put that time out of their minds and went on to live full and productive lives.

It is for the wives and families who bore the burden of their Vietnam veteran's torment.

It is for fathers and mothers who lost sons, sons and daughters who lost their fathers and wives who saw the promise of a lifetime together with their husbands die with them.

I hope and pray this record meets with their approval.

*"There is no such thing as closure for soldiers who have survived a war. They have an obligation, a sacred duty, to remember those who fell in battle beside them all their days and to bear witness to the insanity that is war."*

Lieutenant General Harold G. Moore

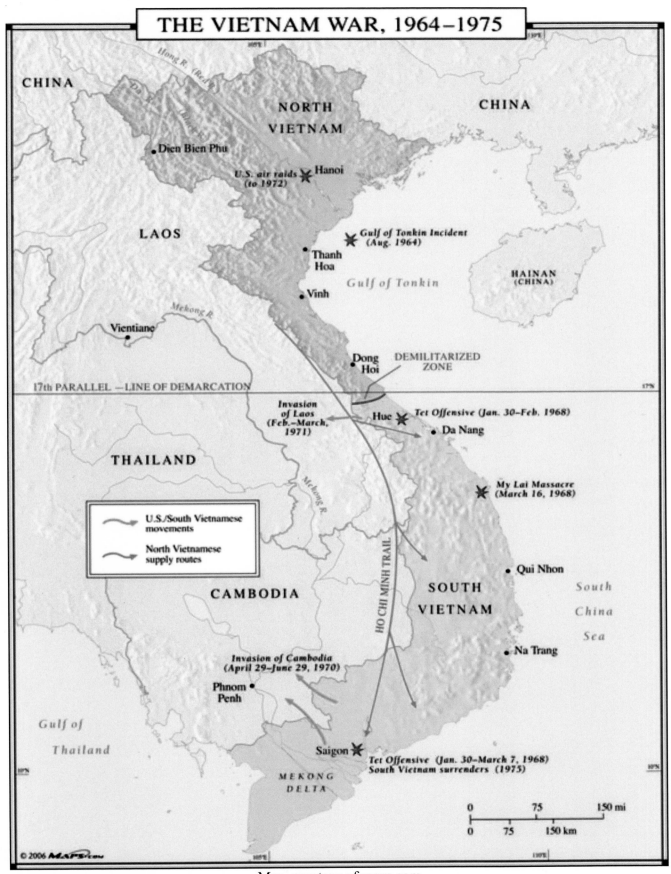

# THE VIETNAM WAR, 1964–1975

**CHINA**

*Hong R. (Red)*

**NORTH VIETNAM**

• Dien Bien Phu

**CHINA**

U.S. air raids ✳ • Hanoi
(to 1972)

**LAOS**

Gulf of Tonkin Incident ✳
(Aug. 1964)

• Thanh Hoa

*Gulf of Tonkin*

**HAINAN (CHINA)**

• Vinh

*Mekong R.*

Vientiane •

Dong Hoi • DEMILITARIZED ZONE

17th PARALLEL — LINE OF DEMARCATION

Invasion of Laos
(Feb.–March, 1971)

Hue • ✳ Tet Offensive (Jan. 30–Feb. 1968)

• Da Nang

**THAILAND**

*Mekong R.*

My Lai Massacre ✳
(March 16, 1968)

→ U.S./South Vietnamese movements

→ North Vietnamese supply routes

**CAMBODIA**

• Qui Nhon

**SOUTH VIETNAM**

*South China Sea*

HO CHI MINH TRAIL

Invasion of Cambodia
(April 29–June 29, 1970)

• Na Trang

Phnom Penh •

*Gulf of Thailand*

Saigon • ✳

Tet Offensive (Jan. 30–March 7, 1968)
South Vietnam surrenders (1975)

**MEKONG DELTA**

| 0 | 75 | 150 mi |
| 0 | 75 | 150 km |

© 2006 MAPS.com

Map, courtesy of maps.com

3

# Contents

# Introduction

One evening in 1985, my wife and I watched an episode of the television series, *"M.A.S.H."* It was an emotional, touching episode, highlighting the bonds men form in combat. It prompted me to call a friend I served with, in the Mekong Delta, in 1968, in the *"The Brown Water Navy."* When he answered the phone, I excitedly said, *"This is Sater! How are you doing?"* He wasn't doing well. He told me he was *"stoned, shacking up, and out of work."* His answer, and the tone of his voice, hit me hard. It meant everything to me that friends who fought alongside me had the happiest lives, possible. I wanted more for men who had been through so much. We ended the awkward conversation, quickly. It was clear he didn't want to reconnect. I was emotional, when I hung up the phone.

At that point, I had not yet fully opened up to my wife about my Vietnam experience.

Seeing my torment, and wanting the best for me, she simply asked,

### *"Why not forget it? It happened long ago!"*

I struggled to find the words to answer her question, and to help her understand. Late that night, I put my thoughts on paper, and gave it to her, the next morning. I don't usually write poems, but this one poured out of me. She cried. That's when I opened up to her about my nightmare of the Mekong, sixteen years after I came home.

# "It Happened Long Ago"

She said, "Why not forget it?  It happened long ago!"
The deepest wounds, cut to the heart,
Will always heal slow.

The nightmare of the Mekong,
Of death, despair and fear,
Could not be left in Vietnam.

It's fresh.

It's crisp.

It's here.

My body's strong.  My mind is sound.
I suffer from no pain,
But once a man has been to war,
He's never quite the same.

For I know war for what it is.
No glory in the fight.
It's friends who die, and crippled kids,
And voices crying in the night.

I know the chill of Monsoon rain,
The heat of tropic sun,
The loneliness and heartache,
The power of a gun.

For some it never happened,
And most will never know.
Except for those who fought the war,
It happened long ago.

Terry Sater, 1985

This book has been in the making for decades, but couldn't be finished, until now. For the first twenty years after coming home from Vietnam, I was too close to it. Later, I couldn't figure out how to tell the story without risking pain, or heartache to those I served with, or their families. I've done my best to avoid that.

*"No event in American history is more misunderstood than the Vietnam War. It was misreported then, and it is misremembered now."*
President Richard M. Nixon

I'm at the point in life that I want to pass the history of *my* slice of the Vietnam War, on to my grandsons; Alexander and Asher. Other Vietnam vets may want to pass it along to their grandchildren, and their grandchildren. We don't know what they will be taught in school, but at least they will have the truth, as someone who was there, saw it. In a few years, my grandchildren will be old enough to read this. In a few years, I, and many of my brother Vietnam veterans will probably be gone. This is the time for this book.

A veteran friend advised me to skip all references to politics. There are many reasons why I should follow his advice, but I believe discussing the Vietnam War, or for that matter, *any* war, without addressing the politics, makes as much sense as writing a drunk driving accident report, without mentioning alcohol.

In this day of *"trigger warnings," "safe spaces,"* and being *"politically correct,"* some of terms here, may offend. They make *ME* cringe. This is a gritty, sometimes irreverent, real account of my Vietnam experience.

One morning, around 1990, my young daughter, Dina, came into our kitchen while I was eating a bowl of cereal. She was reading my diary from Vietnam and was upset that I had used the term *"gook."* She told me, *"Dad, that isn't very nice!"* I was surprised that with everything in my diary, that one word stood out and upset her. At first, I explained that it was a different time and it was during a war in which people were trying to kill me and my friends, while we were trying to stay alive, and kill them. That didn't work, so I tried to take the humorous approach and said it didn't mean anything more than a list of other racist terms that I rattled off. At that point, I fell on the floor, laughing at my feeble attempt at comedy. She looked down at me, totally disgusted. Then, I explained that she felt the way she did, because that was the way we raised her. I considered editing those terms out, but decided against it. It was the 60's. We were at war and I was just a kid. I wouldn't use those terms, today, but if I changed them here, it would be dishonest and cowardly.

I'm not a war hero. I did nothing heroic, but many that I served with, *were* heroes. I did nothing extraordinary, but I served in an extraordinary and historical unit. Some that I served with died. Most were wounded. My wounds are the haunting memories of young lives wasted in a cause our country couldn't commit to win decisively, but wouldn't disengage from, either. They just kept us there, in the meat grinder. I am a witness to war, passing on my perspectives and experiences. I saw the war from two different angles. During 1966 and 1967, I served on the largest warship in the world, and at the time, the world's only nuclear powered aircraft carrier, the USS Enterprise. "The Big E" launched combat aircraft on *"Yankee Station,"* off the coast of North Vietnam, in the South China Sea. Later, I fought in close combat, in the Mekong Delta, aboard what was jokingly called the world's smallest aircraft carrier, an armored troop carrier, with a helo pad. This isn't just MY story. It is the story of many people, living and dead. I am here to tell *our* story.

The words and pictures that follow are from letters, my diary, personal audiotapes, official military records, books, and historical information from the Mobile Riverine Force Association. In some cases, I melded sources together, such as blending the details of an official operations report, into an entry in my diary, in order to provide a narrative that would be easier to follow. Other times, I added memories that weren't in my diary, but actually happened. Again, I did that simply to make it easier to read and follow.

In essence, I have taken pieces of a very old jigsaw puzzle and put it together, to the best of my ability. Some of the jigsaw pieces are old and faded. Some are missing. I tried to make them fit, in order to give you a better picture of what we went through. If I wasn't exactly sure where a piece of the puzzle went, I put it where my best guess told me it belonged. I am grateful to Lt. J.G. Robert B. Conaty, one of the officers of River Assault

Squadron 13, who was kind enough to send me his personal journal, which offered many details on operations that were not available to me, otherwise.

My letters home represented a different world than the one I kept in my diary. I kept the dark reality of Vietnam to myself, captured in my diary, until I no longer could stand to record it there. You will understand why.

In my diary, I recorded the capricious malevolence that struck those around me. In letters home, I was on uneventful patrols and having fun times with my friends. Many of those who lightened my heart with letters from home are gone now, but in their letters, they live on, connected to future generations. When I was in Vietnam, the seemingly mundane life I read about in letters were like rays of light, in a dark world. I cherished every word of normal, *"boring"* life, back home. As I wrote this book, I was struck by the contrast between the normality and saneness of the world at home and the humid, violent, and dangerous foreign world I lived in.

Woven into the fabric of this history of Vietnam and the 60's, is my family's history. The letters to me, from home, may seem trivial to some. I ask you to read them not as you are now, in a comfortable chair, in your soft bed, or on a beach. Imagine reading them far from home, lonely, dirty, tired, sweaty, seeing death and misery, and not knowing if you will ever see home, again. You are building emotional calluses, as a coping mechanism. You joke about death and dying. As you read them, imagine yourself knowing that with one careless misstep, you may fall into the Mekong, your mouth, throat and lungs filling with muddy brown water, while your body is swept away. The mundane and the trivial news from home meant that somebody, somewhere, cared about you. Imagine that you know from newspapers that many Americans at home thought you were a ruthless monster, a *"Baby Killer."* They didn't know you, or what you were going through, but they *hated* you.

As I write this, I am much older than my mother and father were, when I was in Vietnam. My children are roughly twice the age I was, when I was in Vietnam. As a father, I know it must have been harder for my mother and father, than it was for me. It was harder for my girlfriend, Judi, than it was on me.

I've always enjoyed reading personal accounts of past wars. Movies tend to focus on the *"glory"* of war. History books have a way of making war a sterile, impersonal thing. They don't fully impart the humanity or, inhumanity of war. History addresses the causes, strategies, and statistics of war. They don't convey the stifling heat, the loneliness, the fear, or the courage. They leave out the crying voices of innocent children and battle fatigued men. They don't express the bonds of men who face life and death together on a daily basis. Sterile history books are more likely to tell of the statistics of war than daily bouts of dysentery, ringworm, *"jungle rot,"* or infections that can threaten life or limb in hours. They don't show the crazy things you do in war to occupy your mind and lighten your heart.

In 1965, I was living a carefree life. It was the year I graduated from Mercy High School. I worked and I partied, but I never knew anyone who had been killed, or used drugs. My life was a cross between the T.V. series, *"Happy Days,"* and the movie, *"American Graffiti."* I was a poor student, but I had fun. A friend of mine heard teachers talking in the hall, one day. One teacher was telling the other that *"Terry Sater will never amount to anything because he doesn't have a serious bone in his body."* At that time, it was probably true.

Most of my buddies had nice cars. Frank Judge had a '60, white Corvette, hard-top convertible, with red scoops and a red interior. It was awesome. John Brune had a '47 Chevy coup. Very nice. Jerry Kochner had a white '59 Chevy Impala that was pristine. Tom Donovan had a red, 1960 Plymouth Valiant, with *"three on the floor."* It wasn't too flashy, but it was far above what I drove. I had to borrow my father's 1958 white and red Edsel station wagon. It had a push button automatic in the center of the column. The bench seats were worn, and you had to put towels across them, to keep the springs from snagging your clothes. It was embarrassing.

My first memories of Vietnam go back to nebulous *"background noise,"* as I graduated high school. I heard about a conflict *"over there,"* but really didn't know what it was about. Older men than I were planning my generation's path towards our destiny in Vietnam. Most Americans couldn't even <u>find</u> Vietnam on a map. The notion of the U.S. getting embroiled in a long war that would take over 58,000 lives was inconceivable.

As I was working and going to college, it occurred to me that if I didn't do well enough in school, I could be drafted. My father, Dale, had served in the occupation forces, in Italy, as a Tech 5 Sargent. The Army didn't appeal to me. I didn't like the idea of sloshing through the jungle and I knew the Navy offered good training. My older brother, Tom, had served in the Navy. When he joined the Navy at seventeen, I was eleven. I had a kid brother's hero worship and hung on every word of his wild and exotic Navy exploits. I thought his uniform was *"cool."* His ship, the destroyer, USS Furse, DDR 882, cruised the Atlantic and the Mediterranean. It was part of the U.S. naval blockade, during the Cuban Missile Crisis.

During the summer of '65, Larry Lapp, a friend who belonged to a nearby church's "Young Adults Club," introduced me to some of his friends. He drove me to Phil and "Gussie" Simon's home. Mr. and Mrs. Simon were on the front porch. Phil had a cigar in one hand and a whiskey and water in the other. He had a hearty laugh. I liked him immediately. His wife had a warm and friendly manner that made me feel at home. I didn't know it at the time, but Larry had gone into the house, to fix me up with their sixteen year old daughter, Judi. Unseen, she peeked out of the window and told Larry, *"Are you JOKING? He has glasses!"* As Mr. and Mrs. Simon and I sat on the porch, talking and laughing, Judi rushed by, putting a scarf over her light brown hair and curlers. We were abruptly introduced, as she passed by. I can't, or won't say which I noticed first, her beautiful blue eyes, or her shape. Either way, she was only sixteen. I was an older college man of eighteen.

In time, I got to know her brother, Steve, and her sister, Fran. I started enjoying many activities with their church group. We had campouts, car rallies, and parties. In the background, there was always news of the vague, incipient conflict, in some strange land, across the Pacific, in Southeast Asia.

In mid-December, the ASYA Club went Christmas caroling. Judi and I got into the back seat of my friend Ed Bahr's car, who was with Judi's cousin, Bobbie Antel. I put a box of mistletoe over Judi's head and kissed her. Since it *was* a whole box of mistletoe, I was able to negotiate more than one kiss.

My first *"official"* date with Judi was two weeks later, on New Year's Eve, December 31, 1965. We spent the entire night partying with her brother, Steve, his girlfriend, Pat, and Ed and Bobbie. Judi was a lot of fun, and we hit it off pretty quickly. She also had a kiss that had us celebrating *"Happy New Year"* for every time zone, until we all attended Mass services together, the next morning.

As the war and the draft heated up, my friends and I had to make serious and difficult choices. The choices were to either risk being drafted into the Army and hope that we weren't sent to Vietnam, or join the Air Force or Navy. Two of my best friends decided to risk the draft. John Brune was drafted into the Army and received orders to Germany. Frank Judge was drafted, and spent most of his two years in Colorado. In April, of 1966, John Bailey and I joined the Navy on the *"Buddy Plan,"* as well as their *"120 Day Plan,"* which meant that I would leave for Boot Camp, on July 10th.

It was during those 120 days that I fell in love with Judi. I couldn't turn back. I had signed the papers and was committed. It was during 1966 that The Righteous Brothers came out with their song, *"Soul and Inspiration."* It said everything about how I felt about Judi. She loved me enough to sit next to me in a '58 Edsel station wagon! Where could I find another girl who would do that? I had a difficult time imagining her waiting for me for four years, but I prayed she would.

# Preface
# Our Path into the Quagmire

One motivation in writing this book was to gain a better personal understanding of how we as a country, got involved in Vietnam. I searched for one decision, or one monumental moment, that would explain why we fought the war in Vietnam. For some, the research may have been a difficult and painful journey. For me, it was enlightening and cathartic. I have a better understanding of what happened, when it happened, and why it happened. There was no ONE decision, or one moment that clearly marked our way down that path. The list of ingredients in our recipe for involvement in Vietnam is more like a *"witches brew"* of many things.

**1847-1862**. France gained control of Vietnam, making it their colony.

**May 19, 1890**. Nguyen Sinh Cung was born in central Vietnam.

**1901**. The Socialist Party of America, a democratic-socialist and social-democratic political party in the United States, formed in 1901 by a merger between the three-year-old Social Democratic Party of America and disaffected elements of the Socialist Labor Party which had split from the main organization in 1899.

**1919**. Nguyen Sinh Cung petitioned for independence at the Versailles Peace Treaty talks that ended World War I. He was ignored.

**September 1, 1919**. The Communist Party of the United States of America was founded.

**November 6, 1927**. *"Communism is like Prohibition. It's a good idea, but it won't work."* Will Rogers

**February 3, 1930**. Nguyen Sinh Cung presided over a meeting establishing the Vietnamese Communist Party.

*"It doesn't matter a jot if three-fourths of mankind perish! The only thing that matters is that, in the end, the remaining fourth should become communist."* Vladimir Lenin.

**May, 1941**. Nguyen Sinh Cung adopted the nom de guerre *"Ho Chi Minh,"* or, *"Bringer of Light."* Ho formed the Vietnamese Independence League, or Vietminh. In later years, the South Vietnamese government gave it the derisive label of *"Viet Cong."*

**1941**. The U.S. military intelligence agency Office of Strategic Services, or "OSS" formed an alliance with Ho Chi Minh and the Viet Minh guerillas, against Japanese troops occupying Vietnam during WWII.

**March 9, 1945**. The Japanese installed Bao Dai as their puppet after ousting the French colonial government.

**May 8, 1945**. Victory in Europe Day, generally known as V-E Day, VE Day or simply V Day. The Allies of World War II accepted the unconditional surrender of Nazi (National Socialist German Workers' Party) Germany's unconditional surrender of its armed forces. This marked the end of World War II in Europe.

**July, 1945**. The allies divided Vietnam at the 16th parallel. Chinese Nationalists disarmed the Japanese north of the parallel. The British did the same thing south of the 16th parallel. During the Potsdam Conference in Germany, the United States, Great Britain, the Soviet Union and other allies received a request from France for the return of all French colonies in Indochina. Virtually all of Southeast Asia, Vietnam, Laos and Cambodia all returned to being French colonies.

**August 1945**. Japan surrendered unconditionally. Vietnam's emperor, Bao Dai, abdicated. Ho Chi Minh's guerrillas proclaimed a provisional government in Hanoi.

**September 2, 1945**. The USS Missouri served as the stage for the surrender of Japan, in Tokyo Bay.

**September 2, 1945**. Ho Chi Minh proclaimed the independence of Vietnam, saying, *"We hold the truth that all men are created equal, that they are endowed by their Creator with certain unalienable rights, among them life, liberty and the pursuit of happiness. This immortal statement is extracted from the Declaration of Independence of the United States of America in 1776. These are undeniable truths."*

**September 26, 1945**. Viet Minh guerrillas who mistake him for a French officer killed Lt. Colonel A. Peter Dewey, an OSS officer. Before his death, Dewey filed a report stating his opinion that the U.S. "ought to clear out of Southeast Asia."

**March 5, 1946**. At Westminster College, Fulton, Missouri, Winston Churchill gave his *"Iron Curtain"* speech. *"From Stettin in the Baltic to Trieste in the Adriatic, an iron curtain has descended across the Continent."*

**December 19, 1946**. 30,000 Viet Minh launched a large-scale attack against the French in Hanoi.

**February 7, 1950**. Senator Joseph R. McCarthy charged that the U.S. State Department harbored Communists, launching the era of *"McCarthyism."* McCarthy's crusade caused politicians, celebrities and the media to fear appearing *"soft"* on Communism.

**June 27, 1950**. President Harry S. Truman ordered, *"...acceleration in the furnishing of military assistance to the forces of France and the Associated States of Indochina (i.e., Cambodia, Laos and Vietnam) and the dispatch of a military mission to provide close working relations with those forces."*

**June 30, 1950**. President Harry S. Truman ordered U.S. troops into Korea following North Korea's invasion of the South. He also sent 35 U.S. troops to Vietnam as Military Advisors.

**December 23, 1950**. Vietnam, Cambodia, Laos, France and the U.S. signed a *"unified pact of common interest."*

**By the end of 1951, French casualties in Vietnam exceeded 90,000.**

**July 27, 1953**. The Korean War ended in an armistice, dividing the country at the 38th parallel. The lines of truce stand to this day.

**January 5, through February 16, 1954**. In over a dozen ambushes fourteen French naval craft (The predecessor to the American Mobile Riverine Force) are sunk or damaged, with nearly 100 men killed or wounded by the Viet Minh during the French occupation of Vietnam.

**March 13, 1954**. 12,000 French forces were surrounded by 75,000 Viet Minh at Dien Bien Phu. When the French asked the U.S. for help, President Eisenhower warned Congress that the loss of Indochina would set off a chain reaction of nations falling in Southeast Asia "like a row of dominoes." The administration did not receive support from Congress for intervention.

**May 7, 1954**. 9,500 French at Dien Bien Phu surrendered. The last French radio message is, *"We're blowing up everything. Adieu."*

**July 20th and 21st, 1954**. The Geneva Accords were signed by the French and Viet Minh, establishing the independence of Laos and Cambodia, while splitting Vietnam along the 17th parallel. The demilitarized zone was created and a cease-fire agreed to. The French withdrew from north of the DMZ. Ho Chi Minh set up a

Democratic Republic, with nationwide elections scheduled for two years later. The U.S. refused to sign the accords.

**September 8, 1954**. The South East Asia Treaty Organization (SEATO) was formed to coordinate protection of the area against communism.

**October 9, 1954**. The last French troops left Hanoi. Vietnam, Laos and Cambodia had been French colonies since the late 1800's. Ho Chi Minh assumed power the next day.

**January 1, 1955**. The United States began direct aid to South Vietnam.

**January 24, 1955**. *"(Communism is) the opiate of the intellectuals…. But no cure, except as a guillotine might be called a cure for a case of dandruff."* Claire Boothe Luce, Newsweek

**October 26, 1955**. Ngo Dinh Diem declared himself President of the Republic of South Vietnam.

**August 1, 1956**. *"Vietnam represents the cornerstone of the Free World in Southeast Asia. It is our offspring. We cannot abandon it, we cannot ignore its needs."* Senator John F. Kennedy

**September 5, 1956**. President Eisenhower sent U.S. advisers to train the South Vietnamese Army.

We should never have had Ho Chi Minh as our enemy. He petitioned for independence for Vietnam at the Versailles Peace Treaty. We ignored him and supported the colonialist desires of the hapless French. Ho was an ally, in our fight against the Japanese in WWII. He quoted the American Declaration of Independence in his own Declaration of Independence. We looked the other way when Diem did not hold elections in 1956, as promised in the Geneva Accord. We weren't supporting democracy. We supported the colonialist French and a series of corrupt dictators and opportunists.

**October 4, 1957**. The Soviet Union launched Sputnik I, a basketball sized 183-pound satellite. The American public feared the Sputnik launch would develop into the eventual threat of intercontinental ballistic missiles.

**October, 1957**. The first guerrilla attacks against Diem's government were launched.

**January 1959**. North Vietnam endorsed the resumption of armed struggle in South Vietnam. Soon after, construction began on a network of roads and trails that would someday be known as "The Ho Chi Minh Trail."

**July 8, 1959**. Vietminh guerrillas fired on a South Vietnamese Army mess hall, near Bien Hoa, twenty miles northwest of Saigon, killing two Vietnamese soldiers, an eight year old boy, and two American soldiers. Major Dale Buis and Master Sergeant Chester Ovnand were the first Americans to die in what would be called the Vietnam era. Nine years later, the Mobile Riverine Force operated in the area.

**July 17, 1959**. Lying, to avoid American opposition to his revolution, Fidel Castro declares, *"I am not a communist and neither is the revolutionary movement, but we do not have to say that we are anticommunists just to fawn on foreign powers."*

**May 1, 1960**. Francis Gary Powers U-2 spy plane was shot down by a SAM-2 missile, over the Soviet Union. President Eisenhower learned on May 7th, that Powers was alive.

**December 31, 1960**. The American military commitment to South Vietnam totaled 900 advisors.

Many partisans try to put the responsibility for the Vietnam War on President Dwight D. Eisenhower. Although he had some hand in it, the United States was not really in a *"war,"* until the presidency of John F. Kennedy. Even though Eisenhower sent advisors to South Vietnam, that in no way obligated President Kennedy to send combat troops to Vietnam. We will never know what action President John F. Kennedy would have taken if he had lived, but it was under his presidency that it became our war. That is not to disparage him. I have actually always admired him. It is simply fact.

**January 20, 1961**. In his inaugural address, John F. Kennedy declared,
"Let every nation know, whether it wishes us well or ill, that we shall pay any price, bear any burden, meet any hardship, support any friend, oppose any foe to assure the survival and the success of liberty."

**January, 1961**. The first American combat soldier was killed in action in Vietnam. By year-end, American troop strength was at 3,200 men.

**April 17, 1961**. Approximately 1,300 members of a CIA-supported counter-revolutionary Cuban exile force invaded the beaches of Playa Girón (Girón beach), on the east bank of the Bahia de Cochinos (Bay of Pigs).

**May, 1961**. French President Charles De Gaulle to President Kennedy, referencing Vietnam. *"I predict to you that you will, step by step, be sucked into a bottomless military and political quagmire."*

**May 13, 1961**. President Kennedy sent 100 "Special Forces" personnel to South Vietnam.

**June, 1961**. *"Now, we have a problem in making our power credible, and Vietnam is the place."* John F. Kennedy, following the Kennedy – Khrushchev meeting in Vienna

**August 13, 1961**. Construction of the Berlin Wall began.

**September 21, 1961**. The Army's 5th Special Forces Group was activated at Fort Bragg, S.C.

**December 2, 1961**. Americans should remember, communists don't always admit to being communists, when they are just getting started. Fidel Castro waited until he felt the time was right, to declare, *"I am a Marxist-Leninist and shall be one until the end of my life."* He went on to state, *"Marxism or scientific socialism has become the revolutionary movement of the working class. If we had paused to tell the people that we were Marxist-Leninists while we were on Pico Turquino and not yet strong, it is possible that we would never have been able to descend to the plains."*

**December 11, 1961**. Thirty-three helicopters and four hundred air and ground crew arrived in South Vietnam aboard the U.S. Aircraft carrier USS Core. By year's end, the U.S. had 3,200 military personnel in Vietnam.

**January 11, 1962**. In his State of the Union Address, John F. Kennedy said, *"Few generations in all of history have been granted the role of being the great defender of freedom in its maximum hour of danger. This is our good fortune."*

**February 8, 1962**. The U.S. military headquarters opened in Saigon. From 1960 through 1962, thirty-two U.S. military personnel lost their lives in South Vietnam.

**February 22, 1962**. The South Vietnamese Diem regime was corrupt, ineffective and unpopular. Early in the morning, two South Vietnamese pilots, who had taken off in a sortie that appeared to be directed at Vietcong in the Mekong Delta, instead dropped their payload of bombs and napalm on Diem's presidential palace. Diem and his family escaped.

*"Fairness"* has become a central concept of political campaign rhetoric in politics, but it is now, has always been, and will continue to be elusive in economics, in war, or in life. That fact was best articulated by John F. Kennedy, on **March 21, 1962.**

*"There is always inequity in life. Some men are killed in a war and some men are wounded, and some men never leave the country, and some men are stationed in the Antarctic and some are stationed in San Francisco. It's very hard in military or in personal life to assure complete equality. Life is unfair."*

14

**May, 1962**. *"We are winning the war."* Secretary of Defense Robert McNamara Report.

**December 31, 1962**. There were nearly 12,000 American military personnel in Vietnam.

**May 1, 1963**. The Diem government permitted Catholics to fly religious flags over the city of Hue in honor of the Archbishop's birthday (the Archbishop was Diem's brother). The Buddhists were prohibited from displaying the same gesture.

**June 11, 1963**. Buddhist monk Quang Duc sat in a busy Saigon intersection and poured gasoline on himself. With his hands pressed together in prayer, he lit the gasoline and burned to death. His last words were contained in a document to reporters, pleading with Diem to show "charity and compassion" to all religions.

**September 2, 1963**. President John F. Kennedy to Walter Cronkite, *"If we withdrew from Vietnam, the Communists would control Vietnam. Pretty soon, Thailand, Cambodia, Laos, Malaya, would go."*

At this point in our history, Democrats, Republicans and all Americans were united in defending capitalism, and fighting all collectivist, oppressive ideologies that called for a dominant, powerful central government, restrictions on personal liberty and not only equal opportunity, but income redistribution and equal outcome. America was united in fighting socialism, Marxism and communism.

**November 1, 1963**. Diem's generals captured Nhu and his brother, killing them the next day.

**November 1963**. There were 16,300 American advisers in South Vietnam. A total of seventy-eight Americans had been killed.

**November 15, 1963**. Robert McNamara announced that 1,000 advisors would be pulled out of Vietnam in early December and said the US military role would end by 1965.

**November 22, 1963**. President John F. Kennedy was assassinated in Dallas, Texas. Lyndon Johnson assumed the Presidency of the United States of America.

**November, 1963**. Lyndon B. Johnson to Henry Cabot Lodge, U.S. Ambassador to Vietnam. *"I am not going to lose Vietnam. I am not going to be the president who saw Southeast Asia go the way China went."*

**1964**. The number of American combat deaths in Vietnam climbed to 137 for the year. We had 23,300 advisers in South Vietnam. A total of 225 Americans had been killed in action, in the fledgling Vietnam War.

**April 1964**. The American Ambassador to South Vietnam, Henry Cabot Lodge, Jr. *"I would not be surprised to see the Mekong Delta totally cleared of Communist forces by the end of 1965."*

Our leaders were not always candid, or honest. Deceit was involved from the beginning, through appraisals of our opportunity for success, "body counts," enemy troop strength reports, to assessments of the ability of the South Vietnamese to fight and win, or even our commitments to winning the war.

**June 20, 1964**. General William "Westy" Childs Westmorland was officially appointed Commander, Military Assistance Command Vietnam ("MACV") in Saigon.

**August 2, 1964**. Three North Vietnamese gunboats in the Gulf of Tonkin attacked the U.S. destroyer Maddox. Two nights later, the Maddox, and the destroyer, the Turner Joy, were reported attacked by North Vietnamese gunboats. Confusion of the facts and a lack of evidence leave some doubt that the attacks actually occurred.

**August 4, 1964**.  President Lyndon Johnson and Secretary of Defense Robert McNamara authorized an air strike against targets in North Vietnam.  Twenty-five PT boats and 10% of North Vietnam's total petroleum storage capacity were destroyed.

**August 5, 1964**.  On my seventeenth birthday, Lieutenant J.G. Everett Alvarez Jr. was launched from the deck of the U.S.S. Constellation in his A-4 Skyhawk.  He was shot down over Hon Gai, North Vietnam and became the first American pilot captured by the North Vietnamese.  He spent more than eight years in captivity.

**August 7, 1964**.  Congress passed the *"Tonkin Gulf Resolution,"* authorizing Johnson to take "all necessary measures to repel any armed attacks against forces of the U.S. and to prevent further aggression."

**August 7, 1964**.  *"All Vietnam is not worth the life of a single American boy."*  Senator Ernest Gruening of Alaska, who, along with Senator Wayne Morse, voted against the Gulf of Tonkin Resolution.

**August 10, 1964**.  Congress gave LBJ wide powers by adopting the Gulf of Tonkin Resolution.

**October 16, 1964**.  China tested its first Atomic Bomb.

*"Far from being a classless society, Communism is governed by and elite as steadfast in its determination to maintain its prerogatives as any oligarchy known to history."*  Robert F. Kennedy

**November 3, 1964**.  LBJ was re-elected as President of the United States with 61% of the vote.

**During the fall of 1964, the U.S. turned down a secret offer of peace talks by North Vietnam.**

**December 20, 1964**.  General Khanh and young officers in the South Vietnamese Army, including Nguyen Cao Ky and Nguyen Van Thieu, seized control of the government.

**February 7, 1965**.  Viet Cong attacked the American airfield at Pleiku.  LBJ ordered retaliatory raids.

**March 2, 1965**.  Sustained U.S. bombing of North Vietnam began, under the code name *"Rolling Thunder."*

**March 8, 1965**.  U.S. Marines went ashore at Da Nang as the first Marine combat ground troops to be deployed to Vietnam.  Captain Lee Peterson stated, *"We're not going in to fight, but to free the ARVNs (Army of the Republic or Vietnam) to fight.  It's their war."*

**March 11, 1965**.  *"Operation Market Time"* commenced as a joint U.S. Navy and South Vietnamese Navy effort to block the infiltration of North Vietnamese supplies into the south.

**March 21-25, 1965**.  Twenty-five thousand civil rights marchers left Selma, Alabama, in a march to Montgomery, the capital of Alabama.

**April 1, 1965**.  General Westmorland convinced LBJ to increase U.S. force levels in Vietnam to 33,000 men.

**April 22, 1965**.  The first combat between U.S. Marine ground troops and VC occurred.

**May 20, 1965.  North Vietnam restated its peace proposal, which the U.S. had already rejected.**

**June 18, 1965**.  Nguyen Cao Ky assumed power in South Vietnam as the new Prime Minister.  Nguyen Van Thieu serves as the official Chief of State.

**July 28, 1965**.  Johnson announced that he would send forty-four combat battalions to Vietnam.  This increased the U.S. military level to 125,000 men.   The monthly draft doubled to 35,000.

*"I do not find it easy to send the flower of our youth, our finest young men, into battle. I have spoken to you today of the divisions and the forces and the battalions and the units, but I know them all, every one. I have seen them in a thousand streets, of a hundred towns, in every state in this union, working and laughing and building, and filled with hope and life. I think I know too, how their mothers weep and how their families sorrow."* President Lyndon Johnson

Popular Song, *"I Feel Like I'm Fixin' To Die Rag."* 1965
*"Come on, Mothers, throughout the land,*
*Pack your boys off to Vietnam;*
*Come on Fathers, don't hesitate!*
*Send your sons off before it's too late!*
*You can be the first one on your block,*
*To have your boy come home in a box!"*
*"Country"* Joe McDonald

<u>August 4, 1965</u>. President Johnson requested an additional $1.7 billion for the war.

<u>October 10, 1965</u>. Ronald Reagan, told the Fresno Bee, *"We should declare war on North Vietnam. We could pave the whole country and put parking stripes on it, and still be home for Christmas."*

<u>October 22, 1965</u>. I received my notice to report for draft registration.

<u>October 28, 1965</u>. The St. Louis Arch, the country's tallest monument, was topped off.

<u>December, 1965</u>. We had 184,300 troops in South Vietnam. It was estimated there were 70,000 to 80,000 Viet Cong and Viet Cong sympathizers in the Mekong Delta. 1,594 Americans had died for the cause.

<u>July 28, 1965</u>. President Johnson announced American combat forces in Vietnam would reach 100,000.

<u>November 14th, through 16, 1965</u>. The U.S. Army engaged the North Vietnamese army in heavy combat in the Ia Drang Valley. The 1st Air Cavalry lost 300 men. The NVA lost 1,200. The American forces won so decisively that North Vietnam decided to focus their combat strategy on guerrilla warfare.

<u>December 31, 1965</u>. There were nearly 200,000 Americans deployed in South Vietnam. American casualties reached 5,300 wounded and 1,350 killed.

<u>January 12, 1966</u>. President Lyndon Johnson State of the Union address. *"...war is always the same. It is young men dying in the fullness of their promise. It is trying to kill a man that you do not even know well enough to hate… therefore, to know war is to know that there is still madness in this world."*

<u>January 29, 1966</u>. In what was considered a major escalation of the war, the U.S. began bombing around Haiphong Harbor and Hanoi.

Idealism played a part in our commitment to the war, but so did common human frailties. Arrogance and pride played a part. Kennedy was stung by criticism over the Bay of Pigs fiasco. He needed to look *"Presidential"* and tough. Johnson didn't want *"any damn Dinh Binh Phoo."* He was concerned how history would see HIS role in the war. Nixon didn't want to be *"the first American President to lose a war."* We couldn't imagine a small, backward country like Vietnam being able to stand up to us.

Religion played a part. Diem was Catholic, in a largely Buddhist country.

Fear played a part in our quicksand involvement in Southeast Asia.  Sputnik, the Chinese "A-Bomb," McCarthyism, the Cuban Missile Crisis, the Berlin Wall, and Khrushchev's shoe banging at the U.N., all added to the climate of fear.  We went to Vietnam out of fear of the threat of global communism.

**June 27, 1969.**  Life Magazine published pictures of 217 of the 242 men who had been killed during the week of May 28th.  One of the men had said in his last letter home,

*"You may not be able to read this.  I am writing it in a hurry.  I see death coming up the hill."*

# Chapter 1

## Boot Camp

I said goodbye to Judi and my family, on the morning of July 10th, 1966, at my home. I didn't want her, or anyone, to go with me to the train station. John Bailey and I left for boot camp, taking a train from St. Louis to Great Lakes Recruit Training Command at Great Lakes, Illinois.

John and I both enlisted with the Navy's promise of becoming "Aviation Electrician Mates," working on the electrical systems of aircraft. During my first boot camp roll call, the Petty Officer in charge called out *"Seaman Apprentice Sater!"* I spoke up, correcting him that my *"rate"* should be listed as *"Airman Apprentice."* He said, *"Sorry, Fish!"* The Navy's enlistment promise lasted until my first roll call. I was a *"Seaman Apprentice."* This change was my first lesson in the realities of Navy life and my first step towards Vietnam. I broke my glasses during the first week of Boot, and was held back a week until they made new glasses for me. John Bailey went on. I didn't see him again, until 2013.

The first couple of weeks of boot camp were tough. I was homesick and missed Judi. The Navy was doing what it intended to do, which was to break down individuality. My head was shaved in seconds. My dental appointment was a similar experience. They didn't spend a lot of time fixing teeth. If I had a cavity, they pulled the tooth. They pulled so many teeth on the upper right side of my mouth, I spent most of my life chewing food with just the left side of my jaw. When we received our shots, we went through a gauntlet of medics, shooting us in both arms. I wore a denim uniform and leggings. We weren't sailors, yet, worthy of wearing *"bell bottoms."* We marched everywhere in formation. We were constantly reminded of our insignificance. Rumors are rampant in any military setting. We heard one man was shot and killed, trying to escape Boot Camp. Of course, we also believed they put *"saltpeter"* in our food to damper our sexual urges.

I was surprised to learn that I scored high in the Navy's overall "GCT/ARI" intelligence tests. I also learned a valuable lesson, when the Company Commander barked out the question *"Who has a GCT/ARI above 60?"* I proudly raised my hand, along with one other recruit. We spent the next few hours scrubbing garbage cans, although the Navy term was more akin to *"excrement cans."* I never raised my hand again.

**I receiving training on "sound powered phones."**

**Judi's first letter, July 11, 1966.**
She wrote almost every day. Each carried the intoxicating scent of *"Ambush"* perfume. Only a few of her letters are here. Most were *"edited,"* years ago, in our back yard....... in a fire we built.

*Dear Terry,*

*Well, it's twelve hours since you left, so I decided to write you a letter and then send it when I get your address. I hated to go to work. I just felt terrible, but I'm glad I did. It made me feel a lot better except for one thing. All the electricity went off in Clayton at 2:40. The air conditioner went off and I thought I'd die. It was 104 again. Tomorrow it's supposed to get up to 108! Man, I think I'll melt.*

*My first bus ride was this morning, too. Steve brought me home from your house, then I caught the bus at 10:08. I almost missed the bus because I was standing on the wrong side of the street, but I made it.*

*You know, I think you were right in not letting us come along with you, downtown. We all would have made a big scene. Here it is only twelve hours since you've left, and I already miss you terribly (you big skinny goof). I'm still waiting for you and Frank to buzz by here or at least call. You know what? I think I love you!*

*I feel like going to bed around 8 o'clock. I had three hours sleep today, but I guess you feel worse than I do. I bet you didn't get any sleep, and haven't gotten much by now, either.*

*You know, I think if I write to you a lot, I'll probably run out of things to say, because the only thing I know about is work, and that's not exciting. Let me tell you, it sure feels funny writing to you and writing that I love you. I'd much rather be telling it to your face. Just think, you only have 3 years, 364 days, 11 hours, 27 minutes, and 43 seconds (roughly) in the Navy, then you are all mine. I think we can last it, don't you?*

*Well, I guess I'd better stop writing for now. I have to wash my uniform, and I feel like going to bed now, even though it's only 6:50. I'll close for now. Be good and God Bless you!*

*With <u>All</u> My Love,*

*Judi*

**Letter from thirteen-year-old brother, Pat.  July 18, 1966**
*Hi Terry,*

*How ya' bin? Have they been rough on you? Mom hasn't done anything but talk about you. The day after you left, she started cleaning up your room. She picked up the shirt you wore last night and stuck it under her pillow. I heard her say she wouldn't wash it. Have you started counting the days 'till you get out yet? Mike and I moved into your room, it's too hot downstairs, but don't worry. We are only using one of your drawers. We call it our summer clubhouse. I even brought the short wave radio set upstairs. Steve (Ma-2-Z) is taking Mike and me to a baseball game tonight, Cards-Cubs. If you are really interested, I'll keep informing you on what place they are in. Presently they are tied for sixth place. By the by, "Boss" had her pups. A litter of seven, though three of them died. I even saw one of them being born right in front of me, although it died later. The four remaining pups are healthy and strong, and we are going to keep two males, Peanuts and Sloopy.*

*Your Landlubber Brother,*

*Pat"*

**Letter from eleven-year-old brother, Mike**
*Hi Ter,*

*How ya do-in. Steve is taking Pat & me to the baseball game today. When do you come home on leave? How's the chow? Are you bald yet?*

*Mike*

*Letter from eight-year-old sister, Sharon. ("Rip" was a nickname. "Ter," is short for Terry. A tear is the same as a rip)*
*Hi Rip,*

*Thanks for the post card you sent me. I like it very much. Well, I'm going in fifth grade next year. On my report card I made 5 E's and I got a certificate award in spelling. And I will be in advance band, next year. I was in the Spring Festival. As soon as I walked in to play my clarinet, half of it fell off on the floor 'cause I put too much cork grease on it.*

*I joined a softball team. First I was on a very little team and then I got moved up cause I was too good for them and my very first game we lost 32 to 7, but I got 2 home runs and I got somebody out at third base.*

*Well, how do you feel? I hope you come home soon. Well, I have to close now. Have fun!*

*Sharon*

**August 12, 1966.** The Beatles played Busch Stadium, in St. Louis.

**September 1, 1966.** The first administrative unit of the Mekong Delta Mobile Afloat Force was commissioned at the Navy Amphibious Base in Coronado, California. Shortly after, the unit was designated Task Force 117 (TF-117), and was code-named the Mobile Riverine Force (MRF).

**September 23, 1966.** Boot Camp Graduation. Mom and Dad drove up with Judi, Nancy, Judy (my sister), Pat, Mike, Sharon and Tim. I was easy to spot during the passing in review. I was the *"Guide On,"* carrying the company flag on the front, right corner of the class. My company lined up in formation from my position.

I was able to leave the base for a while, after graduation. Dad towed a camping trailer from St. Louis, to Great Lakes. They found some excuse to leave for a while, to give Judi and me time alone. We chuckled when they honked the car horn upon their return.

**October 2, 1966.** Irving Berlin sent a birthday message to Groucho Marx;
### *"The world would not be in such a snarl if Marx had been Groucho instead of Karl."*

**October 3, 1966.** The first trainees for River Assault Squadron 9 reported for training to NavPhiBase, Coronado, California.

**(Left) Judi and I, after my Boot Camp Graduation. (Right) My sisters, Judy and Sharon, brothers Pat and Tim, my dad, Dale, brother. Mike, plus Judi and I.**

# Chapter 2

## *"The Big E"*

Soon, I was out of boot camp and thrilled that my orders were to report to the U.S.S. Enterprise on October 24, 1966, at Alameda Naval Air Station, San Francisco.

The USS Enterprise, also known as *"The Big E,"* was commissioned on Sunday morning, September 24, 1961, at a cost of $451 Million. She was the largest, longest, tallest and mightiest warship ever to sail the seas. I once read that to appreciate the Enterprise, you had to imagine driving down a road at thirty miles an hour and seeing a large shadow pass over you. As you turn to your left, a ship twenty-five stories high, weighing 90,000 tons and longer than eleven football fields quickly passes by. Over 5,400 sailors wave as they leave you behind. In 1966, *"The Big E"* was in a class by itself. The name *"Enterprise"* has been part of naval history since 1775. She was the seventh ship to carry the proud name. At her commissioning, the Secretary of the Navy, John B. Connally, Jr. called her a worthy successor to the highly decorated, USS Enterprise of World War II. *"The Fighting Gray Lady"* fought in the Battle of Midway, and participated in raids on Tokyo. She was one of the primary targets of the Japanese attack on Pearl Harbor. Fortunately, she was delayed from entering port the night before the attack, due to engine problems.

The nuclear powered Enterprise made her maiden voyage on January 12, 1962. The Big E and other ships of the Second Fleet were there for the 1962 Cuban Missile Crisis to set up a *"strict quarantine of all offensive military equipment under shipment to Cuba."* The blockade was put into place on October 24th. The first Soviet ship was stopped the next day. The crisis ended on October 28th, when Premier Khrushchev agreed to remove all of the missiles from Cuba.

During 1964, the Enterprise, the nuclear powered cruiser *"Long Beach,"* and the nuclear powered frigate *"Bainbridge"* completed *"Operation Sea Orbit,"* a historic 30,565 mile voyage around the world, without a single refueling or replenishment. *"The Big E"* was transferred to the Seventh Fleet in November of 1965 and became the first nuclear powered ship to engage in combat when she launched aircraft against the Vietcong on December 2, 1965. She launched 125 sorties on the first day, dropping 167 tons of bombs and rockets on V.C. supply lines. The next day, Enterprise set a record of 165 sorties in one day. She served six combat deployments to the Gulf of Tonkin during the Vietnam War. She was known as the *"Carrier with Class."*

<u>October 26, 1966.</u> The aircraft carrier U.S.S. Oriskany (CVA 34), was launching air attacks against North Vietnam, when a seaman improperly handled a flare that ignited munitions. After a three-hour struggle to stop the inferno, the fire was finally brought under control. Twenty-five pilots and navigators as well as nineteen other officers and enlisted men died in the blaze. The Oriskany was forced to sail from "Yankee Station," off the coast of North Vietnam, to Subic Bay for repairs and personnel replacements.

**Letter Home. November 7, 1966, as the Enterprise sat at its pier, in Alameda, California.**
*Dear Folks,*

*I am not sure what I can talk about, since I just talked to you for quite a while on the phone. Talking on the phone always makes home seem close, but not close enough. Sometimes when I am up in the observation tower, or in the Captain's Plot, I look at the gyrocompass and just look out to the east. Isn't that a tearjerker?*

*I have been going on liberty just about every night, and consequently, haven't had the time to write. I had liberty tonight, but I didn't go because I put my request chit in for a school and the Chief I told you about that kept telling me I "didn't need a school" denied it. He said I have to be on board ship for a year before I could apply for a transfer. I knew he was wrong, so a little while ago, I went down to the Education and Training Officer and talked to him. I told him "somebody" told me I had to be on board a year before applying for a transfer. He said that was wrong and that I should put in my request about three or four months before this next cruise is up. So then I ordered a correspondence course on electricity and left.*

*I have ten days in the states before I leave, but one way to think about it is that the sooner I leave, the sooner I get back. I sure wish the Admiral would get the lead out of his, uh, <u>anchor</u>.*

*All My Love,*

*Rip*

On November 19, 1966, the Enterprise left Alameda Naval Air Station and sailed into the Pacific, towards the Tonkin Gulf, off North Vietnam, also known as *"Yankee Station."*

On Sunday morning at dawn, November 26th, the *"Big E"* pulled into Pearl Harbor, Hawaii. As part of Navy tradition, we were *"manning the rail,"* lining the decks and all rails. I was on the flight deck, at the fantail.

Contrary to popular belief, the U.S.S. Arizona is no longer a commissioned Navy warship, however, she received our Boson's pipe salute as we steamed past her, out of reverence and respect. I had cold chills as I wondered what it was like on a similar Sunday morning, on December 7th, 1941. The Japanese sneak attack left 2,403 dead, 188 destroyed American planes and 8 damaged, or destroyed battleships. Even today, oil still seeps from the Arizona

**I took this photo of the USS Arizona Memorial, from the observation deck of the Enterprise.**

The Governor proclaimed it *"Enterprise Day"* in the state of Hawaii the day we pulled in.

We left Hawaii on November 28th. Between Hawaii and the Gulf of Tonkin, our Captain announced that two Soviet *"Bear"* bombers were approaching the ship. We scrambled fighters to meet them. They flew under, over and around the Soviet bombers until they were convinced to steer clear of The Big E.

**The nuclear powered frigate USS Bainbridge supported the Enterprise task force.**

**Letter Home, November 28, 1966**
*Dear Folks,*

*I am sorry I haven't written. I throw myself at your mercy! I have no excuse, except that I am always, studying, working, eating, or sleeping (more or less in reverse order of importance).*

*Today we left Pearl. We weighed anchor at 6:00 a.m. and moved to a different pier, then left again at 1300 (1:00 p.m.). I had to "man the rail" again today when we left. I was kind of disappointed that the only send-off we had was about sixteen hula girls and no crowd. You can see why, after being treated like "war heroes" when we got here. My faith was restored, however, when we reached the mouth of the harbor and saw a large crowd, waiving to us. We passed a country club-swimming pool, and the pool was empty because everybody was next to the fence waving to us. It's not just because it's a ship, either. These people see as many ships as you see <u>cars</u>! This may be "the ship that God forgot" for the crew, but there is consolation in seeing hoards of people waiting to gaze at the "Queen of the Seas" as civilian admirers call the ship. It is also nice to be treated to a drink because you are from "The Big E," or pick up a Hawaiian newspaper and read "Aloha, Carrier Enterprise" sprawled all over the front page.*

*"The old man" came on the loud speaker system today and congratulated us on the "Operational Readiness Inspection" we had the last few days. We broke record scores for any attack carrier. We may get the "E" for efficiency badge to wear on our right sleeve. Tom knows about it. Ask him.*

*I was going to go into town last night and get bombed, but I changed my mind. Being broke reinforces your will power.*

*Can you send me some of my record albums? Send me the one by "The Association," "Soul and Inspiration," by the Righteous Brothers, Johnny Rivers, and Bob Kuban! The records have to be in good condition, too! It's pretty expensive equipment we are using here. I have to admit, I don't do much work here. There is a television in the shop, and when we are out of reach of shore installations, the ship has its own videotapes. Tonight I am going to watch "The Sandpiper" on television. We have an expensive hi-fi record player and AM-FM radio. I can go down to the snack bar and buy candy, or soft ice cream anytime I want, or soda. I am off at 8:00 P.M. and get up at 7:30. Yeah, I have it easy, and I travel, but I know where I would rather be!*

*It seems unbelievable when I look back to my school buddies. Frank Judge is in the army. John Brune is in Germany. John Bailey is in Florida. Bob Kelly is dead of cancer. Jerry Kochner is going into "boot" on December 9<sup>th</sup>. Danny and Dave Booher are on the east coast. Charlie H. is engaged and in Germany. Tom Judge is in Vietnam, and Bill Koch is heaven knows where! Then there is Ken Baumer in Subic Bay, Steve Simon engaged and sweating the draft. Alvin Susaki's deferment is up, and Larry Lapp is in the monastery. Boy! A lot has happened! Now, little brother, Pat is just entering the cycle I have gone through. You could give him a rough idea of what's to come, but he wouldn't believe it. Can you picture Pat in uniform? I guess you don't want to. Can you see him as a pallbearer for a friend? How about going out the door to catch his classes at college, or bringing his girlfriend over? And Mike is right behind him! I better shut up. I already have the rest of the kids away from home!*

*We should reach Subic Bay, Philippines, in ten days. I won't get any mail until we get there. That is kind of disappointing. We got mail today, but there was only four letters for the whole division, so I know they messed up. The last time we had mail call was the 23<sup>rd</sup>. Then, I got several letters. By the way, thanks for the Thanksgiving Day card. I got a letter from Mr. & Mrs. Simon, thanking me for the spiritual bouquet. It was nice to hear from them.*

*Use this info with discretion, but we are supposed to stay in Subic for seven to ten days. Then, we are supposed to be "on the line" for sixty-five days! Do you have any idea what it's going to be like to see nothing but water for over two months?*

*I am going to start my beard after we leave Subic. Everybody grows one. It's the tradition. Besides, when I start shaving for the benefit of 4,999 sailors, I know I've been away from Judi too long!*

*Well, I am pretty tired right now, and besides, there is a chief that is here and he has been yelling like mad for the past ten minutes because we are all "sitting on our butts." So, I will sign off for now. I'll try to write at least once a week or something like that.*

*Love,*
*Terry*

**Letter Home, Undated**
*Hi, Folks*

*Please frame this certificate for me. It really is signed by the Captain. I have entered the "Domain of the Golden Dragon!" I have crossed "The 180<sup>th</sup> Meridian!" It means I have entered the far western Pacific. Today is my first day with a combat unit. The Enterprise became part of a task force with the Bainbridge and several other carriers. This morning we had the Kitty Hawk, the Ticonderoga and another carrier with us. It's getting crowded out here! I got your letter. The St. Louis Post-Dispatch is a great Christmas present! Thanks a million! Speaking of millions, I intend to pay off my phone bill within the next few months.*

*Love,*

*Terry*

**Letter Home. December 15, 1966**
*Hi, Folks,*

*We left Subic today at about 8:30 am. Out of the days I had liberty, I went to Olongapo once, went swimming at Grande Island once (and it's the most beautiful island in the world!), went to the E.M. Club and bowling once and stayed on the ship for two liberties. I stayed on the first time because I was too lazy to get in dress whites and the second time, because I was broke.*

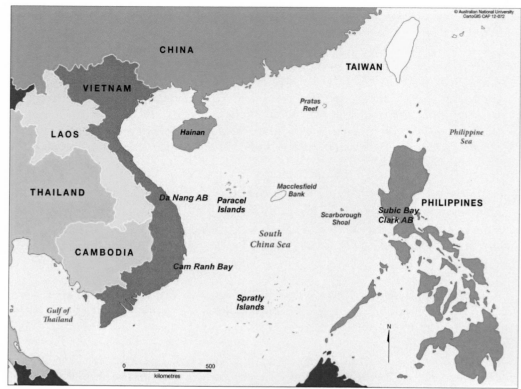

Map, courtesy of gentleseasblogspot.com

*We should be "on the line," tonight or tomorrow, somewhere between North Vietnam and Hainan Island. It is about a thousand miles from Subic Bay, to Hanoi, so we'll be traveling pretty fast! "The Line" is our combat operations area, where we will be launching aircraft against North Vietnam. This morning in the Electronics Technician shop, the guys were talking about how many planes and pilots we would lose. You would never get this info from the newspapers back home, but on the last cruise they lost twenty-one planes and twenty-five pilots and navigators (some planes have two people). Since the North Vietnamese have a much better air force than before, the "scuttlebutt" is we will lose more, this time. They say that once, a jet took off and its engines failed. The ship cut it in half and the pilots were lost. Once they almost saved a pilot. A chopper lifted a guy about 100 feet over the water and the cable broke. The pilot vanished.*

*I would appreciate it if you would send a family picture and some pictures from when I was home. I have two packs of slides being developed right now. I know there are pictures of Hawaii in them, and I got pictures of planes taking off to intercept the Russian "Bear" bombers that wanted to get a look at us, plus pictures of everybody all over the 011 and 012 levels, looking for them with binoculars. Once there were four of the "reconnaissance bombers" on our radar screens. None of the other ships with us knew anything about them from their radar. I can't remember what the rest of the pictures are of. There are a couple of me manning the rail. One of them showed how I could lean into the terrific wind at almost a 45-degree angle. You should get the pictures in about three weeks!*

*I guess I'll put this in with my Christmas card to you. I hope you have a very Merry Christmas and don't worry about me, Mom! Instead of moping about me being gone, make it a happy Christmas for the kids, OK? Maybe I will say "Hello" to Bob Hope for everybody! Anyway, Merry Christmas and Happy New Year!*

*All My Love, Your Non-Combatant Combatant Son,*

*Terry*

*P.S. We aren't even going to be close enough to <u>see</u> Vietnam!*

**Christmas card to newborn nephew, Bryan Sater, who was born on December 8<sup>th</sup>, 1966. December 18<sup>th.</sup>**
*Dear Bryan,*

*Merry Christmas, kid! I just now got the news about you! How do you like the world? I guess you have a little more room, now. Do what your folks, and your big brother tell you. I'll put your name on a 500 pounder, so you can say "Hello!" to "Charlie!" Merry Christmas, everybody, and Happy New Year!*

*Seaman "J.G."*

*Terry*


**Letter home. December 30, 1966**
*I think that since I am almost on the other side of the world, it is the 29<sup>th</sup> at home. Tomorrow night is New Year's Eve. A Chief put up a sign here in the shop that says "Happy New Year 1967." We were all thinking about adding a "?" to it, but we decided it would cause "hate and discontent in the ranks," so we didn't. Did you know that the first time I took Judi on a date was last New Year's Eve?*

*For the past couple of days only our A-6 Intruders have been flying, because it has been raining something fierce in North Vietnam and only our A-6's are "all weather" planes (radar equipped for bombing). They blew up some oil depots yesterday, the biggest oil depot in North Vietnam was one of them.*

*Today I was playing a tape of the Beatles "Rubber Soul" album. Boy, those Chiefs have no appreciation of music! All I ever hear is "Turn that down, will ya?" We had an inspection of all the areas in the island today. I had to clean up the shop and got an "Outstanding" on it.*

*Yesterday we were relatively close to North Vietnam. It might have been sixteen miles or less. See how far sixteen miles looks on a world map!*

*I am getting along pretty well in my Basic Electricity Course. They are assigning me the "Pathfinder" radar to learn, and I mean learning how it <u>works</u>, not how to watch the radar screen!*

*I just thought I'd drop you a line to let you know I'm OK. I'll write a longer letter to you soon.*

*Love,*

*Terry*


<u>**December 31, 1966.**</u> The war was heating up. The death toll for Americans for 1966 was 5,273. U.S. Forces in Vietnam reached 385,300 by the end of 1966.

**Letter home, Sunday, January 22, 1967, Subic Bay, Philippines.**

*Hi! Dad, Mom, Tom, Rosie, Nancy, Les, Tommy II, Bryan, Judy, Pat, Mike, Sharon, Tim, and anybody else who wants to hear!*

*Well, the weather here in Subic is completely different from the Gulf of Tonkin. I caught a cold there, but I'm getting a sunburn, here. I went snorkeling, yesterday on Grande Island, and I plan on doing it tomorrow, all day. The water around here is fantastic! I borrowed a snorkel, some fins, and a mask. I had a ball! I never went out any farther than where the water was about fifteen feet deep, because at the time we were having a division party with free beer and I had a few in me. We had a pig roast and played football!*

*We are supposed to leave Thursday (the 26th) and head for Manila. We leave there on the 30th.*

**During January, 1967, the first elements of the Mobile Riverine Force, River Assault Squadron 9, River Assault Division 91, arrived in Vietnam.**

**Letter home, Thursday, February 2, 1967.**

*Hi, Folks!*

*I'm back on the line again! Last night at 7:30 our position was about 125 miles north of Da Nang, heading further north. The weather is terrible. It is monsoon season, and it is ALWAYS cloudy, chilly, and drizzling. That is, except when it is cloudy, cold, and pouring down! I have decided not to even go outside unless it clears up. I was standing in the hanger bay, yesterday, watching them get ready to replenish from an ammo ship and the biggest wave I've ever seen surged into the hanger bay, spraying up to the flight deck. I just caught some of the mist from it, but some guys were drenched.*

*I have no word from the school yet, but I have come a long way in the Basic Electricity course. It is fascinating, but at times very difficult. When I don't understand the book, any of the E.T.s in the shop are glad to sit down with me for an hour at a time and help me out. I have only turned in three of the tests for the course, but I have done well on all of them.*

*I saw something funny in the hanger bay, yesterday. You have to be very careful, walking through it. There is equipment on the deck, so you have to keep an eye on where you step. There are also airplane wings, right at your head level, so you have to keep an eye on what might be above you. I saw a guy going through the hanger bay too fast, and he walked right into a plane wing. It knocked him out, cold! Two officers were walking, and talking, oblivious to the poor guy. They stepped over him like he was a log across a wooded path!*

*A buddy of mine heard his brother, who is a Marine in Vietnam, was going home because he was wounded twice and was awarded two Purple Hearts, but now he isn't, because he has to have three Purple Hearts to go home. Do you know what the chances are of getting shot three times in Vietnam and living to tell about?*

*Well, I guess I'll close now. I'll try to write again soon.*

*Love,*

*Terry*

**Letter home, Sunday, February 12<sup>th</sup>, 1967.  A week after Dad's 50<sup>th</sup> birthday.**
*Hi, Dad!*

*Judi just told me in a letter I got the day before yesterday that it was your birthday Feb. 3<sup>rd</sup>, so Happy Birthday! No, the enclosed cash isn't a birthday present.  It's for my phone bill.  I'll try to pay the rest off as best I can.  If it is OK with you, I won't send TOO much money until after we leave Hong Kong next month.  I want to buy a set of "gabs" (tailored gabardine dress blues).*

*We lost three planes today, two A-5 photo recon Vigilantes and an F-4 Phantom, but I won't have any details 'till tomorrow.  I know for sure that the crew of one Vigilante was rescued.*

*I will begin E.T. school in June or July.  If school starts before the Enterprise gets back, they will just fly me off. Imagine ME, flying across the Pacific!  The first six weeks of the school are in San Diego, the rest in Frisco.  I just <u>have</u> to pass.  It's my only chance at getting something out of the Navy.  It's different when I can't depend on you and Mom to MAKE me study!  Well, anyway, I'll be home in June or July.*

**Dear Mom, Dad, Nancy & Les, Tom & Rosie, the Simons, Grandpa, Grandma, and everybody!**

*It's about 8:00 p.m. ("2000" Nav time).  I am sitting here very calm, but rather excited about what will be happening, tonight.  All of the radars are tied down, the planes fastened to the flight deck, and all loose gear has been stored away.  We are waiting, along with the fourteen other ships, for a typhoon to hit.  We left the line today and we were supposed to be in Subic Bay by Saturday, the fourth, but you just don't go into a harbor during a typhoon.  That's why there are fourteen ships with us.  The highest winds we have been in so far this cruise are 65 mph, or 70 mph.  We will probably be taking 10-degree rolls, which aren't very much compared to the other ships.  I would hate to be on a "tin can" right now.  They will be climbing the walls… I mean "bulkheads!"  I can feel big waves hitting us right now, but we aren't rolling at all.  Usually, a wave hitting a ship this size is like throwing a bucket of water against a brick wall.  Our antennas and safety nets are going to take a terrific pounding, though.  We will probably pull into P.I. (Philippine Islands) Monday.  I don't want to give you the idea there is any "danger" for us, with this typhoon.  We will probably roll quite a bit, compared to the way we usually do.  I just think it's neat!  Anyway, I'll let you know how it turns out.*

(Most ships have everything bolted to their decks, such as tables, benches, etc.  The Enterprise didn't.  As we went through the typhoon, the tables and benches in the mess halls and ward rooms were tipping over.  The ship took water OVER THE BOW!  For an aircraft carrier like the Enterprise to take water over the bow, was remarkable!  It damaged antennas and equipment around the flight deck.  At that time, I had the good fortune of having a berthing compartment (where I slept), right in the middle of the ship.  It was like lying on the middle of a "see saw," with my head and my feet going up and down.)

**On February 15, 1967, the Viet Cong sank a US minesweeper and damaged three others on the Long Tau River. The Mobile Riverine Force began search and destroy operations in the Rung Sat zone, a V.C. stronghold, which bordered the Long Tau River.**

During February 1967, we pulled into Hong Kong.  It was a three-day visit I will remember as long as I live.  I cannot imagine anywhere in the world that has such a diversity of people, cultures and economic classes in such a small area.  There were open-air meat markets selling everything from pork, to cats and dogs.  Next door was the "Hong Kong Hilton," a first class, high rise hotel.  The Enterprise sat in the harbor in *"full dress."*  She was lit up like a Christmas tree.  You could see her for miles around.  She was a beautiful sight.

Someone had stolen my wallet just before we pulled in, by reaching across my bunk while I was sleeping, so I didn't have much money. I offered a $50 reward for its return, because I needed my I.D. to get off the ship for liberty. The wallet was quickly returned. I am certain the guy who returned it was the one who took it, but I couldn't prove anything. Fortunately, you didn't need to be rich to have a good time in Hong Kong. I went to Bonwit Tailors and had three shirts made. I picked out the fabric and enjoyed Chevas Regal scotch while the tailor measured me. The shirts cost a grand total of $3.00 each. One thing I have always regretted was passing by a *"Chairman Mao,"* shop, selling the *"Red Book,"* and other communist propaganda. It was *"off limits"* to us, but I wish that I had gone in and bought a Red Book as a souvenir.

**I had to get my picture with this Hong Kong shop keeper's little girl.**

**Letter Home, Wednesday, April 26, 1967.**
*Hi People!*

*I'm on watch right now and just thought I would drop a line to let you know I am alive. I'm sorry I haven't written, but when we are in port, I do well to write at all.*

*Has Judi told you the news? I am a Seaman now, instead of a Seaman Apprentice. It's really nothing spectacular, but it is $20 a month more and a half-hour more liberty! This time in port, though, I have been back on the ship early every night. I haven't even taken the "SA" stripes off my shirts. I don't really care if people think I am an "SA" instead of an "SN," as long as the disbursing clerk knows the difference!*

*I have picked out Judi's graduation present and a set of Noritake china that I liked pretty well. I will have to buy them next time in port which should be about May 19th or 20th, because I should have enough money by then. The china should run me about $50.00 or $60.00. I will keep it on the ship until we reach the states, then I will mail it home, but I haven't decided on sending Judi her present or waiting until I get home to give it to her. It's a "Lady Hamilton" watch.*

*There is a "tentative" schedule out concerning the rest of the cruise. Here it is;*
> *April 28 – May 19; On the Line.*
> *4 days in Subic.*
> *May 23 – June 20; On the Line.*
> *2 Days in Subic;*
> *Head Home!*
*We are supposedly going to pull into Frisco the morning of July 6th, but it is too early to tell for sure when it will be. I hope it's a little earlier than that.*

*Last Saturday, I went to a division party on Grande Island and a couple of us went to the top of the island, to an old World War II fort. It was occupied by the Japanese during 1942, until the end of January 1945. On January 30, 1945 US Army troops landed on Grande Island supported by US Navy carrier aircraft from Task Group 77.4. It was really something. There was a wall, where the Japs executed the Flips and was all shot up. There was an enemy trench and watchtower, too. Nothing has been done to this fort, either. That's what makes it so neat! It isn't a public park or anything. It belongs to the military base. The next time we pull in, I will get some pictures of the place. That's about all around here. I'll try to write again soon.*

*Love,*

*Terry*

**Me, on top of the Grande Island, Fort Wint 10 Inch Gun emplacement. It wasn't even used when Japan took over the Philippines, during WWII. With the pullout of all U.S. Forces, from Subic Bay and Grande Island, it now serves as a resort area.**

### Letter to Mom, Monday, May 8, 1967
*"Happy Mother's Day," Mom!*

*I'm really not too cheap to buy a card. I just never can make up my mind picking one out, so I write!*

*Today I attended a lecture on the various radar systems on the Enterprise. I went to one a couple weeks ago, too. I didn't do it out of personal ambition, understand. I HAD to go. I am glad I did go, though. The Enterprise carries nine or ten different radars, each with its own specialty, all of them interesting. One radar can fool enemy aircraft's radar to make them think we are someplace we aren't. Another radar locks on our aircraft and guides them all the way to the fantail. Two different radars can detect a plane, depending on its size, up to about 500 miles away. One sends out a single beam radar, locks on the aircraft and a computer gives the aircraft bearing, altitude, speed, and direction. Isn't that fantastic? Our aircraft transmit a certain code. If a plane doesn't transmit this code, WE transmit a SAM missile! It isn't really that final, but you get the idea. The Tacan radar is used for telling the Enterprise aircraft from the Hancock's, Kitty Hawk's, etc. There are several other surface-air search radars like the SPN6 and SPN12. The "Pathfinder" is a harbor navigation aid that will cover the immediate area of the ship. The bow and fantail even show up on the radar screen. It will detect mines, if our lookouts don't. Well, what do you think our chances are of being taken by surprise? By the way, the Enterprise is theoretically "unsinkable." It has a double hull and is supposed to easily take torpedoes. If it starts to sink, it isn't supposed to sink below the Hanger Bay, and if we were sunk in the Gulf of Tonkin, the water isn't deep enough for it to go all the way under in a lot of places.*

*Love,*

*Your Second Son*

**Me, at one of the radar screens in the Operations Electronics shop.**

**Letter Home, Saturday, May 27, 1967**
*Hi Folks!*

*We leave <u>today</u>, for sure. We will be in Subic until June 3rd or 4th.*

*Today a guy was teaching me how to solder terminal points in a circuit. He said I'll be a "very ambidextrous E.T.," because one minute I hold the soldering gun in one hand, then the next minute I'm holding it in the other. I figured I would just let him think that. The <u>truth</u> is, I felt all thumbs and it didn't feel right in <u>either</u> hand! He said I did pretty well, though. A few days ago he taught me how to use an oscilloscope to measure the voltage at different points in some of the equipment here. It was fun!*

*We had an "Alpha Strike" yesterday. Our aircraft hit a thermo-power plant near Hanoi. I think Uncle Ho should put gas lanterns in his place, if you ask me.*

*Yesterday I was on an ordinance working party. I was sitting on 24 tube shaped objects and a guy told me to get off them because they were warheads for missiles that the planes were going to carry. It wasn't really dangerous. It's just that the thought of sitting on 24 missile warheads seemed rather awesome at the moment. Not very dignified, but it is a picture to think about.*

*I can't wait to get in port and buy Judi's watch and the china. I'm going to have to borrow about $30 from one of the guys though, because payday is the day before we pull out and I will have liberty at 4:00 p.m. that day. The stores are closed then.*

*Mom, I hope you liked your flowers, and you are over your cold! They sell order forms here on the ship, so that's how I got them. They only sell them for holidays and special occasions, like Mother's Day, though. I realize I haven't written for about two weeks. Remember though, the way they deliver mail, the letter I write tomorrow may arrive a couple days after this one.*

*Love,*

*Terry*

**Letter Home, Sunday, May 28, 1967**
*Hi, Folks!*

*We pull in, tomorrow. The weather is a little rough, right now, but it always is when we are between Subic Bay and the Tonkin Gulf. I went to the base of "the island" a while ago, and had a rough time opening the hatch to the flight deck so that I could see what the weather was like. It was windy! We are taking small rolls, too.*

*I just had chow. It was pretty good. I had two small steaks, fried potato halves with sour cream, pumpkin pie, ice cream and a salad. When I'm home I probably won't want any big fancy dinners. Eating takes too much time that I could use for "play time!" Maybe sometime, Mom & Dad, Tom & Rosie and Nancy and Les can go someplace together with Judi and me.*

*In about a half-hour I have to go down to the flight deck because the division is having their picture taken on one of the aircraft elevators for the "cruise book."*

*Even though we pull in tomorrow, I'm not doing anything, because I will have the duty. We didn't get mail today or yesterday, so I guess we will have some waiting for us in Subic.*

*Just think, I'll be home in about five weeks! That isn't too long, considering I've been gone twenty-nine or thirty weeks by the time you get this letter. I wish I could be home for the 4th of July, but it will be the 6th.*

*Mom, I don't know if you heard that Johnny Rivers album that you sent me, called "Changes," but I just thought I would tell you it is one of the favorites of the guys here in the shop. The only trouble is that sometimes I don't notice the sound of a jet warming up on the flight deck and when the "cat" (catapult) launches it off the deck, the whole ship shakes and the needle starts dancing all over the record.*

*A couple of days ago I was watching "flight ops" from the 011 level on the top of the island. When a Phantom or a Vigilante would go into A.B.'s (after-burners), I had to turn around and hold my breath. Even at such a great distance, the heat from those engines made it feel like my hair was going to catch fire and my face shrivel up. We have to face the wind when we are either launching or recovering planes because when we launch it gives the planes an added lift. When we are recovering, it makes it easier for the planes to come down easily.*

*Sometimes E.T. school scares me. I never <u>expected</u> an electronics school! In "Boot" they talked like asking for E.T. school was like asking for the moon, because it was such a difficult rate, one of the most technical and skilled jobs the Navy has. Now it seems that when guys around here talk electronics, I almost understand what they are talking about! I'll make it through the first few weeks OK, because that will cover basic stuff like electricity and I'm already familiar with that. It's advanced math and electronics that scares me.*

*Did Judi tell you about how I had to buy a new pair of shoes because somebody stole mine from near my rack? The guy in charge of the sleeping compartment told me I could have a pair of the unclaimed, lost shoes in the compartment, but I just couldn't see wearing somebody else's shoes, so I had to buy a new pair for $8.50.*

*I have to "man the rail" tomorrow. That's getting old. The only time I want to man the rail is when we are passing under the Golden Gate Bridge!*

*I guess I'll close now. I'll have more to write about in port. Would you call Judi and tell her I have duty tomorrow and that I'll be staying on the ship? I'll write her tomorrow. I haven't had a chance, tonight.*

*All My Love,*

*Terry*

**Secretary of Defense Robert McNamara visited Saigon, July 7th, through July 12th, 1967. He ordered an increase of 55,000 troops in Vietnam.**

**The aircraft carrier Forrestal suffered the loss of 134 crewman and 21 aircraft during a fire, on July 29th, 1967, while off the coast of Vietnam.**

**On September 15th, 1967, the Viet Cong ambushed the Mobile Riverine Force on the Rach Ba Rai River at "Snoopy's Nose." The V.C. slunk away during the night, leaving seventy-nine dead comrades.**

We pulled into Subic Bay, Philippines, several times. Most of the time we were conducting air combat operations on *"Yankee Station,"* off North Vietnam. Every day we got news of what our bombers did over Vietnam and learned which planes were lost. My primary job was working in *"the island"* superstructure on the flight deck, in "O.E." Division (Operations-Electronics), but I was also assigned work details, such as taking on ordinance, for strikes against North Vietnam. I put my young nephew's names on some of the bombs for luck.

I came to love the sea. I spent many hours during our cruise simply staring at white capped waves. I also enjoyed it when I could watch flight operations, refueling and replenishment operations. Sometimes, when we had time off, we would sun ourselves in the nets that surrounded the four and a half-acre flight deck. It was great to lie in the bow net, with the salt air blowing, watching the flying fish swimming ahead of the bow.

**My favorite spot on the Enterprise, lying in the bow nets, six stories above the ocean!**

There was one terrifying moment, when, lost in my thoughts, I was suddenly shaken by the roar of the afterburners of an F-4 Phantom. When a jet is shot off the catapult of an aircraft carrier, the nose goes up and the afterburners are wide open, blasting downward. If the F-4 had taken off with me in the bow net, I would have become a *"crispy critter."* It was a relief when I realized they were simply testing the engines of the fighter. It was chained to the deck.

The shipmates that I worked with were Electronics Technicians. They were educated, what we used to call *"slide rule,"* types, before hand held computers were invented. I made good friends and enjoyed their company. We often went on liberty together in Subic, and the local town of Olongapo. To get to Olongapo, you had to leave the Navy base and cross a small bridge over the Kalaklan River. The river doubled as Olongapo's sewer system. We called it *"Shit River,"* for obvious reasons. It was said that you weren't a man until you were able to cross *"Shit River"* and survive the stench. Kids would sit or stand in canoes in the river, and dive in to retrieve coins that servicemen tossed in. Olongapo was easily as wild as any untamed city of the Wild West. Prostitution, murder, fighting and corruption ruled Olongapo. San Miguel beer flowed twenty-four hours a day, seven days a week. When you walked into a bar, the bar girls would lure you with the seductive words, *"I love you, Joe! No shit! You buy me drink?"* If you insulted them, or otherwise pissed them off, you could easily get a broken beer bottle thrust into your face, or midsection. During my first liberty in Olongapo, I drank six San Miguel beers, very fast, because I wanted to impress my *"old salt"* shipmates. They had to carry me back to the Big E. I did not accomplish my goal. They put me into the middle *"rack,"* still in my uniform. The racks were like large shelf units, maybe five or six inches thick, with reading lights and storage. During the night, the entire rack wall section collapsed. When they found me in the morning, my arm was sticking out of the collapsed racks. They immediately assumed I had died in the wreckage. The simple truth was that I was so drunk, I was unaware of the catastrophe.

On another visit, I was standing on a corner, in my dress whites' uniform, when a kid came up to me with shoe shine kit. He asked if I wanted a shoe shine. I shook my head, *"No."* He looked up and said, *"I'll put polish on your uniform!"* Before I could say anything, I noticed a Filipino cop glaring at me and moving his hand to the gun on his hip. I got a shoe shine.

One night, about eight of us were in the Enlisted Men's Club, on the base in Subic Bay. An equal number of guys from the deck force sat at the table next to us. Everyone was drinking. I noticed that the deck guys kept staring at the guys at our table, in a decidedly unfriendly way. Over the objections of my buddies, I turned to one of the deck hands and asked *"Something bothering you?"* He answered *"No,"* and seemed to back off. I turned to each at the table, in turn, and received the same response, until the last man said, *"Yeah. You!"* I said: *"O.K., Let's take it outside!"* We got up and walked outside. I led, with my challenger following behind me. As I went through the door to the outside, a shout rang out *"He's got a knife!"* I turned to see him pull a knife from his boot. He barely had the knife out, when a nearby Shore Patrol grabbed him and took the knife. He was taken away. If the Shore Patrol hadn't been there, this might have been a very short story.

We were at sea, during Christmas Eve Mass. I sat, surrounded by F-4 Phantoms, A-6 Intruders, A-4 Skyhawks, and other planes, with hundreds of sailors. During his sermon, the Chaplain asked those were writing home telling their families they had been *"wounded in action,"* to please stop! I couldn't believe people would do that, or that families would believe it. We were far out to sea. The flight deck is an extremely dangerous place, but the only men at risk in <u>combat</u> were the pilots, copilots and navigators.

**Letter from nine-year-old sister, Sharon. Tuesday, June 6, 1967**
*Dear Terry*

*Thanks for the 2 dollars you gave me. Mr. and Mrs. Simon gave 2 dollars too and Father Smit gave me 1 dollar. Judi Simon gave me a dress and necklace to go with it and Judy Sater gave me a bracelet. We were out of school June 1 and I got an award for good work and I passed to fourth grade. I got the most stars for spelling in the room.*

*Your sister,*

*Sharon*

**Letter home, Tuesday, June 20, 1967**
*Dear Mom, Dad, Grandma and brothers and sisters,*

*This is a special occasion. One hour ago, the Enterprise recovered its last aircraft this cruise for combat operations. It's an odd feeling. The combat operations are over now, and the way I feel is pretty close to how I felt graduation day. I'm glad it's over, but I'm also proud as hell of my ship! The Skipper says we re-landscaped "Uncle Ho's yard" with 14,100 tons of bombs. It would have been more if we had better flying weather the first half of the cruise. 14,000 tons of bombs weren't delivered without a cost. Fourteen pilots and navigators won't be returning home. At 2:30 this afternoon, the "Intrepid" will pull alongside and we will transfer aircraft handling equipment to her. She takes the load, now. Officially, Oriskany is our relief.*

*Tomorrow I am supposed to check out of OE Div. I'm pretty happy about it! I'll be home just a few days after you get this letter and I can hardly believe it! I just bought two rolls of slide film and I may buy more to cover my flight home. If I do by chance stop in Japan and Anchorage, Alaska, there will be a lot of pictures to take. Come to think of it, there will be a lot to take pictures of, no matter how I come home!*

*I will be "in transit" from Subic as soon as we pull in. I get off the ship and stay in a barracks for a few days until they fly me home. I'll buy Fran & Steve's china and soak up sun so that I look a little darker when I come home. I can't wait!*

*See you soon!*

*Terry*

**From the Enterprise Cruise Book**
*"The waters about 100 miles east of North Vietnam, where the Gulf of Tonkin joins the South China Sea, are known to the men of the United States Seventh Fleet and the world as "Yankee Station." These waters became well known to the officers and men of ENTERPRISE, for before they completed their last mission they were to spend 132 days at Yankee Station. During that time, they would fly a total of 13,471 sorties. Before this cruise was over, they would deliver 14,100 tons of bombs."*

I was fortunate to be given the opportunity to sign up for E.T. (Electronics Technician) school due to my overall test scores, performance on the Enterprise, and staying out of trouble. The Enterprise was in port in Subic, but would be going back to *"Yankee Station"* in the Tonkin Gulf. I was to fly back to the states for a month's leave, and then report to Basic Electricity and Electronics School, in San Diego.

**On June 24, 1967, I sent the following "Radiogram" to Judi, through the "Amateur Radio's Public Service Net Serving Midwest USA",**
*"Hi, Judi. I leave the ship today. Will be in the Philippines for a few days and then fly across the Pacific and half the country to be with you again. It won't be long now, Judi. Love, Terry*

I left the ship June 25, 1967. Two days later, at "0600," I caught a bus to Clark Air Force Base, to catch flight # W234 at 1315 Hours. Part of the route followed the path of the infamous *"Death March of Bataan."*

Ten hours after the attack on Pearl Harbor that Japanese planes hit Clark Field, the main US air base on the Philippine island of Luzon. Japanese forces captured 76,000 prisoners. Many were sick, wounded, or starving. The prisoners were forced to march sixty-five miles to their final destination of Camp O'Donnell. Thousands died during the march. Many were beaten to death, shot, or bayoneted. Two and a half years later, General Douglas MacArthur fulfilled his promise to return to the Philippines and liberate it from the Japanese.

The bus ride along the trail of the Death March of Bataan was a chilling link to my earlier experience in cruising past the Arizona memorial and Corregidor. Those experiences left an ineffaceable mark on my sense of history, the sacrifices made by those Americans who went before us, and the debt we owe them.

We arrived at Clark at 0900. From Clark, we flew to Yokota, Japan. We spent a couple of hours there, before going on to Travis Air Force Base, which took nine hours. From Travis, I took an hour and a half bus ride to San Francisco. My flight took me to Los Angeles, Kansas City, and finally, home to St. Louis.

By this time, the United States was deep into the ground war in Vietnam. I knew our Navy was fighting on the rivers in the Mekong Delta, but it was generally considered a volunteer force and I never imagined I would someday be a part of the elite force and wear the distinctive camouflaged green beret, myself.

During the summer and fall of 1967, the MRF was constantly in action. In June, *"Operation Concordia"* trapped four hundred Viet Cong near Ap Bac. ARVN units and sailors of the MRF killed over 250 of the enemy while losing forty-six men. The riverine force cut off the enemy's line of retreat and took heavy fire, wounding fifteen sailors.

**The first helicopter pad fitted Armored Troop Carrier (ATC) arrived in Vietnam, July 22, 1967.**

On July 29th, 1967, an electrical anomaly discharged a Zuni rocket on the flight deck of the USS Forrestal (CVA-59), starting a chain-reaction of explosions, while conducting flight operations in the Gulf of Tonkin. The devastating fire and explosions killed 134 sailors and injured 161. The monetary damage exceeded $72 Million (equivalent to more than $509 Million, today), not including damaged aircraft. The Forrestal managed to make its way to Subic Bay, Philippines. It never returned to the Gulf of Tonkin. .

The Seventh Fleet put an enormous amount of ships and other resources into the area of operations at *"Dixie Station,"* off South Vietnam and *"Yankee Station,"* in the Gulf of Tonkin. This included a number of aircraft carriers. Quite a few of them had nicknames. The Oriskany was sometimes referred to as *"Firefly,"* due to its fire in 1966. Other carriers that sailed with the Enterprise, or *"The Big E,"* included the Coral Sea, the Kitty Hawk *("The Shitty Kitty"),* the Ticonderoga *("The Tico"),* the Ranger, the Constellation *("The Connie"),* the Intrepid *("The Fighting I"),* and the Bon Homme Richard *("The Bonnie Dick").*

The *"Skipper"* of the Enterprise was Captain James L. Holloway III. Captain Holloway inspired confidence and pride. He seemed to respect and care about his men. We respected and cared about him. One day at sea, I was sitting in line for a haircut on the barbershop floor when the captain entered the area. As was the tradition and the requirement, someone yelled *"Attention on deck!"* Captain Holloway smiled and told the sailor who yelled it out, *"Hey! What are you trying to do, make enemies?"* Captain Holloway went on to become Vice Admiral Holloway, Commander of the Navy's Seventh Fleet, from 1972 to 1973. From 1974 to 1978 he served as the Navy's Chief of Naval Operations, the top position in the largest navy in the world. As of this writing, the Admiral is still enjoying his retirement, at ninety-four.

I had only been in the Navy for one year, at this point. I used to joke with my father that I was amazed at how much he learned, while I was in Boot Camp. The truth is, it was I who learned. When I was a kid, Dad was a strict disciplinarian. I got the belt, or smacked, whenever he felt the need. Once I was in the Navy, I saw him in a different light. He was just a guy, working hard to feed a family of eight kids and raise them the best he could.

I saw the whole world differently. Once you've seen poverty, REAL poverty, in places like the Philippines, or Hong Kong, you have a deeper appreciation for how fortunate Americans truly are.

When you see sacred places like Pearl Harbor, or Corregidor, and travel the trail of the Death March of Bataan, you absorb a sense of the pain and sacrifice of those who served before you. It instills a deeper appreciation for what we as Americans have had passed down to us.

**USS Enterprise CVAN 65.  Photo courtesy U.S. Navy**

# Chapter 3

## Electronics Technician Schools

After a month at home, I left for Basic Electricity and Electronics School, in San Diego.  I made good friends in B.E.E. School.  We drove to Yuma and Phoenix Arizona on a weekend lark.  One of the guys heard about a party, in Yuma.   We ran a *"taxi"* service with Frank LaBate's Chevy Impala convertible to the Tijuana border.

**On August 11th, 1967, Gerald Ford, House Republican Leader, accused Johnson of *"pulling punches"* in the bombing campaign of North Vietnam, while sending more Americans to die in the ground war.**

**Letter Home.  Saturday, August 26, 1967**
*Dear Mom, Dad and Everybody,*

*Hi!  I guess you're mad, huh?  I kind of got the message when Judi said you wanted to know if I was "still alive."  I guess it looks like I'm really having too much fun to write and all that, but it's really not true! I'm sorry I haven't written, but I do get pretty busy. My liberty is usually limited to going out for coffee after class, which means about 1:00.or 1:30 a.m., until between 3:30 and 4:30 a.m.  Sometimes we come back to the base at dawn.  I guess that sounds wild, but it's just that those are the only hours we can run around.  We either go to a classy place called "Mr. B's" and drink coffee for hours and act rather "adult," or we go to "Oscar's," and act like <u>idiots</u> there.  This town is "unfriendly" towards "Squids," so we always go in civies.  At Oscar's, the management is pretty friendly to us because usually, five or six of us go in at once and that's almost a whole dollar profit for them.  Sometimes, if we are in a real good mood, we blow our cool by using Navy jargon and letting those who don't know it that we are "Gobs," "Squids," or whatever you want to call us.  We'll say something like, "Well, let's go back to the <u>BASE</u>!"  One time, the waitress came up to us and she had a badge that said she was a "trainee," so one guy said, "That's something like a "Seaman Apprentice" isn't it?"  She said "Not quite!" and stomped away.  Another time, we went out to a park near here where they have a big bell, which was donated to San Diego by the Japanese.  It is rung by swinging a big log, which is pretty big and is suspended by a heavy chain.  It is not meant to be rung.  We got this idea due to the fact that it is surrounded by a wide, deep moat.  We jumped the moat, to get to the bell.  The first time we rang it, I drove the "getaway" car. The second time we rang it, four of us managed to jump the moat and gave a joint effort in swinging the log as hard as we could.  Pretty juvenile, I guess, but there isn't much as to do!  It was a challenge!  Anyway, after eight hours of electronics theory, I'm almost ready to stand inside the bell while they ring it.*

*As for school, we just finished the hardest part of it, which is "Inductance and Capacitance in a Parallel Circuit."  I scored a 70, which at first disgusted me and then I found out that a "Charlie" or "C Track" class, which covered the material in a week and a half, had a class average of 69, with two of the guys flunking it.  My class covered it in three days and nobody flunked it.  62.5% is passing.  Now we start studying transformers and have the test on that on Tuesday.  The final exam is Wednesday.  Thursday, we have off.  Friday, I leave for Frisco and Treasure Island ("T.I.").  My average is a low of 75, approximately.  It has dropped in the last few weeks, but the material is also getting harder.  Anyway, all I care about is passing with a decent average.*

*When I get up to Frisco, I have to get to the ship and see my buddy Shane and see if he kept any mail for me after I left the ship.  I also want to see if he picked up my I.D. bracelet and the ring.  Besides, I'm anxious to hear how the trip back to the states was on my old "boat."*
*I'll close for now, and try to write as soon as I get up to Frisco.*

*Love,*
*Terry*

**Letter Home.  Sunday, August 27, 1967**
*Dear Folks,*

*I have half an hour before class starts, so I guess I can write a short letter to you.  We have our first test today. This is sort of an "A Track" class, in High School.  Remember me, the "C Track" flunkie?  They say that according to our test results, we are the "cream of the crop" and they have figured out our predicted averages. Mine is 84%.  Passing is 65%.  Only three guys have lower predicted averages than I do in this class.  One guy has the same as me, and several guys hit around 84.3%, 84.6% and so on.  I would feel more comfortable being at the top of a low class, than at the bottom of a high class.  There are twenty-three guys in the class.  One guy has a predicted average of 99.9%.  The test today covers "matter," atomic structure, electromagnetism and electrostatics.  As you can see, they are moving us pretty quickly.  It still kind of scares me, but I'll never have another opportunity like this and I can't use that good china in an old shack!  It should be a good sized house with pillars in front!  Anyway, after all I went through to get this course, I have to pass it!*

*I can't wait till Christmas.  Among the other things, I want to see the china!  Really, Christmas isn't that far away.  By the way, I'm sorry if I ever seemed crabby or nervous when I was home.  After the first four days home, I started dreading to leave, even though I tried to push it out of my mind.  You may have noticed I never volunteered to talk about when I was leaving.  It made me nervous when people asked, because I just didn't like to think about it.  I think I almost bit some heads off the day before I left, so now you understand why.  One day, Mom said something about me "pacing the floor" when I was home.  The thing is; I felt like I was in a race with time, like I had to beat the clock.  I had to be doing something, because soon, my leave would be over.*

*I have a pretty crazy schedule.  School starts at 5:00 p.m. and lasts until 1:30 a.m., except on Fridays and then it lasts until midnight.  They give us a five-minute break every forty-five minutes and an hour for chow at 9:30 p.m...  The rest of the time is completely devoted to electricity and electronics, with math interjected periodically.  The instructor throws out facts a mile a minute and if you don't get it, "Too Bad."*

*The food here is terrible!*

*Love,*

*Terry*

After graduation from "BE&E" school, I reported to "Advanced Electricity and Electronics School," at Treasure Island Naval Base, in San Francisco, September 1, 1967.

**On September 3rd, 1967, Nguyen Van Thieu was elected President of South Vietnam.**

Classes commenced on September 4th.  Advanced Electronics School was a very arduous school.  In high school, I only had one semester of freshman Algebra.  During this school, I was force-fed Algebra, geometry, calculus, and trigonometry, as well as advanced electronics theory. I failed my second quiz and *washed out* of ETA school on October 31, 1967.  I was devastated by the failure. I just didn't cut it. It didn't matter that many others had also washed out. I really wanted to accomplish becoming an "E.T."

The second blow came when I received my new orders.  In shock, I read my orders to the *"Mekong Delta Mobile Riverine Force training at Naval Inshore Operations Center, Vallejo, California."*  It was more than the fact that I was going to Vietnam.  My plans of becoming an E.T. were dead.  Soon, I could be as well.

I tried to avoid going to Nam.  I am neither proud, nor embarrassed by that.  I wrote to the Bureau of Naval Personnel, stating that I requested to be returned to *"The Big E"* and to continue working towards the Navy's already considerable investment in my electronics training.  That request was turned down.  When I went home on leave, I called "BuPers" (*Bureau of Naval Personnel*) and tried again.  The voice on the other end of the phone said that if I was worried about getting killed, I didn't have to, worry, because the Mobile Riverine Force *"hasn't lost a boat yet!"*  The irony and humor in his claim wouldn't hit me until I arrived at Dong Tam, their base in the Mekong Delta.  I tried not to worry the family or Judi about the danger of the Mobile Riverine Force duty.  I told them the unit was a patrol, or policing outfit that really didn't see action.

**On the plus side, I was able to be home for Christmas leave, 1967.**

# Chapter 4
## *"S.E.R.E."* Training

On December 28th 1967, I reported to *"Fleet Airborne Electronics Training Unit, Pacific, U.S. Naval Air Station,"* North Island, in San Diego California.

**At this point, the U.S. had 485,600 troops in Vietnam. 15,979 Americans had died there.**

One day in early January, I sent home an audio tape on the lectures we were receiving, to give us a basic understanding of what we should expect and what was expected of us, in Vietnam. It began;

*"Right now, I'm walking up to the baseball field, facing San Diego Bay.*

*They gave us a lecture today on the physiological warfare that the Viet Cong and North Vietnamese used. They gave the example of "Hanoi Hannah." She would pick out a popular American name, like "Bill," and a typical family circumstance like a married guy in the service, whose wife and family was living in San Diego. Then, she would play romantic music, getting everyone listening to her, homesick. Softly, she would say, "Has that got you thinking about your wife, Bill? Well, don't worry about it. She's with your friend, in San Diego!" She knows there are a lot of "Bills" in Vietnam, with many having wives in San Diego. She knows she will rattle a lot of guys with tormenting comments, like that.*

*She'd follow that up with a "Tom," in San Francisco, "Bob," in Long Beach, and so on.*

*Fortunately, there's not that many "Terry's." Plus, I'm not married and my girl is in Overland, Missouri. I don't think she'll be saying anything that hits a cord with me.*

*Tomorrow, I get my combat boots and my "greens." I have to buy some heavy socks. I'll have to start breaking in the boots, for the hiking they're going to have us doing, around the Marine base, at Camp Pendleton. Most of the guys have been wearing them all week, getting them ready. I'll just be starting, tomorrow. Maybe I'll smash the upper leather parts with a hammer, to soften it up.*

*It's Thursday afternoon. I just got my boots and my green fatigues. The cap has a Marine insignia on the front! It is disgusting that I have to wear a Marine insignia! Tell that to my "Jarhead" buddy, Ed Bahr!*

*We're hearing lots of lectures. I'm still aggravated that I got these orders, so I haven't been paying a lot of attention to them. I've been reading "Valley of The Dolls."*

*It's now 6:00, in the evening, and it's kind of chilly out. We knocked off at 4:30, after having lectures, all day.*

*I just finished talking to Judi, about forty-five minutes ago. I know I'm running up big phone bills, but I can't help it. It's worth it to me.*

*I was in the barracks, a few minutes ago. We have coal oil heaters. They just finished putting six gallons of coal oil in the heater. It wasn't working, last night. It was pretty chilly. I couldn't stand getting out of bed, this morning. I had two blankets and it was still cold, even though the blankets are really great. When I get out of the Navy, I'd like to have a couple of them!*

*Tonight, Judi was getting on me about the fact that I'm not making any friends, yet. It kind of bothers her. I have talked to a lot of the guys. I'm not the "loner" type, but sometimes, it does a guy good to be completely on their own. I'll get around to making friends.*

*One of the things they are talking to us about that does interest me is the "R&R." They say they'll give us five days, every three months. Somebody told me that by the end of our year, over there, we'll have twenty-five days of R&R out of the country, and three days R&R, in the country of Vietnam. The rest of the time, we're on duty. I don't know if they give us "liberty," or not.*

*Tomorrow, they're supposed to give us the details on taking R&R. If they give us R&R as much as they're saying they will, I'll get around to seeing Hawaii, Bangkok, Australia and maybe Japan. I would like to get to Bangkok, or Australia, but I figure if I can get to Hawaii, I can call home from there.*

Over time, my petulance with my orders gave way, as a grudging pride in the unit started seeping in. I started paying more attention to the lectures. One of the lectures that stayed with me was the one on the difference between a *"Lawful Order,"* and an *"Unlawful Order."* It was drilled into us that we had not only the *"right,"* but the <u>responsibility</u> to refuse any order that violated the Uniform Code of Military Justice. We could also refuse orders that were not strictly under the normal performance of duties, for example, a sailor who outranked me, couldn't tell me to shine his shoes, but he could tell me to *"swab the deck."*

We were also taught the **"CODE OF CONDUCT FOR THE U. S. FIGHTING MAN"**

   *1. I am an American fighting man. I serve in the forces which guard my country and our way of life. I am prepared to give my life in their defense.*

   *2. I will never surrender of my own free will. If in command, I will never surrender my men while they still have the means to resist.*

   *3. If I am captured, I will continue to resist by all means available. I will make every effort to escape and aid others to escape. I will accept neither parole nor special favors from the enemy.*

   *4. If I become a prisoner of war, I will keep faith with my fellow prisoners. I will give no information, or take part in any action which might be harmful to my comrades. If I am senior, I will take command. If not, I will obey the lawful orders of those appointed over me and will back them up in every way.*

   *5. When questioned, should I become a prisoner of war, I am bound to give only name, rank, service number and date of birth. I will evade answering further questions to the utmost of my ability. I will make no oral or written statements disloyal to my country and its allies or harmful to their cause.*

   *6. I will never forget that I am an American fighting man, responsible for my actions, and dedicated to the principles which made my country free. I will trust in my God and in the United States of America.*

Prior to the Vietnam War, violation of ANY of the code, could result in a Courts Martial. After learning of the atrocities inflicted on P.O.W's, it was determined that requiring strict compliance to such a demanding code was not always realistic. Today, it stands as a guide to personal conduct.

Following some classroom training, we were sent off to *"S.E.R.E."* (*Survival, Evasion, Resistance and Escape*) training. Only a limited number of people in the military typically undergo this training, such as those in Special Forces, pilots and air crews.

**Audio tape home, immediately after SERE training;**

*"I'm in the barracks, at Mare Island. It's after dark, around 7:30. The temp is about fifty-four degrees. I just got off the phone with you. I'll try to talk. My voice is rough, but getting better. I am fighting a cold, cough and severe bronchitis. I went to sick bay this morning and got some "GI Gin." That's government-issue cough syrup. I have been taking a lot of cold pills.*

*I started S.E.R.E. weighing 165 pounds, at 6'2." I lost twenty pounds and I'm having a little trouble walking. It was very cold at night and I shivered so much, the muscles in my legs, butt and back are all cramped up. I can hardly bend my legs. I walk like "Frankenstein!" In class today, they were teaching us the military organization in Vietnam and the political structures of the provinces and districts. They also talked about what our jobs would be over there. From what I hear, the kind of boat I would be on would be a river assault boat that will carry troops and be out for four or five days, then in for at least three and then out again. Every four, five, or six months, it goes into the yards for a while and that's when everyone gets R&R.*

*I really enjoyed the tape from you last week. Mom, thanks for congratulating me on stopping smoking. Right now, my throat is very ticklish. Every time I think of a cigarette, it makes me sick. Tim, I think you did a great job singing "Yankee Doodle Dandy." I think it is the best "Yankee Doodle Dandy" I have heard in months!*

*As for the SERE training, I don't know what I should or shouldn't tell you. Judi probably told you it was confidential. It is spelled S. E. R. E., for "Survival Evasion Resistance and Escape." The "Resistance" phase is the most confidential. We started Monday morning. They got us up at 4:30. We "mustered" at 5:30. They gave us army jackets and sheath knives. They also gave us a box breakfast. We had to have that eaten by 8:00, that morning. I finished it at 7:30. I figured we weren't going to be eating much in the days to come. I didn't get anything else to eat all day Monday or Tuesday. About one o'clock in the morning, on Wednesday, I got a quarter cup of rice and two or three cups of rice broth.*

*On Monday, they taught us survival, until about 3:15. Then, they had us hike and jog to the camping area, which was about three miles. We jogged "double-time" about two miles of that. It was on a beach. We had parachutes for sleeping bags. You fold them over, several times. The parachute material is supposed to have a high insulation value. It didn't keep me very warm. I still don't understand why they gave us parachutes. I doubt we will be issued parachutes on the boats.*

*For food, they told us to catch crabs, along the rocky beach. Red crabs, maybe two or three inches across. Since there was one-hundred-thirty-one of us, there wasn't that many crabs for us to catch. Since the only real meat was in the claws and there was so little of it, I didn't even bother. The thought of eating them raw, was revolting to me. Instead, I just starved.*

*The next day, we went to Warner Springs, near San Diego, by bus. When we got there, we pitched camp. After camp was set up, we went to the night evasion course. The course was 540 yards long and 30 yards wide, at the narrowest point. They had four to six so called "aggressors," against us. They had M-1's, or shotguns, with blanks. They would shine a flashlight on us and say "Freeze!" or simply shoot us with blanks. When they shot us, we knew we were "shot." I didn't make it all the way through the course, but I wasn't caught, either. They gave us a time limit. I think it was two hours. I got about fifty yards from where we were supposed to get to, before the time ran out. I had just gone underneath some concertina wire, which consists of rolls of barbed wire, when some Lieutenant got caught in it. I helped him out of it and then I helped another guy out, so, consequently, I didn't make it to the finish point on time. After the concertina wire, there was something like tumbleweed, or real thick bushes. Further down, there was a railroad tie fence. This is where our C.O. got caught, trying to get underneath it. He was too big. I managed to find a place that was pretty well hidden. Somebody had gone that way before and had dug a hole underneath the fence. I got under the fence, across the road. There were large boulders, similar to what we used to see at "Elephant Rock State Park," in Missouri. Once you peeked over that, you could see a machine gun tower, which, of course, did not have real ammunition. That's the narrowest point, and the most dangerous. It had "aggressors" waiting for us, most of the time. This is where most of our guys were caught. I made it past there, then I went down behind the machine gun nest and on to the concertina wire.*

*It was a pitch black night. You couldn't see your hand in front of your face. The temperature was pretty cool, but the stress and the exertion made me sweat. That's where I got stuck. I got turned around a couple of times, in the dark. It may seem kind of odd to you that it took me two hours to go 500 yards, but most of it was on my hands and knees, or crawling on my stomach. It was through rugged terrain, in the Cleveland National Forest. In this "night evasion," they told us that when you are evading, you have to stay away from all trails, roads, river beds, or anyplace that looks traveled at all, so I was crawling underneath bushes. By the end of the course, I was picking cactus needles out of my wrist, with my teeth.*

*It was pretty rough. It looked like a combination of forest, desert and rock canyon. I climbed a tree at one point, to try to see where the finish point was and to rest for a while. The most important rule I learned, was NEVER, NEVER hit one of the "aggressor" instructors. While sitting there in the dark, one of the other trainees was captured by the instructors just below me, at the base of the tree. He made the mistake of hitting one of them. I sat in the tree, listening to his beating. It never occurred to me to try to help. He shouldn't have hit the instructor. Secondly, there were enough instructors that I could not have taken them all on. I know he was very badly hurt, but I have no idea what became of him. The "aggressors" were all around me, gathering guys up. I froze. They never did see me. They did get quite a few of the guys.*

*That night, when I went back to the tent, there were eleven guys in it. It was so crowded, I didn't even try to get in, so I slept by the fire. Around two or three in the morning, it started raining, so I put a big piece of cardboard over me. A Lieutenant made me take it off, because he was afraid the soaking wet cardboard was going to catch fire, so I sat by the fire, in the rain.*

*The next day, we tried to catch food, like rabbits, and find edible plant life. We made a stew with one or two trapped squirrels and some animals they provided, including pigeons and rabbits. I remember a rabbit's head in the stew and one of the guys eating the eyes, as a joke. I ate some cactus. I didn't like it at all. You don't eat the cactus needles. You are supposed to peel the skin off the cactus, with a knife and wipe the blade each time you take a swipe with it. If you don't, you put needles back on the meat of the cactus and you will be digging cactus needles out of your tongue, your throat and your stomach. It didn't have much taste. It was kind of mushy. The most important thing in survival is water. Cactus has liquid in it that will keep you alive.*

*That same day, I made a wooden knife that I could use to escape from the "P.O.W." compound, but I'll tell you more about that, later. Anyway, I lost it.*

*The next day, we started our hike. It was a navigational exercise. We broke camp at 5:30 a.m. They gave us two coordinates. It was through all kinds of mountains. We started marching at daylight. Most guys ran out of water around noon. Some guys drank out of a stream. I stretched my water, almost all the way. I remembered from Boy Scout hikes to elevate my feet when I rested and don't rest for much more than five minutes. The other guys didn't do that. I think it helped me a lot, because the other guys seemed to tire out a lot quicker.*

*We had to carry a tent and some other stuff, with us. We took turns, starting at the front of the line. The Lieutenant carried it first. We passed it every time a guy got tired.*

*One thing that was unusual about this week was that there were a lot of Lieutenants and Lieutenant "J.G.'s" (Junior Grade). They weren't really treated like officers. They were treated more like regular guys, because you really couldn't have the usual "pomp" that is associated with the officer-enlisted man relationship. It just doesn't work on a hike or something like that. You can't be bothered with saying "Yes, Sir," "No, Sir," or saluting. We did what we were told, though. We showed them respect. On this hike, the Lieutenants carried the tent their share of the time and we carried it our share of the time. There wasn't anybody getting off easy because of rank. We had trouble getting our bearings, but we got to our coordinates about 2:30 in the afternoon. We had flagged down a truck and asked for directions! There were six squads. They started us out at five minute intervals. I think only two of the squads made it to the place we were supposed to get to without getting lost. Four of the squads got lost. We were four miles from the place we were supposed to be. That's just in one direction. We went through all kinds of trouble to get to where we were supposed to be. When we got to the coordinates they had given us, they gave us two more coordinates, which was to our camp site for that night. During that leg of our hike, I noticed one of the older guys in the group was tiring awfully quick, holding up the squad. A couple of times, he was coughing so hard that he threw up. Right after we scaled down a big cliff, I noticed he was throwing up blood. I asked him if there was anything special he could tell me about the problem. I pointed it out to the Lieutenant and we found out that he had a bleeding ulcer and wasn't telling anyone. He talked to a medic, who just told him to drink a lot of water.*

*We marched for an hour and a half in the dark before we got to camp. It was a "cold camp," meaning we couldn't have a fire. It was the forest rule. We pitched our tent in the dark. For dinner, we each dipped two fingers into a can of "Spam" and got enough to equal about two or three spoonful.*

*They woke us at 5:30 in the morning, for our day evasion exercise. We started the course two hours later. They spread all one hundred and twenty-nine of us out in a straight line, on a tract of land approximately a mile and a quarter long, over hills, through the woods. When they fired a gun, we all started heading towards a certain point. We were told to head southeast and to keep the sun to our left cheek. By 8:00 a.m., eighty-three of the guys had been caught. They came close to me one time, but I managed to evade them. I finally managed to get close to the spot that was our final objective. I crossed a road and got to a clearing at the top of a hill. There was a helicopter flying nearby. They told us that if the helicopter came near us, we could flag it down to pick us up, so I took off my jacket, my green shirt and my "skive" shirt and started waving it at the helicopter. The chopper flew right past me. He saw me. He just didn't want to pick me up.*

*They caught just about my entire group by this time. I followed a creek bed for a while. I was so tired; I was just about ready to give up. I didn't know if the exercise was over, or not. They were still firing M-1 blanks, just as in the night evasion course, but I hadn't heard any gun shots for a while. I met only one or two guys within forty-five minutes, so I thought maybe the exercise was over and I was one of the last ones there, lost or something. I finally made it to the spot when the siren went off, signaling the end of the exercise. It was frustrating. I was closer to the point we were supposed to get to than I had thought. If I had gotten there on time, they would have given me a piece of fruit and a cup of water. A lot of guys risked a lot and ran a lot, just for that prize, because we were all starving and thirsty, by that time. As I was coming in, the "aggressors" were there. They had twenty-four to thirty-four of our guys lying on their stomachs, with their faces in the dirt. This was the beginning of the "POW" phase.*

*They had "captured" us. They made it as realistic as they could and they were rough. They put us in a truck and took us to the POW camp. When we got to the camp, they ordered us to file out and go into the compound. They had us strip down to our skivvies and then they checked each article of our clothing, for weapons. If we had an escape plan, we would simply declare; "I have an escape plan." The "aggressors" would then say; "What is it?" We would then explain; "I got between you and your rifle and I shot you," or "I had concealed this knife and stabbed you when you turned your back." If they thought the plan was viable, they could then tell us "OK, make it!" As I recall, we only had one escape in that manner. After we stripped down and they finished going through our clothing, they gave our clothing back. As I started to walk away, one of the aggressors called me back. He was dressed in a pressed green military uniform and a crisp green cap with a red star on it. He spoke to me in a strange Korean/American/Vietnamese accent. He took my glasses and asked if I really needed them. I thought I would try "reverse psychology" and replied; "No, I don't." He smirked and said "Good! I'll take them!" They do that to all of the guys, because it makes it much harder to try to escape. I know that, because they had a tower guard and I could hardly see the top of the tower, let alone see if the guard was in the tower or looking in my direction.*

*They took us in to the main gate of the P.O.W. camp and lined us up in front of the command post. They gave us a long and firm lecture on the futility of trying to escape. Following the lecture, they lined us up in front of a trench and had us strip down again for another inspection. After the lecture and the inspection, they ordered us to pick up all of the pebbles and rocks in the compound. We had to run while we did it. After we did that for a while, they had us work at filling up a trench with our hands.*

*The temperature swings were extreme. It was scorching hot during the day and bone-chilling cold at night. Periodically, they would form us in lines, for inspections. A few of us, including me, passed out during the inspections. During one inspection, my throat was making involuntary gurgling sounds, from lack of water and food. I kept passing out and then coming to when I hit the ground. I was afraid of getting a beating for passing out, so I would jump back up quickly. As soon as I stood up, I would pass out again. I hit the ground three times in the span of several minutes. When I hit the ground the third time, I was coming to, and saw the guy in line next to me bend over to help me up. One of the guards yelled at him to get back in line.*

*They had all of us sit and listen to communist propaganda lectures. They seemed pretty realistic, both in their messages and in their strange, "B" movie accents, kind of a cross between Korean and German. They utilized everything they had learned from earlier wars, especially the Korean War. Their used every conceivable angle to undermine morale, unity, and military discipline. They tried to find every possible "chink" in our mental and emotional armor. They came at us on religion, telling us how ridiculous it was to believe that a virgin could have a child. Communists don't want you to worship God. They want you to worship the state.*

*They hit us on race, singling out a couple of the colored guys. The aggressor pointed at one of them and asked him if he felt equal to the white guy next to him. The aggressor yelled at him, "He doesn't think you are!"*

*After they worked the race angle for a while, they tried to chip at the military discipline and structure of the group by trying to undermine the officer - enlisted man relationship. They told us how the officers felt they were better than all of the enlisted men. They told us that the officers thought the enlisted men were "dirt." They had a large propaganda board, with pictures of Mao Tse Tung. The speaker pointed at the picture and said; "See, Comrades, he wears the clothes of the WORKER! The peasant! Not the military man, like you do! We are for peace, not for war!"*

*He was a very good speaker, but we were so tired, from a lack of sleep and sheer physical exhaustion, that a couple of the guys fell asleep during the lectures. The aggressors would angrily snatch them up, or smack them. We had to bow from the waist to an aggressor, when we would speak to them or be spoken to, by them. We were instructed before the training that the "American fighting man" is not supposed to subject himself to degradation "in the face of the enemy," but that bowing was a customary sign of respect in the culture of the far east. They said that bowing was not a form of degradation. It was simply showing respect. They told us that the oriental could not stand to "lose face," so we should never put them into a position that they will feel they have lost face. They conveyed to us that if we did, WE would be the ones who lost face, teeth, or some other part of our body. Some of the guys seemed to be swayed. It was amazing to me that in a very short time, in an artificial setting, guys were succumbing to the psychological manipulations of our trainers. I really didn't feel affected by the lectures, at all.*

*We were told prior to the POW phase that if we escaped and made it to a wooden shack a hundred yards away from the POW camp, we would win a sandwich, an orange and a glass of milk. One of the formidable challenges to that escape, however, was the tower guard. I knew I would never be able to escape from a prisoner of war camp if I had been captured. While some had a hard time catching the tower guard with his head turned, I couldn't see the top of the tower! One member of our class did make many escape attempts. He would be roughed up each time he tried. The first time he attempted it, they handcuffed him. The second time, they put him in leg irons. The third time, they chained his handcuffs to his leg irons.*

*When we wanted to use the latrine, we had to yell to the tower guard; "Sir! Tower guard, sir! Request permission to use the head sir!" When our guy in handcuffs and leg irons made the request, the tower guard replied; "You want to do WHAT on my head?" He shouted out "TAKE A PISS, SIR!" He got a terrible beating for that. I am certain that if he had it to do over again, he still would have said it again.*

*One night, I had to go to the tower guard to request permission to use the head. One of our guys was at the base of the tower to instruct us how to request it properly. I was freezing cold, bone-tired, sleep deprived, famished, dehydrated, and sick. When I yelled out the request, I left something out, or got the words mixed up. Our guy at the base of the tower had to do push-ups as punishment for my mistake. When I requested it again, I messed up again and he had to do a bunch more push-ups. He begged me to PLEASE get it right this time! I did, but felt terrible for the guy that had to take my punishment.*

*Our commanding officer of the class had it worse. Probably much like they would do in a true situation, the ranking officer of our group was beaten regularly and humiliated, constantly. He was tied up and paraded around the camp in a wheelbarrow. This was done to try to break down morale, respect, and military bearing.*

*The camp looked much like you would expect a real POW camp to look. It was barren, mostly dirt and mud. We had bunkers, half buried in the ground, with pot-bellied stoves in the middle, for heat, but we were not allowed to be in them very much. They smelled of musty dirt, sweat and smoke. Barbed wire and guards ringed the camp. Oriental music played over speakers. They had a bulletin board, plastered with propaganda. Flood lights on tall poles ringed the camp. The lighting was so bright, you could read a newspaper by them.*

*Being good American POW's, we would take every opportunity to deface, or rip down the propaganda. We learned later that was a big mistake. They told us we should have studied the information to learn how our captors thought and used that information against them, to survive in the event we were really captured. They told us we had to get into their heads, to keep them from getting into ours!*

*They called us in for interrogations, five or six at a time, into a different part of the compound. They kept guys there for quite a while. It made us nervous. They didn't call me until we were ready to be served chow, which was a watery oyster soup. I heard it was pretty sickening. I didn't get to eat. They called my prisoner number, "number 101," in for interrogation. I went in with five other guys. I was at the head of the line. I had to put my hands behind my head. The guy behind me had to put his hands around my neck. The guy behind him had to put his hands around his neck, and so on. They took us into a small building and put seven of us into a very small "hot box." I didn't have enough room in it to lift my head, or move my feet. They kept us in that box for twenty minutes to a half-hour. On the plus side, I was finally warm for a change. On the downside, all of us were filthy and stunk. If it was a real prisoner of war camp, we probably would have been left in it a lot longer. We had to keep yelling out a "roll call" of our prisoner numbers, starting with the lowest number and going up to the highest. While I was in this hot box with the seven guys, they had other guys in single, small boxes. One guy in the small boxes was funny as hell and seemed to have a high tolerance for pain. The goal of the "aggressors" was to get us to "confess" to our war crimes, signing a document. This guy would start screaming "I'll sign! I'll sign! Just let me out and I'll sign!" I could hear the guards let him out to stand in the box. After a couple minutes of standing and stalling, they would order him to sign the confession. His voice would ring out; "Fuck you!" Then we would hear them pound on him and shove him back in the box. That scenario was repeated several times. I also heard one colored guy screaming for help because he was getting bad leg cramps. The guards asked him if he would sign his confession for "war crimes." He said he wouldn't sign, so they left him in the box. He kept screaming in pain, but received no pity, or help from the guards.*

*After a while, they took all of us out of the larger box we were in and shoved us into the smaller boxes. As the seven of us were getting out of the larger box, they were letting the guys out of the smaller boxes. When they opened the box of the colored guy who was yelling, he tried to stand up, but fell over, flat on his face. He didn't have circulation in his legs. He tried to get up again, but fell over, again. He tried to stand several times, but kept falling over. The boxes looked like grain boxes. They were slanted on the bottom and they were barely shoulder wide. They told us to stand in the box, with our feet crossed, then get down on our knees, then put our heads down into the box. After we got down, into the box, they closed the lid on top of us. The box was extremely tight. I tried to uncross my feet several times, but I couldn't. I did wiggle my toes and tried to move my feet and legs as much as I could, just to keep the blood circulating. After hearing the other guy yelling about cramps and falling over several times, I didn't want that to happen to me. My feet kept going to sleep on me while I was in the box with the seven of us in it. I didn't want that to happen, either. They had given us a few hints prior to going into this phase of the training. They told us it was important to keep your mind occupied. There were six air holes in the box, which was constructed of plywood. I counted each of the layers of plywood and studied how the box was constructed, in the smallest, most insignificant ways. I did isometric exercises and thought about what kind of food I wanted to eat when I was finished with the training.*

*It was clear that being in the boxes affected people differently. A couple of the guys fell asleep in the boxes and unfortunately, they snored. That enraged the guards, who would beat on the boxes and scream at the guys in them. There were some, however, that were extremely distressed with being in the boxes, suffering from claustrophobia. They would howl, holler and plead to be let out of the boxes. The guards would tell them they had to sign the paper. When the prisoners would say that they wouldn't sign the paper, the guards would then tell them that they were going to "turn the crank," to make the boxes even smaller. There was no "crank" on the box of course, but they did have something that made a sound like there was one. If the guys in the box would have stopped to think about it, they would have remembered there was not a crank on the box when they got into it. Regrettably, their minds were playing tricks on them and they were terrified.*

*After a while, they took us out of the small boxes and led us into small, separate rooms. Each one of us had our own interrogator. The "rooms" were actually small, dark, metal "Conex boxes," set two or three feet off of the ground. They were in a row, separated by thin metal walls. An interrogator took me into one of the rooms and ordered me to sit on the floor. We had to be careful to call this part of the training an "interview." If we referred to it as an "interrogation," they would beat us. I had five spotlights in my face. He used the "friendly" approach with me, for the most part. I sat on the floor, with my back against the wall, legs crossed. There was a desk, six feet away. My "interviewer" sat on the desk. I couldn't see his face, due to the lighting, I could only see him from his chest, down. His face was in the dark. He had a .38 revolver sitting on the desk, next to him, as an unspoken threat. It reminded me of an old 1940's war movie. The guy in the box next to mine was getting smashed against the wall, constantly. The noise and concussion of each hit reverberated against me, physically, and got inside my head, emotionally.*

*My interrogator asked me if I wanted a cigarette.*

*I replied; "Sir, no thank you, sir."*

*They warned us not to be a smartass with the interrogator, or play "John Wayne." We were taught that it does no good to go into the situation with the macho idea of telling the guy to "Go to Hell." We'd only get our face bashed in. They urged us not to try to be a "hero." We were advised to be respectful, but not answer any questions. The interrogator sat in front of me, blowing smoke in my face. I wasn't sure what he thought that was accomplishing. Maybe he thought it would make say that I really DID want a cigarette. He kept asking me questions besides my name, rank, serial number and date of birth. He asked me where I was from. He asked me if I had a girlfriend. We were taught they would try to get us to answer easy personal questions, so they could wear us down and drop our guard. The thinking was that if they can get you into the habit of answering trivial, personal questions, before long, you'd be spilling valuable tactical and strategic information. I kept telling him that under the articles of the Geneva Convention and what my country allowed me to say, I could only tell him my name, rank, serial number and date of birth. He told me that the Geneva Convention didn't matter and didn't apply to me. Then he started asking me if I had enough clothes and if I was warm enough. I stiffly replied that I was not allowed to engage in conversation with him. He told me that it was in the "Code for the American Fighting Man" that I could communicate my health and welfare. I knew, however that the only way I could do that would have been through the chain of command of my superior officers. An American POW cannot put himself in a position to negotiate individually for better treatment.*

*When I told him that I couldn't talk to him about it, he became threatening and asked me; "How would you like it if I took all of your clothes and threw you out, into this cold, mountain winter?"*

*I blurted; "I wouldn't like that, sir!"*

*I knew he WOULD do that. He threw a Geneva Convention pamphlet into my lap and told me to read it. I didn't look down, or pick it up. I stared blankly, into the lights. We had been taught that in the past, American POW's had been photographed picking up a piece of paper, or a book, and a photograph was then used as propaganda, saying the American POW was "reading his confession." For the same reason, a POW should never sign anything, even a subscription to a magazine. You aren't supposed to shake hands with the enemy, because they could say you are being "welcomed into the Communist Party." You are also not to subject yourself to a news interview, as a Vietnam American POW did, who was shown bowing from the waist.*

*He continued to ask questions. I got tired of answering "Sir, my country will not allow me to answer that, sir!" I began to simply stare at him in silence.*

He asked, "How would you like if I walked out of here, closed the door behind me, locked it and left you here for two weeks? What do you think would happen?"

I replied with a deadpan expression and said, "Well, I suppose by the time you came back, I would be dead."

He asked, "Do you think that would be worth it?"

I said, "Sir, yes, sir."

I felt hypocritical, sounding so "brave" in a training exercise. I KNEW he wasn't going to lock me in the box for two weeks. I knew they weren't going to shoot me, or break my bones. I DID believe they would take my clothes and put me out into the freezing winter night. I wish I could know that if it came to it, that I could say something like "I regret that I have only one life to give for my country," but nobody really knows what they will do until they are faced with a life and death decision. That is one of the most stark, vivid revelations.

In the end, he told me I was "stubborn" and he didn't think he was going to get anything out of me. During our "debriefing" of the training, they told us that if we went through a second "interview," it meant the instructors felt we could be broken easily. I wasn't called back. Eighty-three were. They were probably wrong.

We were taught how to resist giving the enemy information. I did not say that we were taught to NOT GIVE information, just to resist it as much a possible and to give as little information as possible. One of the main lessons I learned was that ANYBODY can be broken. It's just a matter of how long, or how much pain or fear you can stand before you break. Some people say "torture" doesn't work. I believe most people who have been a POW and been tortured, would disagree.

When my "interview" was over, I went back to camp and requested that I be readmitted into the compound. They didn't let us get to sleep until about 3:30 or 4:30, and then they got us up at 4:30 or 5:30 in the morning. They immediately called for an "inspection."

Most of the guys really got the hell beat out of them. Our Commanding Officer got smacked around constantly and the Lieutenants were hit often. During one inspection, the camp commandant and his immense goon of an aid stopped in front of me. The Hulk towered over me. He actually blocked the light from the surrounding flood lights. I stood in the cold darkness of his shadow. The commandant barked; "I.D.!" My freezing fingers fumbled with the button of my left shirt pocket to get my I.D. card out as quick as I could. It was more difficult than it should have been. My fingers were numb. Finally, I got it out and presented it to him, for his inspection. They moved down the line, but out of the corner of my eye, I saw The Hulk scowling back at me. Suddenly, he turned and came stomping back, towards me. I was terrified of what was about to happen to me. He brought his arm back, behind him, took a full swing, and smacked me hard across the face. I rocked back.

The Hulk sneered in a fake accent; "That's for not getting your I.D. out quick enough!"

I felt great relief. The fear was gone! The fear was worse than being hit! I was elated!

The next morning, they lined us up. The "Sergeant Major" screamed at us;

"Do not move! None of you are to so much as move an eye, or a finger! If you move so much as an INCH, I will secure the problem!"

This meant that if we moved, he would end our POW training exercise. We were so tired, confused, fearful, and already affected by the disciplined training, we did not move. We couldn't believe that if we moved, the training exercise would be over and we could finally get some sleep, take a hot shower and eat good food.

The Sergeant Major walked up to our "XO" (Executive Officer, the second in command) and shouted;

**"Did you hear what I said? If anybody moves, I will secure the problem!"**

*When it sunk in, all of us started jumping up and down, yelling and throwing our jackets in the air. We looked like mad men. We were tired, unshaven, wild haired and filthy. We looked insane, with sunken eyes, from lack of sleep, food and water. We were laughing and smiling like imbeciles. With the problem secured, they broke out a breakfast of one bowl of oatmeal, a half canteen of milk and an apple or an orange. I am certain that I have never enjoyed a meal as much as I did that fabulous banquet. I drank down the oatmeal like a crazed animal. We had learned that when you are really starving, the roof of your mouth hurts. Mine did.*

*That was the conclusion of my SERE training.*

I probably could have gotten out of going to Vietnam by flunking the S.E.R.E. training, but how can anybody intentionally fail a test like that? A test that measures who you are, in so many ways? I couldn't.

The back of my Survival, Evasion, Resistance and Escape diploma testifies;

*"The individual listed on the reverse side has received the training listed below while attending the FAETUPAC SERE training school completing on the date indicated (January 12th, 1968);*

I.    *CLASSROOM PHASE*              II.    *FIELD PHASE*
    *Moral aspects and code of conduct*       *Land navigation*
    *Survival psychology*                     *Night evasion*
    *Area survival (tropics, desert, arctic)*     *Day evasion*
    *Sea and seashore survival*             *Compound exercise*
    *Edible foods*                          *Interrogation*
    *Land travel*
    *Camouflage & evasion*
    *Geneva conventions*
    *Communist indoctrination methods*
    *POW resistance & escape*
    *Survival medicine*

On January 15, I signed up for a $10,000 life insurance policy at a cost of $2.00 per month, naming Mom and Dad as beneficiaries.

I have the greatest respect, and empathy for any American P.O.W. Even though I went through the extremely tough, brutal, S.E.R.E. training, I know it was NOTHING compared to actually being a prisoner of war. Still, I struggle with one question. We were told during our S.E.R.E. training that anybody can be "broken," under "enhanced interrogation" techniques. Senator John McCain is an outspoken critic of *"waterboarding,"* or *"enhanced interrogation."* He says they don't work. In 1969, as a Prisoner of War in Hanoi, he gave an anti-American propaganda broadcast. During the broadcast, he said; *"I, as a U.S. airman, am guilty of crimes against the Vietnamese country and people. I bombed their cities, towns and villages and caused many injuries, even deaths, for the people of Vietnam."* If torture, or *"enhanced interrogation"* doesn't work, why did he make that broadcast?

# Chapter 5

## River Warfare School

I reported to the Naval Inshore Operations Training Center, Mare Island, Vallejo, California, for two months of River Assault Craft training, January 14, 1968.

I still didn't feel like I fit in with the Riverine Force at this point, but the unit did have a certain *"panache"* to it. There was real pride and an appreciation of belonging to a history making military unit. My buddies in ET school were *"slide rule"* types. These guys weren't. You could say the guys in the Operations – Electronics Division of the Enterprise were kind of like the cast of *"The Office,"* or, *"The Big Bang Theory."* These guys were hell bent for leather, rough and tumble, adventurous guys, more like *"The Dirty Dozen."* Most were volunteers for *"River Rat"* duty, either because a friend or family member had been killed in action, or they simply wanted the experience of combat. I still wore my blue ball cap from the Enterprise. It wasn't long before I made several good friends, though, including radioman Pat "Grif" Griffin, Engineman Freddie Arens, from Boston and Seaman Jerry Ranson, from Chicago.

As a group, we didn't walk anywhere. We jogged to cadence, as class 14-R, pounding our right foot, to give each chant a rhythm. One chant was,

> *"14-R's the best class goin'*
> *Vietnam is where we're goin'*
> *Will we live or die?*
> *We'll live!"*

At the time, there was only River Assault Squadrons Nine, and Eleven. Another chants was,

> *"Riv Ron 9 and Riv Ron 11*
> *When we die, we'll go to heaven"*

River Assault Craft training at Mare Island was unique. Vietnam represented the first time since the Civil War and the days of the *"Ironclad"* and *"Monitor"* that the Navy battled on rivers.

America conducted riverine operations during the Revolutionary War. In 1775, after the battles of Lexington and Concord, the Americans and British struggled over control of the Hudson River-Lake Champlain-St. Lawrence River waterway. During the War of 1812, Americans again fought the British on waterways.

From 1835 to 1842 the American army and Navy opposed the Creeks and the Seminole, in the Florida Everglades. They utilized all sorts of boats and canoes, manned by soldiers, sailors and marines.

Riverine operations were dynamic during the Civil War, especially along the Gulf Coast and along the Mississippi River.

During the 20th Century, the American Navy patrolled the Yangtze River after the Boxer Rebellion in China, patrolling 1,500 miles of the river.

Much of what we were being taught was being learned by *"trial and error,"* based on what was happening in the Mekong Delta at the time, and from the French *"Dinassaut"* operations in Indochina from 1947 to 1953. Our instructors were Army, Navy and Marine Corp. personnel.

**The siege of Khe Sahn began January 21, 1968. There had been a U.S. presence near Khe Sanh since 1962, when a U.S. Army Special Forces camp was established in the nearby village of Lang Vei. Khe Sahn became the home of the Third Marine Division's 26th Marine Regiment, the Ninth and 13th Marine Regiment and the South Vietnamese 37th Ranger Battalion, for a total of 6,000 men.**

**The North Vietnamese built up forces around Khe Sanh with elements of the North Vietnamese Army's 304th, 320th, 324B, and 325C North Divisions, for a total of somewhere between 15,000 and 20,000 troops. President Lyndon B. Johnson told his generals,**

## *"I don't want any damn Dinbinphoo!"*

**North Korea seized the U.S. intelligence ship U.S.S. Pueblo, AGER-2, on January 23, 1968.**

### Undated Audio tape home

*Today, we had another day of training with the .38 caliber revolver. My ears are messed up. They usually have cotton for us to stick in our ears, but today, they didn't. They had fifteen of us lined up on the firing range, in standing position, firing the .38's. At first, it didn't seem bad, but after a while, there was a lot of ringing in my ears. This is our third day of training on firing the .38. We'll be doing it tomorrow, too. Our boats get issued .38's, but we won't be wearing them when we are in Vietnam, which they refer to as "in country." We just keep them on the boats.*

*The first day, I wasn't a very good shot, but yesterday, I was much better. I put six rounds in the bullseye and four close to it. We were firing ten rounds at a time. They had us firing at a slow rate, first, then speeding up. We were directed to fire with both hands, not one hand, like they do in movies. They drilled into us to take a breath and let half of it out, while squeezing the trigger and trying not to blink. It was fun, but I can imagine circumstances where it wouldn't be. I think tomorrow, they'll be scoring us on the .38. After that, they'll start training us on the M-14's, or the new M-16. Then, they'll start training us on various machine guns.*

*They taught us about grenade launchers. They have a new one, the "Mark 19." It can fire four hundred rounds a minute! These boats have a real <u>arsenal</u> on them!*

*A big commotion around the door to our barracks woke me up in the middle of the night. There was a bunch of guys, facing the "Neptune," our enlisted men's club. There's a Navy ship in port, and the crew of it was on liberty at the Neptune. They started knocking the "RAG" sailors (River Assault Group) and PBR (Patrol Boat, River) sailors. There was a big brawl, with beer bottles being thrown and chairs being broken. The Shore Patrol busted in and started arresting everybody, so the riverine guys ran into our barracks to hide from them.*

*I've been hearing a lot about the Enterprise, lately, going into Japan and causing riots because it is a nuclear powered ship, which "may or may not" have nuclear weapons on board. The news anchor was having trouble pronouncing the name of the Japanese city the Enterprise was going to; Sasebo, Japan, where our Navy has a base. He was struggling with "Say....see.....bow?"*

*I see it is also going towards North Korea, in response to them taking the USS Pueblo. Everybody here is angry about our ship being taken. You can imagine why sailors would feel that way. I know if I was on a ship that had been taken within international waters, I'd sure as Hell expect the U.S. to come and get me back! I'd hate to think my country would just scratch me off as a loss, for political reasons! Everybody here supports sending a large Navy task force, as well as Marines, if necessary, to get them back. I think if we just sent a couple carriers off their coast and told them to release our guys or we will bring HELL down upon them that would be enough. An intelligence ship like that has a lot of top secret stuff on it. I just hope they had time to destroy everything of value before it was taken. I can see why they didn't try to fight back. They only have some automatic weapons on them. I'm sure the Pueblo would have been sunk if it tried to fight back.*

*By the way, don't worry about my voice. I'm still recovering from the bronchitis I got during S.E.R.E. I'm popping pills and swigging "G.I. Gin." I sleep with my pea coat over my blanket. I should be better, soon.*

*I don't know if I'm going into Frisco, next week, or not. It takes a lot of money. It only takes $1.20 to get there on Greyhound, but eating off base is expensive. I should get paid, tomorrow. Last payday, I only got $23.00.*

*I imagine these phone bills will be coming in, next week. I'll send you as much as I can and send the Simons some money. Once I get over, "in country," I should be able to send more and make up for all the phone bills I've driven up, so far. They say that in Vietnam, all you need is five or ten bucks a month!*

*In class, today, they were teaching us the military organization in Vietnam and the political structure of the provinces, districts and the country of Vietnam. They told us what our jobs are going to be, over there. They say our boats will be out for four or five days, then in for at least three and then out, again. Every four, five, or six months, the boat will go into the yards, for overhaul. That's when everybody gets R&R. I don't know if we get it wherever we want it, or not.*

We were instructed in every phase of operating a river assault craft. Every crew member was cross trained to perform every other crew member's job, in case casualties required any of us to take the helm, call for help, or man a gun. We were trained to crew any type of river assault craft, whether it was an Armored Troop Carrier (ATC, or "Tango" boat), an Assault Support Patrol Boat (ASPB, or "Alpha" boat), or a Monitor. We were trained on every weapon we were expected to operate.

We were each given a training guide, composed of 130 pages of mimeographed study material, stapled together. I have one of the few remaining copies.

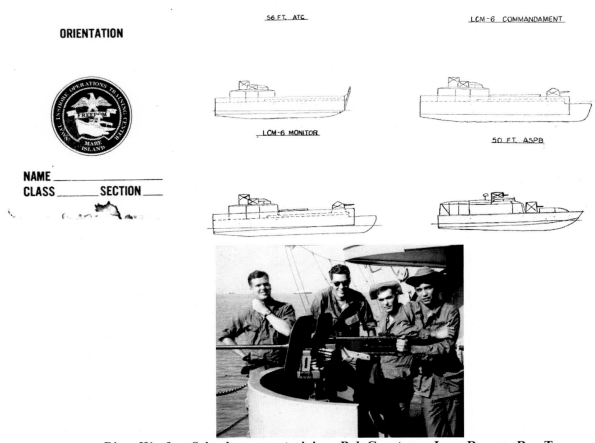

**River Warfare School gunnery training. Bob Grout, me, Jerry Ranson, Ron Tope.**

SPECIAL OPERATIONS DEPARTMENT
U. S. NAVAL AMPHIBIOUS SCHOOL
CORONADO, SAN DIEGO, CALIFORNIA

CI-1111
GJK:rjb
30 September 1966

HANDOUT

## DEFINITION OF INSURGENCY AND RELATED TERMS

INSURGENCY - A condition resulting from a revolt or insurrection against a constituted government which falls short of civil war. In the current context, SUBVERSIVE INSURGENCY is primarily Communist inspired, supported, or exploited.

COUNTERINSURGENCY - Those military, paramilitary, political, economic, sociological and psychological actions taken by a government independently or in conjunction with friendly nations to prevent or defeat insurgency.

INTERNAL SECURITY - The state of law and order prevailing within a nation.

INTERNAL DEVELOPMENT - The strengthening of the roots, functions and capabilities of government and the viability of its national life toward the end of internal independence and freedom from conditions fostering insurgency. (AR 320-5)

INTERNAL DEFENSE - The full range of measures taken by a government to protect its society from subversion, lawlessness, and insurgency.

SPECIAL WARFARE - Embraces all the military and paramilitary measures and activities related to unconventional warfare, counterinsurgency, and psychological operations.

UNCONVENTIONAL WARFARE - Includes the three interrelated fields of guerrilla warfare, evasion and escape, and subversion. Unconventional warfare operations are conducted within enemy or enemy-controlled territory by predominately indigenious personnel, usually supported and directed in varying degrees by an external source.

GUERRILLA WARFARE - Military and paramilitary operations conducted in enemy-held or hostile territory by irregular, predominately indigenous forces.

COUNTERGUERRILLA WARFARE - Operations and activities conducted by armed forces, paramilitray forces, or non-military agencies of a government against guerrillas.

COVERT OPERATIONS - Operations which are planned and executed as to conceal the identity ◆ of or permit plausible denial by the sponsor. They differ from clandestine operations in that emphasis is placed on concealment of identity of sponsor rather than concealment of the operation.

SUBVERSION - Action designed to undermine the military, economic, psychological, morale, or political strength of a regime.

WARS OF NATIONAL LIBERATION - The propaganda term used by the communists to dignify their efforts toward covert aggression.

COLD WAR - A state of international tension, wherein political, economic, technological, sociological, psychological, paramilitary, and military measures short of overt armed conflict involving regular military forces are employed to achieve national objectives.

We were assigned a boat and crew for training. I was on an "ASPB," or *Assault Support Patrol Boat.* A tough talking Boson's Mate 1st Class, Ken Carrol, was my boat captain during this phase of training. He was a trim, *"squared away,"* twenty-five year old married guy. We'd take our boats on simulated operations in the marshes north of San Francisco, around Vallejo. Staff from the school would *"ambush"* us with automatic weapons, AK-47's and other weapons, loaded with blanks. One day, Carrol saw me sitting on the bow of the boat, dangling my legs over each side of the bow. He screamed at me, calling me a *"stupid son of a bitch,"* and other colorful terms, not nearly as nice. He said I'd fall off the boat and drown as soon as we got to Nam. I didn't object. I knew he was right and that what I was doing was stupid.

**An Assault Support Patrol Boat (ASPB) during River Warfare School**

During search exercises of sampans, instructors would strike a flare and toss it on a boat to simulate a grenade, training us on very real possibilities and conditioning us to stay on our toes.

We called one of our guys *"Wheezer,"* due to his raspy, wheezing voice. During one search exercise, an instructor in a sampan asked *"Wheezer"* to strike the end of a flare he held out. Wheezer said; *"Sure"* and did it. The instructor said, *"Great, Dumbass! You just killed your crew!"*

We received intensive, extraordinary training in swimming, unlike anything else at the time, with the exception of SEAL, or Coast Guard rescue training. We had to demonstrate proficiency in swimming the length of the pool using just our arms, or just our legs, or just one arm or one leg, to get us used to the idea that we could either lose the use of arms, or legs, or actually *lose* our arms or legs, and still swim to shore, or to another boat.

In one exercise, we lined up at the deep end of the pool, facing the water. We put on a flak jacket and helmet. Then, in random order, someone would hit us from behind, knocking us into the pool. We had to remove the flak jacket and the helmet, at the bottom of the pool, and swim to the surface. As we broke the surface, we were told to splash our arms as though we were trying to dispel a coating of burning fuel that could be making the surface a burning hell. We were told no one could finish the school without passing this phase of training.

We also had exhaustive training in First Aid. The Navy Corpsman instructor was memorable. He was an excellent teacher, focused on teaching us how to tender first aid to combat wounds. As good as he was, if you started to doze off due to the exhaustive physical aspects of our training, he would fire a .38 pistol into the air, with blanks, startling you awake.

When it came to our "liberty," some of the guys loved going to the bars and getting into brawls. They'd start slugging, for any reason, at the drop of hat. One of those guys got into a fight with Freddie. I was told Freddie pulled a knife on him, but I don't know if it is true. I wasn't there. He beat him so bad, Freddie spent some time in the hospital.

One of the guys has remained in my memory because he seemed to relish fighting so much. He bragged that he couldn't wait to get to Vietnam and *"kill gooks."* He had me wondering if there was something wrong with *me*. I didn't want to get into fights and I wasn't looking forward to killing, or being killed.

At the end of training, just before we left for Vietnam, I went to the Chaplain, worried that I might not be able to pull the trigger in combat. I wasn't a conscientious objector, and it wasn't that I was more afraid of dying than anyone else. I was simply afraid I would not be able to shoot to kill, potentially putting my crewmates at risk. I was more afraid of failing to do my job than of dying. Nobody really knows what they will do in a combat situation until they come face to face with it. He tried to calm my fears, but I was still unsure.

Just before we completed training, a sweaty, potbellied, balding insurance salesman walked into our barracks; He came up to us, as we were watching TV, or lying in our bunks, giving us his pitch. He told us we needed to buy life insurance policies on ourselves before we went to Vietnam so our parents would reap the benefits if we were killed. What kind of a person does something like that? Did he also make sales calls in hospital ICU's, or cancer wards? Good sales people are empathetic. This guy was a sick sociopath. He left in a hurry, denying his family the benefits they would have reaped, had he stayed.

**January 31, 1968.** The Tet Offensive began, at 3:00 a.m. We were all glued to the TV in our barracks. The Mobile Riverine Force was heavily engaged in combat throughout the Mekong Delta. The Viet Cong attacked many places, including Saigon, and the river towns My Tho, Can Tho, Vinh Long, and Chau Doc. By the end of the day, it had spread to over one-hundred towns, villages and cities across South Vietnam, with over 80,000 North Vietnamese and Viet Cong fighting. Our TV showed the Mobile Riverine Force fighting in the area around Saigon. This was three weeks before we would be going there. The Tet offensive cranked the war up a notch and proved to be the turning point of public opinion about the war. The Viet Cong lost the battles of Tet, but before it was over, the American public showed it had no taste for a war like this one.

On February 1st, 1968, during the Tet Offensive, Saigon police chief, General Nguyen Ngoc Loan, was photographed shooting a Viet Cong guerrilla in the head. The prisoner, Nguyen Van Lem, was reported to be a Captain in a Viet Cong assassination and revenge platoon, responsible for the killing of South Vietnamese policemen and their families. The photographer, Eddie Adams was told by the police chief that Lem had killed one of Loan's officers and wiped out his entire family. The photo was splashed all over newspapers, magazines and television, around the world. It was extremely detrimental to the way the South Vietnamese government was viewed. I sometimes wonder what the average person would have done, in General Loan's place, if Nguyen Van Lem had killed <u>their</u> friends and family.

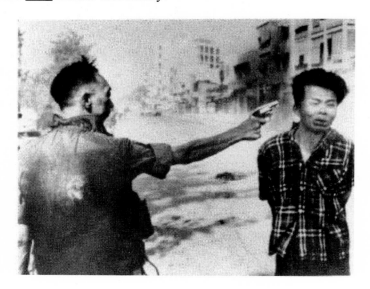

On February 6, the U.S. Army Special Forces camp at Lang Vei, near Khe Sahn, was overrun by North Vietnamese and Viet Cong forces who were supported by nine Soviet PT-76 tanks.

On February 15, 1968, an Air Force F-4 Phantom became the 800th U.S. aircraft lost in the 3 year air war over North Vietnam.

### Audio Tape Home
*Hi, Everybody!*

*I'm standing out on the barracks balcony. It's sometime in the evening. I feel like kind of an idiot. A lot of people are walking by, while I'm talking into this tape recorder.*

*I got off school yesterday at 3:30, came back to the barracks and hit the rack until this morning. This morning, they formed us up, to get shots. I got three shots: typhus, typhoid and diphtheria. I got three shots in Coronado, too. They told me they are making a pair of prescription sun glasses made for me. They don't know if I'll have them before I go to Vietnam, or not. If they don't, they will just send them to me, over there.*

*As I said on the phone, we will be going to San Clemente Island, this Friday. We'll be down there for about a week, for gunnery practice. We'll be on an "LCU." That's a "Landing Craft, Utility."*

*We'll be firing the 40mm cannon. We have had class room instructions on it. They are mounted on the bow of our "Monitors." We will be trained on a number of other weapons, as well.*

*We have already been trained on the M79 grenade launcher. It looks like a sawed off shotgun, except with a huge barrel. The 40MM grenade looks like a huge bullet. I use one of the brass from one, to put my change in, at night. They had us firing them at some oil barrels. I was surprised that it doesn't have much of a kick! You can even fire it with the stock up against your chest. It is accurate and pretty deadly.*

*One thing I'll never forget is throwing the hand grenade. We threw them at tires. I never thought I'd be scared to throw a grenade. When you get in the pit, they have you put on a helmet, like that would do any good if the guy next to you dropped a grenade at your feet. Of course, it doesn't explode when it hits the dirt. It has a timing mechanism in it. It takes fifteen pounds of pressure to pull the pin of a grenade. It's not like in the movies, where a guy pulls the pin with his teeth!*

*In the movies, they always seem to "lob" the grenade with a stiff arm, but they told us to throw it like a baseball. We had to get it over a ridge, to be safe. They told us that if we tried to lob the grenade, stiff armed, we probably wouldn't get it over the ridge and it would blow up pretty close to us! The first grenade a guy threw, landed under a tire and it blew it up into the air, fifteen or twenty feet.*

*They didn't have "practice" grenades. We only threw live grenades. Everybody who wasn't throwing a grenade was back twice as far as the guy throwing the grenade, but there was still shrapnel coming back as far as we were. One guy got a shrapnel cut in his leg. After a while, I got farther back, behind a hill.*

*One colored guy said: "There ain't nothin' gonna happen! Let's go see what's gonna happen over the hill!"*

*I said: "I'll tell you what. You get closer and tell us what's happening, O.K.?" He stayed with us.*

*We had instruction on shotguns. We fired them from our shoulders and from our waist. I LOVED firing from the waist! That was cool! We were firing at cardboard boxes, in a field. I don't know if I will shoot any Viet Cong, but if I run into cardboard boxes, over there, they're DEAD!*

*The .38 caliber pistol is pretty neat. I may target shoot with that, when I come home. I know how you feel about guns, Mom, but when I get home, I'm going to have a shotgun, a 38 and maybe an M-16!*

*Mom, I keep thinking about the guy that was talking to you about how dangerous it was over here, on the boats. That makes me mad! If I saw him, I'd punch him in the face! Nothing makes me madder than some character dramatizing this stuff and talking to mothers, or wives about how dangerous it is! It's ridiculous! I don't know WHAT they are trying to prove! Anyway, if it WAS dangerous, you'd be able to tell it from me! I'm a Christian and I'm a patriot, but most of all, I'm a devout <u>coward</u>! You know if it was dangerous, I'd be screaming it to you! The "Brown Water Navy" and all the small boats over there are really mopping up the Viet Cong, with the smallest percentage of casualties of any type of unit in Vietnam!*

*One thing we'll be doing is promoting the South Vietnamese "Chieu Hoi" program, which means "Open Arms." If a Viet Cong turns himself in to the government, he comes forward with a card which says he is surrendering. We have been told that they are distributing these pamphlets that say; "Chieu Hoi the Green Boats." The PBR's and boats of the Mobile Riverine Force are all green, for camouflage. They told us a lot of guys have itchy fingers, over there and that if a guy comes in to turn himself in, with his hands over his head, to take him prisoner, but if he makes one false move, he's had it! So anyway, don't worry! We'll just be patrolling, doing routine stuff. Just don't worry about it! That bothers me more than anything you could do!*

## BREAK

*This is Sunday afternoon. We just got back from San Clemente, around noon and I got all kinds of mail! Mom, I got the fudge and the cookies you sent! Thank you!*

*I guess I'll start off, telling you about the week in San Clemente. We got there and back on a DC-6 Mercer Airlines. It was ancient! Some of the guys were afraid to fly on it. It was a bumpy ride. I got close to getting air sick, but fought it off. Flying doesn't normally bother me. Someday, I'd like to sit down with maps and figure out how many miles I've flown. I know it's a lot.*

*San Clemente is a dinky little station, with a handful of naval personnel and few civilians. They told us we had to stick around one small area because of some areas are "off limits." The island is twenty-seven miles long and two to four miles wide. It is forty-one miles from the mainland.*

*There are goat herds, all over the island. During gunnery practice, I heard we killed forty of them. Most of us tried to avoid hitting them, but we WERE guilty of trying to herd them in different directions. On the way back, I heard we really only killed four. I guess you could say that for some guys, gunnery practice "got their goat."*

*Monday afternoon, we had to load all the ammunition on an LCU. That's a "Landing Craft, Utility." It was supposed to take an hour, but we were doing it from 12:30 to 4:30, because they were so slow getting truck loads of ammunition down to the boat. Then we had the rest of the day off.*

*Tuesday, they woke us up at 4:30. We were out until 6:30, in the evening.*

*Wednesday, they woke us up at 4:30 and we came back at 9:30, after practicing night firing. That day, I fired the 40mm cannon. It takes two guys. It has a "pointer" and a "trainer." The "pointer" aims the gun up and down, and the "trainer" aims it sideways. The guy that points it up and down also fires the gun, with a foot pedal. It's a powerful cannon. I fired one hundred rounds. I fired about fifteen rounds, single fire. Then, they had me fire it on automatic, three or four rounds at a time. It was something like a slow motion machine gun. The water was rough. It was hard to fire, with the boat going up and down. I didn't try to adjust the gun up and down. I just waited for the rolling of the boat to point the gun to the right position and fired it. It worked pretty well. Some of the guys fired into the water, twenty yards from the boat.*

*During the night firing, they used tracers. There were tracers during the day, too, but they aren't as obvious. They had us firing at the shoreline. It was pretty miserable, sitting in this little boat, in rough water, at night. We saw seals all over the place. When we looked down from the bow, we saw a five or six foot shark, just below the surface, probably hunting the seals. There were porpoises and all kinds of small fish.*

*Thursday, we got up at 4:30, again. We didn't use up all of the ammunition like we were supposed to. They assigned me to the commissary working party, loading food onto a pickup truck that was going to take the food down to hillside, to the pier, to be loaded onto the LCU, for our lunch.*

*After we loaded it, we started to pile into the back of the pickup, but the colored guy driving it said; "Sorry boys, but I can't take you down in the back of this truck! You'll either have to wait here, or walk down."*

*Two of the guys got into the cab of the truck. The other four of us decided we'd walk, taking the long way down, following the road, instead of just climbing down a steep hillside. On the way, we were laughing about how funny it would be if the boat left without us, and we'd be stuck there, all day, laying in our racks!*

*When we got to the bottom of the hill, we could see the boat, with its ramp down, loading food and ammunition. We were hidden from their view, and decided to stop there for five minutes and take a break. We figured that if we got there, we'd just have to help unload all the stuff off the truck that we just loaded onto the truck.*

*After stalling a few minutes, we continued on. When we got to the other side of the building, we discovered the boat was on its way out. It was far out, so we started walking down the pier. When we got to the end of the pier, one of the guys asked if we should yell for the boat. We decided we should, just to enhance the plausibility of our story, so we called out, in voices barely above a whisper; "Hey! Wait for us! Don't leave us here!"*

*Following our insincere effort to hail the boat, we decided to leisurely stroll to the operations and communications office and report our plight. The Petty Officer on watch called the boat, over the radio. The lieutenant on the boat replied with frustration that they couldn't come back to get us, so we should just go back to the barracks, or the pool hall, to occupy our time. We put on our best long faces, appearing disappointed and on the verge of crocodile tears. We walked out. Once we were clear of the building, we were laughing and jumping up and down, overjoyed with our good fortune. I turned and saw the Petty Officer standing in the doorway, watching us. When the boat came in that night, we explained to the lieutenant that we were "screaming our lungs out," for them. We probably overplayed our hand, but we escaped retribution.*

*Friday, we had the day off. We watched a low budget movie about sea pirates. It didn't have big stars in it. In one shot of a sea battle between French and English sailing ships, you could see a modern barge ship, in the distance. The captain of the sailing ship said his ship had a draft of twenty fathoms. A "draft" is how much of the ship is underwater. A "fathom" is six feet, so this guy was saying his 18th Century sailing ship had a draft of one hundred and twenty feet! We laughed about that one!*

*When I was in the enlisted men's club, on San Clemente, a buddy from Chicago, came in and said: "Guess what! My brother quit the syndicate!" He told me the "syndicate" is like a gangster Bell Telephone. "You can find it fast in the Yellow Pages!" I thought it was a riot! He said his brother quit because several of his buddies got "sent up" for four or five years. My buddy was in it, once. He delivered booze down south, and got $200, for driving down there. Some of his buddies stole box cars full of cigarettes and booze. I told him I wanted him to tell you guys about it, on the tape. He said; "No. I don't want them to think I'm a hoodlum!" The funny thing about it is that the guy is a devout Catholic. I can't recall hearing a bad word out of him. He's the one who went to Mass with me, on Sunday. He doesn't smoke pot, or do drugs. He told me about the murder syndicate, in Chicago. He said you get a contract with a "torpedo" for a set price. He said that's "big time" and he never messed with that.*

*He said there are juke box, cigarette and pin ball syndicates. It's really interesting when you talk to somebody that has first-hand experience in this kind of stuff!*

*On Saturday, we got up at 4:30, again, and had breakfast. Then, we turned in our linen and blankets. When we got to the plane to fly back, they couldn't get one of the engines on the DC-6 to start. They had to work on it, for a while. When we finally got into the air, everybody was a little jittery.*

*I guess I can answer some of your questions from your last letter.*

*Mom, I understand you are worried about tigers, in Vietnam. I knew there were tigers in Vietnam. I even heard our guys have killed them, over there. You may have heard that the tigers were going into villages, stealing sampans and going out to our boats, in the middle of the Mekong River. Rumor has it, they have dragged sailors off the boats, by their collar, or something.... O.K. So much for that....*

*Mom, I'm sorry that what I told you about the S.E.R.E training up upset you. The worst thing about it, was the cold. The hunger was bad, but now, I just can't stand to be cold! My muscles were sore and cramped, just from unending shivering from head to toe. It's a valuable education for anybody who could be captured. I'm just glad I won't be cold in Vietnam!*

*They told us when we started S.E.R.E. that before it was over, we'd know hunger, thirst, cold, heat, pain, boredom and fear. They were right! I did. Before the training, I thought that maybe I'd be a LITTLE hungry, but I was STARVING! I lost twenty pounds! I now KNOW hunger. I know thirst. We felt the cold and the heat, intensely! I know pain! I can't say boredom was a problem, but I certainly know fear. I do think the training was very useful, though. I'd hate to go through it again, but I'm glad I went through it. It tells you something about yourself. It gives you an idea if you would break easily, or not, if you were captured. That's worth something to a person. I think it is an invaluable part of our training and a way to weed out men.*

*As for what you were saying about the Navy, I have to admit that when I got the orders for Nam, I was a little bitter, and even though I have issues with the Navy, I'm proud of my uniform, I'm proud of this unit and I'm proud of the Navy. I'm just doing my part to protect our country. It's a good feeling, actually. I don't think I'm too good to go to Vietnam and do my part, when you consider everything Americans have done in all of the wars throughout our history. Too many men have died to protect what we have now, for me to say; "You can't send me." So, I guess I'll go over there and do my part.*

*I know you said they're not going to get Pat, Mike and Tim. I know you and Dad are the parents, but still, I think you ought to leave it up to them, whether they go, or not. Pat's asthma and concussions might be an issue if he tried to join, or if they tried to draft him. To Pat, I'd say if you can't get out of it, just bite the bullet, so to speak, and do it. But, if you have a choice, I hope you forget about it. It may depend on your circumstances, when you are at that age. I don't think Mike or Tim would have any problem joining, if they wanted to.*

*Mom and Dad, if the kids want to join, I'd recommend not discouraging them. I just think it's a decision they have to make, on their own. It's a big decision for a guy. Since I've been in, I've seen a lot, overseas, and I've seen sides of life I never knew existed. I think I'm a lot more mature than I was when I joined. I could be better off, in some ways, if I hadn't joined, but there is no way of knowing!*

*A Marine major instructor told us the commands in Vietnam are pressuring the training staff to "Send more over! Send more over!" They are pushing to cut the classes shorter, but he is fighting it, because he believes everybody should have as much training as possible, before they go to Vietnam. He instructs us in small arms. He calls us "Sailorinors." He says; "You're not really sailors. You're not really marines and you're not really soldiers!" The major's trademark was his patent leather combat boots.*

*Tell Timmy that anytime he wants to sing a little song on a tape, I really enjoy them! The one about the horse was real cute! I'll play it for some of the guys, here, soon. Sharon and Mike can play their trumpet and clarinet, too, so I can keep track of their progress!*

*Today, we were out on the boats. They're LCM's. They call them "Mike boats." We were out on them all day, today and yesterday, practicing. It's mostly for the coxswains, or "coxn's," or "helmsmen," to practice handling the boat. The rest of us have to get used to operating the ramps, handling the lines and other deck duties. Yesterday, we were practicing pulling up to other boats and to the pier, or beaching the boat, dropping the ramp, just as we would do in Vietnam, transporting troops.*

*It was raining all day, yesterday and this morning. It was bad to be out in it. When I was a kid, I thought it would be great to be out on a boat, all day, but right now, it's just hard work. There's not much fun in it. Yesterday, we were out all day, then we brought it in and had to hose it down and clean it. This morning, we* took it out, beached and dropped the ramp into the mud, again. They say there are three ways to do something; "The RIGHT way. The WRONG way and the NAVY way!"

Judi told me Mom was worried about me going over there. Mom, you really don't have to worry! The boats travel in groups of at least three. Sometimes, there are as many as fifteen of them. Each boat has different armament, but the "Monitor" has a 40 mm cannon, an 81mm mortar, machine guns and grenade launchers. They have thick armor, all around them! Grenades and rockets just bounce off! The only people that have anything to worry about are the people on the PBR's. They have a fiberglass hull. They're fast, but everything goes right through them! You don't have to worry about me. I'll be on the safest boats on the river.

Judi also told me that Grandpa saw a sailor going overseas and you were worried it was me. They don't work that fast. They have to make a reservation for me at Travis Air Force Base. They will not be coming to the barracks and telling me; "Grab your stuff! You're leaving for Vietnam, right now!" I would at least have plenty of time to call you. Just don't worry about something like that!

We will be out on the boats, all this week. Next week, we're supposed to have a couple night operations, operating as we would in Vietnam. Instructors, dressed in Vietnamese garb, will "ambush" us, from various spots, firing blanks at us, with machine guns and small arms. We will be firing blanks, back at them.

I also heard that when we get to Vietnam, we will be sent to Subic Bay, for additional training, for a month. That would be one month less I would be in Vietnam, so that's some good news for you!

Today, they had me at the helm of the LCM. I didn't like it. I was satisfied sitting around, or doing whatever else they wanted me to do, but I didn't want to "drive" the boat. It's got two shafts, with rotating handles, on each side of the wheel. Each controls one of the two engines. It's like driving a car that has two steering wheels, two brakes and two accelerators. You have to work both of them, at the same time. For example, if you want to turn right, or to "starboard," you back down, or turn off the starboard engine, while you rev forward the "port" engine, while you turn the wheel to the right. I am getting the hang of it, though.

I got paid today. I got a terrific $28.00. I'll send part of it home.

It was raining off and on, today, for the third day in a row. Monday, it rained all day. Yesterday, it rained and today, it rained just a little.

I got my glasses, today. They were supposed to be prescription sun glasses, but they are just regular glasses. Now I have four pair of regular glasses! How does the government screw stuff up that is this simple?

I wish I could tell you when I'll be leaving here and give you a schedule. I did hear they are cutting our classes by one week, but I don't know for sure.

I have tomorrow off. I have the watch in the office, here, from 2000 to 2200, tonight. Tomorrow, I'll just catch up on my sleep, or watch TV.

BREAK

I'm out on the balcony, again. It's raining, but I'm under the porch area. I just finished my watch and thought I'd finish this up, before I hit the rack. I called Judi a while ago.

Tomorrow, we're going out on the boats, again, practicing handling them. I'll be taking the helm, more.

Hopefully, I'll find out when our "port call" is. That's when we're flown out of Travis. I hope we get four to six days leave before we fly over.

There's a party going on across the street, at the enlisted men's club. The class ahead of us, "12-R," is graduating. They have the whole top floor of the Neptune Club. They graduate tomorrow and leave pretty *soon. I don't know how much leave they got. I know some of the PBR classes are getting four to six days before they go over. I saw PBR's on the river, while we were training, yesterday. There were six of them. They are small boats, made out of fiberglass. They don't have much armament on them. I also saw an "ATC." That's an "Armored Troop Carrier." It's a small boat, used for carrying troops. It's protected all over. It has big steel grates all around it, to deflect grenades and rockets.*

*I think I'll close, for now, so Goodbye! I'll write, soon!*

**Our concerns over the condition of the ancient DC-6 were well justified. Lieutenant Larry Irwin, curator of Navy Gunnery Training, Camp Roberts, California, later wrote;**
*"Before Camp Roberts was used as a live fire training facility, the trainees were flown from Travis AFB down to Coronado Island off San Diego. From there they embarked on a couple of LCMs that were outfitted with .50 Cal, 20MM and 40MM cannons. The boats circled around the west side of the island and commenced live fire training against the hillside, scaring the hell out of the resident goats. The Navy switched to Camp Roberts mainly because the contractors who provided the aircraft to fly us to Coronado didn't have the money to properly maintain their two planes. On the return flight from Coronado on what turned out to be the last flight, the larger of the two planes, in which I was riding, was streaming smoke from the two out board engines and upon landing bounced twice before settling to the ground. The Air Force Police met the plane at the end of the runway and ordered the pilot to pull off the runway and stop the plane. We had to de-plane and walk about 1.5 miles to the terminal. The plane had to be towed to its final stopping place. We were told later that it was strewing parts and oil on the runway which tends to upset the Air Force. Too close for comfort."*

**February 18, 1968**. The U.S. State Department announced the highest U.S. casualty toll of the war in Vietnam. In the previous week, 543 Americans had been killed in action. 2,547 were wounded.

**February 23, 1968.** 1,307 enemy artillery, rocket and mortar rounds were fired into Khe Sahn: almost one per minute.

**February 27, 1968**. CBS Evening News anchor Walter Cronkite reported; *"the bloody experience of Vietnam is to end in a stalemate."*

**February 29, 1968**. Robert S. McNamara resigned as Secretary of Defense.

**March 16, 1968.** Company C 1/20th Infantry, commanded by Captain Ernest Medina entered a hamlet known as My Lai (pronounced "Me Lie"), a reported VC village. Lieutenant William Calley's 1st Platoon led the force. Over the next four hours, over 300 men, women and children were killed. He was convicted of first degree murder of 22 civilians and given life in prison. He was released on parole in 1974. What is it that makes men do such things? Those who never face such circumstances take comfort in telling themselves that they would never, could never, do such horrible and repulsive acts. But who can be so certain?

**From the book *"NAM"***
*"Patrolling near My Son in February, Calley's radioman was shot. For three days the company tried to penetrate My Son but were driven back. Two men were killed by booby traps. Another was hit by sniper fire. The patrols blundered into a nest of booby traps, but when they extricated themselves unscathed, two more were cut down by sniper fire. On their next assignment they were heading for the rendezvous point when an explosion tore through the early morning stillness and a man screamed. There was another explosion and another scream. Then another explosion and another and another and another.*

*They had stumbled into a minefield and, as men rushed forward to aid their wounded buddies, there were more and more explosions. Severed limbs flew through the air; medics crawled from body to body and always more explosions. It went on for almost two hours, leaving 32 men killed or wounded.*

*On 4 March the company was mortared and most of the men's personal possessions were destroyed. Ten days later, two days before the assault on My Lai, four men – including one of the company's last experienced NCO's*

*(Non-commissioned officers) were blown to bits by a booby trap. In 32 days, Company C – whose field strength was 90 to 100 – suffered 42 casualties and had scarcely seen the enemy.*

*Calley had seen atrocities committed by the VC too. One night, the VC had captured one of his men and they heard him screaming all night, seven klicks (kilometers) away. Calley thought the VC had amplifiers, but they didn't. They had skinned the GI alive, leaving only his face, then soaked him in salty water and torn his penis off."*

What Lt. Calley and his men did was insane, but so was the world they were living in.

**March 16, 1968**. Senator Robert Kennedy, former Attorney General of the United States and brother of slain President John F. Kennedy, declared his candidacy for the Presidency.

On March 19th, 1968, I checked out of River Warfare School and flew home for a surprise weekend liberty, before going to Vietnam. I landed in St. Louis and caught a cab to Judi's house, arriving at 1:30 a.m. Her mom and dad welcomed me. When I went to Judi's room and woke her, she said; *"What are YOU doing here?"* and put her arms around me. After a wonderful weekend, I left for the airport, unsure of my future.

The night before my River Warfare Class left for Vietnam, I went to a phone booth and called my brother, Tom, to tell him I had changed my *"next of kin"* information to list him, rather than Mom and Dad. I didn't want Mom and Dad to get bad news from the grim faces of Navy officers showing up at their front door. I had told Judi and the family that the Mobile Riverine Force simply patrolled the rivers, but was not really in combat. I confided to Tom that it was actually a high casualty unit, and I may not make it back.

**In the book, "My Father, My Son," Admiral Elmo Zumwalt said this about casualties in the Delta;**
*"When we first began the patrol along the canals and smaller rivers, I think we caught the Viet Cong off guard. But it did not take them long to respond and set up ambushes, because the canals and rivers were often so narrow the men in the river patrol boats could easily be hit from either side by enemy fire. The swift boats and PBRs were especially vulnerable because they had so little protection. Swift boat hulls were made of aluminum only one-eighth of an inch thick. The PBR hulls were fiberglass. The enemy could hit them with B-40 rockets, which are like the old bazookas, automatic weapons, and hand held rockets. And under cover of dense foliage that grew along the riverbanks, the enemy attacked the boats without being seen. Our river patrol casualties reached an unacceptably high rate of 6% a month. That meant anyone serving a year's combat tour on the riverboats had a 70-75 percent chance of being killed or wounded. We had to reduce those risks considerably."*

The bus trip from Mare Island to Travis Air Force Base was both an inspirational lesson in life, and a very embarrassing and shameful moment. Six of my graduating class sat across the back seat of the bus. We were facing a year in Vietnam. We had mixed emotions of anxiety, fear, loneliness and bravado. Most had a hangover, or still had a buzz. The bus was full of civilians, including women and children. Our language was inexcusably offensive. Suddenly, a Navy officer in *"civvies"* walked to the back of the bus. He leaned forward; bracing his hands on the seat backs in front of us, leaning over and putting his face close to all of us. In a very hushed voice he told us he understood how we felt. He had just returned from Vietnam. With disgust in his voice, he told us we were not honoring the uniforms we wore, or the men who had served or would serve in Vietnam. For the rest of our ride, we sat in silence, not because we were afraid of what the officer might do, but because we were shamed by the truth of his words.

# Chapter 6

## The Heat of Tropic Sun

Seventy-two of my classmates arrived in Vietnam. At that time, the River Assault Force, or Task Force 117, consisted only of River Assault Squadron 9 and River Assault Squadron 11. They were just starting River Assault Squadron 13. Soon, they would also launch River Assault Squadron 15. Thirty of us went to River Assault Squadron 13. Although I wasn't overly superstitious, the number of my river squadron DID give me pause. Forty-two, including two of my best friends, Freddie and Grif, went to River Assault Squadron 11.

**March 21, 1968.** I made the first entry into my diary. Judi's name and address is on the inside cover, so that it would go to her in the event of my death.

**First Diary Entry, Thursday, March 21, 1968**
*"I am on the plane to Saigon right now. We will arrive in about five hours. The whole trip from Travis is supposed to take about eighteen hours, counting our stop in Yokota, Japan. We were supposed to stop in Anchorage, Alaska, but for some reason, we didn't. It is a strange feeling, going to Vietnam. I have been afraid of the idea for the past couple of months, but right now, I am more homesick than afraid.*

*Most of the class has been drunk all day. I suspect that's always the way it has been when men are sent off to war. I am scared. Whenever I say something like "when I come back," I feel like I'm kidding myself. Nobody can be sure they will be coming back, alive, anyway. There are seventy-two of us in class "14-R." I can't believe all seventy-two will live. Every unit has its casualties.*

*I have to keep a sort of daily record, or diary. If anything happens to me, maybe what I say in these pages will comfort Judi, Mom and Dad. If I get back (and I plan on it), it may help Judi understand me better. If I am going to ask her to marry me, she has to understand me. She seems to have an uncanny insight into me now, though. If anything does happen to me, I don't want Judi to be a grieving "widow" for a lifetime. She has too many years of happiness ahead of her to become sad, or bitter.*

*I want Mom and Dad to remember they have five more kids at home and they owe all their love and attention to them, instead of thinking or talking about me. If, in the next twelve months, something happens to me, I carry the consolation that I am protecting my loved ones at home. I have to believe in something like that."*

A tape recorder captured the final minute of landing. I was having a conversation with Jerry Ranson. The plane went into an extremely steep approach in order to reduce the possibility of being shot down. It seemed like the plane was going in at a forty-five degree angle. We practically stood up in our seats. If it wasn't for the seat belts, I would have slid onto the floor. A *"Stewardess"* (not *"Flight Attendant"*) addressed the passengers.

*"Gentlemen, kindly extinguish all cigarettes, at this time and remember, please refrain from smoking until you are well inside the terminal area. Also, please check to make sure your tables and chairs are in an upright position for landing."*

After hitting the runway, you could hear the deafening roar of the engines, and feel the strain, as the aircraft fought to come to a halt much quicker than normal. They didn't want the aircraft too get too close to the perimeter, within range of mortars, or guns, when it came to a stop.

As the engines were shutting down, the stewardess came over the sound system one last time.

*"Gentlemen, we have just landed at Tan San Ute Airport. The local time is 7:15 a.m. and the ground temperature is 80 degrees. For your own safety and comfort, please remain seated until the aircraft has come to a complete stop and we have been cleared to disembark! On behalf of Captain Saunders and the entire crew, it has been our pleasure serving you for this portion of your flight. Thank you and Good Morning!"*

As I stepped out of the plane, the heat and humidity hit me in the face. It felt as though I had walked into an enormous steam bath. I had trouble breathing. I was in awe of the world I now lived in. Over the course of the war, 997 men died during their first day in Vietnam.

**Diary, Friday, March 22, 1968.**
*I didn't have time to write last night. We were busy all day, getting to our base at Dong Tam. Last night we had a mortar attack. It scared me to death at first, but after a few minutes sitting in the bunker, I wanted out again. They were hitting on the army side of the camp. Some of the mortars were coming from the "friendly" village, to the east. I could hear and see the machine gun fire. The "Dog Faces" captured three hard-core V.C. They will probably let them go in a couple days. A real nice colored guy I talked to says this place could be overrun anytime, if Charlie really wanted to. A type of barbed wire, "concertina wire," is the main defense.*

*I am glad about one thing, though. I can call home!*

The base was named *"Dong Tam"* by General William Westmoreland, because it meant *"united hearts and minds,"* in Vietnamese, and is easy for Americans to say. It was made by dredging the My Tho River. The place didn't even exist until it was created by Navy Seabees and the Army Corps of Engineers.

**Dong Tam. The *"Route 66"* canal is visible, on the left.**

**On March 22nd, President Johnson announced General William Westmoreland would step down as U.S. commander in Vietnam to become the Army Chief of Staff. On the same day, over 1,100 rounds of rocket and mortar fire hit the marine base at Khe Sahn.**

A few notes to explain the information, military jargon and terms contained in the official Operations Reports, and in my diary. They describe the activity of the Mobile Riverine Force's day to day operations.

There are many references to various military units. I realize those references may be tedious for the casual reader, or slow their reading. I have spent considerable effort in providing unit designations because one of my primary audiences for this book is the men who belonged in those units and their families. I want the great-grandchildren of a soldier or sailor to be able to say, *"Oh! This is where our great-grandfather was, on this day, in 1968, and this is what his unit did!"*

Time is stated in military time, based upon a 24-hour clock. "0700" is 7:00 A.M. "1400" is 2:00 P.M. "2300" is 11:00 P.M.

"KIA" means, "Killed in Action." "WIA" indicates "Wounded in Action."

A "kilometer" is 0.62137119 miles.

The combined Army/Navy Mobile Riverine Force was abbreviated to *"MRF."* The group of ships that served as our support base in the middle of the major channels, was called our "Mobile Riverine Base," or "MRB." The Mobile Riverine Force was designated as TF (Task Force) 117. *"Swift Boats,"* or, PCF's (Patrol Craft, Fast) made famous by John Kerry, was designated as Task Force 115. A "PBR" (Patrol Boat, River) was featured in the movie *"Apocalypse Now."* PBR's belonged to Task Force 116. Task Forces 115, 116, and 117 served as the forerunners of today's Special Warfare Combatant Craft Navy. They learned from everything we did in Vietnam, both good and bad.

There were ultimately four River Assault Squadrons. River Assault Squadron Nine was the first. Riv Ron Eleven was the second to form, followed by River Assault Squadron Thirteen, and finally, Riv Ron Fifteen. Each Squadron was comprised of two Divisions. The 1st Division of River Assault Squadron 11 was "Riv Div (River Division) 111." The 2nd Division was Riv Div 112, and so on. My new boat would be T-131-3, or ATC 131-3. This indicated it was an Armored Troop Carrier in River Division 131, in River Assault Squadron, or *"Riv Ron" 13.* They were referred to as *"Tango"* boats. The operations reports could be confusing at times. Boats of different divisions were sometimes mixed, yet the operations reports do not usually indicate that.

The following organization chart provides a representation of the allocation of men and boats to River Assault Squadron 13. The organization charts for the other three River Assault Squadrons would be very similar.

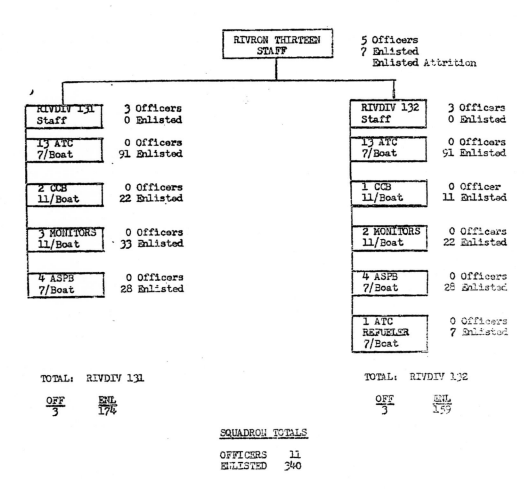

RIVRON THIRTEEN STAFF — 5 Officers / 7 Enlisted / Enlisted Attrition

| RIVDIV 131 Staff | 3 Officers / 0 Enlisted | | RIVDIV 132 Staff | 3 Officers / 0 Enlisted |
|---|---|---|---|---|
| 13 ATC 7/Boat | 0 Officers / 91 Enlisted | | 13 ATC 7/Boat | 0 Officers / 91 Enlisted |
| 2 CCB 11/Boat | 0 Officers / 22 Enlisted | | 1 CCB 11/Boat | 0 Officer / 11 Enlisted |
| 3 MONITORS 11/Boat | 0 Officers / 33 Enlisted | | 2 MONITORS 11/Boat | 0 Officers / 22 Enlisted |
| 4 ASPB 7/Boat | 0 Officers / 28 Enlisted | | 4 ASPB 7/Boat | 0 Officers / 28 Enlisted |
| | | | 1 ATC REFUELER 7/Boat | 0 Officers / 7 Enlisted |

TOTAL: RIVDIV 131

| OFF | ENL |
|---|---|
| 3 | 174 |

TOTAL: RIVDIV 132

| OFF | ENL |
|---|---|
| 3 | 159 |

SQUADRON TOTALS

| OFFICERS | 11 |
|---|---|
| ENLISTED | 340 |

**The purpose, or mission of River Assault Squadron 13, as with all of the River Assault Squadrons, was spelled out in the official history of Riv Ron 13.**

*"The basic mission of RAS 13 is to support the Mobile Riverine Force in South Vietnam. The primary mission of RAS 13 is the safe transportation of men and material to and from an area of operation in a riverine environment and the support of those forces in the area of operations. ALL assault craft used by RAS 13 are designed with this basic mission in mind. In addition to transportation of troops and equipment, RAS 13 performs a variety of secondary missions, such as interdiction of hostile water traffic, security for the Mobile Riverine Base, waterborne resupply of assault forces, mine sweeping operations, direct and indirect fire support to assault forces, blockades of hostile beaches, waterways, and riverine armed reconnaissance element operations."*

As you would expect, the official mission statement didn't really cover everything we did. Although some viewed the river assault boat crews as nothing more than *"bus drivers"* for troops, we did much more. We carried the 9th Infantry Division, the Army of the Republic of Vietnam, Vietnamese Marines, Cambodian mercenaries, Vietnamese Regional Force/Popular Force troops, Green Beret, Navy SEAL's, Vietnamese Police, "Co Van" U.S. Marine Advisors, Vietnamese *"Kit Carson,"* or *"Tiger Scouts,"* South Vietnamese Navy trainees, and whoever else we were told to carry. Sometimes we'd spend days, or weeks with the 9th Infantry, or some other unit. Sometimes we'd be out by ourselves for days, or weeks at a time. At times, they would send single boats out in different directions, in hopes of drawing fire and giving away the enemy locations.

We challenged the enemy in their strongholds, refusing to concede them refuge in the Rung Sat Special Zone, or the U Minh Forest. We hunted them until they ambushed us, and then we made them pay the price for it.

**An article in the December, 1968 issue of National Geographic said in part,**

*"First, the war. I saw it blazing most fiercely in South Viet Nam, where the U.S. Navy's "miniature battleships," painted green and built expressly for combat along the Mekong Delta waterways, pitted their rapid-fire cannon against Viet Cong rockets made in the Soviet Union and in China.*

*Those deadly rockets spewed from bunkers hidden in dense greenery, sometimes along canals so narrow that the boats could not turn around. "It's like the old days," said the commodore of the River Assault Flotilla, "Exchanging broadsides at 15 to 20 yards, point-blank."*

"I (The letter "I") Corps" was roughly the top 1/4 of Vietnam that bordered the DMZ (Demilitarized Zone) and North Vietnam. "II Corps" was to the south of I Corps, followed by III Corps. The Mekong Delta was "IV" Corps. As noted in the reports, several boats of the MRF were sent to I Corp for action.

As I arrived at the Navy side of the Dong Tam base, I looked out at the boat repair area of the docks. They were repairing boats that had been blown up, shot up, damaged, sunk, or simply in for routines maintenance or overhaul. The irony of the calming words from the Bureau of Naval Personnel rang in my ears....I laughed. *"We haven't lost a boat yet!"* That's when I knew. They only lost the <u>crews</u>!

While I was sorting that out, I noticed an army officer sitting on the bank, looking thoughtfully into the harbor and the late afternoon sun. As I approached, I saw the cross on his fatigue shirt that indicated he was a chaplain. He flashed a friendly smile and held up a rough, hand-made shovel. With pride, he said; *"Look at this! I just took it off a dead gook!"* This man of God introduced me to the surreal reality of my new world.

I wasn't just far from home. I was far from everything that was clean, comfortable, safe and sane. We arrived thinking we were facing an enemy in black pajamas, but it was more than that. Our enemy was anger, loneliness, boredom, and fear. It was rats, snakes, leeches and mosquitoes. It was stupidity, carelessness, recklessness, and our own foolish, youthful sense of immortality. It was periods of endless rain, or choking dust in the blazing sun. It was demons we brought with us and demons that found us, there. It was bad luck, no luck, heartless fate and eerie premonitions. It was the muddy, mighty, and unforgiving Mekong River.

In the article in the December, 1968 issue of "National Geographic Magazine," titled *"The Mekong. River of Terror and Hope,"* by Peter T. White, he noted that the Vietnamese call the Mekong the *"Cu Cu Long Giang," "The River of Nine Dragons."* The Minister of Information in Saigon, Ton That Thien, explained that the Mekong actually splits into only eight primary branches, as it flows into the delta and out to the sea, but eight is an unlucky number to the Vietnamese. They were compelled to make the number either seven, or nine. They accomplished that by finding a small, narrow branch that was less than ten miles long, and made it the "ninth."

He also explained, *"The Lao and Thai of the Lower Mekong Basin share a common tongue and speak of the river as "Mae Nam Khong," meaning "Mother River Khong." What does "khong" mean? Nobody can be sure. The contraction of Mae Nam Khong into Mekong was made by Westerners. The Cambodians, or Khmers, call the river Tonle Thom, The Big Water."*

The Mobile Riverine Base ("MRB"), experienced the worst attack in its year of operations in the Mekong Delta, Friday, March 22, 1968. It was my second day in Vietnam. Nine rocket and mortar rounds were fired from the south bank at the Benewah, a barracks ship, and the LST, Washtenaw County. The USS Benewah took two 75MM recoilless rocket heat rounds on the port side of the ship. There were no personnel casualties. One of the rockets penetrated the bulkhead on the forward mess decks, rupturing a steam line and air vent, damaging a fan room and spraying the area with shrapnel. The second rocket hit just forward of the port accommodation ladder about a foot below the waterline. This blast opened a one inch hole, and ruptured two ballast tanks, causing minor flooding, which was repaired.

The Washtenaw was targeted with five mortar rounds from another location on the south bank, just after the attack on the Benewah. Several of the rounds hit close, but they all missed.

Immediately after the attack, two ASPB's on BID (*Base Interior Defense*) patrol fired on the areas of attack with 20MM cannons and 81MM mortars. Washtenaw, Benewah and Askari strafed the south bank with 40MM and 3 inch gun fire. The two ASPB's, Colleton and Benewah continued Harassment & Interdiction fire on the south bank throughout the night.

Just before the attack on the MRB, Dong Tam was hit by one of the heaviest mortar attacks in weeks, absorbing seventy-three 120MM and 81MM rounds. Three personnel were wounded in the forty minute attack.

**Letter home, Saturday, March 23, 1968.**
*Hi, Folks!*

*You'll have to excuse the pen. The dust is so bad here, it even gums up my pen. The monsoons haven't started yet. I doubt if they will for a while.*

*I guess I can tell you about my trip. The trip to Saigon was O. K. It got tiresome sitting so long and it was almost impossible to judge time, since we kept jumping from one time zone to another. Landing at Tan San Ut airport was a weird experience. The heat was something else and everywhere you looked, there were armed guards and jeeps mounted with machine guns. Vietnamese soldiers with sub-machine guns were everywhere. Bunkers were all over the place. There was a huge, gaping hole in the roof of the main terminal, due to a mortar round. Most of the people were military personnel and it seemed odd to think that all the uniformed men, whether they were short, tall, fat, skinny, blond, or dark headed, all of them are here to kill. It seemed even odder when it occurred to me that I wear the uniform too.*

*There was a bus to pick us up and take us to the heliport, but it didn't come for a long time, so we sat in the bar and drank "33" beer. After about 3 ½ of them, I was feeling pretty good! The bus finally came and took us to a motel in Saigon where we checked in. Then, they told us they didn't have any beds for us. It was being used as a barracks and they had beds in the halls and all over the place. We hung around long enough to eat. Then, the bus came to take us to the heliport.*

*At the heliport they said THEY were filled up, so they took us to a small airport and THEY were filled up. We went back to the heliport and after four or five hours, we left there on a Sikorsky helo for Dong Tam. I sat near the open door and had a good view of everything. The outskirts of Saigon was pock marked with craters from bombs and mortars. When we arrived at the army side of the base (the heliport), nobody was there to meet us, and so we had to carry our sea bags from one place to another, trying to find out where we were supposed to go. There were about seven of us in this group. I flagged down a jeep and he gave three of us a ride. A truck grabbed the other guys.*

*They have us on working parties right now. They don't know where to put us on the boats. Right now, our barracks is on the land base. Monday or Tuesday, we move out to a barracks ship, in a main channel of the Mekong River, just outside Dong Tam harbor.*

*It is safe here. Charlie (V.C., "Viet Cong," "Victor Charles," "Chuck") only bugs the army side once in a while for harassment, but I haven't seen anything yet. I found out they are counting the whole month of March as our time in Nam and the rumor is they usually just keep the "RAGS' (River Assault Group) here for ten or eleven months, instead of twelve! Every little bit helps! I also found out they aren't going to pay us for about three weeks. I already have two weeks pay coming to me. It should be a big check. I don't need any money here, though. They only pay us once a month.*

*I've seen the hats we wear. We can wear just about anything. The "RAGS" usually wear the Aussie "Digger" type hat, with one side folded up, or fold up both sides and wear it as a cowboy hat. Some wear the black beret or a green camouflaged beret. You can compare it to the "Rat Patrol" (TV Show) jokers. There isn't any spit'n polish in this bunch. It's a change from the "Big E." It's almost hard to believe there is any real action here. I can see a Vietnamese village from my barracks. They are supposed to be "friendlies," though. They bring their women in during the day to work in the chow hall, raking, planting grass or something.*

*I guess one thing I can talk about is our defenses. I'm not supposed to, though. We have PACV's (Patrol Air Cushion Vehicles), which have Charlie very scared. I checked them out, today. The dragon teeth and eyes painted on the bow could scare anybody!*

*Then there is the huge fleet of monitors, ASPB's (Assault Support Patrol Boats), ATC's (Armored Troop Carriers) and so on. They are putting flame-throwers on the monitors. That's a terrible weapon, but necessary. The Army sets up the perimeter. We have a special type barbed wire, with tiny blades like old Viking's axes on it. It can rip a man to pieces. We also have a weapon I never heard of, before. It is a "beehive" mine that is either tripped or command detonated, which sends out tiny darts for several hundred yards. There is also a "beehive" round for the 105 Howitzer. It fires 8,000 "flechettes" or darts. We also have Huey and Cobra choppers with the mini-guns and rockets on them.*

*I guess I'll close for now. I have the 2-6 watch in the morning! I'll write tomorrow! My address is still kind of up in the air. I'll give it to you tomorrow, for sure!*

*All My Love,*

*Terry*

When I first reported to River Warfare School, Judi was upset that I wasn't making friends, too quickly. I resisted for a while, only because I didn't like my orders and I didn't want to go to Vietnam. Eventually, I did start making friends, but I don't think I ever mentioned their names to Judi, or the family, until I arrived in Vietnam. Looking back, I understand why. The mere fact of putting our feet on the soil of a war zone brought us closer together. In training, we were *"running mates,"* going on liberty together. Perhaps adversity deepens bonds. I've read that in making a sword, both strength and flexibility are needed for the best blade. The metal must be forged in a crucible until it is white-hot. Then it is quenched in cold water. The process may be repeated many times. That was us. We leaned on each other for strength, for laughs and for our lives. As time went on, we were forged under fire, then quenched with cold beer. The process was repeated, many times.

Two of the guys who were friends of mine in River Warfare School were Freddie Arens and Pat *"Grif"* Griffin.

Freddie was a twenty year old, red headed Irish Catholic engineman, from Boston. He always tried to act tough, but he was usually just kidding. One day, I asked him what his middle name was, and he told me it was Vincent. I followed that up with asking him what his *"confirmation name"* was. Confirmation, admits a person into full participation in the Catholic Church. Freddy didn't want to tell me. He said it was *"stupid."*

He told me *"I didn't like it when that cool dude with the weird hat slapped me!"*

I asked; *"You mean the bishop?"*

Freddie replied; *"Yeah! He said my name as "Frederick Vincent VINCENT Arens! He said "Vincent" again, so I don't think I should use Frederick Vincent Vincent Arens!" That's stupid, man! Ya' know?*

Pat *"Grif"* Griffin, like Freddie, wasn't a very big guy. Nobody ever called him by his first name. We called him *"Grif."* He was intelligent, with a wicked sense of humor. He had a curly mop of dark hair and a wispy mustache. Like me, he wore glasses. He was twenty-one, and from Topeka, Kansas. We got together whenever we could, even though Grif and Freddie were assigned to River Assault Squadron 11, and I was with Riv Ron 13. Whenever I could, I'd ride on their boat, meet them in Dong Tam, or on the barracks ship.

**Diary, Saturday, March 23, 1968.**
*Well, seven of us got into trouble last night. We had been drinking, but that's not why we got into trouble. We had a mortar attack, and after a while, Jardine, Griffin, Freddie, several other guys and I sat on <u>top</u> of the bunker. We looked like spectators at a fireworks display, awed by the noise, concussion and bright colors. Between the half moon, our flares and Charlie's mortars, it was pretty bright. It was stupid, I guess, but they weren't hitting near us, so it <u>seemed</u> safe at the time.*

*The straight skinny around here is that Charlie is going to get the "Green Monsters" (the boats and us) and the army on the other side of the base. Last night two rockets hit the barracks ship. It didn't hurt anybody, but it flooded one compartment. One rocket hit aft above the water line. If it had hit amidships, it would have hit the ammo and JP-5 fuel and blown her out of the water. Anyway, like I was saying, Charlie says he is going to get us between the first and sixteenth of April. I think the place <u>could</u> be overrun. They won't give us guns on the base because they are afraid we'll hit the "straight legs" (the 9<sup>th</sup> Infantry guys) around the perimeter. They <u>do</u> have an armory, down by the riverbank, and if the perimeter falls, <u>then</u> we get guns. When HQ sends up a green flare, it means, "ground attack." That's the bad one! We had TWO mortar attacks last night. Charlie tries to mess up our sleep. He sleeps during the day and keeps us awake at night.*

*I am more confident I'll be coming home now, unless they put me on an ASPB. Those guys are really getting it!*

*I've started smoking again. There's nothing else to do! I miss Judi terribly already.*

**On March 25th, President Lyndon Johnson met with his inner circle, the so-called *"Wise Men."* They were high-ranking insiders who represented the political elite of the nation. The group included Dean Acheson, secretary of state under Truman, Henry Cabot Lodge, Abe Fortas, Averell Harriman, Maxwell Taylor, Clark Clifford, Arthur Goldberg, Cyrus Vance, Omar Bradley and Matthew Ridgway, who was the commander during the Korean War. They reached a consensus that there was no end to the conflict in sight and advised Johnson against further escalation. After meeting with them, Johnson said to his military leaders, General Wheeler, and General Creighton W. Abrams;**

*"Our fiscal situation is abominable... What will happen if we cut housing, education, and poverty programs? I don't give a damn about the election.... The country's demoralized... I will have overwhelming disapproval in the polls. I will go down the drain... How can we get this job done? We need more money---in an election year; more taxes---in an election year; more troops---in an election year; and cuts in the domestic budget---in an election year. And yet I cannot tell the people what they will get in Vietnam in return for these cuts. We have no support for the war..."*

Judgement was passed on the war just as I arrived. The powerful elite decided that the war they sent us to, was folly. My friends and thirty thousand others died <u>after</u> Johnson and our leaders decided we weren't going to fight to win. At the same time, a Harris poll reported that 60% of the public believed the Tet Offensive was a standoff, or a defeat for America, even though it was actually a major military victory for the United States and a crushing defeat for the Viet Cong and North Vietnamese. President Johnson should have either done what was necessary for us to win the war, or brought us home and pulled the U.S. out of the war in Vietnam. David Lloyd George once said, *"Don't be afraid to take a big step if one is indicated. You can't cross a chasm in two small jumps."* Johnson continued the war taking small steps, leaving us in the chasm.

**Audio Tape Home, Sunday, March 24, 1968**
*Hi, folks!*

*This is Sunday night and I'm standing behind my barracks, facing the perimeter. There's nothing going on here, really. The boats go out every day and have little skirmishes, once in a while. Dong Tam seems to be a really secure place. I can't believe how BIG this place is! It's HUGE! And it's still in the construction stage! The barracks, or "hootches," are sand bagged half way up and the rest is screened in.*

*I'm not given any kind of weapon. They have an armory, down by the river bank. If Charlie ever tries to take the place, then, and ONLY then, do they give us guns. They don't let us have them right now, because the Army is out on the perimeter, all around the base. They're afraid that if they give us guns and we hear shots, we'll start firing and maybe hit some of the Army guys. I guess that makes sense.*

*Right now, I see a large truck approaching from the perimeter, way off in the distance. It's throwing up a cloud of brown dust, behind it. They're building up a huge earthwork. I imagine they'll put gun emplacements on it. They have concertina wire, claymore mines and other stuff surrounding the base. .*

*It's been clear, every night, here. There are lots of stars out. The temperature is wonderful, at night, but during the day, it gets awfully hot. One bad thing about the base, at least this time of year, is the dust. It is terrible! They're trying to plant grass in a lot of the areas of the base, but it won't grow. I thought that being in the delta, it would be like marshland, but this is more like a dustbowl.*

*They don't have us doing much, right now. I don't have a boat assignment, yet. They have put me on working parties, filling sand bags for bunkers and to stack around the "hootches."*

*I hear tomorrow, they'll be sending me out to one of the ships in the harbor. I think I'll buy a Polaroid camera, in their ship's store.*

*There is a helo circling over me. You can probably hear it. They have a huge helo force, here. They fire "mini-guns." Their rate of fire is so fast that the tracers make it look like a laser beam! The helo above me is coming in for a landing, very close to me. They stir up a lot of dust... Everything in our hooch is covered in it. I'm glad I got to ride on one from Tan San Ute Airport to Dong Tam. It was quite an experience.*

*A guy told me today that to take this base, Charlie would need 8,000 hard core Viet Cong. They've been capturing fifteen and sixteen year old V.C., lately. That's kind of sad.*

*I heard they knew enemy forces were building up around Khe Sahn and that to take this place, they would have to do it by surprise, but they wouldn't be able to do that, because there are so many patrols out, all the time. Dong Tam has an enormous amount of air power, artillery, infantry and Navy units, here. Half the base is Army and half of it is Navy.*

*They have a "MARS" radio station. I can go in there, at any time, to call home. For the first three minutes, it costs $6.30, for station to station calls.*

*They had a BBQ steak dinner, today, next to the chow hall. It was surprisingly good! I'm not eating C-Rations, yet. I haven't even SEEN any! I'm trying to eat healthy. I'm taking at least two salt tablets a day and once a week I take a malaria tablet. Everybody takes them as a preventative.*

*They have Vietnamese women working in the chow hall, like "coolies." They throw smiles at us, during the day. At night, they probably help their men fire mortars at us. The V.C. are pretty good with mortars. I fired eight mortars, during training, on San Clemente Island. Of course, I didn't fire at anything in particular. They just had the tube pointed up in the air and I dropped the mortar in, firing off, into the practice field.*

*I think about the last time I was home, a lot. Even though it was a short time, I think it was one of my most enjoyable. I really had a good time. I do get nervous, though. I'm used to Navy life, now. I guess I have changed since I joined the Navy. While I was home, I couldn't help thinking about coming over here. That added to my nerves.*

*I've been drinking a lot of beer, lately. I like it when I can get Budweiser, partly because it reminds me of St. Louis. Sometimes, our enlisted men's club, "The Windjammer," only has Pabst Blue Ribbon, Hamms, or Carling Black Label. Last night, they ran out of everything except "Korean Crown." It was so disgusting, it was even hard to drink after drinking a lot! The rumor is that it has formaldehyde in it, as a preservative. I haven't been getting drunk, lately, but the beer sure tastes good in the middle of these hot days! I'm broke and for the last couple of days, buddies have been buying me beers. They cost fifteen cents at the "Windjammer."*

*I guess I'll sign off, for now. Last night, I had the two to six watch, just standing around the barracks. I almost fell asleep! I'm glad I didn't! Out here, that would be a bad scene!*

### Diary, Sunday, March 24, 1968.

*I had the two to six watch this morning, in Dong Tam, patrolling around our "hootches." I almost fell asleep on watch, then I heard somebody yell, "I'm going to get my .38! I'm going to KILL that son-of-a-bitch!" One of the boat crew guys was drunk. While he was getting his .38, I found out that he had been begging a guy to fight him, so the guy decked him with one punch, splitting his lip open.*

*When he came out of his hooch, he was wearing his flak jacket and a .38 in a hip holster. He just finished fastening the buckle of the holster. One guy grabbed his shoulders and called for me to grab his gun. They were facing me, in the dark. I couldn't see if he had his gun out, or not. I lunged forward in the dark, not knowing what was going to happen. He didn't have his gun in his hand, but he was going for it. I pulled his arms back and one of us took his gun. It was empty! A bluff like that can cost you your life!*

*The "straight skinny" is, Charlie is going to take the place between April first and tenth and if they come, the army is going to pull out, leaving us here! I hope that's not true!*

Fist fights happened often, in Dong Tam. When you have that much testosterone, booze, bravado, and anxiety, it happens easily. One night, a guy I knew walked behind one of our guys I came over with, and slapped him on the back of the head. As the guy who did the slapping walked on, another poor guy happened to be walking behind him. The guy who got slapped on the back of the head spun around, smashing the innocent guy on the nose, breaking it and splattering it across his face. He laid on the ground, choking on his own blood. We were afraid he going to drown in it, but we got him to sickbay as quick as we could, and he was fixed up.

During our first few days in Dong Tam, we had exhausting and distasteful duties. We were put on back breaking work details, filling sandbags for bunkers, or to stack around *"hootches."* One morning I was on the odious *"shit detail."* Fifty-five gallon barrels were cut in half and placed under the out-house latrines. We had to lift a large plywood flap and pull the filled half barrels out from the latrines, pour kerosene or diesel fuel on the contents and burn it. The stench was unbearable. We wore rags over our faces. They didn't help much. It was not only repulsive, but dangerous. Poisonous snakes sought warmth in the tubs during the night.

A 12' sign at Dong Tam read;

**Dong Tam RVN**

| Monsoon Acres | Sun City Homes |
|:---:|:---:|
| (April-Nov.) | (Dec-Mar) |

A Waterfront Development
Engineered and Built By
**Naval Construction Battalion Nine**
**Delta Detachment and Naval Support Activity – Saigon**
Homestead Sites Courtesy of
**9th Infantry Division**
Offering

| Boating | Hiking | Outdoor Living |
|:---:|:---:|:---:|
| No Down Payment | | One Year Leases |
| Immediate Occupancy | | with Options |

One day, a young, junior officer drove me off base to a field, to guard pallets of supplies that had not yet been brought into the gates of the base. When we got to the field, I asked for the weapon I assumed would be provided. He told me I didn't need one. I made it very clear to him he was NOT going to leave me in a field, surrounded by jungle, to guard supplies, without a weapon. I'm pretty sure cursing and threats of bodily injury was involved. I was a young, skinny, twenty-year old enlisted man and he was an officer, a little older than me. I didn't care. He looked at me and grudgingly handed me his .45 caliber automatic and drove off.

After a while, a Vietnamese figure came out of the jungle and approached from the distance, with the sun behind him. I pointed the .45 in his direction, yelling *"Di di mau!"* I was telling him to LEAVE! He dropped to the ground, not like a guy trying to make himself a smaller target, but like a sack of potatoes, or a puppet that had his strings cut. I looked at the gun, trying to figure out what the hell happened. I hadn't fired it.

Later, when the Jeep came to pick me up, we drove by the spot where the guy fell to the ground. There was a young teenage boy, lying in the arms of his old *"mama-san."* The boy appeared to be having an epileptic seizure. His head was shaking from side to side, and he was drooling. Apparently, seeing a gun pointed at him triggered a seizure. I felt bad about it, but would still do it again, if faced with the same situation.


In an effort to eliminate Viet Cong activity on the south bank of the Song My Tho, across the river from the Dong Tam base, a powerful tear gas was sprayed in the area. The V.C. often used the area to fire mortars into Dong Tam, especially during the night. The chemical that later became known as *"Agent Orange"* had already defoliated the area, which was designated a *"free fire zone."* Basically, that meant if we saw anyone moving in the area, we were free to fire on them, if we suspected they were Viet Cong. The ships of the MRB and the river assault boats that protected the ships with 24/7 *"BID"* patrols would also hit the area with nightly *"H and I,"* or *"Harassment and Interdiction"* fire. We would fire on suspected and known areas where the enemy would often hide, establish ambushes, fire rockets, or use as infiltration and escape routes.

**Diary, Monday, March 25, 1968.**
*Charlie hasn't bugged us for two nights, now. The mortar attacks happen so often, I have a feeling we will have at least a few mortars, tonight. I've checked out the "PACV's" (Patrol Air Cushion Vehicles). They are groovin' machines!*

*This morning we're building bunkers again. We fill sand bags and stack them up around framed walls. I feel more like a soldier than a sailor. A lot of the guys are anxious to see action. Myself, I would be satisfied to stay right here! I have no desire for "action." I know I'll be seeing it before long, though. One thing that keeps bugging me is that Charlie has kids thirteen to sixteen years old with them. I don't think I could stand the idea of killing a kid my brother Pat or Mike's age. I'm only twenty, but I feel much older.*

**Diary, Tuesday, March 26, 1968.**
*I didn't add any more last night because Freddie, Jardine, Bouling, Smith, and I got plowed at "The Windjammer," the Navy enlisted men's club, in Dong Tam. We weren't mortared last night. Only the first two nights at Dong Tam. Tonight I am on APL-26, a barracks ship. They call it "The Apple." It is pretty nice. It makes me miss "The Big E." I am assigned an ATC, or "Armored Troop Carrier," for Riv Ron 13. I think I will be on a "BID" patrol boat until mine gets over here. We circle the ships in the river, guarding them from any sort of attack or mine. I think it is an easy and safe job.*

*When we see a clump of vegetation, or anything suspicious floating the river, we get close enough to it to either throw a concussion grenade into it, or shoot it with a shotgun. The goal is to minimize the opportunity for the enemy to plant mines on the ships. We are also there to respond to enemy attacks from either bank.*

*On the boat to My Tho, a junk went by with a family in it. A little girl smiled and waved to me. I returned both.*

*Eight V.C. were mowed down, in, and around heavily fortified bunkers, by the guys in the 3rd of the 60th Infantry, and helo gunships. Three of the grunts were injured by booby traps. One was wounded by sniper fire.*

I sent home an audio that tape a few of us made, the night of March 25<sup>th</sup> at Dong Tam. Daryl Jardine had a great talent in writing new lyrics to popular songs. Jardine was kind of a short guy, with blond hair. He was a Radioman, Petty Officer Third Class. He had a big personality, with a great sense of humor. He revised the lyrics for the song *"Downtown,"* by Petula Clark, so that it became "Dong Tam." In the song, *"libs"* is short for *"Liberty,"* or time off. The song, *"Yesterday,"* by the Beatles, became *"Civilian Days."* Here's a picture of Jardine (with the sunglasses). I'm on the left. I can't recall the name of the other "River Rat." We're enjoying drinks at *"The Windjammer,"* our enlisted men's club, in Dong Tam.

**I sent this note, along with the audio tape, which is transcribed, here.**
*"Hi, Folks!*

*You'll probably have trouble with this tape, because my batteries were really worn down during most of it. If you have any old batteries, put them in, so the tape will be played about the same speed it was recorded in. I had to do a lot of censoring in it. In the song, "Dong Tam," that a buddy of mine made, I didn't know how to erase one word without it being conspicuous. In one part, Freddie talks about a green flare and a ground attack. He's just joking! Don't take him serious!*

*Send a tape, soon!*

*Terry"*

**Audio tape home. March 25, 1968**
> *"This is Radio City, Moscow, speaking! Hello, everybody! I've never really talked into a tape recorder, before! My name is Freddie! Hey! There goes another flare, man! We better make it for the boats! No, we better NOT make it for the boats, 'cause they'll probably get us, anyway! Let's just hang around and watch them kill everybody, then we can die quietly!"*

**The tape then cut to five of us singing a couple choruses of *"Cops of the World."***

*"Cause we're the cops of the world, boys!*
*Yeah we're the cops of the world!*
*We'll spit through the streets of the cities we wreck.*
*We'll find you a leader that you can't elect!*
*Those treaties we signed were a pain in the neck!*
*Cause we're the cops of the world, boys!*
*Yeah we're the cops of the world!*

*We've rammed in your harbors and tied to your ports.*
*Our pistols are hungry. Our tempers are short.*
*So bring your daughters around to the port*
*'Cause we're the Cops of the World, boys,*
*Yeah we're the cops of the world!"*

**We followed that up with *"Dong Tam,"* sung to the tune of the Petula Clark song, *"Downtown,"* recorded in 1964. At one point in the song, you can actually hear a 105 Howitzer being fired.**

*"When you're in Nam and war is driving you crazy,*
*You can always go... Dong Tam!*

*All of the shells and rockets making you jumpy,*
*You can always go... Dong Tam!*

*Listen to the sound of all the mortars landin' 'round 'ya,*
*With Charlie waiting just outside to get the chance to pound 'ya!*
*How can you win?*

*The flares are much brighter here!*
*You can dance on your bunker and drink all your beer!*
*Here at Dong Tam! What shitty "libs" we got!*
*Dong Tam! Waiting here to get shot!*
*Dong Tam! Charlie is waiting for you!"*

Imitating a radio announcer, Freddie playfully introduced the guys who sang on the tape,

*You are listening to the wonderful music of Daryl Jardine and his version of "Down Town!" O.K. Here's the guys what's gonna' sing the next little tune for ya!*

*My name's Bouling!*

*Mine isn't! .... Jardine!*

*Mine's something else! Smith!*

*SATER! They KNOW me!*

*Oh! Do they? And I'm Freddie!*

*O.K. All set? Jar, you start it off!*

*Wait a minute! I gotta finish my samich!*

*You wanna a beer to wash it down?*

Jerry Ranson joined us for a rendition of the Beatles tune; *"Yesterday."* Jardine changed it to *"Civilian Days."*

> *Yesterday, all my troubles seemed so far awaaaay,*
> *Now I went and joined the Naaavy. Oh I believe in Civilian Days.*
>
> *Suddenly, I'm only half the man I'm supposed to be,*
> *There's an officer over me. Oh, I believe in Civilian Days.*
>
> *Why I had to go I don't know, they wouldn't say.*
> *I signed something wrong, now I long for civilian days!*
>
> *Civilian Days, life was such an easy game to play!*
> *Now I need a place to hide away. Oh, I believe in Civilian Days!*

The next night, Tuesday, March 26th, Freddie and I added a little more in the audio tape,

I started it out, "Hi, *Everybody! I'm here with Freddie Arens. He's the guy from Boston I told you about, when I was home!*

Freddie chimed in, *"The weird one."*

> *Yeah. The weird one on the bus. I was telling them we were making fun of you, the way you say "Bawston," and "Hawvid," and "cah!"*
>
> *I hope you didn't tell them the OTHER stuff!*
>
> *No. I didn't tell them any of the other stuff. You wanna tell them where we ARE right now?*
>
> *We're on the RIVER, right now! Where we at? We down by Vung Toe, or what?*

I was never sure if Freddie was kidding, or not. I corrected him, looking forward to his response;

> *"My Tho"* (pronounced "Me Toe.")
>
> *I had the wrong toe! The town of Vung Toe is up that way!*
>
> *I ain't never heard of Vung "Toe!"*
>
> *"Vung Tau?"*
>
> *Is that near Kansas City?*
>
> *Don't be messin' my mind up, now!*

Pulling Freddie and the conversation back to reality, I said,

> *We're on the APL 26, the barracks ship, in the middle of the Mekong River. We have our boats all around us.*

Freddie dryly added; *"The stars are out."*

> *Yeah. The stars are out.*

With the playful banter that always cracked me up, Freddie added the obvious, *"The sun's down."*

*The sun's down. We're not supposed to be out here, are we?*

*Here's the army, coming from a patrol, right now. They're unloading their stuff on the pontoon, next to "The Apple."*

After a long pause, Freddie seriously mused, *"Seems like we could buy a weapon off one of those guys."*

*I want to get a 38, man! How many 38's they got on a boat?*

*We've only got two on my boat!*

*Only two 38's on a boat, and I know I wouldn't get one!*

In his comical, self-depreciating way, Freddie responded,

*The captain has one and the chief engineer, the cool engineer has the other one. Not me. I'm just the "lesser cool engineer." I'm just a "baby snipe."*

*Freddie's a "snipe!"*

*"Baby snipe!"*

*I don't think they know what a "snipe" is.*

*A "snipe" is..... Engineering Department. We're the dirty, grubby guys that run around in the bilge.*

I asked Freddie, *"Why do they call you "snipes?"*

*I don't know!*

*Don't you know?*

*I'm only a "boot camper!" I don't know why they call me a "snipe!"*

Freddie was exaggerating by joking that he was just out of *"Boot Camp,"* which he wasn't. I tried to explain to Freddie, my understanding of why enginemen are called *"Snipes."*

*They call you a snipe, because on the big ships, the snipes are always down in the engine room. A snipe is a little animal that has beady eyes, never sees the sun and just sticks his head up, out of the hole, every once in a while!*

Freddie chuckled. *"You're lookin' for to get hurt, ain't ya?"*

*No! That's the way they got the name! That's the way I heard it!*

With feigned anger, Freddie: laughed. *"You're cruisin' for a brusin'!"*

*That's the way I heard it!*

*Hang on. I gotta check what's on the other side of this.*

*Freddie's gonna check what's on the other side of a tarp, right next to us. I don't know what's on the other side of it. We're on the very top deck of the APL.*

*It's sleeping quarters!*

*It is? Hey! I'd rather be up here, ya' know it? The breeze?*

*No. I'd rather be down in there in air conditioning!*

I liked the idea of sleeping topside on the ship, with all of its amenities.

*This is "cool," up here, though!*

*No it's COOLER down there!*

*Let's take a walk, down there! Let's go down to the pontoon!*

I agreed with Freddie. I hoped we could get Grif in on the conversation.

*OK. Maybe we'll find Griffin down there. He's another cool head. We can talk to him.*

*(As we walked, we passed a radio playing the song, "Sunny," by Bobby Hebb. One line in the lyrics stood out in cruel irony; "Now the dark days are gone, and the bright days are here.")*

*Freddie and I are sitting out on his ASPB, now.*

*It's not an ASPB! It's my "yacht!"*

*Oh, O.K.!*

Freddie was very proud of a lawn chair he bartered for, bought, or stole.

*Notice the cool "chea" I got? You better explain what I just said! They won't understand.*

*Oh! By "chea," Freddie means "chair." He's sitting on his little aluminum lounge chair. That's his Boston accent!*

Freddie lit a cigarette. I commented that we missed Freddie's crewmate.

*Griffin is supposed to be on this boat too, but he's not here. He's a radioman.*

*No. He's probably in taking a shower. I told him he better! No. I'm only foolin'*

I reflected on the diversity of our jobs and geography.

*This is kind of a mixed group. An "E.T. striker," a "snipe" and a radioman.*

*It's a cool group, though!*

*It IS a cool group! It's the "In Crowd," man!*

*It's a "happening!"*

*If you hear a weird sound, like somebody's messing with cellophane, it's the boat radio! Terry's going to give you his address!*

*Does anybody ever call you "Fred," instead of "Freddie?"*

*Yeah…. When people are mad at me… . Once in a while, somebody weird calls me "Frederic." My mother calls me…… I can't tell you what my mother calls me! Can I say what my mother calls me?*

*Sure!*

(Freddie, had a funny, but obscene word, for what his mother supposedly called him.)

*Oh, sorry! I had to bleep out what Freddie said his mother calls him! Oh! My address! It is; "Sn Terry Sater B50-92-57, River Assault Squadron 11" and below that, put "Riv Ron 13," because I'm temporarily attached to Riv Ron 11……*

Freddie was sitting in a spot that could not be seen from the shore, behind a .30 caliber machine gun.

*I'm not going out there with this cigarette lit. I might get zapped! Wait a second! I might get a Purple Heart out of it!*

*Freddie's cool on Purple Hearts. He wants to get a Purple Heart!*

*I got this .30 cal. aimed right at you, man!*

*You do? Nice guy!*

*That's O.K. You gotta' crank it once before it will fire!*

*You "gotta crank it before it fires?" The .38?*

*No. The .30 caliber!*

*Has it got ammo in it?*

*Oh yeah. It has 600 rounds in the little box, next to it.*

*My good buddy was just pointing a .30 caliber machine gun at me that has 600 rounds of ammo in the little box next to it! His boat has a .30 caliber machine gun on each side of the stern.*

Typically playful, Freddie explained;

*It has the cover on it! You can't fire it with the cover on it! You can, but it will put holes in the cover! You don't want to do that. They'll write you up! Destruction of government property!*

*I'M government property! O.K. back to my address! I'll never get the address finished! After Riv Ron 13, put down "FPO San Francisco, California, 96601," Next to "Riv Ron 13," put "T-131-3."*

I nudged Freddie, saying; "Tell 'em how come I didn't write last night! What was I doing last night?

*"Uh, ya were at a "pahty" with me!*

*It was a BIG party, really!*

Freddy agreed. *"Only two of us ended up getting wiped out! You had to go hit the rack! We started drinking that Korean crap!"*

*Yep! "Korean Crown!"*

*That was some raunchy stuff! Isn't that the stuff that has thermaldahide, or something like that in it?*

*I still think it's not "thermaldahide." I think it's "peraldahide."*

*Maybe it is! I don't know. I just know that I heard it messes up babies, or something.*

*Messes up babies?*

*Yeah. Women take it for medicine, or something. I don't know! And then, when they have kids, it messes the kids up, with arms, legs missing, or something like that.*

*People that do that must be weird, too.*

*I think it must have been some kind of hoax, like it was supposed to be good medicine, or something. I don't pay much attention to that stuff.*

*Neither do I.*

I tried to list the other guys in our drunken binge, from the night before;

*We were all drinking, last night. There was Freddie, Jardine, Griffin, and Bohling....*

*Oh man, you can't name them all!*

*There was a whole bunch of guys. We were drinking a whole bunch of booze. Freddie was buying it all! He's a big spender!*

*My last fling, man! Ha!*

*I hit the rack before the rest of the guys, just after I threw up!*

*You DIDN'T!*

*I DID! All of a sudden, I started tasting the pizza coming up!*

*The pizza we had for chow?*

*Yeah!*

*Oh, man! I NEVER eat that stuff! That's pathetic! That spaghetti kept bouncing up and down on me!*

*I could have gone back and drank some more, but I was tired, then. After I threw up, I felt O.K. That pizza was just bad! It was weird, too, because I had the pizza hours before.*

As a proud Irish-American, Freddie offered his advice;

*You shouldn't eat that whop slop before you're gonna' drink, anyway!*

*Freddie, tell them about all the advantages of this place, the barracks ship! Tell them about how different it is from Dong Tam!*

*Oh, it's rather cool!  We don't have any dust!*

*Yeah!  That's a BIG thing!*

*That's a REAL big thing!*

*Tell them about the music machine!*

*They have a juke box in the chow hall.  I haven't even checked that thing out!  I don't even know how it works, 'cause they haven't got any coins!*

*Hey!  That's true!*

*I mean, you don't stick paper in it!*

*Freddie, I don't think they know about the money situation!*

*Oh!  The money situation is BAD!  Send some!  No!  Ha!  No!  Don't send any money!  We're only foolin'!  They took away all our money and gave us these little pieces of paper what says we got money!  "Funny money," we call it, 'cause it's funny to look at!*

*What do they actually call it?  The real name?*

Freddie insisted, with a laugh; *"Funny money!"*

*"M.P.C."  "Military Police Certificate."  Even the NICKELS are paper!*

Changing the subject, Freddie broke into a verse of *"Cops of the World."*

> *"We've rammed in your harbor and tied to your port!*
> *Our pistols are hungry!  Our tempers are short!*
> *So bring your daughters around to the port!*
> *'Cause we're the Cops of the World!"*

Freddie explained.  *"It's kind of stupid, but anytime we're sittin' around and got nothin' to do, we start singin'!  Ha!  Ha!  It kind of keeps the morale up!"*

I nudged Freddie to talk about one of the guys in his crew.

*"Another thing that keeps the morale up is "Wheezer!"*

Freddie was a decent and loyal guy, who didn't want to say an unkind word about one of the guys from our training class.

*Don't say that man!  He's still my coxswain!*

(The "coxswain," or *"cox'n,"* is the helmsman, or, the guy that *"drives"* the boat.  *"Wheezer"* was the guy who lit the flare for our *"aggressor"* trainer, in River Warfare School, and was told that he just blew up his own boat.  Many of us thought he was dangerously inept.)

*Is he?  They're still trying to get him off the boat, though, aren't they?*

*Hmmmm. Hey, we're going out tomorrow at 7:00 O'clock and we won't be back until 7:00 O'clock the next day.*

*Tell them about "BID Patrol." That's what I'm going to be on, tomorrow, with the boat captain I'll be getting. We're going out with one of the other boats.*

Freddie was pleased that they were going to be patrolling the east bank of the river.

*We get the east bank! Nothing ever happens on the east bank! "Bid Patrol!" "Bid," as in "Bed," without an "E," only it's an "I." "Base Interior Defense" Patrol. Actually, it's "BIDP" Ha!*

Comforting my family at home, I added; *"It's a safe job, though!"*

*Is it? Not on the north bank, it ain't! Everybody wants to do something on the north bank! On the other bank, all they ever do is just snipe at you and stuff! That's cool, 'cause you can't fire back at them! Those little "zipper eyed" son of a …….*

After a break, I began the conversation again.

*We're on the stern of Freddie's ASPB, right now. I'm sitting on the engine cover of Freddie's engine.*

Freddie urged me, *"Tell them what kind of engines we have!"*

*I don't know what kind of engines you have!*

*"V1271's!" Two V1271's!*

*Yeah! Two "V1271's," if you want to pass that around to the neighbors, or anybody! We're sitting in front of an 81MM mortar, and we've got the two .30 caliber machine guns in front of us. The flag on the boat is waving in my direction, about five feet in front of me.*

I switched gears to something that had been on my mind, all day;

*I was going to call my girl, today, at 1300, because, you know… that would be 7:00 p.m., stateside, at my home. It would have cost $5.70, for three minutes, or something like that, at the MARS radio station. I stuck around for an hour, but they couldn't get through and I had to leave. I can't afford to be calling home right now, anyway. I don't know when we're gonna get paid. I owe this one guy, Ranson, $24.00. He lent me part of the money for my airline ticket home. He's a nice guy.*

*I owe Freddie some money, too! I've been mooching cigarettes and beer off him, and I borrowed a buck to buy some soap the other day.*

Freddy jumped in, dismissively;

*No you don't! Big bleeping deal!*

*What time is it, Freddie?*

*About eight o'clock. Oh! Excuse me! "2000!"*

*What else can we talk about?*

*I don't know, man! I'm classified!*

*You're classified?*

*Yeah! Top secret material, right here! Less than two feet from you!*

*Oh! I'm honored!*

*You should be!*

## Next Night

*Hey, Freddie, tell them about you running into the anchor chain of the barracks ship, last night!*

*I ran into the BLEEPING anchor chain last night!*

*Because you were the coxswain on the ASPB?*

*Yeah. 'Cause I was the cox…. cox…….*

Freddie was distracted by the loud roar of an ATC tying up next to his boat, banging into it hard. He shouted;

*Alright! Shut those engines down and quit hitting my boat!*

I explained to my family, listening to the tape;

*An ATC just pulled up next to us and tied up.*

Freddie added;

*Hear that noise? That's why they call us "The Green Monsters!"*

I began again, anxious to pull the story out him.

*O.K., Freddie. Tell them why you ran into the anchor chain!*

*Cause I kept watching this nut! He had a grenade and uh… uh… uh…See! If I don't SWEAR, I start stutterin' to try to make up for it!*

*Oh, that's alright! STUTTER, then!*

*Anyway, 'cause I kept watching this weird guy, Wheezer, with a grenade, 'cause I didn't know if he was gonna throw it in the water, or throw it at me! He kept fumbling with it! He's kind 'a soft headed! I kept trying to watch him, but he walked to where I couldn't really see him and I tried to watch him and I really couldn't and when I turned around to see where I was going, there was a bow of ship right in front of me! I spun the wheel as best I could to keep from hitting the bow, but I caught the anchor chain! See! And I didn't even swear in the whole thing!*

*And what was Wheezer doing?*

*Wheezer was running around the boat for the next fifteen minutes, while we were checking to see if we had any damage done, with the um…. "Gosh darned" GRENADE in his hand!*

*He finally tossed it in the water, though?*

*Oh yeah!*

Some weeks later, *"Wheezer"* had guard duty on a pontoon, alongside a ship in the MRB. He started to throw a concussion grenade into the Mekong, but fumbled and dropped it. He was standing on the edge of the pontoon. He could have kicked it into the water, or, he could have run for cover. Instead, he bent over, picked up the grenade, and brought his arm back to throw it. It went off in his hand. A concussion grenade doesn't have the shrapnel that a fragmentation grenade has, but it can be deadly at close quarters. He died of shock. His death almost seemed predetermined, from our training, at Mare Island. It was his third, and final grenade encounter.

**Diary, Wednesday, March 27, 1968.**
*Griffin and Freddie took off on BID patrol, on their ASPB, "A-112-1," today. I pray to God their boats don't get hit. The ASPB's are kind of the "destroyers" of the river assault fleet. They are fifty feet long, and about fifteen feet wide, at the widest point. They are faster than our ATC's, or "Tango" boats. The ASPB's can do fourteen knots, or about 16 MPH. The Tango boats only do about half that. They have a draft of under four feet. They have more armor than a PBR, or a "Swift" boat, but less than the other boats of the MRF. It's almost like they are too fast, but not fast enough, and too armored, but not armored enough. Charlie has really been tearing them up with B-40 rockets. Griffin is a radioman and he will be in the coxswain's flat, where the coxswain, or helmsman, radioman, and boat captain would be. He is pretty level headed, but those B-40's have been wiping out coxswain's flats. Freddie has an intense hatred for Charlie because a good buddy of his was killed here. He may get reckless because of his hatred and catch a shell that way.*

*We had quarters today and I missed it. I overslept. I got a small chewing out, but even a <u>big</u> chewing out would roll off my back anymore. I don't care enough! We also had a "beer call" on the pontoon, tied up next to a ship. We got two beers. I gave one away. I wasn't in the mood for it.*

*Ranson, Miller, Roy and Underwood got here, today. Ranson missed the boat when we left Dong Tam the other day. He says they got mortared hard last night. One hit a crane.*

*Several of the guys are just getting here from the states. They were drunk at Travis, and got a "Captains Mast" for it. One was cut from 1st Class P.O. to 2nd. One was cut from 2nd to 3rd and one, from Seaman, to Seaman Apprentice.*

*Well, nothing is new. I guess I'll sign off. I haven't been worrying about getting zapped lately. Maybe it's only because I haven't seen death or mutilation yet. It is happening, all around me. I see it in the distance, or hear rumors about things that have happened, but so far, nothing close to me.*

**Letter to Judi, Wednesday, March 27, 1968.**
*Hi Judi!*

*I'm sitting in front of the jukebox in the chow hall, right now. They are playing the Temptations "You're My Everything." You are.*

*They gave us a briefing today. They said we won't get paid until the 13th or 15th of April. Now don't send money! I wouldn't put it past you, but it wouldn't be worth it, because there isn't anything I need and by the time this letter gets to you and I get your reply, I'll be paid, anyway! They also said we aren't going to be doing anything until our boats get here in April, sometime. Probably late April. They may send us out on other boats, once in a while, though. It kind of makes you wonder why they could only spare us for four days leave, doesn't it? They have more <u>men</u> than they do <u>boats</u>, here!*

*They just announced Mass is going to be held in the Mess Hall. I better go, because over here, you never know when they will have it. Sometimes they can't get it in on Sunday.*

*I hear they are moving this thing back to Dong Tam sometime this afternoon. They have sure been moving us around enough! I just heard that they will probably let us off this thing Monday and put us back on the base at Dong Tam, because after some guys come back off operations Monday, they won't have any room for us. Since our boats aren't in, they have no reason to keep us here. It really makes me mad, how they were in such a hurry to get us over here and now we just sit around and nobody knows what to do with us! Don't get me wrong. I would be satisfied if I never went out on the boats.*

*All the ships are moving to Dong Tam from My Tho, tomorrow. We moved about half way, today. I am going to send you a map I found today in "The Old Reliable" paper, the newspaper of the 9th Infantry Division. They are the boys my ATC will be hauling around. It is perfect for you to keep track of where I am. If I could have found another paper, I would have sent one to the folks. Maybe they can copy it. You can see where I traveled from Tan Son Nhut airfield to Dong Tam by helo, and up river from Dong Tam to My Tho.*

*Well, Hon, I guess I'll close for now. So until same time, not quite the same place, tomorrow, I love you with all my heart, Honey. I always will.*

*Terry*

Eight Viet Cong were finished off, Thursday, March 28th, in operations ten miles northwest of Dong Tam. Charley Company of the 4/47th Infantry slew three Viet Cong. Army gunships took out five. Two soldiers of Charley Company of the 4/47th were killed by snipers. One other was seriously wounded.

At least in the Mekong Delta, snipers were not usually our biggest concern. If they were good, they could have picked us off the boats, pretty easily. It did happen, but not often. They were more effective with mortars, mines, automatic weapons and rocket propelled grenades.

The two battalions swept south after being transported twelve miles up the Kinh Xang by boats of Riv Ron 9, to their objective beaches. The troops were landed at 0615. Nine boats remained in the AO (Area of Operations) to provide command and communications support.

**Martin Luther King Jr. led a march in Memphis, on March 28th, which turned violent. King was led from the scene. One 16-year-old boy was killed. 60 people were injured, with over 150 arrested.**

**Diary, Friday, March 29, 1968.** .
*Today, I had the 1600-2000 watch in the radio shack, on the pontoon, alongside "The Apple." I also have the "dog watch," from 0400-0800 in the morning.*

*This afternoon, Jack Meeks, from my training class, was in the chow line and he called me over and asked me if I knew "Corky Martin." I told him, "I went to E.T.A. School with him!" He met Corky when he went over to the "Askari," one of the repair ships. Corky came up to him and asked if he was in Class 14-R and if he knew me. I'm going to go over and see him tomorrow, if I get the chance. It will be good to see him.*

*I'll be glad when I start getting mail. It's starting to make me edgy! Oh, I forgot! Corky asked one of the guys if I got married. When they said I didn't, he said he was going to kick my ass! I think that's funny. He knows I want to, and I think he thinks a lot of Judi, because of the way she has stuck by me.*

*Two Viet Cong were killed by helicopter gunships. Soldiers of the 3/60th Infantry took one VC prisoner. Four soldiers were wounded. Two, from machine gun fire, and two from booby traps.*

*A crewman aboard a Riv Div 92 monitor received facial wounds when a shell cooked off in his 40MM mount, Friday morning.*

*An Army helicopter was shot down, but there were no casualties.*

**Diary Entry, Saturday, March 30th, 1968.**
*I saw Corky today! It was really hard to believe he was here! I didn't tell my boat captain I was going. I told several others, though. I just grabbed one of the small boats that ferried between ships. He said he should kick me for not marrying Judi, yet. I hope he can come with me on leave.*

*I went with Grif and Freddie today, for "racetrack," so that the APL could shift anchor. Every time the ships move, the boats that are tied up to them go in big circles, or "racetracks," until they can tie up to the ships, again. We sat on the bow and listened to the radio as we moved up and down the river. Sometimes we were only fifteen or twenty yards from the bank. At Mare Island training, I never thought I would expose myself like that, without my flak jacket and helmet on. It just seems different, now that I'm here.*

*The MRF killed ten Viet Cong, six miles east of Cai Be. Eight, by helicopter gunships and two by men of Alpha Company of the 3/30th Infantry.*


Sunday, March 31st, River Division 92 assault boats were ambushed with machine gun fire from both banks as they were backing off the banks of the Nam Thon River, after loading men from the 3/60th. They returned fire and returned to the Mobile Riverine Base at 1715.

In another incident, a column of boats moving down the Kinh Xang River, north of the Dong Dinh Bridge had two rockets pass between an ATC and a Monitor, exploding on the opposite bank. The boats returned fire with all weapons, including the newly installed flamethrower on Monitor 92-2.

**On March 31st, President Johnson announced that he would not seek, nor accept the nomination of his party for President, in the next election.**

**General Westmoreland ordered the Marines at Khe Sanh to be relieved by the first US Air Cavalry Division, on April 1st.**

On April 1st, the ARVN Seventh Division conducted a *"Traildust Mission,"* dropping what would become to be known as *"Agent Orange,"* on the south bank, across the river from Dong Tam.

On the same day, at 1651, six infantrymen from Bravo Company, of the 4th of the 47th were wounded by a command detonated booby trap. Two V.C. were sighted running from the vicinity and were taken under fire, without success. The six wounded men were evacuated to Dong Tam by an ATC, or *"Tango"* boat.

**Diary, Monday, April 1, 1968.**
*I saw Cork again, today. I can't believe he's here. It's almost like having a friend from home, here.*

*I watched three Seawolf helos attack a V.C. position near here, while I was out on A-112-1, Freddie and Grif's ASPB. It was awesome to watch. It was kind of exciting, but when I stop to think about what those rockets can do to a human body………..*

*I hear our boats will be here the 20th. I will enjoy working on mine. I want something to do.*


Dong Tam and the *"MRB"* were under constant mortar attacks. On Tuesday, April 2nd, the 4/47th conducted a sweep of the area, looking for the Viet Cong doing the attacks. They killed two V.C. and destroyed one hundred seventy bunkers and three huts. They also captured eight Chinese communist grenades and fifty rounds of machine gun ammo.

One U.S. soldier was wounded, when he threw a grenade into a HAY STACK, to *"check it out."* He was evacuated to the 3rd Surgical Hospital at Dong Tam.

**The "U.S. Naval Forces Vietnam Monthly Historical Supplement" reported;**
*"On 2 April, while the MRF was anchored in the vicinity of Dong Tam, a homemade booby trap was discovered aboard USS Colleton (APB36). The explosive device, which consisted of C-4 explosive, shaped like a grenade, with an attached claymore detonator, was found in the auxiliary engine room, alongside a pipe. MRF EOD personnel disarmed the device. This marked the first-known possible attempt at sabotage against a ship of the MRF. The source of the booby trap was not determined; however, a thorough investigation was initiated by the Naval Investigative Service, along with the implementation of more stringent internal security procedures and inspections."*

**April 3, 1968. Letter from my girlfriend, Judi's father, Phil Simon**
*Hi Terry,*

*I sure am glad the shoes feel good. I know what you mean about changing them at the end of the day, as my work shoes are heavy, too.*

*I am sorry I showed so much emotion when you left, but your going is like losing a son for awhile, and I am quite a sentimental slob.*

*I'm sure glad you are taking things in stride. One thing I want you to remember is that the Good Lord is on your side. Thank Him every morning for letting you live another day (I do). Ask His forgiveness, every night. Pardon me for preaching. I didn't mean to.*

*Now back to the weather we are having. Tonight it's pouring raining so hard it came up over the sidewalk, and came through the wall in our basement. It's kind of funny, we keep hoping for rain, and then when it comes, we want to shut it off.*

*I was going to put siding on the garage. Steve, Pat, Larry and Fran came over, but no go. It rained most of the day. Was going to ask you to help, but knew you couldn't make it. Maybe we will make it next Sunday.*

*Well, "Toto" (that's what Tommy Two, your nephew, calls you, he was over here last night),*

My nephew, Tom Sater

*I'll come to the end of the speel. Hope I did not bore you too much. Gussie says "Hi" and "Don't go near the water!"*

*So long, and may God Bless*

*Phil Simon*

Phil Simon treated me as a son, even when I was just a young kid, hot for his daughter. "Gussie" was Judi's mom, Augusta.

**Diary, Thursday, April 4, 1968**

*The boats and the Army came back off ops, today. Riv Div 91 and Riv Div 92 took the 4/47th and 3/47th Infantry, seven miles from My Tho, at a spot called "The Crossroads." The Navy boats had two killed and forty-six wounded. One of the wounded isn't expected to live. He caught a B-40 in the head. The two killed were a chief and a radioman. They were in the coxswains flat of a monitor. It was an ambush that really chewed our boys up. It happened less than three miles southwest of where the MRB was anchored. A total of ten men were killed, including six soldiers, two sailors and two Vietnamese. One-hundred-nine were wounded, including seventy men of the 9th Infantry Division, thirty-seven of the boat crews and two Marines.*

*Twenty-one VC had been killed by evening, at 2000, but enemy fire prevented a better count of V.C. bodies.*

*The whole ship is full of guys hobbling around. Some of them with their arms in slings, some with their knees or feet bandaged up. I think this makes five from the MRF killed this month. Yesterday, I had asked Rich Twigg (our 1st Class P.O.) if I could go on this operation. He said I couldn't. War is a filthy thing. It's too bad we need it for "the pursuit of happiness."*

**On April 4th, Martin Luther King Jr. was in Memphis Tennessee. As he stepped onto the balcony of his hotel, James Earl Ray fired one bullet into his neck, killing him. Following his death, Robert Kennedy gave an extemporaneous speech in which he pleaded for everyone to *"tame the savageness of man and make gentle the life in this world."* Rioting took place in Washington D.C., Detroit, Boston, Kansas City, and many other cities, killing forty-six people.**

**Letter Home, April 4, 1968**

*Hi Folks!*

*This is just a note in case you're worrying about me. I'll send you a tape as soon as I get one to record over.*

*Nothing is really new. I have trouble sleeping at night because I do so much of it during the day! They haven't got anything for us to do. Yesterday I asked if I could go out on operations with some of the boats and they said I couldn't, so I just slept all day. It may sound funny to you that I asked to go out on operations, but I'm going crazy, not getting any mail and not having anything to do! Newspapers and magazines are treasured here. I think I read the same issue of "Time," every night!*

*It has been awfully quiet, here and I'd like to have some training on one of these ATCs (They call them "Tango Boats." ASPB's are "Alpha Boats" and Monitors are "Mike Boats."*

*I ran into a soldier from Clayton today. He had "St. Louis Mo" on his flak jacket! He just came off of operations.*

*They have a movie every night here on the mess decks. I saw one, tonight. It was "Mysterious Isle."*

*After every operation they throw a beer party. I guess we'll have one tomorrow. The beer is usually as good as the movies. My guys keep getting "Carling's Black Label." The straight legs (9th Infantry) always wind up getting Miller High Life. I guess that's one of the things about war that I'll have to put up with! I guess I'll close for now. Don't worry about me.*

*Your ~~sailor marine soldier~~ son,*

*Terry*

On Friday, April 5th, the 4/47th Infantry swept the area of the previous day's firefight. Fourteen Viet Cong were dispatched. Fourteen *"friendlies"* were wounded.

In two days of fighting, twenty-two U.S. and two Vietnamese men were killed in action. Another one hundred twenty were wounded, as of 1930, Friday. Echo Company, of the 3/47<sup>th</sup> Infantry suffered twelve killed and thirty-four wounded. Thirty-seven Viet Cong were obliterated. Three were captured and cuffed.

I always admired the courage of the 9<sup>th</sup> Infantry Division guys, and not just in those dramatic moments of a firefight, the scenes that you remember in war movies. Nobody knows when their time will come. In a war, sometimes just getting up in the morning and putting one foot in front of the other shows courage.

A third Navy man died Friday from wounds suffered in Thursday's vicious assault on the boats of River Assault Squadron 9. He was FN Douglas George Morton, a crewman on Monitor 91-2.

Other sailors who lost their lives in the battle were BMC Samuel C. Chavous, and BM3 John D. Woodard, crewmen of M-92-2. They were fatally wounded when an RPG-7 rocket exploded in their coxswains' flat. Thirty-three other Riv Ron Nine personnel, three UDT Det Golf men and two Marines assigned to the Flotilla's riverine survey team were injured.

**Diary, Friday, April 5, 1968.**
*We had another "Beer Call," today. It helped me keep my mind off looking for mail that never came. It will probably start getting here when we go to pick up our boats! I got the word that four of my crew will be going on BID patrol, tomorrow. Ruff, Zepp, Tom Bohl, and I are going. I am just getting to know them pretty well. Ruff's brother and father were killed over here on December 1<sup>st</sup> and December 4<sup>th</sup>. His brother was a Marine and his father, a pilot. He thinks he has a score to settle with Charlie.*

*Bohl is Catholic and comes from a family of about fourteen brothers and sisters. He's not a bad guy. He's kind of quiet, but friendly.*

*Rudy Mahanes is ex-army. He's very intelligent, kind of a "playboy," now that he is divorced from his wife of about eighteen months. He is from Florida and is really a nice guy.*

*I still don't know much about Tommy Snow or our Boat Captain. Snow is from the south, a CT (Communications Technician) dropout. Our captain is a real "lifer," besides being a First Class Gunner's Mate. Not real bright, though.*

Our boat captain was grouchy and didn't seem to give a damn about us. If there wasn't work that needed to be done, he'd make something up. We didn't like him, at all. One day he sent one of the crew up to the ship we were tied up to, for sandwiches. When the crewman came back with a bologna sandwich for each of us, our captain was in the well deck, out of sight. Each of us took his sandwich and rubbed the bologna over various parts of our bodies. Places I won't go into here. Afterwards, we put his sandwich back together and waited for him to join us. When he joined us, we sat quietly, with perverted smirks, watching him devour his sandwich. Later, he was taken off the boats and put into a staff position. I think the higher ups saw that he was not a leader, and not fit to be a boat captain.

**Diary, Saturday, April 6, 1968.**
*Right now, I'm in a hammock on one of the "Alpha Boats," on BID patrol. The only thing I don't like about it is that there is probably mail on the APL.*

*The MRB is shifting anchor to four miles southeast of Ben Tre. A soldier was medevacked out, today, with a suspected case of malaria.*

*During the first three days of the ongoing operation, eighty-two Viet Cong were sent to whatever eternity that waits for them, and four were captured. Thirty-seven allied people died in the fighting. One-hundred-fifty-three were wounded.*

**Undated Letter to my girlfriend's father, Phil Simon**
*Hi, Mr. Simon!*

*This is just a short note to you. I'll write one to you and Mrs. Simon, too, but I wanted to tell you that you didn't have to apologize for being emotional when I left. My Grandpa did too, and my Dad gets that way. I'm kind of a "sentimental slob," myself. Judi could tell you that! I consider myself lucky that I've got great folks. I've also got Judi and I think SHE has great folks. I've made out, all around!*

*I appreciate your prayers, very much. It makes it a little easier over here, knowing I am remembered in prayer. I'll remember you in mine. Take care of yourself.*

*Yours,*

*Terry*


Helicopter gunships brought hell down, taking out eighteen Viet Cong, on Sunday, April 7th, during a four-day operation in Kien Hoa Province. Over the four day operation, eighty-seven Viet Cong were eliminated.

Two soldiers were injured, Sunday, resulting in a four day total of one-hundred-fifty-five Army, Navy, Marines and allied Vietnamese wounded. Thirty-six other allied personnel lost their lives in the heavy fighting along the Ba Lai River, on Thursday and Friday.

**Diary, Monday, April 8, 1968.**
*It was too hard to write on the boat Saturday. I had the wheel from about 4 to 7 Saturday evening, and 3 to 5, Sunday morning. I had to rely on the radar an awful lot on Sunday morning, because I lost my regular glasses and I had to use my prescription sunglasses. I piloted the boat totally by looking at the radar screen. I could not see the shore, except on radar. I was the only one awake on the boat.*

*The Benewah had a close one. A boiler room fire broke out, close to midnight and could have developed into a real disaster, but the fire fighters on board put it out, avoiding many casualties.*

*Dong Tam got mortared, last night. It was pretty bad.*

*A helo with mini-guns sprayed the beach, down from me. At night, the mini-gun looked like a laser beam, when it was fired at a focused target. Every fifth round was a "tracer." When they were spraying an area, it looked like a firehose, with bright red water, flowing out. We have enormous respect for chopper pilots. They provide close air support when things get hot!*

*One day, I watched an F-4 Phantom attack a Viet Cong machine gun position, perhaps a mile or two away. The fighter jet came down at a forty-five degree angle, strafing the enemy position. Each time it pulled up, for another pass, the V.C. fired a stream of machine gun fire up at the fighter. That was repeated several times before the fire from the ground finally stopped.*

*I got a package, card and four letters from Judi. They improved my moral 200%!*

*I had a working party from about 8:30 or 9:00 'till around 10:00 or 10:30.*

**Diary, Tuesday, April 9, 1968**
*Last night, I was staying on a ship, in the middle of the Mekong. The air conditioning was off in the compartment, so the pontoon next to the boat was <u>full</u> of guys sleeping there. I slept on the bow of an ASPB, with a blanket to cover me and a life preserver for a pillow.*

*I hit the beach in Dong Tam today, with Corky.  The MRB moved here from My Tho, at 1400 and arrived at 1515.  We met Freddie and Grif at the "Windjammer."  All of us got plastered.  Corky was late getting back and he may get "put on the pad," or on report.  I hope not.  I got back by coming back on the "Captains Gig!"  Corky knew the cox'n for it.*

*I got a letter from the folks, Mr. Simon, two letters and a card from Judi.  Now that's a "mail call!"  I even got an Easter basket from the family!  My moral is high.  All I need is mail, to keep me happy!*

**Tuesday, date unknown - Letter from my mother, June Sater.**
*My Darling Boy,*

*I have thought of you constantly since you left.  In fact, I find it hard to concentrate on anything else.  I was so worried about you landing at TSN airport, with all the shelling going on there.  It was in the paper that they shelled it with fifteen rounds and this was when I knew you'd be arriving there.  Well, I was vastly relieved when they said there were no injuries.  I am trying to do better, and keep up my spirits, but I do have my ups and downs.  Generally I am much better than I was.  I started driving again Friday.  Monday I got out a little bit, too.  I took Grandma Foster Monday and she enjoyed it.*

*Judi had received your card and letter and had called and read parts of it to us (Dad & I).  Say, who are you trying to kid, signing "Your Pal, Terry"?  Huh?  Ha Ha!*

*Well, Dear, it's now Thursday, 10:30, and I took Nancy to work and kids to school, and then laid down.  I was very sick, so I went to sleep and slept very deep, till Aunt Louise came and woke me up.  This medicine Dr. Votaw gave me Tuesday, just knocked me out.*

*We got your letter yesterday and I was sure glad.  It was a very interesting letter.  I found Dad reading it two different times and I read it to Mrs. Simon, and Grandma.  It sounds like you are in a regular dust bowl.  I thought the monsoons were over and that that is the reason the Americans have launched a new, big offensive.  They also say the North Vietnamese are launching a new one down the rivers and we have been bombing several sampans, lately.  I'm sure glad they weren't shelling when you came in for a landing.  It was pretty stupid of the Navy and really awful that you all got shunted all over the place.  You didn't complain, just explained, but I'll bet you were really dog tired, disgusted and hungry.*

*Well, darling, I know you're not a killer and I'm sure most of the servicemen are like you and just want to get it over with and go home, so don't let yourself feel bad about it.  Terry, don't even trust the "friendlies."  They might prove to be "enemies."*

*Well, if they count March and ten months, that would bring you back home last of December, or last of January.  We'll all try to keep busy till then and start looking forward to that day.*

*I just saw your sister, Judy on the Charlotte Peters Show.  The Mercy High School cast and Judy's group of singing nuns and cast of "Sound of Music" were on TV and your sister really looked good.  I didn't know she wasn't going to have her glasses off and I didn't know her.  I thought one looked like her and I waited until they showed all their faces before I realized it was Judy.  She was so pretty.  She's really going to be busy this weekend.  We're going to see it Saturday night.  Tom and Mary, Judi "Si" and her girl friends are going, also.*

*I haven't seen your Judi since you left.  I was feeling too bad at first.  I knew she was too and then I think it makes her feel bad when she comes here for the first time after you leave.  For nostalgic, etc. and also, she probably will wait till I'm more cheerful, as I haven't been very cheerful since you left.  Darling, I am far behind on my work, now.  I have to take it slow.  Guess I'll close for now.*

*Love, Always,*

*Mom*

**On April 11th, Secretary of Defense Robert McNamara, called up 24,500 reserves for two-year commitments and announced a new troop ceiling of 549,500 American military personnel in Vietnam. The total number of Americans *"in country"* peaked at a little over 540,000, at that point.**

River Assault Squadron 9 embarked the 3/47th and 4/47th, at 0320, on April 11th, and beached at 0730, in three provinces. Three-hundred-sixty-four enemy bunkers were destroyed. A *"Pys Ops,"* or Physiological Warfare Operation was conducted from the boats.

On Friday, April 12th, an infantryman drowned while crossing a stream. Another soldier was shot in the leg by another man, whose pistol discharged as it was being cleaned.

### Letter home, April 12, 1968
*Hi Everybody!*

*I'm on "BID" patrol, right now. I just wanted to thank you for the long letter and all the goodies. I still have a lot of it in my locker. It will take a while to use it up! The lemonade is very good! They give us Kool-Aid at lunch and dinner, but it's not very good and it's usually not cold. I carry packs of lemonade in my pocket and mix it with ice water, every chance I get.*

*They gave me a "G.Q." station on here in case anything happens (Nothing ever does on BID, though!). I'm supposed to use the grenade launcher and M-16 on the fantail. That's something straight out of a John Wayne movie! The grenade launcher is a mean weapon!*

*I'll be taking the helm on here, before long. We take two-hour watches. I'll probably have it again tonight, or in the morning.*

*I was surprised to hear about your plans for the shop. I hate bookkeeping and all that stuff too, so I don't blame you. It will be nice to have the basement all fixed up. If I get home in time, maybe we could have a New Year's Eve party, or a Christmas party. At least I should be there for a Valentines Day party!*

*I was glad to hear about Dad getting that plaque from the Boy Scout's Troop 644. You really deserved it, Dad! It got me thinking how you always found time to take a bunch of scouts camping or bringing us back, or making "fake" camp fires for indoor events, and supplying the troop with meat for campouts, or getting me the things I needed. I haven't got a trophy for ya, but I do thank you a whole bunch for all you did for me while I was in scouting. It's a good program and it does more than teach guys how to tie a square knot! I'll close for now.*

*Love,*

*Terry*

### Diary, April 13, 1968. Saturday
*Tomorrow is Easter. I'll be on BID patrol. I've been getting it every other day! I got a tape from Judi and everybody at home. It's so wonderful to hear the voices.*

*We had beer call, today.*

*I'm getting better on the helm and starting to know the ropes on the radio. There has been nothing written here the past few days, because there is nothing to write about. I'm bored!*

Three sailors were injured, Saturday, April 13th. A chemical gas launcher malfunctioned aboard a monitor, M-91-2, south of the MRB. One sailor was taken to the Benewah for treatment, but was later rushed to the Colleton for emergency surgery. Two crewmen received minor wounds. A fourth member of the crew was blown overboard by the explosion. He was picked up by A-111-1, which was on BID patrol. He was not hurt.

Sunday, April 14th, soldiers of the 3/47th and the 4/47th took sniper fire as they operated in Kien Hoa Province. Ten Viet Cong were killed. Dozens of bunkers and V.C. flags were destroyed. Enemy weapons and munitions were captured, including forty rockets, 102 grenades, 48 mortars, 2 Claymore mines, a five-foot Bangalore torpedo and an estimated 8,000 rounds of automatic weapons ammunition. Other material captured included 200 entrenching tools, 6,400 blasting caps, hundreds of batteries and a large quantity of medical supplies. At about 0830, a Tango boat was rocked by an explosion about six feet in front of it, as it was beaching. It was believed to be a B-40 rocket. There were no casualties, or damage.

**Diary, April 16, 1968**

*Today has been a day to remember! Freddie is in sick bay…. blood poisoning, all the way up his leg, from a cut on his toe.*

*I got paid $250. Lost $40 of it, side betting on a craps game. Jerry Ranson was trying to teach me how to play, but I wasn't very good at it. I don't know if I'll tell Judi, or not. If it makes her as sick as it did me, there wouldn't be much sense telling her.*

*We had a man overboard, tonight. They got him out alive. He was a crewman of A-92-6. He was rescued about 2215, after falling from the pontoon alongside the Benewah and floating several hundred yards downstream. It's a small miracle they got him out. Usually, if you fall in the Mekong, you are dead.*

*Yesterday was bad. The MRB, was attacked with rockets and recoilless rifle as it was anchored east of My Tho. The Tom Green County, one of the LST's, was hit with three rockets from the south bank. The Benewah, and the APL right behind us, were hit with one or two and the refueler, a converted "Mike 6," was sunk, after throwing flames forty feet up. All three crewmen of the refueler jumped overboard and were picked up by A-92-2.*

*Altogether, eighteen personnel were injured. None were killed. Two of the guys I trained with received Purple Hearts in the action. The eighteen wounded included four crewmen of the Tom Green County, five members of the Benewah's ship's company, four soldiers and five assault boat crewman. The hostile fire was suppressed by the ship's 40MM cannon, three-inch gun and machine-gun fire. The area was also hit by Army artillery and an Air Force air strike.*

*Two hours after the attack on the MRB, Grif and Freddie's boat, A-112-1, found a body floating down river with his arms tied behind his back, over a pole. No head. I couldn't sleep last night, thinking about it. It was wearing American "greens." If I die, I don't want it to be like that. A few of us talked about how we would want it, if we "had to go," over here. I decided on something like a .30-cal across the chest, for reasons too long to go into. It's big enough that I would go quickly, but small enough I wouldn't be mutilated, completely.*

*The boats of River Division 111 also found a floating booby trap with a Viet Cong flag and propaganda materials, near My Tho. It was all destroyed.*

*Well, to a cheerier subject, I bought a Polaroid, today. It cost $90, with extras. It's a real good one, the "Model 230."*

*Oh yeah! I forgot. Charlie never <u>did</u> try to take Dong Tam between the 1st and the 10th!*

The discovery of the headless body stayed with me in my dreams for years. With each month, horrific visions from additional experiences merged into one epic nightmare montage. I couldn't get the image out of my mind. I was angry at myself that I couldn't. How was the guy captured? Who was he? The Operations Report said that it was a Vietnamese body, but Grif and Freddie told me he was wearing American greens. I can't help but wonder if it was decided that it would not be good for morale to report that an American had been captured, tortured and beheaded. Grif and Freddie told me it was an American body. What did he go through before he was decapitated? Those possibilities were explored in my nightmares, for decades.

On April 16<sup>th</sup>, ten V.C. were killed and three captured. Two men of the 9<sup>th</sup> Infantry gave their lives in the action and thirty-one, wounded.

**Letter from Mom, Wednesday, April 17, 1968. She was 46 years old.**
*Dear Terry,*

*I am so anxious to hear from you, since the attack Sunday on your Riverine Force. They say fourteen sailors were wounded, but went back on duty. I just wonder if this is true. We were all so stunned when we heard the news that we weren't sure we heard it right. Dad had me call the station. Now you can just forget about telling me how you guys are not in much danger. I've been so scared ever since and the news is not good. It looks like the V.C. are getting ready for another big sweep all around Saigon and I imagine if they've attacked your group now, they'll be coming back over and over. We're wondering if this is the same barracks ship that you've been on. I'll send the clippings from the St. Louis Globe Democrat and St. Louis Post-Dispatch, although I know you already know all about it. You can see how it was reported. Judi "Si" called yesterday from work, when her mother told her what I'd read to her and wanted to know about it, too. Said she too, had heard only the part about the Riverine Force had been attacked, but didn't know what they said about casualties. Judi had just called Monday night and read your long letter. It was very interesting. So, now you are going out on patrols. I'm so worried about booby traps. These damn VC are so ingenious. Be careful!*

*Mrs. Simon called to tell me Judi got a letter. I was so glad.*

*I was talking to a lady and she told me a friend of hers was home (on leave), a young man, from the River Patrol and he said it is really something, over there, that going down the river, they (VC) hide behind bushes and shoot at them, etc…. There is sure a lot of action going on over there. I guess I'd be better off not to watch the news, but can't help it.*

*Judi called last night and read your letter dated April 11<sup>th</sup>. It was very amusing. I really laughed a lot. Judi was so funny, too. I told her I'd start getting together some goodies to send you. Of course, I know you haven't even gotten my first box, yet, and that cost nearly $3.00 to send.*

*Tom said you were on this patrol on the 12<sup>th</sup>, so apparently, the next day is when the VC attacked your group. So, I guess by Monday or Tuesday we might hear from you about the attack.*

*You'll be an "uncle" again, soon! Mary is due Thursday, so it's any day, now and I'm sure hoping for a girl. Imagine this, "Dorothy Virginia". I blew my top. I said "Don't you dare saddle my granddaughter with a name like that!" I know they meant well, wanting to name it after her mother and me, but I've always hated my name. I will close this time, and mail this. Take care of yourself.*

*Love, Always. Lots of hugs and kisses, Judy Sa said to tell you "Hi." Dad will write soon.*

*Mom*

On April 18<sup>th</sup>, three River Division 111 sailors were decorated with Bronze Stars for action on December 4<sup>th</sup>. They were BM1 Robert D. Julian, BM3 William R. Wolverton, and EN3 Gerald R. Vinopal. A Gold Star in lieu of a third Purple Heart was presented to HM1 Royale J. Pariseau of River Assault Squadron Nine Staff.

**Thursday April 18, 1968. Audio Tape Home.**
*Hi, Everybody!*

*I hear we are picking up our boats at Vung Tau, on the coast of Vietnam, and then taking them twelve or fifteen miles away, to Cat Lo. That may be on the map I gave Judi. I'll be there before you find out where it is, probably. There are seven men in a crew, with four boats going down, so that's twenty-eight of us going down there, plus some guys helping us work on them, like my buddy, Corky, as an E.T., helping to install the radios and other stuff. I'm not going to be a radarman on the boat. The ATC's don't have radar. I imagine they'll put* me on the 50's and 30's, because they usually put the gunner's mate strikers on the 20MM cannons. I won't be a radioman. I won't go into it, but I think it's safer for me to be on the guns, than the radio.

These guys are really a motley bunch. I guess because you have so many rates on one boat. Each boat has gunner's mates, a bosn's mates, radiomen, and an engineman, or a "snipe." Everybody is so different. We range in age from eighteen to about forty-five.

I guess I could tell you about my boat crew. There are seven of us. A Gunners Mate First Class, is our boat captain. He's a quiet guy. I don't think he's too bright, really. I haven't talked to him, much. One guy's father was a jet pilot and was killed over here, on December first. His brother was a marine. He was killed on December fourth. If we ever have to take captives on our boat, I'm afraid of what he may do if we turn our back. He says he will kill them. Then there is Rudy Mahanes. He's a pretty good guy. He's an expert diver, from Florida. I know him pretty well. He's very polite and well spoken. He always says "Pardon me," instead of "Huh?" like I do. He went to Gunner's Mate School and dropped out.

There's Zepp. He's a little guy, but pretty gung ho! We took a "John Wayne" picture, in front of the boat. He's got an M-16. I've got an M-79 grenade launcher.

Tommy Snow, is from the south, Tennessee, I think. He's a great guy. He went to Communications School and dropped out. I guess we're just a bunch of rejects, but a pretty good boat crew, actually.

Mahanes is a green belt in judo. We've become friends. He said he will work out with me. He's going to teach me some Judo. I don't like calisthenics. I need something I can work out with. Maybe Judo will do it.

**From left to right, Tommy Snow, Rudy Mahanes and Teddy Underwood.**

*In just a second, you'll hear the machine gun firing in the background* (There is the sound of a machine gun, firing in the distance). *It's a boat on BID Patrol, firing at the bank, maybe in a practice area. It's firing red tracers. It sounds like a 50 caliber machine gun. Tracers are bouncing up into the black sky, at different angles. It's firing in all different directions. I don't see return fire. It's fading. It sounds like the boat is moving away. You may not be able to hear it, now.*

*I fired the M-16, a lot. I also fired the Chicom AK-47. It is a good weapon. The VC bury it in rice paddies, sticking lard or something in the barrel, then pull it up and fire it. The M-16 jams if it gets dirty, but it is a wonderful weapon, being accurate and light. We don't have to worry about that on the boat. It's pretty easy to keep it clean on the boat. It does give the infantry some trouble. The AK-47 has a wooden stock and there's not that much to it. It is short, light, simple and sturdy. It's custom made for these short little people.*

*The army was out on operations, last night and the day before, twenty-four kilometers, or fifteen miles, northeast of Dong Tam. They killed ninety-seven Viet Cong and captured three. We had three U.S. casualties, all army. They had gone up "Route 66." There are two areas of the river that are kind of controlled by "Charlie," where he has the upper hand. "Route 66" is straight and long. "Charlie" knows he owns it. "Snoopy's Nose" is shaped just like the cartoon character, "Snoopy's" nose.*

*We can paint names on our boats and gun mounts. The boats have all kinds of weird names. I'm thinking of naming my gun mount "Sater's Spade." The Spade is bad luck for Vietnamese. I saw an ATC, or Tango boat the other day named "Sweatin' Plenty." I saw a Monitor named "Bad News." One of the Alpha boats is called "The Trip." Then there is "Saigon Tea," "Linda Sue," and "The Green Phantom."*

*I've learned a lot about guns and the sound of various guns. I can pretty well tell the sound of each of them. I know something about the power of them. Being here gives you a different outlook on guns, I guess 'cause they're used for different purposes, but of course, with the riots I've been hearing about in the states, maybe there aren't used for different purposes.*

*It's about 12:30. I'm the only one on the pontoon.*

*I just finished watching a movie, "My Blood Runs Cold," with Joey Heatherton and Troy Donahue. It was a weird movie, about reincarnation.  .*

*I had a pair of jungle boots, but I'm trading them to a guy on the Askari for a case of batteries. We're going to trade other things, too, like my G.I. issue "K-Bar" sheath knife.*

*I'm anxious to see our boats. There's supposed to be a lot of innovations and improvements in them. The guys live on their boats instead of living on barracks ships. Some guys are mounting movie cameras on their gun mounts. You can see all the action that I'll ever be in, which won't be much. I don't really relish taking movies of…… well, … you know what I mean. Just giving you an idea of what it looks like behind the gun mount. After spending $90.00 on a Polaroid, I won't be spending much….    I gotta start saving some money.*

*I think we moved anchor. The ships don't look like they're in the same positions they were in, earlier, today. I'm on the pontoon, now, on the APL.*

*The army is out here, on the "Apple." They're going out on an operation, pretty far from here. I think up "Route 66." They have their packs all over the pontoon. I don't envy the army. They've got a rough job.*

*A boat nearby is firing a 20MM cannon in slow, short bursts.*

*Judi wrote me about Tom hitting a coat hanger with his lawn mower and it going into his ankle. It sounds pretty bad to me. I hope he gets well, soon, and it doesn't cause any complications, with the baby coming. As soon as Mary Rose has the kid, send me an air mail letter real quick, I don't know if you can get me a telegram to me. I don't think you can. If there is ever an emergency, contact the Red Cross, and they can get me on the telephone, very quickly.  I was reading on the bulletin board how a message came in from somebody's wife that there was an emergency at home and they had him on the phone talking to her in half an hour.*

*You can learn an awful lot about life, in a place where there is so much of the opposite.  I've seen things that I didn't really understand, or appreciate before I came here.  We don't take a lot of prisoners, but we treat captured prisoners a lot better than the VC, or the North Vietnamese do.  I've heard a lot about both sides.*

*I was sitting in the berthing compartment, today.  Five guys were helping me record a tape.  They get a kick out of it.  Most of them don't have tape recorders and they are surprised at how their voice sounds.  My voice probably sounds a lot different than it normally does.  My nose is stopped up.  I have a cold, because of the air conditioning. They enjoyed doing it.*

*I can't believe what just happened!  I turned off the microphone for a second, and right after I turned it off, about four shots from a 40MM cannon went off, from a Monitor.  It may go off again. (Two cannon booms) There it goes!  I don't know what they're firing at.  I can't see the flash.  Oh, yes. (Two booms)  It's way up river.  The flash goes, and then the sound gets here.  On certain sections of the river, they can have practice fire. I believe that's what they're doing.  I can't see any fire coming back at it.  It's something way up the river.  (Four rapid cannon booms) Come to think of it, I do see some enemy fire, way up river.  It's from one of the hostile banks.  I'm not sure though.  It might not be.  It looks like machine gun fire.  It's only a flicker, from here.  Dong Tam just put up some more flares. (Four rapid cannon booms) That's a 40MM cannon, firing on automatic (Four rapid cannon booms).  I'm not sure if this is practice, or if it is enemy fire, but it looks like machine gun, up river, though.  Come to think of it, there's supposed to be some more army coming in at around 2030 (8:30 p.m.).  They may be firing on the boats bringing them here.  The monitor may be helping them out.  That has to be a forty.  It has stopped, temporarily.  I don't know what the story is.  I still see the flashes, up river.  I wish I had binoculars, or a Starlight scope, it would be a big help.*

*Dong Tam has four bright flares in a row up, right now.  They're lighting up the area.  They stay in the air for an awfully long time.   Over to the right of them I see the silhouette of the Askari and to the left of it, I can see the outline of the Monitor.  Far over to the right, is where the machine gun fire is coming from.  The moon isn't out, but the stars are very bright.  I can see My Tho, way down river.  We're anchored right outside Dong Tam, right now.  Everything is quiet.*

BREAK

*I'm back again.  It was machine gun fire.  The Monitor was doing recon by fire.  They'll fire into a bank to see if that's where the enemy is.  If there is, they'll fire back.  It's a game of cat and mouse.  I'm going to go inside, right now.  The army should have been back, by now.*

I took a break long enough to call my buddy from E.T. School, *"Corky,"* on the repair ship, the USS Askari, over the radio.

*"Therapy," this is "Green Dragon One."   Therapy, this is Green Dragon One, over!  Therapy, is Corky there! This is Terry.  I'll be over pretty soon.  We just finished eating chow!"*

"Corky" replied: *"Can you make it over to (Garbled)."*

I replied; *"Say again!"*

Corky answered, *"Can you make it over to Delta Tango?"*

I replied, *"Yeah, I could make it over to Delta Tango!*

Corky answered; *I'll meet you at the Windjammer!  The club!*

*O.K.! I'll meet you at the Windjammer! Over and out!*

(BREAK)

*Hello!*

*It's night. I just got back from Dong Tam. You heard me talking to Corky, on the Askari. I met him, at the Windjammer. "Therapy" is the call sign for the Electronics Technician Shop of the Askari. They have their own frequency, at 76 megacycles. I made up the code name of "Green Dragon One." They have a lot of code names, here. "Delta Tango" is the phonetic alphabet initials for Dong Tam.*

*While I was over there, I was bargaining. They were handing out boots, the other day. I got some "jungle boots" I was going to send home, but I didn't know how to send them. They are a size 11. I didn't know anybody that wore that size. There was a guy from the Askari E.T. shop that wore a size 10 ½, but they only have them in full sizes. He's going to get me a case of batteries that fits my tape recorder, for the boots. If you are in the riverine force, you can get boots anytime you want them. They guys on the ships can't get them.*

*We had a good time in Dong Tam, playing shuffleboard.*

*Right now, I'm sitting on the pontoon next to the APL and there's a generator going. Flares are going over Dong Tam. I can see the Askari. It's not too far from us.*

*I just got the word that we're going to get our boats on the 26th of April. We'll be in Vung Tau for four days. It is one of the R&T center for Vietnam. After we pick up our boats at Vung Tau, we'll take them to Cat Lo, a few miles away, then bring them up river, to Dong Tam.*

*I requested R&R for August 2nd or 4th, which would get me out of Vietnam for my birthday. I put down Australia, Bangkok and Tokyo, for my choices. I would have put down Hong Kong, but I might as well go someplace I haven't seen.*

*I got your tape, the other day. I keep playing it, over and over. I enjoyed it. I play it when I'm on BID patrol, when I'm driving at night.*

*The army had operations, today. I think they came out pretty good. I counted the boats. There were about fifteen of them. The monitors are getting meaner and meaner, as far as armament goes. They used to have just 40MM cannons. Now they are putting dual Zippos, flame throwers on them. They can put out a stream at 250 feet, for four minutes, or one at 250 feet for eight minutes. They may be horrible, and they may be inhumane, but they are necessary in saving our lives from a tenacious enemy that is dug into concealed bunkers.*

*There is a lot of tree line landscape around Dong Tam, but it is safe. It is a huge base. I was on BID patrol, near My Tho, the other day. Not much tree line. Lots of water buffalo, straw, or grass huts. Just like you would expect Vietnam to look. Sampans go up and down here, all day long. Kids pick up our C-Rations we don't like and toss in the river. One time we traded one case of C-Rations for four watermelons.*

*Something funny happened in the chow hall of the barracks ship, "The Apple," last night. When they have movies, the first row is open for anybody, but you can't see very well. You're looking straight up. The second row is reserved for the people that run the ship. The third row is reserved for the mess cooks and cooks. The fourth row is also reserved for the ship's company. The fifth and sixth rows, along with the tables on the sides, are open for the Army and the riverine sailors, but you can't see anything from those seats. It only goes back six rows.*

*Rudy Mahanes, and I decided we were going to sit in the seats where the cooks and mess cooks sit. We weren't gonna move unless somebody told us they were going to put us on report, unless we moved. So, we were sitting there, and this guy came up and told us we were going to have to move. Before I could say anything, Rudy* jumped up screaming and yelling, and saying "things are going to have to change!" I thought he was gonna deck the guy!

It was really funny! I almost started laughing! Rudy told the guy he didn't have the nerve to throw him out, himself, and that he would have to get the Master at Arms. If Rudy would have played it cool and just sat down, I think the guy was so timid, he would have left us alone, but Rudy overplayed it, making such a big deal out of it, the guy went and got the Master at Arms and we had to move.

Tomorrow night, we're going to have a little protest and put up bulletins, or posters in the passageways of "The Apple," saying that the riverine sailors and the Army are getting cheated, because the ship's company gets head of the line privileges for chow, and they get the best seats reserved for the movies. Anyway, we're going to protest! It's just something to do!

When I was on the Enterprise, the ship's company didn't have any privileges over the air wing guys, the "Airedales," but on this thing, the captain pampers his crew. It isn't fair. These poor Army guys wallow around in the rice paddies, getting shot at, but these guys have it made! They should be able to get a good seat for a movie!

Well, I'll close for now and I'll write, soon!

**Diary, April 21, 1968.**
I decided to keep a financial record. I sent Judi a money order for $60, on the 15ᵗʰ. I have to know how much I can manage to save and how long it takes to pay back debts.

We moved to Vinh Long last night for "Ops." I don't know how long we'll be here.

**Diary, April 23, 1968**
We're still at Vinh Long, in the middle of the Mekong Delta. Three sailors were seriously injured on a River Division 92 Zippo. Freddie is back from sick bay. He lost a _lot_ of weight!

I traded a pair of boots for twenty-seven batteries and sold six for $1.25. I should have done better, but the boots would have been too big for me, anyway!

I'm anxious, but a little apprehensive, about getting our boats in three days. It's a thirty-six hour trip bringing them up river from Cat Lo, which is near Vung Tau, on South Vietnam's east coast. We will be bringing them to Dong Tam. I'm almost sure Charlie will try to get us. He could tell they are new "Green Boats," and equally green crews. The new Riv Ron will mean a lot more trouble for him. If he is smart, he _will_ try to get us as we bring the boats up river.

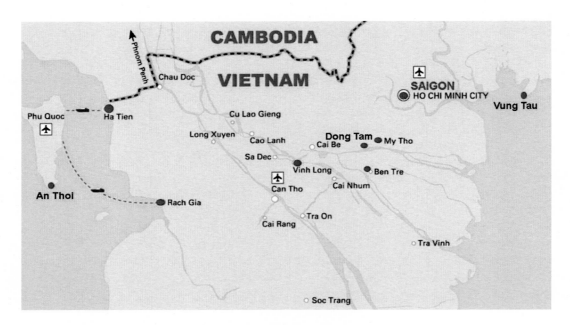

In the early morning hours of April 23rd, a sentry on the LST, USS Tom Green County spotted a swimmer with a face mask on the surface of the river, just ten to fifteen yards off the starboard quarter of the ship. The Tom Green County and the other ships of the MRB were four miles east of Vinh Long. The sentry shot at the swimmer, but didn't know if he got him. The boats on "B.I.D." patrol saturated the area with concussion grenades, which undoubtedly woke every sailor sleeping on the ship, while hopefully causing damages or fatalities to one or more of the enemy divers.

Thirty minutes later, two other sailors of the Tom Green County spotted a small light, below the surface of the water. Boats immediately searched the area and blanketed it with concussion grenades once more. A hull inspection didn't reveal anything suspicious.

**Navy historical records from April, 1968 described the V.C. attempts to mine LST's, saying;**
*"According to captured enemy documents, the Viet Cong sapper squads normally practiced at "dry runs," to probe the target's defense, prior to an actual mining attempt. It proved interesting to note that both sightings were near the MRF support LST; suggesting that she was the priority target within the MRB, presumably because of the large ammunition supply on board."* The full impact of that truth would not be realized until November.

On the morning of Tuesday, April 23rd, MRF forces annihilated forty-six Viet Cong, six miles northwest of the ships of the Mobile Riverine Base, in the Giao Duc District of Dinh Tuong Province. Four Vietnamese Marine were killed and twenty wounded, in the savage fighting. The Army's 4/47th Infantry was moved in, hoping to surround an estimated V.C. company. In the fighting that followed, the 4/47th and the Vietnamese Marines were each credited with fifteen V.C. killed. Artillery killed another eight, while gunships accounted for six.

Three sailors were injured at 1645 when their boat was blasted with a rocket hit in the coxswain's flat. Zippo 111-7 was providing fire support to the Vietnamese Marines when the invisible enemy attacked from heavy jungle cover. All three injured crewmen were medevacked. One was reported to be seriously injured.

**A "Zippo" flamethrower, hitting enemy positions.**
Photo, courtesy olivedrab.com

Also on Tuesday, the MRF was visited by General William Westmoreland, Military Assistance Commander of Vietnam. He was briefed on MRF operations by Commodore Salzer and LCOL Conlin, USMC, Acting Executive Officer, 2nd Brigade. Other attending the briefing were Major General Hay, Commander, II Field Forces, Vietnam, Major General Ewell, Commanding General, Ninth Infantry Division and Brigadier General Knowlton, Asst. Div Commander, 9th Inf. Div.

# Chapter 7

## The Power of a Gun

The crest of my unit, River Assault Division 131, gave a nod to the popular TV show, *"Have Gun – Will Travel."* It was the story of a professional gunfighter named *"Paladin."* After fighting in the Civil War, he settled into San Francisco's Hotel Carlton where he awaited responses to his business card which featured the picture of a chess knight, and the words, *"Have Gun, Will Travel ... Wire Paladin, San Francisco."* It aired from 1957, to 1963, starring Richard Boone. The River Assault Division 131 crest modified the motto to *"Have Guns Will Travel."*

**Diary, April 27, 1968**

*After spending a few days outside Dong Tam, I am on an LST heading down river to pick up our boats. It is "2200," now. In a few hours, we will be in the South China Sea. We are supposed to spend about four days working on our boats. I am pretty sure I will be in the well deck of the boat, with four .30 cal. machine guns and two 50's.*

*A letter from Judi really cheered me up, today. I sure miss her. I try not to think about how many months there are ahead without seeing her, or talking to her. It's hard not to count days or weeks.*

*It's "2245," now. I went topside, because it felt like we were out of the river. Sure enough! We are in the South China Sea! There may be a little "sailor" in me. I love the salt air and watching the shadowed waves lunge at the hull, while white caps leap to touch the deck. It's restless, tonight. I guess because of the rain today. This is the first rain since I got here! It's the calling card of the monsoons!*

Sunday, April 28th, thirteen men of the river assault boats were wounded in vicious ambushes, while withdrawing troops from the Cam Son area and beaching them, just west-northwest of the MRB. Eleven sailors were wounded in the most severe attack, at 1145. The boats were hit with a barrage of rocket, recoilless rifle and automatic weapons fire from both banks. They took at least five B-40 rockets. They returned fire with all weapons, including the *Zippo's* flamethrower. Six of the eleven wounded were aboard the monitor.

Boats of River Division 92, and Division 112, were in the first incident, at 0910. The boats in the rear of the column were hit from both banks. Tango 92-7 was struck with a B-40 rocket. There was only one other minor casualty, a crewman of Grif and Freddie's boat, A-112-1, was injured. I don't know who it was, or how he was injured. The combined firepower of a team of Seawolves and the boats finally silenced the enemy weapons.

**Tango 3 (on the right), after offloading from a cargo ship.**

I took this picture when we were picking up T-131-3 *"Tango 3."* An LCM-6 is bringing it to the dock. You can see how the ATC's were made from the LCM-6's, like the one on the left. The sides were widened, with bar armor and Styrofoam, to absorb rocket hits. The "A Frame" support framing for the green canvas top is pushed to the front of the coxswain's flat. If you look into the well deck, you can see the seats are in place for ferrying troops. The mounting brackets for the six machine guns in the well deck have protective "boots" over them. The gun turrets on top, towards the stern have covers over them, but don't yet have the Mark 19 grenade launcher, or two 20MM cannons in place.

**April 28, 1968, Letter from home.**
*Dear Terry,*

*I still haven't gotten any new stationary. I went shopping, last night, with your Judi and your sister, Judy. Since you gave her that long list of things you wanted, we thought we better get started on it. So Judi Si paid for the tennis shoes and I bought the shorts and got some boxes of candy. I will send a box in the morning and Judi will send a box in a few days. I got out your Explorer shirt and Judi cut off the sleeves and took it home to hem. She'll send it, later in her package to you.*

*I'm sure sorry we're so slow about getting tapes ready. We enjoyed yours, so much. It brings you so close to home and helps all of us feel a part of your life.*

*We finally heard word from you about the attack we were all so concerned about. Sure glad you were confined to living quarters and you didn't say how your crew member got the Purple Heart, so next time, tell us.*

*Guess you are now picking up your boat, as it must be the 30th, where you are. It's the 28th, here. I sure hope you have a safe voyage back to your base. If you went up on the 26th, you must be getting ready to head back.*

*I think I really enjoyed this tape more with you just talking to us, than all the others. Once in a while, it's nice.*

*We had a lot of fun, last night. Those two nuts, Judy and Judi were giggling so hard, trying to sing that song to record it and then, we turned on your tape and Judi and I listened quietly for an hour. I will give it to her, in a couple of days, to take home and hear again, over and over, and so her folks can hear it, too.*

*Hope you like the candy. I wanted to get you some good Mavrakos Candy, but didn't get there. I just finished wrapping your package. Hope everything is satisfactory. Be careful.*

*Love Always,*

*Mom*

**Letter from the Commander of River Assault Flotilla One, Captain R.S. Salzer.**

*Dear Family and Friends of River Assault Flotilla One.*

*In response to several requests that I have received, I will now describe how a typical operation is planned and executed.*

*We select the area for each of our many operations on the basis of the latest intelligence information regarding current locations of enemy forces, in coordination with appropriate Army commands and Vietnamese authorities.*

*Our planners then go to work to draw up the details of the operation. Some of the things that they must consider are the number of friendly troops and assault craft required to do the job, how many boats of each type will be required, what waterways can and cannot be used due to depth, width or other factors such as vegetation growing in the water, and what the tidal situation is in the target area. The tides are very severe in this part of the world and have great bearing on our operations. Frequently, we must plan our transits so that we cross shallow areas at high tide or pass beneath low bridges at low tide. Once, down south of Can Tho, we even jacked up a bridge a few feet so that the boats could pass beneath. It is imperative that all such matters be carefully planned in advance, but we must be careful to ensure that the planners do not compromise the security of an operation by too much coordination or identifiable reconnaissance.*

*The Army and Navy staffs then go over the operation in complete detail to see if we can find any weaknesses or faults in our plans. At the conclusion of this meeting, the plans are typed on stencils, duplicated, and distributed to the various Army and Navy commanders who will participate in the operation. The operational area is also cleared with local Vietnamese military authority to avoid conflicting with any ops they may have planned in the same vicinity. Perhaps 12 hours prior to the beginning of the mission, we hold what we call a "back brief" for all our commanders. They then go back to their respective units and brief their personnel on the operation.*

*Many of our operations feature dawn or predawn landings. Thus the troops often board the boats for the transit to the operational area between midnight and four o'clock in the morning. Regardless of the early hour, we always have a hot breakfast ready for both the boat crewmen and the infantrymen before they go.*

**(Comment: The night before an operation, boat crews would be preparing the boat for the operation, cleaning weapons, loading food, water, ammunition, fuel, etc. After that, they would write letters, never knowing if it would be their last, and hopefully, getting a little sleep. Most of the time, we didn't have time to go on a ship for a hot breakfast. I don't blame the commander. He probably just didn't know.)**

*Three assault boats at a time come alongside the pontoons beside each barracks ship to embark the Army troops. Although we operate at darken ship conditions in the Delta, we do use a few red lights of low candlepower, covered on the sides and focused downward on the pontoons, to provide the small amount of visibility required for the infantrymen to assemble their packs and safely climb aboard the ATCs (Armored Troop Carriers).*

*Once the ATCs are loaded, the boats form into a column and begin the trip to the op area. Leading the formation are two to four ASPB (Assault Support Patrol Boat) minesweepers followed by a Monitor and then a group of ATCs. Other Monitors and flame throwing ATCs are interspersed among the ATCs to protect the troop-laden convoy. The Squadron Commander controls the actions of his boats from aboard a CCB (Command and Communications Boat) which is usually near the middle of the column. The Army artillery barges, escorted by other Navy assault craft, will have left earlier so that they will be in place and ready to fire prior to the time the troop convoy begins moving into the dangerously narrow waterways near the operational area.*

**(Comment: At one time, ASPB's may have always led the column, but in my experience, that wasn't the case. My ATC often led the column, *"sweeping."*)**

*Enroute to the landing site many of the soldiers will be catching a few hours of sleep. The first part of the journey will be along one of the larger rivers where the boat crewmen will be able to relax somewhat, although all gun mounts will be manned and ready for action should the column be attacked.*

**(Comment: Two boat crewmen would be manning their 20MM guns, in Riv Ron's 13 and 15. One would be manning the Mark 19 grenade launcher. Two crewmen in the well deck would be manning the six machine guns and making sure the engines were operating properly. One crewman would be the coxswain,** *"driving"* **the boat. The boat captain would be standing, or sitting behind the coxswain. Nobody in the crew would be** *"relaxing."***)**

*As the boats near their objective area and turn into one of the hundreds of small streams, everyone becomes more alert. Most areas of the Delta are heavily populated, and therefore, we do not open fire unless first fired upon. In some unpopulated VC-dominated regions where we have every reason to expect enemy ambushes, we may "recon by fire," while going through such areas. By firing at suspicious spots and bunkers with cannons and grenades, we can sometimes surprise the enemy into opening fire prematurely. At the least, it tends to spoil his aim.*

*Finally, we reach the area where the landing is to be made. We may have "softened" the beach for the ground assault with jet air strikes, with helicopter gunship ordnance, artillery fire, or by fire from the boats. We always stand ready to provide supporting fire to the troops prior to, during, and after the landing. The Monitors, CCBs and ASPBs continue to cruise in mid-stream with every weapon at the ready as the ATCs are beached to debark the troops. After the Army has gone ashore, the boats will frequently take up blocking stations to prevent escape of the Viet Cong by sampan.*

*The troops will normally stay ashore for two to three days, although we may move them by boat to many different locations during that period of time. By the end of three days, every sailor and soldier is ready to return to the ships for a warm shower, hot meal and clean bed.*

*As I have said numerous times before, I have never worked with a more dedicated, resourceful and professional group of men than we have in our force. They are doing the job they came here to do.*

*I am sorry that I don't have the time to send personnel letters of appreciation to the many of you who have written to express their support of the task we are trying to achieve. In a country such as ours, no war should ever be described as a "popular" one, but I cannot understand or excuse those Americans who are lending moral support and encouragement to the Viet Cong to continue their terrorist acts against their own countrymen and their ambushes of our forces. It is good to be reminded that this noisy group is definitely in the minority.*

*Sincerely,*

*R.S. Salzer*
*Captain, U.S. Navy*
*Commander, River Assault Flotilla One*

**The** *"U.S. Naval Forces Vietnam Monthly Historical Supplement"* **summed up action for the month.**
*"During the month of April, the Mobile Riverine Force (MRF) operated primarily in Dinh Tuong and Kien Hoa provinces. Total losses inflicted on the enemy by the assault forces of the MRB amounted to 285 Viet Cong killed, 11 prisoners captured and 1,665 structures destroyed. MRF casualties during the same time period were 41 killed (3 USN, 34 USA, 4 Vietnamese Marine Corps) and 264 wounded (66 U.S. Navy, 170 U.S. Army, 28 Vietnamese Marine Corps). After a MRF planning session with IV Corps personnel at Can Tho, on 16 April, the 2nd Battalion Vietnamese Marine Corps became firmly committed to operations in cooperation and coordination with the MRF. The battalion moved to bivouac sites near Dong Tam on the following day and immediately commenced familiarization training with River Assault Division (RAD) 112. During April, PBR's,*

*SEAL's, and Navy armed helicopters of Task Force 116 participated in or supported several Task Force 117 (MRF) riverine operations."*

Around dawn, on Wednesday, May 1st, the Viet Cong fired twenty-five rockets at the ships of the MRB. The Colleton, APL-26 "The Apple," "Tom Green County," and the "Askari" all reported near misses. There were no casualties. The attack was launched minutes after Dong Tam was hit by five 180MM mortar and seventy-five recoilless rifle rounds, wounding six. The ships returned fire. A helo strafed the enemy positions.

**The Commander, Naval Forces, Vietnam received the following message from Vice Admiral Charles K. Duncan, USN, Chief of Naval Personnel, who visited the Mobile Riverine Force on April 18th,**
*"In my necessary brief trip to naval units in Vietnam, I was greatly impressed with the competence, quality, enthusiasm and spirit of our Navy men there. Please express for me to the commands my confidence in their ability to do the Navy's part in winning and bringing peace – and of my continuing personal concern for each individual."*

The monsoons were in full swing, by May 1st, adding to our daily misery. On combat missions during the day, we'd be in our gun mounts, wearing heavy, stinking flak jackets, soaked to the skin, with rain blowing into the well deck, coxswain's flat and dripping into the gun mounts. During the night, it brought a wet chill.

Early in the morning of May 1st, the MRB came under attack from the south bank of the My Tho River, with around twenty-five rounds of recoilless rifle rounds fired at the USS Askari (ARL-30), the USS Tom Green County (LST 1159) and APL-26, the Barracks ship. The base at Dong Tam was hit at the same time.

Later that day, a five-man *"Bushmaster"* ambush team of the 3/47th Infantry was conducting operations, about four miles from My Tho. At 0145, they were approaching to board ASPB's to return to the MRB. Suddenly, they were attacked by Viet Cong. As the soldiers hurried to get to the boats, wading diagonally from the bank, with their weapons, gear and ammo, the river bank suddenly dropped off and they disappeared into deep water. The body of one of the soldiers was found that morning, at 1028. The bodies of the remaining four brave men were recovered by PBR's, on May 3rd. Once again, the Mekong claimed the lives of our men. At times, it seemed the Mekong was more deadly than the River Styx, the river of Greek mythology, a deity that formed the boundary between Earth and the Underworld.

On Friday, May 3rd, Lt. J. R. Nelson, Commander of River Division 112, took multiple fragment wounds to his face when Monitor 111-2 was attacked while supporting a Vietnamese Marine operation. Lt. Nelson was the only casualty of the attack. The officers of the Mobile Riverine Force were among the best I served with, in the Navy. They didn't *"lead from behind."* They were with us, all the way.

The MRF was visited that same day, by Admiral John J. Hyland, Commander In Chief, U.S. Pacific Fleet. The four-star admiral also presented awards to five flotilla personnel. BM1 Vernon M. Ware of River Assault Division 111, was awarded the Silver Star; BM1 Thomas A. Patterson, River Division 111, was awarded the Bronze Star and the Navy and Marine Corps Medal. Lt. Thomas W. Ziegler, the Flotilla Medical Officer, was presented the Bronze Star. BO2 George L. Gadsen, River Division 111, was awarded the Navy Commendation Medal; and BM3 David L. Michaletz, Riv Div 111, also the Navy Commendation Medal.

On Saturday, May 4th, at 1700, a crewmember of Monitor 112-2, BM3 Charles L. Perry, of Columbus, Ohio, fell overboard from the pontoon alongside the Tom Green County, and went under the nest of boats. An intensive search of the MRB anchorage area was launched immediately, without success. His body was found on Monday, by A-112-8, near the barracks ship, APL-26.

During the evening of Monday, May 6th and the morning of May 7th, Dong Tam was battered mercilessly with sixty-three mortar rounds during the night. The attack killed two men and wounded four. The MRB, anchored outside of Dong Tam, went on alert when one of the rounds exploded fifteen yards off the port quarter of the USS Benewah. Over the course of the year, it became impossible to count all of the mortar attacks we experienced. They were simply a part of the daily grind. The Viet Cong hoped their mortar attacks would prove lethal, but were satisfied if they simply harassed us and kept us from sleeping.

Twenty-four soldiers of Alpha Company, 4/47th Infantry, were injured in Cai Be, Monday night, while linking up with the 3/34th artillery, south of the city. Ten were wounded when a grenade was hurled into a cluster of the infantrymen. The other fourteen were injured in the explosion of a command-detonated mine.

Fourteen sailors of River Division 91 were wounded in two ambushes, on the Ba Lai River, eight miles southeast of My Tho, Wednesday, May 8th. It was the same location where three were killed and thirty-eight were wounded in a firefight, just four days earlier. The boats were beaching troops of Charley Company, of the 4/47th Infantry. Six of the wounded were medevacked by Army helo. Two monitors and two ASPB's were hit with RPG 7 rockets, recoilless rifle and automatic weapons fire.

The MRB moved from the Vinh Long anchorage at 0615, to My Tho, arriving after 1100. The ships of the Mobile Riverine Base moved anchor constantly, in order to make our location unpredictable and to lessen the opportunities for the Viet Cong to launch attacks on the MRB.

On Thursday, May 9th, the Vietnamese Marines were suddenly called away, to return to the Saigon area, to counter a Viet Cong threat.

Two 9th Infantry battalions clashed with Viet Cong, south of My Tho. Five V.C. were exterminated with extreme prejudice. Enemy snipers killed one U.S. infantryman, and wounded six others. One man was killed by his own grenade. Accidents with grenades, rifles, handguns, and all other weapons occurred all too often.

Three companies of the 4/47th Infantry fought all day Friday, May 10th, from the south bank of the Song My Tho, opposite Thoi Son Island. The fighting started at 0842 as Bravo Company, of the 4/47th was sweeping west from night positions north of the Ba Lai River. Enemy fire was so intense, a dust-off (medical evacuation) helicopter was driven off by automatic weapons fire. The heaviest fighting occurred after 1700, as the 2nd Platoon, of Charley Company, 4/47th was pinned down by intense fire. All three companies were pinned down at least once in heavy crossfire as contact continued after darkness fell. As of 2045 Friday, five Viet Cong were greased, in the fighting. One U.S. infantryman was killed and sixteen others wounded.

The ships of the MRB departed the My Tho anchorage at 1825, to anchor at Dong Tam at 2040.

The death of Boatswain's Mate 2nd Class Ken Carroll, on May 10th, 1968, exemplified the confusion, muddying rumors and lack of hard facts that plagued the soldiers and sailors who fought in the Mobile Riverine Force, as well as the veterans and families that still struggle to find truth, today. We didn't have instant communications with smart phones, laptops, e-mail, or texting. It took days, or weeks to get information.

BM2 Ken Carroll was the boat captain I trained under, at Mare Island, in River Warfare School. He cussed me out when he saw me sitting on the bow of an ASPB, with each leg straddling the sides of the V shaped bow. He called me a *"stupid son of a bitch,"* and told me that as soon as we got to Nam, my dumb ass would fall over the side and drown. I only say that because the irony still haunts me.

For years, I thought Carroll was on the LST with my group, as we headed to Vung Tao, to pick up our new boats. It was my understanding that at some point during the night, he went out on deck for a smoke, and walked through an open railing, into the Mekong River, or into the South China Sea. It was only during research for this book that I learned that he was assigned to A-111-4, and died at the MRB, outside Dong Tam.

From there, the details are as murky as the Mekong, and seem to be conflicting. The official *"Operations Report"* of Friday, May 17th, reported his death as follows;

*"An extensive search for a man who fell overboard from the Tom Green County at 2200, Thursday, produced negative results. The missing man is believed to be BM2 Kenneth A. Carroll of ASPB 111-4, who was the only infantryman or Navy man who could not be located in a muster, after the incident."*

**The *"U.S. Naval Forces Vietnam Monthly Historical Supplement"* states;**
*"On 16 May, at 2200, Boatswain's Mate Second Class Kenneth A. Carroll, USN, attached to RAS 11, fell into the water between pontoons alongside TOM GREEN COUNTY. An extensive search of the area failed to locate him, and the Navyman was declared officially missing. The body was found two days later floating in the river near the Dong Tam base."*

The Operations Report seems to say that nobody saw him fall in and that they didn't know he had disappeared until the next morning. The historical record indicates that someone saw him fall between pontoons alongside the LST, at 2200. Carroll's death is recorded as having occurred on May 10th, but the Operations Report and the historical record, state it as May 16th, at 2200, or 10:00 p.m. I recorded his death in my diary, the evening of May 16th. The "Virtual Wall" lists his death as occurring on May 18th, the day his body was recovered.

BM2 Ken Carroll was only 25. He was from Ohley, West Virginia. He was a good man. He was right in chastising me for sitting on the bow of the ASPB. He was doing his job and being a leader who cared about the young men under him. He was a good sailor. His family should be very proud of him. I grieve for his passing.

**Letter to Mrs. Simon (Judi's mom), Friday, May 10, 1968.**
*Hi Mrs. Simon!*

*I hope you don't mind this clunky paper, but under the circumstances, it's good that I have <u>any</u>! I am sending this as a "Mothers Day" card. I couldn't find an appropriate card. How many cards do you see for "My girlfriend's Mother"? There's not too many!*

*I hope you are over your little operation. I had my first "operation" about three days ago. It's a different kind, though. I didn't have to fire a shot, but I don't know which I'd rather go through. Sometimes these operations can be interesting, though. Once we beached at a "fire support base," which is made up of barges with Army artillery. I was talking to a "friendly" Vietnamese. We had been eating mango fruit, which has the appearance and texture of a pear, but tastes like a lemon. We also had banana trees around us. I knew there were coconut trees around, so I asked him where they were. He pointed into the jungle, along the river bank and said "over there." He gestured and said in broken English that VC had booby traps around, but he would go ahead of me to watch for them. It was fun talking to him. About six of us went with him, just a few yards out of the area. We got our coconuts. They were green, though!*

*I enjoy talking to these people. They are underestimated. They are very intelligent! When we were at Cat Lo, getting our boats, I gave two Vietnamese sailors a tour of our boat. They were full of questions, although only one spoke English, and he called me "Sir!" Anyway, I answered their questions, except where we were going. It could have been bad if "Charlie" got the word four small boats were traveling from the coast to the heart of the Mekong Delta.*

*Well, this will probably get to you a day or two after Mother's Day, but I hope you have a very happy Mother's Day! Unfortunately, I don't get paid for five more days, so I can't send you anything but my best wishes. I hope you're over your operation, now!*

*Terry*

**Letter to Mom, around Mother's Day**

*Just wanted to wish you Happy Mother's Day! I can't send a card, because I can't find any, so I'll just write you! The mic on my tape recorder is messed up, so I can't send a tape. I'll have it fixed in a few days, though.*

*I'm still recuperating from picking up our boats. We put in a lot of hours. We're awfully busy. Tomorrow we load twenty-six cases of 20MM cannon ammo. We'll have to belt it and stow it, to have it ready for our guns. While we were at Cat Lo, I was thinking about how much I've seen of Vietnam, already. I've seen Saigon, Dong Tam, My Tho, Vinh Long, Vung Tau, Ben Tre, Cat Lo, and a lot of other places I don't know how to spell. I've seen a lot between these places. The only thing about being over here that is enjoyable is talking to the people. I come in contact with them more than I thought I would. They may be poor and uneducated, but I'm finding out more and more how really smart they are. In a short letter to Mrs. Simon, I told her of a couple of instances I've had of talking to them. Two days ago on operations, we were sitting on the boat waiting to pick up troops. We were on the beach (the front of the boat was on the beach, not us) and a couple sampans were buzzing around us picking up C-rations we didn't like, such as bread, crackers, ham & lima beans, chopped ham & eggs, etc. It was fun to throw things to them. We spotted two coconuts in a boat that had three kids about Mike's age in it. We wanted them! We motioned to them to come alongside and we would trade two whole boxes (two complete meals of C-rations) for the two coconuts. They hesitated and we started laughing and joking with each other about how stupid they were and what suckers they were for taking C rations that nobody would have eaten, anyway. Well, they came alongside and wanted the C-rats before they gave us the coconuts, so we did and then we discovered the holes in the coconuts where the milk had been drained out! They were old and all dried up and felt like just shells. They had quite a laugh over it. We sure felt stupid, though! We got even, though. I called them back and gave them an empty can of milk and an empty box of C-rations. They laughed just as hard over that. They have a sense of humor, too.*

*Well, besides all the work I'm doing and going on operations, I'm currently working on my first assignment for Electronics Technician, Petty Officer 3rd Class. My boat captain is putting in a recommendation that I can take the test in August and Corky is working on signing off my practical factors. My course is easier than school, naturally, but it doesn't explain things enough. After I get pretty far in this course, I'm ordering an electronics course from the Cleveland Institute of Electronics and letting the GI bill pay for it.*

*I think our boat captain likes me, because I have been reading manuals on the radios we have on board. I want to understand them to the point I can make emergency repairs on them. He had me uncrate them, help install them and put me in charge of stowing all extra radio gear. We have two fixed radios, two local, two remote control radios (intercom) and one pack radio.*
*I have to close now. I'll write soon!*

*Love,*

*Terry*

Map, courtesy of weather-forecast.com

Five V.C. ate it, Saturday, May 11th, as two companies of the 3/47th Infantry and three companies of the 4/47th Infantry swept west through Kien Hoa Province. Over the course of the four-day operation twenty Viet Cong were eliminated. Thirty-three possible V.C. were detained and six weapons captured. Three soldiers were killed in action and forty-one were wounded in the fighting.

**Formal negotiations began in the Paris Peace Talks, on May 11th, 1968.**

**Letter from my sixty-seven year old, grandfather, Esco Foster. He was my mother's father. Sunday, May 12, 1968. He was still working as an insurance salesman.**
*Dear Terry,*

*Sorry I've waited so long to answer your letter, but you've no idea how hard we have worked this spring and we can sure tell we're getting old, too, because after a hard day's work, we are too tired to move. We worked all day, today, Mother's Day. One of the projects today was building a chicken house for baby chicks. We have 50 White Rock baby chicks being shipped, Thursday. Grandma baked a raisin pie, peach pie, and strawberry short cake. We wish you could have been here. I didn't work on the job in April. There was so much to do, with gardening, cutting grass, chopping up dead trees, setting out new fruit trees, 50 strawberry plants and rose bushes.*

*We have watermelons, cantaloupes, beans, peas, potatoes, cucumbers, radishes, parsnips, lettuce, onions, peppers and tomatoes. We still have to plant sweet potatoes and I haven't even done any spraying, yet, so please don't think that I didn't write because I didn't want to hear from you. I've read your letter over several times. I just had to pick a time to write when I was so damn tired, I couldn't sleep and you know how hard it is for me to stay awake. Usually, as soon as I sit down, I fall asleep.*

*I hope you are as safe, now, as you were in your letter. It may be monotonous, but it's still better than facing enemy guns. If my count is right, this is your 682nd day in the Navy. Hope it is passing real fast for you, although it probably isn't. How is the chow? Have you got your own boat yet? Sure hope you make Petty Officer. You may not be able to read this, as I have to retrace half of it. You know, how a pen won't write because of the oil from your fingers. I've wasted enough effort to write ten pages.*

*We've had a very dry spring, about five inches short of normal, but we had a good, slow, steady rain all day and night, Friday and Friday night and most of Saturday. It was just what we badly needed.*

*Coy Wheeler, one of your cousins, was here in St. Luke's Hospital and we visited with him a couple of hours. They went back home the same day. He received good news, here at St. Luke's, as they told him he did not have Leukemia. He was in the hospital at Paducah and had three cysts cut off his kidney. When he went home, he sent us a paper he carried a story about Wallace School, a school class picture of your Grandma, a sister and two brothers. Needless to say, Grandma was the prettiest girl in the picture. He also sent a story about the location of the school and saying that this area should certainly be made a state park. This may be the reason the forestry service is trying to buy our farm. Well, I guess I should close now, as it is 1:30 a.m. and will try to get about five hours sleep.*

*So answer when you have time and I'll assure you I won't wait so long this time. I still have trees to spray and the house to paint, but I'll still promise to do better this time.*

*Love,*

*Grandma and Grandpa*

Monday night, May 13th, a soldier fell from an ASPB alongside the Colleton, at 2230. He was swept away in dark of night. An intensive search followed, without success. The Mekong claimed another victim.

The next morning, a Platoon leader of Bravo Company, 3/47th Infantry was killed by a sniper, near the hamlet of Vinh Kim, northeast of Dong Tam. Two V.C. were killed in the firefight that followed.

One of the men I trained with, on A-112-2 was wounded the same morning when a 20MM shell *"cooked off"* in his gun mount. In time, it would seem that A-112-2 and A-112-1 were cursed.

Boats of Riv Div 91 entered the Rach Mo Cay, just south of the MRB anchorage, to support a bridge removal project. When the work was done and the boats began to leave, they were ambushed. The *Zippo* covered the V.C. bunkers with its flamethrower. As the Viet Cong rushed from their burning bunkers, the boats and a helicopter team opened up, killing them.

One of the oddities of the Vietnam War was the focus on measuring success, by *"body count."* As someone who has spent decades trying to decipher the intricate puzzles of my experience, I found the answer to one puzzle while playing a round of golf a few years ago, with my son, Chris, and two men who served as Captains in the 9th Infantry Division. As we enjoyed the round of golf at a Mobile Riverine Force Association Reunion, I inquired about how casualty figures were attributed, following a combat action in which the boats were ambushed while carrying troops. Usually, the boats would fight their way through the ambush and then insert troops, after the shooting subsided. Specifically, I asked if they could tell what kind of weapon killed a Viet Cong. I was trying to be subtle, but he caught where I was going with the inquiry. He laughed a hearty laugh.

### *"You want to know about the body count! Yeah, we could tell if you guys killed them!"*

It wasn't that I was looking for credit in killing the enemy. It just didn't make sense that when we were carrying soldiers of the 9th Infantry Division and we were ambushed, twenty or thirty boats would open up with dozens, even two or three hundred, machine guns, grenade launchers, flamethrowers and 105 Howitzers, and the *"After Action Reports"* would say that the boats didn't account for any of the subsequent enemy KIA!

The former Army captain explained that they could tell when a V.C. had been hit with a .30 caliber, or .50 caliber machine gun, or a 20MM cannon, or any of the other weapons of the boats, but the Army claimed them. I was just relieved that I could finally make sense of it.

Forty-seven Viet Cong were killed Wednesday, May 15th in a heated, daylong battle a couple miles southwest Mo Cay. The fighting erupted at 1035, shortly after the 3/47th Infantry was airlifted into the area. When the 3/47th started taking small arms and automatic weapons fire, the 4/47th Infantry was airlifted to a landing zone just west of the enemy. The two battalions closed in on the company-sized V.C. force, calling in thirteen air strikes and steady artillery fire. As morning dragged on to an oppressively hot and humid afternoon, the 2nd Brigade began sweeping across the battlefield, counting the abundant bodies and picking up enemy weapons. Army losses, as of 1930, in the evening, were six killed in action and thirteen wounded. Another nine were listed as casualties of heat exhaustion. Infantry accounted for forty-three of the V.C. KIA, while Air Force planes were credited with three VC killed and fifty-five bunkers destroyed.

### Letter from Mom, Wednesday, May 15, 1968
*Dearest Terry,*

*I've been so nervous and worried about you that I actually forgot to write. Then, it began to occur to me the last couple of days that just because we haven't been hearing from you, it doesn't mean I shouldn't write. I haven't heard from you for two and a half, or three weeks, and Judi for almost two. Even Judi is getting nervous and upset and she usually stays pretty calm.*

*Judi's stomach was all upset last night, and I was telling her that for last two nights, I'd get sick to my stomach and I could just feel it tie up in knots. She said, "You think you've got it bad!" I knew she meant it was getting to her, too. Then, I tried to cheer her up. Her mother told me today that when her Dad brought her home last night, he just made a face behind her, to not say anything and she went to her room, never said a word during supper and later, came out and said she was sick to her stomach. Said she's so worried about Terry and you just can't talk to her. It doesn't do any good. She calls home every day to see if she has a letter and said today, she sounded pretty depressed.*

*Well Terry, where are you? How are you? What are you doing? We think it's probably because you went after your boat and bringing it back, but our question is, "Could it take this long?" I felt all my tensions pile up this morning and when we got no mail, it just pushed me over the brink and I cried and cried. People say, "No news is good news," but then you wonder. Today, I even thought maybe you've been captured and they're just waiting, to be sure before they tell us.*

*Well, I hope you are O.K. and nothing is wrong, because I just don't think I could stand it, if you weren't.*

*Yesterday was a big day for the Sater clan (as you know already, if you received the cable I sent yesterday). Yes, a new baby girl. Mary and Tom say she's a doll. Light brown hair, chubby cheeks and reportedly looks like a Sater. Tom was with Mary the whole time, went into the delivery room with her and helped her. She said today—they were quite a team. Name, oh yes! I think it is Marlene Marie Sater. Pat and Joan are going to be Godparents. They are quite thrilled. Tom said you and your wife will be the next one, but this time they plan to wait about three years, before they have any more. I hope they do.*

*Judi's awfully excited about Fran's baby. Her mother said today; "That's going to be the most spoiled baby." She said every time they go shopping, Judi goes to look at baby things and buys something, all the time. She said she told Judi, "You are going to be seen so much in there, people will begin to wonder." I laughed and laughed. She said this baby should be a happy one, all right, because Judi keeps Fran in stitches all the time, with her carrying on.*

*We are, at present, under severe tornado warnings. Have been all evening. There was one at Rolla about one hour ago and then at Dittmer and is supposed to be heading east to northeast. Tom came by, and then went on home, after his visit to Mary. It's 9:30pm, now. It is raining pitchforks, and lightning a lot.*

*Last Friday was the Senior Mother's Breakfast and I thought of you a lot. Mrs. Kockner and I were talking how it seemed like yesterday since we were there for Terry and Jerry.*

*Tomorrow I hope to get to see the baby, but it is also the concert which Sharon is playing in. At 7:30, we were supposed to go to Holman Junior High, for Mike, so don't know how we'll do it all.*

*May 16th Next Day*

*Well, darling, I'm happy today. Mrs. Simon just called and Judi got two letters, and I imagine Judi will come home for lunch to read them, so now, I know you must be O.K. You can't imagine how relieved I was. Mrs. Simon said; "Well, do you want to hear some good news? Judi got two letters." So now, I will feel like working today. I could tear into things, today. I'm so relieved.*

*I have been waiting to send a tape (a music tape) till we got your new address. I'm assuming that you will have a new address.*

*Tom said last night that it is definitely going to be Marlene Marie and I'm so relieved. He had talked about "Justine," or "Charlene" and I didn't like either one. Guess I will close and get this on the way.*

*Luv ya, luv ya, luv ya.*

*Mom*

The 9th Infantry Division completed a two day operation on Thursday, May 16th, as they swept through and area southwest of Mo Cay and were loaded aboard *Tango* boats. Forty-eight Viet Cong were destroyed and ten weapons were captured. U.S. casualties were six killed in action and twenty-eight injured, including eleven from non-hostile causes.  All units were back to the MRB, by 1130.  The ships got underway thirty minutes later for the three hour transit back to Dong Tam.

**Diary, May 16, 1968**
*Well, little book, I've been pretty busy since April 27th.  We picked up the boats.  They came in on a merchant marine ship at Vung Tau.  One night, we went skinny dipping in the harbor, which was probably a stupid idea.  Harbor Security boats cruised the harbor, looking for V.C. saboteurs.  We could have been mistaken for V.C. and shot at with automatic weapons, killed with grenades, or attacked by sharks.  After we picked up the boats and got them operational, we took them a few miles away, to Cat Lo, through dangerous V.C. territory.  We worked on them for eight days.  We mounted the guns, radios and other equipment, and loaded ammo, water and C-Rations.  We put sand bags around the Coxswain's flat, loaded our personal gear and made them as "homey" as we could.  We beached them and painted our boat numbers on them.  Our boat is T-131-3.  After that, we went to Dong Tam, to join the MRB.  That trip took two days, staying overnight at a PBR base at Ben Tre.  I am the port 20MM gunner.*

*Since the beginning of the month, a few things have happened.  Brooks, Vosguard, Duenaze and Martel have gotten Purple Hearts.  Darvil and Christy have had their 20's blow up on them.  So has Chamberlan's.*

*May 15th I had my first fire fight.  I had been under mortar attacks, many times, but this was the first time I got to shoot back.  We were escorting ten civilian boats and Vietnamese River Assault Group boats, along with an Army LCM-8, carrying artillery ammunition.  We were on the Rach Mo Cay.  The attack happened at the same spot the boats of River Division 91 were hit twice, on Tuesday.  Three sailors were wounded.  This time, Frank Renn, on T-131-2 was wounded.  His was the first casualty of our squadron.*

The above entry into my diary strikes me as odd, forty-eight years later.  I wonder why I said so little about my first firefight, the day after it happened.  Looking back, I can only guess that I was so affected by the experience, I couldn't even talk to MYSELF about it.  I can remember the firefight today, because during River Warfare School, I went to the Chaplain, worried I would not be able to pull the trigger and shoot another human being.  I was on the "port" 20MM cannon.  We had a long column of boats.  Ten, or more.  Automatic weapons and rockets broke the muffled rumble of diesel engines.  Instinct, training, fear, adrenaline and anger took over.  The 20MM had an electric on/off switch, on its pedestal, and a foot stirrup, used to jack the first round into the chamber.  I not only returned fire, I did it instantly, and with everything in me.  I fired steady bursts of the powerful cannon, one to four feet above the bank, blowing away trees, nippa palm, everything.  I learned quickly to vary the height of the line of fire so that it would hit someone whether they were lying down, sitting, kneeling, standing, or in a bunker.  At the same time, I rotated the fire from about twenty degrees off the bow, to seventy degrees to the stern.  The jungle disappeared in front of me.

One main point drilled into us during training, was to lay down such a fierce field of fire that the V.C. couldn't fire back.  We were also taught to fire in bursts that would conserve ammunition, but more importantly, keep the gun barrel from getting red-hot.  If the gun got too hot, the metal would expand, causing a round to jam and *"cook off,"* exploding in the chamber.  I fired at puffs of smoke, not knowing if they were made from rocket propelled grenades coming <u>out</u> of the jungle, or our own rounds <u>hitting</u> the jungle.  It was during this firefight that a herd of water buffalo happened to be drinking at the river.  They didn't fare well.  Fortunately, I don't believe I hit any of them.  They must have been on the other side of the river from my 20.

I don't know if I hit anything other than plant, or animal life.  I never saw the enemy's face.  The Viet Cong were well concealed in bunkers. It was rare for anyone on the boats to see their faces during a firefight.  Still, that day changed me, forever.  It was the day I learned that I would kill if I had to.  Most people think they know how they would react.  They don't.  You don't know, until you are actually in the crucible.  When it happens, your hearing, sight, and situational awareness peak.  Your adrenaline spikes.  You don't think.  You react.

Guys get a kick out of firing guns. It can certainly give you a "rush," but nothing compares to firing a BIG gun, like a .50 caliber machine gun, or a 20MM cannon, when your target is firing back and trying to kill you. THAT'S when you really feel the power of a gun.

The official uniform hat of the River Assault Group, was a camouflaged Green Beret. Each beret had a black ribbon loop on the back of it. The tradition was that the loop was cut after your first firefight. It was our version of the *"Red Badge of Courage."* May 15th, 1968, I cut the loop on my beret.

Forty-one Viet Cong perished, Friday, May 17th, in a heated, four-battalion battle, twelve miles southeast of Saigon. Operating with the 3/39th and 4/39th Brigade, the two MRF battalions were targeted by enemy snipers throughout the day. Some of the 3/47th Infantry were involved in the heaviest action, reporting eighteen Viet Cong took their last breaths. Six soldiers of the Second Brigade were killed and twenty-one wounded in the action. In addition to the VC body count, five prisoners of war were bagged and nine weapons seized. The operation was launched at 2100, Thursday, when artillery barges escorted by boats of River Division 112 departed Dong Tam. The two MRF battalions embarked on boats of River Division 91 and 111 left Dong Tam about three hours later, between 2330 and 2345.

The boats reported a calm and quiet transit to the Area of Operations, except for the artillery barges, which received five rounds of recoilless rifle fire, at 2335, while moving up the Cho Gao Canal. Thankfully, there were no hits and no casualties in the attack. The artillery barges reached the objective fire support base at 0430, while the infantry battalions were beached on tributaries of the Rach Vang at 0800. The boats received sporadic small arms fire during the day. The Navy received credit for one enemy kill, when a Zippo flame-thrower flushed a Viet Cong from a thick growth of nippa palm and he was taken out with small arms fire.

The five ships of the MRF departed Dong Tam at 0700, and completed the sixty-two mile trip to the new anchorage, about 1600. In shifting to the vicinity of the Cua Soi Rap and the Song Vam Co, the MRB crossed through the salt air of the South China Sea for the first time since the first week of November.

The two-day enemy body count rose to well over one-hundred, Saturday, May 18th, as the Mobile Riverine Force killed at least thirty-five Viet Cong in the final battle of a search and sweep operation in Long An Province. After reporting a relatively quiet day, the 4/47th Infantry forced a Viet Cong platoon into the open, late in the afternoon, about 1800. Air Cavalry units, River Assault Craft and ground forces combined to cut down the enemy as they fled across open rice paddies. It was a one-sided fight. The MRF did not suffer any casualties in the maelstrom. The final results of the Can Giouc operation was that 126 Viet Cong were decimated, 180 bunkers were destroyed. Five prisoners were captured, and twenty-two weapons seized. Although contact earlier in the day had been sporadic, the 4/47th infantrymen conducted a search of the scene of Friday's heavy air and artillery strikes, discovering dozens of lifeless, broken enemy bodies and weapons, baking in the tropic sun.

River Division 91 was in one of the day's hottest skirmishes at 1320, when they were caught in a crossfire from both banks of the Kinh Lo, with automatic weapons and rocket fire. The boats were landing elements of the 4/47th Infantry, and returned fire with all weapons, while the troops continued to beach.

Fourteen boat crewmen and one infantryman were wounded, including five crewmembers of M-91-1, four from Z-92-11 and three from A-91-5. In addition, A-91-2 and M-91-3 reported one casualty each. Four of those injured were seriously wounded, while most of the others were patched up in the AO and returned to duty.

The infantry returned to the ships of the MRB late in the evening, when contact broke off around 1900. The cumulative results of the two-day operation, as of 2000 Saturday, May 18th, was that 123 Viet Cong were checked into the Horizontal Hilton, five prisoners of war taken, and twenty-three weapons were seized. Army casualties in the two-day's fighting, were six killed and 28 wounded, including four from non-hostile action.

May 18th, four more boats of River Assault Squadron Thirteen completed outfitting and tests in Vung Tau and assigned to River Assault Squadron Eleven for operations, until the balance of Riv Ron Thirteen boats arrived.

**Letter from my brother, Tom's wife, Mary Rose, Sunday, May 19, 1968**
*Dear Terry,*

*I suppose you have heard by now that you have a beautiful niece. Marlene Marie is just precious. Contractions started about 12:00am, Tuesday morning and at 1:30 am, I woke Tom up and told him to shave. We arrived at the hospital and Tom was with me in the Labor Room, helping me to relax. At 5:00 am we called Joan Hutchins because she works the Delivery Room and wanted us to call her even if she wasn't working at the hospital at that time, so we called her and she helped the doctor. About 6:20am they told Tom to scrub and put a gown and mask and shoes and hat on so that he could watch the birth in the Delivery Room. Every minute was so exciting for Tom and me. Tom didn't want to miss a thing and he didn't. At 6:33am they told me to push and Tom held my head up while I pushed and at 6:35am, Marlene's head came out. When we saw she was a girl, everyone was screaming and laughing and making all kinds of noises, because everyone knew how much we wanted a girl. Tom is so proud. After two days, they bring the baby into the room from 9:00am to 9:00pm and I fed and changed the baby whenever needed.*

*When Tom comes to visit, he has to scrub and put a gown on and then he could hold his daughter. At other hospitals they make you look at you baby through a nursery window and sometimes you can't see them very good from 10 feet back. The grandparents can come to the door of the room and we can take the baby to the door, but no closer. But still, this is better than looking through a window. Yesterday evening, Marlene messed her diaper and Tom wanted to change her. I couldn't believe my ears or my eyes. I had to get a picture of it and I did, about three. Never before did he ever offer to change a diaper, especially a messy one. His daughter is doing strange things to him.*

*Thursday evening a nurse asked us if we would like to talk to some young couples who were taking the Natural Child Birth classes in the hospital, as Tom and I had done. We were both very happy to, so Tom and I were given special permission to leave the 5th floor and to go down and speak to the young couples about our experience. We talked to them for about an hour, answering all their questions and Tom's face just beamed. He really feels as though he was a part of this birth and he most certainly was. I was so thrilled and comforted just having him with me.*

*Today we go home and the time is going so slow. I can hardly wait for Tom to get here. I really miss Tommy and Bryan. My mother is taking care of them and everyday I call them and Tommy tells me about outside and the swing. I suppose we will have to get a swing. Tom is putting up a fence in the back yard so the boys will stay in the yard. Tommy keeps unlocking all the doors and walks through the neighborhood, visiting everyone (just like his father). I get rather panicked when I can't find him. One day I almost called the police. He can also climb over the patio wall, so Tom had no choice but to put up a fence. Tommy tries to say everything and Bryan is still on ball, bird, Da-Da and Ma-Ma. They both are so cute. We bought the boys bunk beds, but we haven't stacked them. Bryan fell out of his bed three times in one night, but he is doing much better, now.*

*The nurse just told me that Marlene now weighs 7lb 11oz. This is very good. At birth she weighed 7lb 12oz, but then they lose weight, but now she is almost back to birth weight again.*

**(Mary Rose stopped the letter here. She picked up again on May 28th)**

Sunday, May 19th, Zippo 92-2 joined two PBR's to burn out a favorite V.C. ambush site along the Song Dong Tranh in the Rung Sat Special Zone, *"The Dark Forest."* The Zippo's mission was completed by 0900, but it stayed in the area when a nearby merchant tanker was hit with a 75MM recoilless rifle round.

Two jets and a helo fire team were called in to strafe the enemy positions, and ARVN troops were beached in the area, to mop up. When PBR's forming a water blockade were assailed with rocket and automatic weapons fire, the Monitor moved in and pounded the enemy bunkers with fifty-two rounds of 40MM cannon fire and machine launched grenades, silencing the enemy action.

On May 19th, the Commanding Officer of River Division 131, Lt. Clarence T. Vaught, arrived in Vietnam and took command of ATC's 131-1, through ATC 131-8. I had been in Vietnam two months.

On Friday afternoon, May 24th, the 3/47th Infantry was sweeping the south bank of the Song My Tho, opposite Thoi Son Island, when a soldier was killed by Viet Cong, at 1630, just as the troops were getting ready to be airlifted out. Three V.C. took the dirt nap, after the firefight that followed. Twenty-eight bunkers were destroyed, along with three wooden mortar plates.

**Letter from Mom, Friday, May 24, 1968.**
*Terry Dear,*

*I started a letter to you Saturday, but decided to tear it up, start all over again and try to be more cheerful. Sorry I am so slow in getting a letter off to you. I think of you almost constantly. I have to take time to sit down and write, and then can't concentrate. Ever since I heard you were within seven miles of Saigon, I've been trying hard not to think about it, but at times, the fear becomes so overpowering that I can hardly stand it, but I promise I will keep trying <u>not</u> to worry.*

*Your letter was very interesting. Saigon has really been in the news a lot for the last two or three weeks. Surprised you haven't heard the rockets slamming into it. I will try to remember what you said, about the newspapers sensationalizing.*

*Well, did you all get your Bengal Tiger on that operation you told us about? You and your sarcasm! Boy… Before you get carried away with being sorry for the army (and well deserved, I'm sure), remember that you'll still be in two years after they go home. Sure wouldn't want you in their shoes, though.*

*How did you get your helmet back, and have you heard from Corky about your Polaroid and tape recorder?*

*I'm wondering when you will be getting R&R. I read somewhere that two people in Thailand are protesting us being there, etc…*

*I've had a fresh worry lately. Every weekend for the last three weekends, I've worried about Les and Nancy wanting to take the boys along to learn to water ski. Saturday was the first time the boys could make it and they went, but never got a chance to ski, so now, I guess they will go this next weekend. I sure wish Dad would go along, the first time. It would be easier. I told Pat when he learned humility and admitted that something could happen, then I'd know I could trust him more to be careful. He's so cock sure, because he's a good swimmer. I think all rivers are dangerous, some a little worse than others. Apparently, those where you are, are worse.*

*I just heard from my sister that my Dad is sick and x-rays showed heart trouble (an enlarged heart), and he was told not to drive, nor mow the lawn, or any exertion and has to stop smoking. Sure hated to hear that. I saw him today at the Cool Valley grocery store and I asked him "How are you feeling?" He said "Not so good." That's all. He reached around me and patted Tim. I sure am sorry things have to be this way.*

*Grandma Sater is sure going down hill, but probably has a few years left.*

*Sure glad Dad finally got a letter off to you. He was so pleased with your letter.*
*Terry, watch out for those rockets, over there. They claim any time now a big offensive is going to start, so keep your flack jacket and helmet on. Too bad you can't wear coats and pants of chain mail, or whatever they called it in those days. I think they were a good idea! And also wear your St. Christopher medal!*

*Glad to hear you're getting all the milk you want. Maybe you will get fatter. Well, back to the salt mines. I've got to go to work, stripping furniture. So, love always,*

*Mom*

# Chapter 8

## Voices Crying In the Night

On May 24<sup>th</sup>, we arrived in Dong Tam with our new boats. I called Freddie on the radio to let him know we were back, and to come over see my new boat. Freddie always made me laugh. He was dependably light hearted. His bright personality countered the darkness. After checking out my new boat and catching up, we shook hands and Freddie caught a boat back to the MRB, just outside Dong Tam harbor, to rejoin his boat.

The next morning, I linked up with some of my buddies at the Dong Tam chow hall, for breakfast. As I sat down, one of them said, *"Did you hear about Freddie?"* I asked what he was talking about. He told me Freddie fell into the river, the previous day, and was dead.

I couldn't speak. On one hand, an emotional callous had already started to build. If you've been in combat, you know what I mean. It's a defense mechanism. You joke about death and dying. You tell yourself and others that it can't hurt you. *"It don't mean nuthin."* You sneer at it. Grief doesn't have an effect on you. You're a hard ass. You're a warrior. You don't hurt.

I kept eating my breakfast. I didn't react. I had been punched in the gut and smacked upside the head. If I spoke, I would have broken, so I didn't.

I was told that he fell, going from a launch, to the pontoon, tied up to the USS Tom Green County, and drowned. It was said that Duenaze, Freddie's crewmate on A-112-1 and one of the guys in our training class, jumped in to save Freddie, but couldn't pull him up, out of the water. At the time, we were told that Freddie couldn't swim, and that he was pulling Duenaze down. We were supposed to be expert swimmers before we graduated from River Warfare School. It didn't make sense. I was angry that they passed him in River Warfare School, when apparently they should not have.

**Freddie always had that great smile. It seems like a cruel irony, or premonition that I had taken this picture of Freddie wearing a life jacket.**

They searched for Freddie's body, but to no avail. Hours after Freddie fell in the deadly river, the Tom Green County was relieved as support for the Mobile Riverine Force, by the USS Vernon County.

It may be hard for young people of today to imagine life before the digital age, before e-mail, 24/7 news and the internet, but in Vietnam, we wrote letters by hand. We didn't have cell phones. Word traveled slowly. Rumors ruled over accurate communications. There were constant rumors of where we were going, what we were going to be doing, when we were going home, who lived and who had been killed or wounded. Half the time, it wasn't true. Almost five decades later, I'm still learning details about when Freddie died.

For most of my life, I wasn't able to shake a sense of responsibility for Freddie's death. I thought that if he hadn't come into Dong Tam to see me, he wouldn't have died. Recently, I learned from historical records that Freddie had gotten back to his boat and tripped on a cleat, as he was going from the bow to the stern. Freddie died at 1919, or 7:19 p.m., not in the early, or mid-afternoon, as I had believed, most of my life. I understand now, that Freddie hit his head in the fall and that's why Duenaze couldn't pull Freddie out of the water. He was probably unconscious when he hit the water. It must have been very hard on Duenaze.

Years later, I looked up Freddie's brother, Peter and spoke to him, over the phone. I called to tell him that friends who served with Freddie still thought of him and always would. I still think of him and remember him in my prayers, constantly. I loved Peter's Boston accent. He sounded just like Freddie. I told him I had copies of tapes I had sent home, in which Freddie and I talked. He told me they didn't have anything with Freddie's voice. I sent Peter the audio tapes I had of Freddie.

The next day, the crew of Tango 131-3 was told that we were to be taken off of the boat we had unloaded at Vung Tau, equipped, painted identification numbers on, and baptized in our first firefight. We were to be split up and assigned to boats that had KIA's, people on R&R, on emergency leave, or simply needed another man to bring it up to full compliment.

When you are in a strange land like Vietnam, living primarily in primitive conditions and people are trying to kill you, stability is comforting. I was being plucked from the guys I trained with and being reassigned to a new boat crew. I didn't like it.

I called Judi, the night before, over the *"MARS"* (Military Auxiliary Radio System) radio telephone system. *"MARS"* is a civilian auxiliary consisting primarily of licensed amateur radio operators who are interested in assisting the military with communications. I only spoke to Judi for three minutes, with a number of radio operators listening to me tell her how much I loved her, and saying *"Over,"* after every intimate exchange. It had a chilling effect on our conversation. When I would say something like, *"Our boats just got into Dong Tam,"* a guy would break in and say; *"Belay that!"* We couldn't say anything about our units, our locations, or plans, or anything. Of course, the Viet Cong knew we were at Dong Tam. They ambushed us on our way there!

In his personal effects, Freddie had written that WHEN he died, not IF he died, he wanted Bill Martel, *"The Rock,"* from his hometown of Boston, to take him home. Today, I wonder if Freddie had some sort of premonition. I am struck by his comment two months earlier, on March 27th, after he, Grif, Jardine, Bohling, Smith, Ranson, and I got together for our "party." Freddie explained that he was buying everybody beers because it was his *"last fling."*

Freddie and Rock grew up together. Rock had to throw together a presentable set of *"greens"* to wear home. At an airport, two M.P.'s, stopped him because his boots didn't have the preferred *"spit and polish."* When *Rock* presented his orders, indicating he was escorting Freddie's body home, the M.P.'s apologized and shook his hand, wishing him well on his journey.

After Freddie's funeral, *"Rock"* risked punishment and stayed home with his wife for a couple extra days. It is hard to imagine coming home from Vietnam for just a couple days, then turning around and going back to the Hell that was Vietnam, but Rock did that. When he reported to the Mobile Riverine Base, officers told him they were surprised to see him so soon. They thought he would have stayed at home for at least a week.

Late one night, I was on the stern of my boat, tied up alongside the pontoon of one of the ships, outboard of most of the boats, when I heard a loud *"SPLASH,"* and frantic yelling. A crewman of the ship we were tied up to, had fallen from his ship, into the river.

*Rock* was halfway between the boat I was on, and the ship. He yelled for someone to get boats out, to rescue the man. While he did that, he grabbed a life ring off a boat and jumped into the black night, into the swirling, muddy, river of death. *Rock* didn't hesitate. He exhibited amazing courage, risking his life to save another. He faced being swallowed by the Mekong, or being swept away and captured by Viet Cong, far down river.

The guy that fell in started yelling to Rock that he was *"going down."* Rock screamed at him to kick off his jungle boots, before the weight of them pulled him under. Shockingly, the guy yelled back that he didn't want to do that, because they were brand new and that he had just bought them off a guy on the boats. The sailors on the ships normally wore Navy issue black lace up shoes, but they cherished a pair of the black leather and green fabric *"Jungle Boots,"* worn by the boat crews, chopper pilots and *"straight leg"* soldiers. Almost comically, Rock screamed at the sailor to kick off the boots and he would get him a replacement pair. The unfortunate sailor who was fighting for his life, was begging Rock for assurance that he would follow through on his promise. Rock screamed again for him, to kick off the boots, promising he would replace them. As they were negotiating, they were drifting farther from the lights of the ships and the river assault boats, into the black night. Finally, the man kicked off his prized footwear, as two ASPB's came in to pluck both he and Rock from the certain death of drowning, or falling into Viet Cong hands.

Rock came through on his promise and got the sailor a new pair of the esteemed *"Jungle Boots,"* and even throwing in a pair of *"Ho Chi Minh"* sandals that he got from someone in the 9th Infantry. The sandals were the favored footwear of the V.C. Their soles were made from old tires.

On Sunday, May 26th, thirty Viet Cong were dispatched and three captured, seven miles from Ben Tre. Boats of River Division 111 were ambushed on the Ong Huong River, at 0715. Two sailors were killed and thirteen injured from the fierce rocket and recoilless rifle fire, as boats beached the 3/47th Infantry. The lead boats bore the brunt of the attack. The Boat Captain, BM2 Ronald Durbin and Radioman Jerry L. Williams, of A-111-1, were killed instantly and two other crewmen were injured. Their boat took two rockets and two recoilless rifle hits. Two rounds took out the 20MM cannon. One hit the mast and a fourth exploded in the coxswain's flat. Four men on A-111-5 were injured in the first attack, as a rocket exploded into their 20MM gun mount. M-111-3, and T-111-6 also took rocket hits, but escaped casualties.

Boats of River Division 91 were also hit, during the day. At 0750, they encountered automatic weapons fire, just west of where the 111 boats were hit. A crewman of A-91-7 was wounded. Later that morning, the Riv Div 91 boats were hit in the same spot as where the boats of Riv Div 111 were hit. Four crewmen of T-91-3 were injured by automatic weapons, rocket and recoilless rifle fire. The boats were attacked several other times during the day, including A-111-2, Z-111-7 and T-111-1, with no additional personnel casualties.

Army forces fought *"Victor Charles,"* all day, calling in heavy air and artillery strikes to pummel the well-hidden bunkers. Sadly, three men of the 3/47th were killed, and twenty-six soldiers were wounded. All, except two WIA were from 3/47th Infantry.

Most of the boats moved out of the AO early in the evening, as the Army settled into night positions.

The MRB relocated to Ben Tre Sunday morning, departing Dong Tam at 0800 and arriving at the new anchorage about 1115.

Nine sailors of River Divisions 9 and 11 were wounded Monday, May 27th, during three ambushes along the Ben Tre River. Four crewmen of T-111-10, one aboard M-111-3, two from T-111-8 and one crewman from M-91-3 and T-91-3 were all wounded in various ambushes by Viet Cong lying in wait with automatic weapons, recoilless rifle and rocket fire. One infantryman from the 3/47th was killed and one wounded, when the troops attempted to land and attack the enemy in the face of the heavy fire. Nine Viet Cong bit the mud, bringing the total to forty-one, for the two day operation which ended, early in the evening.

The troops swept southwest from their night positions, then were ferried by the boats across the Ben Tre River and continued moving west until they were airlifted to a landing zone on the Ham Luong River. The assault boats backloaded the two battalions at this point and returned them to the MRB early in the evening.

**Diary, Monday, May 27, 1968**
*A "PBR" found Freddy's body, floating near My Tho.*

*I was on a working party this morning. This afternoon, a few of us loaded 75 mattresses and 35 racks on a truck and moved them.*

Again, looking back at this diary entry, it struck me as odd that I noted the finding of Freddie's body in such a terse, matter of fact way, moving on to loading mattresses. I just couldn't deal with it. The brusque comment belied the grief that I still feel, to this day.

Lt. Clarence T. Vaught, Commander of River Assault Division 131 had only been in country a week at this point. He called us together for an address by him. By this time, some of his men had been *"in country"* for some time. Many of us had seen combat. We showed up in various uniforms, or *lack* of real uniforms. My mother sent me my Explorer Scout shirt, which was dark green, had short sleeves and was comfortable. I also wore cut off gray Levi's and *"jungle boots."* We didn't wear underwear or socks, because we had no way to keep them clean, or dry. Our feet were frequently wet. Wet socks could cause severe problems. We didn't have regulation haircuts. Grooming and *"spit and polish"* were not priorities. Lt. Vaught stood on a box, so we could all see and hear him. He wanted to communicate to us that henceforth, we would all wear our regulation green army trousers tucked into our boots. We would wear the regulation, long sleeve green army shirts, with the sleeves rolled down, and buttoned at our wrists. The reason for this, he informed us, was so that when rocket propelled grenades started flying, we would not be *"burned by the afterburners of the rockets, as they went by."* All of us just looked at each other. If you *were* close enough for the afterburners of a rocket to burn you, your problem was much more serious than singed arm or leg hair. The person who advised him to issue this order must have done it as a joke. In any case, we never followed that order. I should add that Lt. Vaught became a great leader. I liked and admired all of the leadership of the MRF that I met, or served under.

**Wearing my Explorer Scout shirt on operations with Tango 6. C-Rations are stacked inside the bar armor behind me.**

**Undated-Letter from Mom**

*Dearest Terry,*

*I just read this article in the Sunday paper. It just made me furious and a little sick. I'm getting so fed up with some of our country's tactics. I used to be a loyal American, but believe me, I'm changing. I feel like getting a protest group together and going to Washington and fighting for this boy's freedom. This really makes me sick to my stomach at some of our fine officers.*

*I got your lovely "Mother's Day" letter! It was sure good to see your handwriting again. There is one thing, though, that I'm worried about. You promised me that you were not going to take any chances, or do anything foolish, but yet you followed that "friendly" Vietnamese? How could you really know for sure he wasn't leading you into a trap for the Viet Cong? You are very naïve and foolish if you think you could possibly know he could be trusted. Aunt Louise agreed with me. Said you were naïve and that <u>no</u> coconuts could be worth risking your life for! I do hope and pray that you will never do anything like this again. He could have easily slipped away, after he got you in there and you could have been blown to bits. You know they claim the V.C. pose often as "friendly" and lead our men into ambushes. You may be asking for trouble by going out of your way to talk to them. Not one of them is worth risking your life for. Not to me, and not to Judi, I'm sure.*

*I can see the months ahead are going to be pure torture for me, thinking constantly of you going on these operations, getting shot at, etc. Don't know how I can stand it.*

*Judi got her hair done yesterday and was talking to your sister, Judy. She said she did not want to stay home and Judy told her we were going to the hospital, to see the baby and Mary and Judi said, "Oh, great, let's go with them." Judy said, "Well, we can't go up and see them," and Judi said she didn't care, that was better than staying home, so we picked her up and she looked darling (as usual) and the two of them kept me laughing all evening long. After we left the hospital (the baby sure is pretty), we went by the Matteuzzi's. We stayed there about a half hour, then picked up Pat and his friends at St. Ann's Cinema. Then we dropped them off at a party. After that, we went to the Flaming Pit, where both girls got Bacardi's, me a Brandy Alexander and Dad, a Tom Collins. Judi got a salad, me a baked potato and a glorified hot dog. Dad and Judy got Steerburgers and French fries. We could hear the orchestra in the bar and it was neat. We enjoyed it very much and I think Judy and Judi did, too. Sure did enjoy taking Judi out. We talked about it, Dad and I, and felt like we were also doing something for you, but loving every minute of it. I kept asking Judi where she wanted to go and she finally said, "Well, how about the Mekong Delta?" Pretty cute, huh?*

*Next weekend will surely be a hectic one. Bobbie and Ed's wedding is Saturday morning. Reception that night and Sunday is the St. Bernard Show. This Wednesday is St. Jude's School picnic at Blanchett Park and Thursday is a Holy Day (Ascension Thursday) and Judy's picnic. Monday will be my last painting class, until October. We will learn to paint roses. I'm sure anxious to have more time to paint. There is so much I want to do. I got so many lovely Mother's Day cards and the one your Judi "Si" gave me, she signed, "Luv Ya." I thought that was pretty sweet. Tom and Mary gave me a Fuchsia Geranium.*

*Mary and baby are coming home today. I can't wait to hold my first granddaughter, and see her in the pretty white dress I got her. I will cook a fried chicken dinner and take it over to Mary and Tom's.*

*<u>Please, please</u> be careful and don't take any chances. Try and write.*
*Judi and Judy lit a candle in the Chapel of St. Mary's (for you), last night.*

*Are you <u>still</u> getting good meals? Are you all <u>sleeping</u> on board your own boat, or the barracks ship? Sounds like you've really been busy and working hard. In those pictures of you, the one looked like Dad.*

*My Love Always, XOXOXOXOXOXOXO*

*Mom*

**Letter from Sister-In-Law Mary Rose, May 28, 1968** (Continued from her May 24th letter)

*Have you noticed a couple of days have passed since I started this letter? I don't have any time to myself, anymore. Today is beautiful outside, so I thought I would let the boys play outside on the patio and I would try to finish this letter. Well, I just started and now I hear Marlene crying. I guess I better check her. I hope the boys won't escape while I am gone for about ten seconds.*

*I'm back and they're still here. They are so busy. They don't stop from 7:00 in the morning until 9:00 at night. Sometimes they take a nap at 1:00 in the afternoon and then I have to spank them to stay in their beds.*

*Judy "Si" stopped by to see the baby the other day and gave her the cutest yellow dress, with ruffles on the pants. I'll send a picture as soon as I get them developed. Your sister, Judy and Nancy & Lester and Judy "Si" were all here together, so we played some cards for a while and had a wonderful time.*

*Grandma Bess is in the hospital for tests. She was rushed to the hospital in an ambulance with a sever pain above the eye and while she is there, they are taking all kinds of x-rays. We haven't heard any positive results yet, but we don't expect them to be very good. She is very old and she doesn't have much longer to live. I have been expecting her to die in her sleep anytime, but she keeps holding on. Terry, when she dies I'm going to miss an awful lot. She has been so good to me and I enjoy being with her*

*Tom has been busy. He has started a fence in the back and went in with Pat Hutchins on a garden. They have planted numerous items and now it needs to be hoed and weeded. He also mentioned something about painting the bedroom. Tom is going to have a busy summer. With three babies, I'm going to be a little busy, too. Bobbie and Ed were married Saturday. Tom went to the reception for about an hour and a half, but I just couldn't make it. We were going to take the kids, but we thought it would be too dangerous to take Marlene, only ten days old, amongst 300 people, so I missed out on a good time, just like you. You're thought of often, Terry. Tommy and Bryan are still playing with the little truck you gave them for Christmas. Some of the pieces are missing, but they don't seem to care.*

*Well, take care of yourself and by the way, you sure did have the family in an uproar about following that Vietnamese in the jungle for a coconut. Myself, I think your head must be made of coconut, but maybe you had a good reason, so I can't pass judgement, but please be careful.*

*Love,*

*Tom, Mary Rose, Tommy II, Bryan and Marlene*

Five Viet Cong were neutralized, Tuesday, May 28th, by MRF elements operating west of the MRB in Kien Hoa Province. Four V.C. were taken out by helicopter gunships and the fifth was nailed at 0835 by assault boats, during a firefight on the Mo Cay River. There were no U.S. casualties due to hostile fire.

**Letter home, Wednesday, May 29, 1968**

*Hi Everybody!*

*Sorry I haven't written lately. I haven't got any excuse, except that things get pretty hectic, over here. I'm not doing anything, now. I'm just sitting in Dong Tam, which has the radio code names, "Dry Gulch," "Death Valley," "Bad Lands" and another one something like that. The monsoons are still in the early stages, here, but the dust isn't as bad as when we were here in March.*

*Well, Mom, as for me following that Vietnamese into the woods, he <u>was</u> friendly. He advised me not to go into the woods, but I said we would only go to the edge, not forty yards from a bunch of ATCs, and artillery barges. As for booby traps, I've probably got more training on booby traps than most soldiers. You'll just have to have faith in my common sense. I don't trust <u>any</u> Vietnamese. In the incident with the coconuts, there were four or five guys with me. If the gook (Vietnamese) started to run, we <u>would</u> have known something wasn't "cricket!"*

Vietnam doesn't have "front lines," or "rear lines." The whole country is part of the battlefield and I can't spend a whole year wearing a helmet and a flack jacket, 24 hours a day and living in a bunker. I won't trust a single Vietnamese with my life, but you have to figure that few people understand the Vietnamese and very few want to. I enjoy talking to them, even if it's entirely with gestures. You'd be surprised how you <u>can</u> tell friend from foe. I can tell when we're in VC territory, because either the huts will be deserted, or the people just stare at you. The enemy is everywhere. Once they caught a Vietnamese worker on the base trying to walk out with a complete map of Dong Tam, including the ammo dumps, H.Q. and the docks. They also caught one gook "pacing off" the area between the barracks, so they could mortar us.

I'm not telling you this to worry you. I'm just saying that there's no sense eating my meals in a bunker. I am <u>not</u> naïve or foolish. <u>Nobody there</u> knows what it's like here, so <u>nobody</u> can say what I should do. Newspapers don't tell you. Like I've said, I've had training, the best fighting training the Navy has to offer and I've been here over two months (most casualties occur the first month). I've been in one fire fight, locking my gun about 3 ½' off the ground, and leaning on the trigger of a 20MM cannon, more than ready to kill any V.C. that showed his face. Nothing is keeping me from coming home. There's nothing for anybody to worry about. The best you can do is to trust me and give me credit for some sense. Actually, some Vietnamese can be trusted, to a point. If we pulled out or lose the war, thousands of these people will immediately be killed by the Viet Cong. This war can't be won just by killing. It has to be won by showing we're not imperialists and that we want their friendship. If I make some friends for Uncle Sam, I'd be more proud of that than killing his enemies. I <u>don't</u> want you to worry about me! I'd feel better if you had faith in me!

Well, yesterday, I bought a new suit, or rather, ordered it. It's a Hong Kong tailor. I picked out the material from a sample—silk mohair. I think it's pretty neat. I also picked out the style from a book. The suit will cost $89, with two pair of pants. I won't describe it. I'll just send you a picture of it, in a month or so, when it's ready. I haven't paid anything on it, yet. I should be paid within the next two weeks. I better close for now. I had a pretty rough day. I was on a working party, almost all day.

Love,

Terry

**Letter from Mom, Wednesday, May 29, 1968**
Grandma said the Doctor said she could go home tomorrow. We still haven't talked to him, so don't know what the score is. Maybe we will, tonight.

It rained again, yesterday evening and all night and this morning it's chilly, damp and cloudy. Talk about the monsoons! It hardly misses a day raining, anymore. Guess you're having it there, too.

I never got much sleep, last night. I tossed and turned and flopped all over. I'd wake up thinking about you and how I've just got to do something to get you out of that place. I just can't stand the strain of always wondering if you are O.K. I grab the newspaper and start looking for news to see if they are anywhere near you and all the time I'm reading, the panic mounts 'till I'm ready to scream. Just be careful and please don't go near the Vietnamese people. Don't trust even the children. They may be booby-trapped. I want you home in one piece. Love ya, love ya, love ya!

Long time, no hear from you. Two weeks. Good thing I hear through Judi, or I'd be calling the Red Cross. Judi told me about you all being taken off your boat so abruptly. I really don't understand it, but when I told Dad, he seemed quite pleased and said at least you were safer than being out on patrol operations. I got to thinking about it and realized this is true. I've been so worried about you and constantly thinking about you, out looking for the Viet Cong (and praying you <u>never</u> see one, or encounter one in any way).

I can see, however, how you could be angry and disgusted. Looks like you are being discriminated against. Not much you can do about it, though. So, just go on studying your electronics and <u>maybe</u> you'll be lucky enough to get out of there and on a <u>ship.</u>

*Well, the long Decoration Day holiday is over. We didn't do anything spectacular. I made lasagna and invited Judi Si. She and Judy drove around some and later Judi's Mom and Dad came over and we had whiskey sours and coffee. Sure wished the tape recorder was working so we could have taped some of the conversation.*

*Grandma came home that morning, but has been sick and lays on the couch most of the time. Today, she's up and around for a change. I will sign off, and mail this. My love, always,*

*Mom*

Army helicopter gunships took out ten Viet Cong, Thursday, May 30th. That night, the Navy side of Dong Tam was hit by a vicious mortar attack. Fourteen sailors were wounded in the attack, which came from the south bank of the Song My Tho, directly across the river from the Dong Tam base. Nine of the fourteen injured were crewmembers of the YRSM-17, which took a large 120MM mortar.

The ships of the Mobile Riverine Base made a tempting target for the enemy. Forty minutes after midnight, May 31st, the Colleton took one recoilless rifle round, causing a three-inch hole in the bulkhead of the Weapon's Officer's stateroom. Miraculously, it didn't detonate. Four other enemy recoilless rifle rounds missed all of the ships. The Colleton and the River Assault craft on BID patrol returned fire.

**May, 1968 was the highest casualty month of the war. 2,415 Americans lost their lives.**

**From *"Brown Water, Black Beret"***
*"In June, 1968, the force was expanded by the addition of another River Assault Squadron; in September of the same year, a fourth squadron (15) arrived. With the additions of squadrons 13 and 15 to the original squadrons 9 and 11, the force was subdivided into two groups: divisions 91, 92, 111, 112, and 151 to Mobile Riverine Force Alfa, and divisions 131, 132, and 152 to Mobile Riverine Group Bravo. The two groups conducted separate operations in different parts of the Delta and Rung Sat. The new craft arriving in 1968 were improved versions of earlier designs. All the new ATCs were equipped with armor-plated helicopter flight decks and the weapons complement was enhanced by the addition of two 20-mm aircraft cannon and a Mark 19 long range, 40 mm grenade launcher."*

I was part of Mobile Riverine Force *"Group Bravo."* In some Mobile Riverine Force reports, the author referred to Group *"Alfa."* In others, it was spelled as Group *"Alpha."* Sometimes the boats would be temporarily moved from one group to another, making it difficult to track movement strictly by the official operations reports. That was especially true of the boats of Riv Ron 13, which were *"chopped,"* or transferred to Riv Rons 9, or 11, before Riv Ron 13 was at full strength. Many of the operations of the first Riv Ron 13 boats were obscured and eliminated from unit decorations that were led by River Assault Squadrons 9 and 11.

There were two basic types of ATCs in the Mobile Riverine Force. Both were converted from World War II, LCM 6 landing craft. One type was referred to as a *"Rag Top."* It had a pipe frame over the well deck area, with a dark green, shiny canvas cover stretched over it. The other type of ATC, or *"Tango"* boat had a helicopter deck over the well deck. It was sometimes referred to as a "flat top."

ATC's were specially outfitted for their job in Vietnam with armor plating, bar armor (to detonate rocket propelled grenades) and two feet of Styrofoam (to absorb rocket propelled grenade explosions). The *"well deck"* was the living quarters for the crew, as well as where we carried up to forty troops. It was about eleven foot wide and a little under 23' deep. Our beds, or *"racks,"* were pieces of canvas stretched over a pipe frame, and were hinged to the bulkheads on either side of the boat. Most of the time, we didn't have a mattress. I had one sheet that was dirty most of the time. The boat was open. Some nights, mosquitoes would cover my face completely. Rats and snakes were frequent companions on the boats. Once in a while, something would scurry across my body while I tried to escape into my sleep world. Probably as a direct result of the open air sleeping and being constantly covered with mosquitoes and other insects, veterans of the Mobile Riverine Force often complain of waking up at night, feeling phantom insects crawling over their bodies.

During my year on the boats, I would frequently dream the same dream. I would be home, my body flying above the trees, in a peaceful, clear blue sky. When I laid my head down on the fold out canvas "rack" that served as our beds, it was like popping in a movie to watch. Since coming home, I have read that dreams of flying are a known, subconscious effort to escape whatever your unpleasant reality happens to be.

**The May, 1968** *"U.S. Naval Forces Vietnam Monthly Historical Supplement"* highlighted the increasing problem with rats. *"During the month, rats have been noted aboard the pontoons and boats of the MRF. All available protective measures were taken to prevent the rodents from boarding the ships. Assistance was requested from the local Preventative Medicine Unit at Dong Tam, and they provided rat poison suitable for use on the pontoons and boats. Relocation of the MRB and stricter control of the handling of garbage and refuse have contributed to a lessening of the number of rats noted on the pontoons."*

Each new boat came equipped with bulky, heavy seats, bolted to the deck of the boat, with oversized springs. They were installed to protect the troops in the event the boat hit a large mine in the river. We kept the boat clean by dipping a bucket into the river, and splashing the dirt and mud down to a drain hole and bilge pump that pumped the water out of the boat. The mounting hardware of the seats made keeping the boat clean almost impossible. One of the first things we did with any new boat was un-bolt the seats and throw them in the river.

The 20MM guns came with huge, round sights, designed for use when mounted on ships for anti-aircraft defense, but for our purposes, they were unnecessary. Most of our firefights were at almost point blank range, on rivers or streams that were only as wide as a two or three lane road. We sawed off the gun sights. Whether you were firing the .30 caliber machine, the .50 caliber machine gun, or a 20MM cannon, you *"walked"* the rounds to your target, depending on where the preceding rounds hit. Contrary to most action movies, you really can't miss with a machine gun, unless you are completely blind, or incredibly stupid.

The new boats were equipped with a small commode in the back of the well deck. It was flushed with a hand pump. It even had a little curtain around it. The pumps didn't work. The commodes stank and were probably a health hazard. We ripped them out and threw them in the river. We improvised our own ways of dealing with the lack of that nicety, none of them providing much in the way of dignity, privacy, comfort, or sanitation. Most of the time, we either used a bucket with a rope on it, dipping it into the river to fill it half way, before using it as our toilet, or we simply hung our butts over the bar armor rail of the boat. We used the same bucket to wash ourselves with river water and to wash down the boats after an operation, when they were coated with mud, blood, or both. Our combat environment was high pressure and intense. Our living conditions were primitive, filthy, and cramped. We lacked any small measure of privacy, or dignity. I often wonder how the movement to add women to combat roles would have fared in Vietnam.

On Tango Six, we took a green plastic chair and cut a hole in the middle of it. We then built a wooden frame for the chair, so that it hung out over our stern. We wrapped the frame with canvas on three sides and painted it green, with a small, yellow crescent moon on each side. During one firefight, the crescent moon took rounds from an AK-47. We don't know if the yellow crescent moons simply stood out enough to catch the V.C.'s attention, or they actually thought that someone had to go bad enough that they would remain there during a firefight. One evening, a PBR was tied up behind our boat and was cleaning a .50 cal. machine gun. They fired a round that went through our little "out house," and hit in the bar armor and C-Ration storage, around our gun mounts. Another day a PBR came in to tie up to us and smashed into our prized possession.

**On Blocking Stations, stopping and searching sampans. Our mine sweep gear and our homemade "restroom" is on the right. We kept life jackets, lines, and other gear in the locker in front of me.**

One way we kept ourselves relatively clean, at least at times, was to fill a water jug with river water, set it on a ledge of the boat, next to the gun tubs and wash ourselves under the open tap. We cleaned our clothing and our cooking and eating gear with the river water, also. The water contained much more than "H2O." We know now that the defoliant used on river banks to make the rivers safer for U.S forces was *"Agent Orange."*

When we were tied up to one of the LST's, we ate very well. On the boats; we improvised to make C-Rations," or *"C-Rats,"* as tasty as we could. They were high in protein, low in fat and pretty boring when they were the daily fare. A case would cost the American taxpayer about $35.00. We would trade two cases of them for a bottle of *Seagrams 7*, even after coming to know that it wasn't really *"Seagrams 7."* The Vietnamese would very carefully cut the seal on the bottle with a razor and fill the bottle with some homemade brew. It didn't matter. Turkey loaf and canned peaches were two of my favorites. When the case got down to things like the canned eggs with ham, we would throw it in the river, or trade it to the Vietnamese.

During June, the V.C. tried to avoid large unit confrontations with the MRF. They couldn't beat us. The MRF worked tirelessly to gather intelligence information on planned attacks on cities, towns and military units, moving our ships and boats in search and destroy operations, but the V.C. continued to prove elusive.

On Saturday, June 1st, the Second Brigade infantry clashed with several V.C. squads, southeast of Sa Dec. At 1600 hours, Bravo Company, of the 3/60th, took small arms and automatic weapons fire from enemy bunkers. River Division 91 shifted Charley Company into the area, to outflank the Viet Cong. They fought until night fell, in devastating enemy crossfire. When the fighting broke off at 1940, nine Viet Cong ended their earthly struggle. Seven American men died, one was missing in action and thirteen were wounded in action.

At the same time, Alpha Company, 3/47th, operating a half mile south of the other battalion, began taking small arms and automatic weapons fire from a squad size V.C. unit. They took sniper fire for several hours, reporting ten wounded, including six as a result of non-hostile action.

Two soldiers drowned, earlier in the day, when a sampan they used to cross a stream capsized at 1230. The First Sergeant of Alpha Company, 3/47th Infantry was killed by a sniper's bullet about 1400, in an exchange of fire with six to ten V.C. One Viet Cong was polished off in the clash.

Boats of River Divisions 91 and 111 inserted troops about 0900, on the narrow, bunker lined Nha Man River, and stayed in the AO to provide communications and fire support.

The MRB shifted anchorage Saturday morning, to Vinh Long, departing Ben Tre at 0615, and arriving at the intersection of the My Tho and Co Chien Rivers about 0945. Yard Light Lift Craft-One was relieved by YLLC-5 at 1500 Saturday and departed the MRB for Vung Tau.

Three MRF personnel were wounded Sunday, June 2nd, during a sweep through the Duc Ton District of Vinh Long Province. Two Army infantrymen were injured by booby traps and a crewman of A-111-2 received minor wounds in an attack on River Division 111 at 1605. They were hit as the boats were backloading the 3/47th Infantry for return to the MRB. Minutes later, T-91-5 took a rocket or recoilless rifle hit below the waterline as River Division 91 craft were extracting the 3/60th Infantry. The round did not detonate and the flooding was quickly controlled. The fire was returned and suppressed. Fourteen Viet Cong were K.I.A> in the two-day operation. U.S. casualties were ten killed and thirty wounded.

**Diary, Sunday, June 2, 1968**

*We're in Dong Tam. The day before yesterday, I was in the chow hall, when mortars started coming in. It scared the hell out of me. The chow hall was cleared in a flash. It was a stampede. I saw one guy knocked down, and I went right past him. Another guy was coming in as I was going out. I flattened him with my forearm. I picked him up and threw him. I felt guilty about it, later, but he was an idiot for trying to run into the chow hall while everybody was running out, to a bunker. We have bunkers strategically placed all around the base. One, near the chow hall. Altogether, eight mortars came in. They killed one guy and injured nine.*

*Last night was especially hot. The humidity hung in the air. One of our guys came into the hooch, stumbling drunk, talking about Freddie. Then, he started crying, sobbing like a baby. He kept asking; "Why did Freddie have to die?" I couldn't sleep. It was pitch black in the hooch. You couldn't see anything, but you could cut the tension with a knife. I know everybody was awake. We couldn't talk. I trained with all of the guys in the hootch. I knew all of them. I couldn't tell which one of them it was, because his voice was so distorted by his sobbing and the fact that he was so drunk. I'm certain there were a dozen pairs of eyes, wide open, staring into the blackness, some teary, and some dry, already becoming deadened. We all just laid there, in tense silence, listening to his voice, crying in the night.*

*None of us talk about Freddie. It's almost like he never was. We liked him so well, we have to forget him or it will eat at us. I know if I go, I will quickly be forgotten. It has to be that way. My secret is that I don't think of Freddie as being gone. I try to make myself think he's out on the APL, and I'll run into him sometime.*

*I don't know what to write Judi and the folks. How can I tell them about mortar attacks, or friends dying? During operations the last few days, the boats have at least seven dead and fifty wounded.*

**Shortly after midnight, June 5th, Robert Kennedy was assassinated by Sirhan Sirhan, a Muslim Palestinian/Jordanian immigrant. Writer, George Plimpton, Olympic gold medal decathlete Rafer Johnson and former professional football player Rosey Grier of the Los Angeles Rams, piled on Sirhan and disarmed him.**

**Diary, June 6, 1968**

*I'm on the "USS Bexar," APA 237, at Vung Tau. On June 3rd, Dong Tam was mortared at about 0200 in the morning. It happened again the next night. June 5th. We left Dong Tam at 0600, and started down river to Vung Tau. I don't know how long we'll be here. Quite a while, I imagine. T-131-9 through T-131-13 have completed outfitting and tests and are now joining Riv Ron 13!*

*Lt. Clarence T. Vaught, our new Commander of River Assault Division 131 brought us down here. Commander Perevil Blundell, Commander of River Assault Squadron 13, arrived this week and is also operating from the Bexar, along with all of his staff officers.*

Boats of the MRF beached two battalions of the Second Brigade, on the Cai Lan and Ruong Rivers in Dinh Tuong Province, Friday, June 7th, taking only a few rounds of sniper fire. Two Viet Cong were killed by the infantry and one by artillery fire. A small enemy base camp and several V.C. graves were also discovered.

The next day, one V.C. was dispatched and six were taken captive. Allied casualties for the two days were one KIA and twelve WIA, ten of them, from booby traps. The fatality and one of the wounded in action were Vietnamese Tiger Scouts, working with the 3/60th Infantry. *"Tiger Scouts,"* or *"Kit Carson Scouts,"* were former V.C., or North Vietnamese Army soldiers who defected. They were known as *"Hoi Chanhs."*

The two battalions were extracted by the boats of the MRF, between 1300 and 1345. They were loaded onto the ships of the MRB by 1415 and began the three and a half hour relocation to Dong Tam, in order to reinforce the Army's defensive position, there. Several companies of the 4/47th Infantry were airlifted from the base earlier, to support the First Brigade, which was involved in heavy fighting with the Viet Cong's 514th Battalion.

Forty-four V.C. were wiped out by air and naval forces, Monday, June 10th, in brutal combat operations, southwest of Ben Tre. River Assault boats were involved in the heated fighting, slaying twenty Viet Cong in two battles. In one exchange, the boats killed sixteen Viet Cong, destroyed three enemy sampans and achieved three secondary explosions, while encountering heavy small arms, automatic weapons and rocket fire. The battle broke out just before sunset, when one of three sampans crossing in front of the column of boats opened fire with rockets, automatic weapons and small arms. The sampans should have known they were no match for the Assault Boats. When the boats began to return fire with all weapons, they began receiving fire from V.C. on the east bank of the narrow Tai Phu River. The boats ran the ferocious gauntlet of fire, sinking all three enemy sampans and strafing the enemy bunkers along the shoreline. The ambush occurred at the intersection of the Tai Phu and Ben Tre Rivers, the same point where River Division 92 had engaged in a twenty minute firefight, three hours earlier. One crewman was injured in the firefight.

Four Viet Cong were decimated by sailors of the river assault boats in a pre-dawn battle, just south of *"The Crossroads,"* on the Giao Hoa Canal, at about 0630. The boats received sporadic fire for the next hour, as they continued moving down the Rach Ben Tre, toward their objective beaches. Nine sailors were wounded in the firefight. Seven were aboard Monitor M-111-2, including Lt. Charles Cox, who assumed command of River Division 111, just the day before. Only one of those wounded was considered seriously hurt. Army helo gunships took out twenty V.C., in sporadic engagements throughout the day.

On Tuesday, June 11th, soldiers of the 9th Infantry Division sent one V.C. to join his ancestors, during a sweep of a heavily wooded area, near Ben Tre. Another V.C. switched sides, under the "Chieu Hoi," or *"Open Arms"* program. Six soldiers were wounded by booby traps. Three were injured by an enemy M-79 grenade round. The infantry were loaded onto the boats between 1330 and 1500 and were on the ships of the MRB by 1900. The five ships of the MRB then returned to just outside Dong Tam harbor.

**Letter from Mom, Tuesday, June 11, 1968**
*Dear Terry,*

*Well, so much has happened that I've been too busy to write. In the meantime, received your letter reprimanding me. Quite a verbal spanking, I should say. O.K., I stand corrected, my dear boy. You must understand, however, that it was only my deep concern for someone I love so dearly that prompted me to write as I did. My constant fear for your safety is always uppermost in my mind, and sometimes, drives me to expressing myself pretty strongly. I do not think all my fears are groundless, however. I was just reading an article this morning about a Lieutenant writing home to his wife and telling her that a good friend of theirs was killed when a Vietnamese guard turned on him and pumped 62 bullets into him from an automatic. When your sister Judy told your Judi about you being suddenly transferred, I thought, "Now what?" What are they going to do with you now? I certainly ho... they don't send you anywhere near Saigon. They're bombing the Hell out of that place. I'm sure sorry to hea... about you leaving your tape recorder and Polaroid with Corky. Do you think he will take care of it, and keep i... or you? I sure feel bad that we can't send tapes back and forth. I have decided to send ours back to the ... tory.*

*Needless to say, I was shocked a... heartsick when Bobby Kennedy was killed. We all felt pretty bad, and watched TV through Thursday and Sunday, and all that went on. Ted Kennedy's heartbreaking eulogy to his brother, when his voice broke at the last and he could hardly talk, was, I think, the most poignant part of it all. I did not make phone calls during those days, and stayed very close to the TV. I will miss him. I was just beginning to want him to win the nomination. Now, there isn't a candidate left who appeals to me.*

*Well Darling, please write soon, and let me know what you will be doing. So take good care of yourself, and write. Love, always,*

*Mom*

## The U.S. Naval Forces Vietnam Monthly Historical Summary notes
*"The river assault craft of RAD 131 commenced their first riverine operation on 12 June with a one-company search and destroy operation along the Doi Stream, 3 ½ miles southeast of Saigon. USS Indra (ARL-37), on loan to the MRF for a six-month period, shifted her anchorage from Vung Tau to Nha Be in Gia Dinh Province to provide logistics and repair support for the new squadron. One monitor and three ASPB's from Dong Tam were assigned to the new squadron to provide gunfire support until their own support craft arrived in-country. The Army element involved in this operation was from the 4/39th Inf. Bn., of the U.S. 9th Infantry Division's Third Brigade."*

I had my first firefight was <u>actually</u> on May 16th. The official daily *"Operations Report"* noted that River Assault Squadron 13 *"received its initiation into Delta warfare"* on Tuesday, June 12th, as it supported a one company search and sweep operation on the Rach Doi, northwest of Nha Be, carrying the 4/39th Infantry Battalion, of the 9th Infantry's Third Brigade.

## Post Card to my sister, Judy, June 13th
*Chao Co!*

*How's it going, Kid? Excuse the handwriting ("shell shock," you know! Ha!). I've been meaning to congratulate you on your graduation. I hear you were having trouble. If you didn't make bookkeeping, don't sweat it. I know it seemed of earth shaking importance at the time, but a couple years, and high school is just a memory. I sent you this because here, the rivers are the highways of the Delta. There's probably nothing around this, except grass huts. Sometimes, this seems to be beautiful country. Other times, depressing and forbidding. Running out of room. Better close, Sis.*

*Rip*

**Post Card to my little brother, Pat, June 13th**

*Hi, Kid!*

*Since you're the family playboy, now, I thought you'd like a picture of a fair maiden of Vietnam, squatting in her dugout!*

*Oh yeah, don't knock my spelling, Brain Child! See that grass hut? They don't hold up to well to 20MM cannon fire! I read that in a book, somewhere!*

*No, really Pat, war is O.K. watching John Wayne do it, but it's a filthy thing that should have ended centuries ago, but still seems to be needed.*

*Well, have a good summer, kid, and take it easy. I better not say that. There's a joke that goes with it.*

*Your brother,*

*Terry*

**Post Card to my little brother, Mike, June 13th**

*Hi, Mike!*

*How was school this year? I'll bet you're glad you're out. Keep up your practice on the trumpet I always brag to the other guys how well you play. Are you still practicing your archery? You are getting good at that, too. This is what Viet Nam looks like, next to the ocean.*

*A couple days ago, I took the helm of our boat for about two hours through this stuff. Right now, I'm writing this next to a lantern. It's hard to see. I bet you're really going to be tall when I see you, next. You're growing fast. Well, Mike, I better close, now. Chao anh!*

*P.S. "Chao Anh" is how Vietnamese say hello or goodbye to a man!*

The MRF was visited Friday, June 14th, by General Creighton Abrams, the new Military Assistance Commander, Vietnam. He succeeded Gen. William Westmoreland. He was briefed on operations by Commodore Salzer and Colonel Archer.

I never wrote home about combat, injuries, or deaths, but in one letter, I did confide to Judi that Freddie had fallen into the Mekong and drowned, a month earlier.

**Letter from home, Sunday, June 16, 1968**
*Dearest Terry,*

*How is my boy, who I love with all my heart? I hope, dear boy that your spirits are up, as Judi read your letter, yesterday, and I was awfully sorry to hear of the loss of your friend, Freddie. Glad we have his voice on tape, but terribly, terribly sorry to hear of his drowning.*

*The baby was christened today. Dad and Judy went, but I couldn't as I have an ad in and a few people are supposed to come. Tom called and asked us to come. We are invited over there for lasagna, tomorrow night.*

*I just called Judi and read the postcards you sent the kids. They were really nice and they all really enjoyed them, especially Tim. He thought that was pretty funny, asking him about his girlfriends.*

*I really dread the summer. It will seem like it drags so slowly and I'll be counting off the months till you come home. That's all I think about.*

*Tomorrow is Larry Lapp's birthday, so I am getting off cards to him. Here it is Tuesday. June will be over before we know it. Tom's birthday is the 26th and we've ordered four tickets for the baseball game on the 25th for Dad, Tom, Pat and Mike.*

*Last night, we were over at Mary and Tom's for lasagna dinner. She had Fr. Swabo, her mother and dad, us, Grandma and of course, the God Parents, Pat and Joan. Really delicious. I sure enjoyed Fr. Swabo. He was in very good humor. He seemed surprised when I told him Pat had made "A track," at Mercy High School. Guess he didn't think a Sater could have it in him. He said; "Oh. Well, I'll keep an eye on him!"*

*Mrs. Simon called, yesterday. She said Judi didn't get a letter. Well, Judi called Monday and had gotten two or three letters from you and read them. Well, parts of them, anyway! Ha! Ha!*

*Anyway, she told me about Wednesday being Larry's birthday and also about them all going out to see Fran and Larry's new house and how Judi is all excited about the nursery and can't wait to fix it up. She asked Fran if she would like one of those wooden animals to hang clothes on.*

*Well, Darling, I really can't think of anything else to write.*

*So write soon and Love always,*

*Mom*

# Chapter 9

## Crippled Kids

### Diary Entry June 17, 1968

*I'm on Tango 6, now. They call the boat, "The Animal." They have its scary visage emblazoned on the side of the boat. I'm stationed in the well deck, along with one other guy, four .30 cal. machine guns and two .50 cal machine guns. We left the USS Indra, near the base at Nha Be, early in the morning. We carried Vietnamese commandos on our boat, led by about six Marine advisor commandos, "Co-Vans." One Lt. kept an ear off each V.C. he killed. He wears them on a necklace. Today, he added three. We were in the Rung Sat Special Zone, a Viet Cong stronghold, southeast of Saigon, on the Ong Keo Stream. It was only about forty yards wide. Other boats in the squadron had the Vietnamese 999th Regional Forces Company*

*Before we beached, we started getting fired on, all up and down the column. We had two Alphas, a Monitor, and six Tangos. All of a sudden, one of the Alphas came over the radio with, "We're taking rockets!" "Rockets" is a word that puts the fear of God into you and all you can think about is covering the banks with maximum machine gun, cannon and grenade fire. The two Alpha boats took rockets. Tango 8 took small arms fire. Three Navy guys were wounded. At first, I had the port ".50." It ran out of ammo, so I jumped to the forward ".30." It kept jamming. Tiny took the starboard ".50" and the Viets were loading. The aft ".30" gave me trouble. The lid kept popping up, so I had to hold it down, while I fired. I kept moving from one gun to another because in the seconds it takes to reload a machine gun, you are more vulnerable to being killed.*

*There was an explosion, just off our stern.*

*We fired 3,000 rounds of ammo, just in the well deck. I don't know how many rounds of 20MM and Mark 19 grenades we fired. I can only imagine how many rounds all nine river assault craft fired!*

We got through the ambush and proceeded to our insertion point. When we beached, the commandos got off quickly, but cautiously. It seemed like they just got off our bow ramp, when all hell broke loose. I thought Charlie was going to charge right down our ramp. I couldn't see them, because the jungle was so thick, but I could sure hear the fire. It sounded like they were right on top of us.

Later, I found out contact was made just five meters off our bow. We beached on top of two companies of Viet Cong. We brought the ramp up and stood at it, with M-16's. Within minutes, the commandos had to come back. Charlie was too thick. He was dug in, with bunkers.

An American Marine commando, a major, came stomping back to the boat with three bloody V.C. packs and rifles in his right hand. His left hand was up to his throat, trying to stop blood from seeping out between his fingers, from a shrapnel wound. He didn't look scared, or worried. He looked pissed. He was a big guy, wearing the typical V.C. black "pajamas." He had long hair and a beard. I'll never forget his eyes. He looked like he could burn a hole right through you with a stare. All of the commandos were back on board by 1115.

Tango 131-8 beached a little south of us, and reported seeing Viet Cong moving in the brush. One crewman was wounded when Tango 8 took shrapnel in the coxswain's flat.

A Vietnamese commando had a wounded leg. They brought back a captured Russian rifle, two grenades, three mines, and several packs of personal gear, covered in blood, including diaries, pictures, clothing, ponchos and other personal items. There was a medical kit, too, with bandages that were taken off dead G.I.'s.

As I went through one of the V.C. packs, one photo grabbed me. It was a picture of three boys. I wondered. Was he one of the boys in the picture? Were they his children? His boyhood friends? I can't look at the picture without wondering. I know it will forever remain a mystery.

The boats had a total of ten wounded in the action. Four had to be flown out. Three U.S. Army were wounded in action. At least three Viet Cong were killed in the fierce, close combat.

Tango 132-3 fired an M-79 round at a suspected V.C. position and observed a secondary explosion.

My old boat, T-131-3 had battle damage to its port screw and shaft. An underwater explosion bent two of its screw blades forward and left burn marks. Tango 131-6 reported an underwater explosion at its stern. T-131-11 took a rocket hit dud round that put a four inch hole in the Styrofoam and knocked off a strip of bar armor on its starboard side. A-111-5 observed two secondary explosions while returning fire.

*Monitor M-91-1 had a radio handset destroyed, a hole in the starboard side Styrofoam, below the mortar pit and damaged bar armor. It also suffered damage to its coxswain's flat and radar antenna, due to shrapnel and small arms fire. Five crewmen of M-91-1 were wounded by B-40 rockets and machine gun fire.*

*A-111-4 took two rocket hits to the port side of the coxswain's flat, with an exit hole on the starboard side. Their coxswain flat canopy was destroyed.*

*A-92-5 had an RPG 7 round hit their starboard side, amidships, which damaged their fuel tank and filter. Three crewmen were injured when a B-40 rocket hit just aft of their 20MM mount. A gear locker was destroyed, with the loss of personal gear, due to fire.*

*All boats except T-131-7 suffered varying degrees of small arms and shrapnel damage.*

*When we left, they called in air strikes on the area.*

For most of my life, I believed that I had made a mistake in my diary, listing one of the commandos as a "major." I had it in my mind we carried Navy SEAL's. The Navy doesn't have the rank of major. The Navy equivalent rank would be Lieutenant Commander. While researching for this book, I came across official operations reports that indicated we did indeed carry Marine Advisors.

After the operation, we had a beer blast and steak fry waiting for us on the pontoon alongside the ship. I used my K-Bar sheath knife to open a Bud beer. The beer started squirting out of the can. Instinctively, I started to stop the spray with my thumb. Unfortunately, the knife was still in the can, and I slid my thumb down the blade, cutting it almost to the bone. I went to sick bay very quickly, to get it stitched up. Standing there, among the wounded from the operation, a corpsman came up to me with a clipboard. He asked my name. I asked him if the clipboard was for the Purple Heart. He nodded his head. I asked him to go to the next guy. He asked me what happened. I told him I cut myself. He asked, *"How?"* I told him opening a beer. He gave me a look like he wanted to kill me. They stitched me up and I quickly returned to the boat.

While the boats of Riv Ron 13 and *Group Bravo* were leaving the Nha Be area, Group Alpha was shifting anchorage from Dong Tam to Can Tho, completing the 110 mile, thirteen hour transit, by 1900. Artillery elements and Light Lift Craft-5, which departed Dong Tam at 1400, Saturday, reached Can Tho earlier in the afternoon. Most of the assault boats left Dong Tam about 0200, Sunday and reached the anchorage at Can Tho shortly after the six ships of the MRB.

The MRF's Group Alpha was operating on the Bassac River for only the second time in its sixteen month history. The previous ops in the area were conducted during the latter stages of the Tet offensive, in February.

Army Helicopter gunship miniguns aerated thirty-three Viet Cong, on Monday, June 17th, in support of Second Brigade forces sweeping an area six miles south of Can Tho. Most of the action occurred in the early morning, after boats of River Division 92 beached the 3/60th Infantry on the Cai Dai River. Neither the 3/60th, nor the 3/47th Infantry, which was beached on the Ba Lang River about 0615, encountered significant enemy resistance as they swept toward each other for the remainder of the day. Two wounded Viet Cong nurses were captured by the 3/60th infantry about 1130. The only resistance the boats encountered was a few sniper rounds, during their transit down the Cai Dai and Ba Lang Rivers.

**Letter home. June *"Something."***
*Hi, Folks!*

*I got two letters from you. I guess I better answer them! I lose track of time, here, completely. I don't know if it has been a week, two weeks, or a month since I wrote to you. It's not because I'm <u>enjoying</u> myself, so much, but I'm kept very busy, now that I'm on a boat, again. I didn't knock off until 6:30, today, after cleaning a .50* *caliber machine gun and helping with a .30 caliber machine gun. It's not a _fun_ job, but one I wouldn't complain about. After I knocked off, I took a shower and shaved, on the base we are at. Now I'm writing by kerosene lantern, on the boat.*

*Not much is new. My job on this boat at G.Q. (General Quarters) is in the well deck of the boat, with four .30 caliber machine guns and two ..50 caliber machine guns. The engineman, "Tiny" and I man all six guns. I'd probably take a ".50," if given the choice. They're twice the size of a ".30."*

*There is an operation, tomorrow, but only four boats are going and mine isn't one of them.*

*Oh yeah, in your letter, you said how you were worried about me looking for Viet Cong. Don't sweat it! I only look for coconuts! I wish you guys wouldn't worry about me. I swear, there's nothing to worry about! I hear about all the fighting going on in Saigon and around it. Right now, I'm at Nha Be, a PBR base, about seven miles from Saigon. I haven't even _heard_ a shot, during the two days I've been here! Remember, newspapers sensationalize! On all the operations I've been on, not _one_ of my bunch has been hurt by "Charlie!" There were just a couple guys injured that day the MRB was fired on. They were back on duty, the next day!*

*Mom, don't worry about ways to get me out of here. Once I'm back to the states, my duty will be done, as far as I'm concerned, and they won't be able to put me over here, again. After my tour is up and I'm stationed stateside, I'll feel ten feet taller, every time I see a hippie. I certainly didn't want this job, but I'm proud as Hell that I'm doing it. I'm working hard, at long hours, so the time goes fast. The morale is high, here!*

*If there was something to worry about, I'd tell you. Then again, I can't recall worry doing anything good, anyway. Besides, I wear a St. Christopher medal! The Vietnamese believe religious medals protect you from the V.C.! Really! So much for that subject. Don't worry!*

*How's things, there? Is Grandma feeling better? I hope so.*

**Next Day…..**
*Well shut my mouth! I'm on an operation! I guess I got the wrong scuttle, yesterday. It's nothing big. We are on a search and destroy mission for Bengal tigers that have been stealing C-Rations and cigarettes from the 9th Infantry guys and trading them to the V.C. for toothbrushes and nail files. There has been only one casualty. A guy tried to milk a water buffalo and it turned out to be a bull.*

*We'll be staying here, beached on the river, overnight. I'm going to put flashlights all around my rack, to keep the wild animals and the boogey man away, so don't worry!*

*We are only temporarily based at Nha Be. The chow is very good. It's one of the only places I've been to where you can pick up one or two quarts of milk and put it at your table. At supper last night, I drank two quarts of milk!*

*Well, I'm sitting here in front of a fan. I just finished eating. The army has come back from the field, soaking wet, muddy, tired and bug ridden. They asked if they could sleep topside on our deck, tonight. They've been in the field all day, risking a bullet every minute of it. Meanwhile, I sat here behind bar armor and a foot of solid steel, with six machine guns, two cannons, a grenade launcher, and assorted small arms, around me. They are in good spirits and haven't made a single complaint. There's always somebody who has it worse. I have a lot of respect for them.*

*We did have one little problem. We got a bunch of red ants on the ramp, when we dropped it. Their bites are terrible! I washed them away, with buckets of water.*

*We're supposed to finish up, tomorrow morning and go back to the base.*

*I got my old helmet back from my old boat. It's like a good luck charm, for me!*

*Well, I think I'll close for now. There's nothing new happening. I'll write soon! Remind me, though! I forget!*

*Terry*

I went through a gradual metamorphosis from the person I was when I arrived in Vietnam. It happened to everybody who served there, or for that matter, in any war. You can see it in the letter I just sent home. I tried to get back to the USS Enterprise when I first received orders for the Mobile Riverine Force, but now, it was in my blood. I was a *"River Rat."* I still wanted to become an Electronics Technician, Petty Officer Third Class, but I didn't want it at *that time*. The men I served with were my brothers. While I was on Tango 6, *"Mac,"* the boat captain mentioned the possibility of giving me a field promotion to Petty Officer Third Class, as a Boatswains Mate, or Gunner's Mate. I didn't want it, because I had the goal of becoming an Electronics Technician. It didn't occur to me that I could have taken the promotion and then switched rates, later.

At this point, I was homesick, sick of friends dying and being wounded, but damn it, I was proud of the men I served with. I didn't want to leave them. I had started to lose the comforting feeling that I was protecting the homeland, or doing something that the people of Vietnam appreciated, but I had to finish the job. My personal goals could wait until I got home.

Ten V.C. were eliminated, Tuesday, June 18th, raising the total for the operation south of Can Tho to forty-three killed. Infantrymen shot and killed three Viet Cong in a sampan shortly after midnight. Helicopter gunships added seven dead V.C., while flying cover for the ground forces during the day. The 3/60th Infantry Battalion returned to the MRB early Tuesday evening, leaving four companies of the 3/47th Infantry in the Area of Operations. Allied casualties Tuesday were four wounded, including three by small arms fire and one by a booby trap. In addition, the body of an Army Infantryman who drowned in a stream on Monday was recovered.

**The U.S. Naval Forces Vietnam Monthly Historical Summary for June 18th, reported;**
***"Viet Cong used another of his many hideous booby traps. This one was discovered during a careful inspection of a sampan. The booby trap was a snake tacked to a floorboard in a manner that allowed the snake to strike at whoever lifted the board."***

**On June 19, 1968, President Thieu signed a general mobilization bill, by which all South Vietnamese men between sixteen and fifty became liable for military service.**

Wednesday, June 19th, nine Viet Cong were destroyed, southwest of Can Tho. Four U.S. soldiers died in the action. Nineteen were injured.

At 1500, an artilleryman was killed and thirteen soldiers were wounded, when an Army LCM-8 landing craft was attacked with rockets on the Can Tho River. Ten of the wounded were attached to the 3/34th Artillery battery and the other three were members of the 1097th Boat Company.

Boats of River Assault Squadrons 9 and 11 were attacked twice Wednesday, the same day as the Army LCM-8 was attacked, near the same location. At 0715 a recoilless rifle round was fired at Riv Div 92 boats southwest of the Cai Rang Bridge. Fortunately, with no casualties.

Later in the day, River Squadron 11 was ambushed from the same spot, as they moved down the Can Tho River to load the 3/47th Infantry from a fire support base. Three sailors were wounded in the ambush as A-112-1 took a recoilless rifle hit in the 20MM mount. A-112-1 was the boat Freddie was on, before he died, and Grif still served aboard. One of the men I trained with must have been one of the wounded. I suspect it was Duenaze. I had heard that he was sent to Japan for a serious leg wound. A Seawolf helicopter team hit the enemy positions without mercy, immediately and achieved a secondary explosion.

The Army moved into the Thuan Nbon District after two days of contact, south of Can Tho. The 3/60th Infantry was beached by boats of River Division 92, at 0830. The 3/47th Infantry was airlifted into the area later in the day. The 3/47th Infantry, with the boats of Riv Div 111 and Riv Div 92, returned to the MRB Wednesday night, leaving the 3/60th in the area, along with boats supporting the barge artillery.

The next day, Thursday, June 20th, River Division 112 and the 3/60th fought an estimated V.C. company. The battle continued, well after darkness. Second Brigade elements had the force surrounded, eighteen kilometers, or about eleven miles, west of Can Tho and were calling in air strikes and artillery on the enemy positions.

Eight soldiers of the 3/60th Infantry were wounded by the fierce enemy fire, as of 2000. Earlier in the day, Army units slew fifteen Viet Cong, boosting the total for the four-days of combat to eighty-one enemy killed. During the cover of darkness, the Viet Cong crept away, leaving their fifteen dead comrades where they fell.

River Division 112 was ambushed at 1950, while escorting Army artillery on the Can Tho River. Eight soldiers on T-112-8 were wounded, three seriously, when the boat was blasted with a recoilless rifle hit in the well deck. An artillery barge was also hit in the attack and was badly damaged by exploding 105 Howitzer rounds.

The Vernon County (LST-1170) arrived at Vung Tau on Thursday, June 21st and was preparing Friday, to join Task Group Bravo as its first support LST. Other ships presently assigned to Task Group Bravo included the Indra (ARL-37), which supported Riv Ron 13 in its shakedown operations in the Nha Be area, and Bexar (APA-237) which was stationed at Vung Tau and helped outfit the new RAS 13 boats as they arrived in country.

**Diary, Saturday, June 22, 1968**
*Boy! June 6th, to June 22nd! Big jump! I'm on Tango 6 now. Last op was quiet. It's been so long since I've written, here. I almost feel like quitting.*

*We delivered some supplies to an ARVN base. When the ARVN soldier approached me with a clipboard to sign, I gave him my "John Hancock." By that, I mean I signed the form, "John Hancock."*

**Letter from Dad, Sunday, June 23, 1968**
*Dear Terry,*

*Greetings from "Pop." In writing you this, I am thinking back some few years, when I was in Italy, and received a letter from my Pop. During our daily living, my Dad did not usually comment about his children, as to them being good, or some kind of praise. In his letter to me, he wrote how proud he has always been of his children (It kind of hit me). Anyway, I hope I have shown, through some of my actions (except writing), my fatherly love and pride in your growth to manhood. I believe some of my thoughts to you were lost in the last tape that didn't work out.*

*Many thanks for your Father's Day letter. I enjoyed it very much. I know you must be working with some very brave men. I too worry much about your safety, but know the only thing I can do about it, is advise you to keep your head down and weigh very seriously what you do over there, to avoid an accident. I heard the other day of a sailor killed in an accident on highway 70, along with his father, and younger brother. They were from Ohio, so anything can happen, near and far.*

*In looking at the post card you sent of the three Viet Cong. I suppose it was a picture a few years ago of three who were good friends. I couldn't help but feel a sense of sorrow about them, but when I think of the alternative, it's a job well done, and hope they find a peaceful solution real soon.*

*Terry, I've been writing most of this on Monday evening. Sunday evening, we went to Larry Lapp's home. He had come home for the weekend, and Judi "Si" said we should come over. I showed Mr. Simon and Steve your letter. Mr. Simon sure thinks a lot of you and I suppose partly because you have a knack of making his daughter so happy.*

*Terry, when you write again, please describe your boat, and crew assignments, because then I can get a better picture of things in your future letters, also, your operations.*

*Tomorrow night, Pat, Mike, Tom and I are all going to the Cardinal Ball game. It will be the first time that I have been inside the Busch Stadium ballpark, since it opened in '66. The St. Bernard Club called June and asked if we wanted tickets to go as a group. Grandma bought Tom's ticket because Wednesday, June 26th, is Tom's birthday.*

*About 10 days ago, on a Friday, at Hodimont and Page (where they are doing construction work) I got a traffic ticket for going through a stop sign. Just the day before, they took the signal lights down, and had a temporary sign in the middle, about waist high, along three barrels. Anyway, I got another ticket because my truck license had expired, and I had just found out about it. Anyway, when I go to court, I am going to protest the stop sign ticket (I took some pictures). After the Judge looks at them, I'll let you be <u>judge.</u> Anyway, when you get back, I'll have two tickets for you to any sports game of your choice.*

*Best of everything to my <u>Second Son</u>*

*Dad*

**Diary, Monday, June 24, 1968**
*I'm on BID patrol, right now. We didn't do much yesterday. Last night, I had a few drinks and went to the flick. I've been discouraged lately. I don't know what I'm going to do when I get out. I have little time to really work on my electronics technician course.*

*Lynch has been added to the list of guys getting Purple Hearts in my class. He got shrapnel in the arm and leg. Vosberg got his second wound.*

*I hear my group will be relieved on December 15th. That's too good to be true! I figure I'll stay home three weeks, if it's true. Then I'll be home for New Years! I might be taking my R&R when I want it, August 2nd. It's hard to say, right now. I don't care <u>where</u> it is! I haven't been paid since April 15th. I should be getting a lot.*

*Today we bought a TV! It will be great for morale. It cost $110.00. That comes to $13.75 each.*

*A while ago, I saw a launch trying to sink three sampans, making close passes, like a bull at the Matador. There were just kids in the sampan. I asked Alex to call the ship and report it. The ship must have called them, because they quit.*

**Tango 6, on an operation with our new TV antenna, made from a BBQ grill, proudly on display. We only picked up grainy black and white broadcasts of the Armed Forces Network, but it was worth it!**

On Monday, June 24th, River Assault Squadron 13 and troops of Delta Company's, 6/31st Infantry Battalion conducted an assault and firepower demonstration, for senior officers of Headquarters II Field Force.

**Thursday, June 27, 1968. Letter from Mom.**

*My Dear Boy,*

*I've been anxious to write again, as soon as possible, as I'm worried. I was looking through Life Magazine, the other day and was shocked to discover, or realize for the first time, that there are cobras in Vietnam and that lots of our men have been bitten by them and died! I could hardly go to sleep for thinking about it and just wanted to warn you to be on alert!*

*The news, yesterday scared me, so I could hardly finish reading it. When I saw the part about U.S. Navy boats and sailors near Saigon, I froze. I know you tell me there's nothing to worry about, but how can I help it, when all the talk now, is how two divisions are heading for Saigon and are getting ready for a new offensive?*

*It's now 11:50 p.m., Thursday night and your sister, Judy and I are waiting up for the 12:00 news, to see the River Boat story. Your sister was over the Simon's house, for a few minutes. Your Judi wasn't there. She'd gone bowling, with Diane, but Mrs. Simon said Judi had planned to go to bed early, then get up at midnight, to watch the show, so we are going to see it, too.*

*I will start getting a box together for you, soon, so if there's anything you want, let me know. I've been so busy. I'd kind of forgotten and then, about a week ago, Judi mentioned she'd sent one and it reminded me to get busy.*

*Your letters seem to be coming in three days. That's faster than ever!*

*How do you stand with your Judi, on your phone bills? Have you paid her up to date, yet? According to the way you had talked, before, you would have been able to pay her up, quickly, so I just wondered. She never mentions it and I don't think she likes me to, so I don't know...*

*Next day;*

*Well, we did watch the U.S. Navy Boat Patrol, last night, till nearly 1:00 a.m. Guess it was a mistake, because I started crying through the last one third of it and cried myself to sleep. I realized more than ever, how much danger you are in. They talked about how every day, you are all risking your lives and how lonely it is, too. They showed an operation, with fighting, firing on the shore and the helicopters, flying over. It sure hit home. Please write soon!*

*Love, Always,*

*Mom.*

**Diary, June 29th, 1968**

*We've been on a couple of ops since the last op I wrote about. A couple of days ago, on June 27th, we were in support of Riv Ron's 9 & 11. It marked the first time the 9th Infantry Division and Task Groups Alpha and Bravo worked together in one big operation. We conducted wide ranging reconnaissance-in-force search operations, east of Can Giouc, in Long An Province. River Assault Squadron 9 and 11 boats carried troops of Bravo Company, 3/60th, and all of the 3/47th Infantry Battalion.*

*A few days ago, a Catholic chaplain conducted Mass in the well deck of our boat. It was the most unusual Mass I've ever been to. He started out telling us all to grab a seat, or stand, wherever we wanted to, and that if we wanted to "light up," that was fine with him. Guys were sitting and standing, everywhere, smoking. They say there are no atheists in foxholes. I wouldn't say that's true, but it is good to hedge your bets.*

*Recently, I knew we were going on an op the next morning, and I had to make a choice between going to Mass, and cleaning my gun. I know "God helps those who help themselves," so I cleaned my gun. I'm certain He understood.*

*At the same time, River Assault Squadron 13 and four PBR's left Nha Be at 0530 to set up a water blockade on the Song Rach Cat, in lower Long An Province, to prevent enemy infiltration to the south. The boats traveled the Song Nha Be and were on station at 0859.*

*Our boats, along with the PBR's, inspected 85 junks, 15 water taxis and 278 sampans, in the area of operations. Total results were two V.C. KIA, twenty-four bunkers destroyed, three weapons captured, and five detainees held. This was three or four hours east of Nha Be. Now we are on our way back.*

*I wish all we had to do was to search sampans and junks. It's fun. We give out a couple of cigarettes and cans of C-Rats, and the gooks go ape.*

*I have liberty tonight, but I'll probably stay on the boat, watch TV and write letters.*

*If we get paid July 15th, like I think we will, I should draw at least $600!*

*I guess I know the crew well enough to describe them. I'll start with my boat captain, and go down the line.*

*Don "Mac" McGriff is a 1st Class Bosn's Mate. He's a big guy, powerful. I'd hate to see him <u>really</u> mad at me! By nature, he's pretty easy going, but like anybody else, loses his temper once in a while. He's married to an attractive wife, and has two or three kids. He's a better boat captain than my first boat captain, because he seems more concerned with the crew than petty rules. He really seems to care about us, and wouldn't tell us to do anything he wouldn't do. He even cuts our hair. Instead of finding work for us every day, we do what needs to be done, and then knock off. He doesn't expose us to needless risk, but he has the courage to do what has to be done. He likes to do "fancy work," or "coxcombing" on the rails, bottles, anything that catches his eye. It is an old seafaring art of making fancy knots. His handiwork is on display on the hand rails going up to our chopper pad "flight deck."*

**Boat Captain BM1 Don "Mac" McGriff and I**

*The bad boat captains abuse their authority and take care of themselves, over the men under them.*

*Thom is a 2nd Class Gunner's Mate, and a good one. He's on his 5th year in the Navy, and his last. He extended to come over here. He's tall, has short, dark hair, kind of slim. Real quiet, usually. He's a real nice guy, easy to get along with. He has the port "20." He's smart and knows what he wants out of life.*

*I'll describe a couple of guys every day. It would take too long to describe all of them in one day. You can probably tell I like figuring people out, though.*

*Riv Ron 13 will be leaving Nha Be on Monday, July 1st, for an operation carrying the 199th Light Infantry Brigade.*

Sunday, June 30th, two men of the 3/47th Infantry Battalion were tragically killed and two were wounded by a Viet Cong booby trap, about fourteen miles southwest of Saigon. Four other soldiers of the 3/34th Artillery Battalion were wounded when they accidentally entered an ARVN minefield and a mine exploded. There are no *"front lines"* in Vietnam. Death can find you, anywhere, anytime, and in any manner it chooses.

As July began, intelligence reports were increasing anticipation that a Viet Cong *"Third Offensive"* was coming. The enemy was massing south of Saigon. That was the central focus and driving factor of Mobile Riverine Force operations for that month.

### Diary, Monday, July 1, 1968

*A new month! Time is passing. Not a very profound statement, but comforting! I get a pay raise, today! An E-3 Seaman, with over two years of service now gets $192.00 a month!*

*We have an op tomorrow. I don't think it will be a very big one. Somehow, I seem to have a warning system about these ops. On the night before our two biggest ops I was very nervous. Both times we had firefights.*

*I should have cleaned my gun today, though. No mail today, either. It's depressing.*

*Well, as for a description of more of the crew, today I'll go on to Elrod. I don't know his first name! Elrod is our "Cox'n." He "drives" the boat. He is short, blond, and has a small build. He is from the south. I don't know where, but the accent is obvious. He is a third class Bosn's Mate and my section leader, in a section of three guys, counting him. He hates giving orders. Usually, he "asks favors." He is one of the morale boosters of the boat. Everybody gets a kick out of teasing him. It's just out of fun, though. He's a good guy. We were friends, instantly. We'll probably stay friends.*

*Next is "Tiny," our "Snipe," or Engine Mechanic. After I talk about him, I'll describe Alex. They are "bookends," completely opposite, so opposite they seem to make a pair. They are always arguing. It's funny! Alex calls Tiny "Fat Albert." Alex is the "Intellect." Tiny is not. Tiny says Alex is "book smart," but stupid. Well, the names "Tiny" and "Fat Albert" should give you a good physical description of Tiny. Tiny was married. His wife died in a car accident. He's been in the Navy for five years. He will probably stay in. He has a habit of saying; "Am I right?" after almost everything that he says. From that, his habit of telling sea stories and his "John Wayne" attitude on ops, I'd say he seeks recognition more than the average guy.*

*Tiny gets on my nerves, sometimes. On one "op," he was walking around the well deck with his finger inside the trigger guard, on the trigger, bouncing the barrel of his M-16 on the metal deck. It could have easily gone off, ricocheting rounds in the well deck and getting somebody killed, possibly me!*

*On another op, Tiny came up to me and pointed a .38 in my face. He said he was just kidding, and wasn't serious. I told him if he did it again, I'd kill him. Neither one of us know if I was kidding, or if I was serious.*

*One more thing about Tiny. A few nights ago, we were sitting topside on the boat, in the dark. He watched me when I picked up a metal cup and put it over my cigarette, as I took a long drag on it. I didn't want a VC sniper to see the light of my cigarette, thinking of the old "three on a match" adage. Tiny watched, and I could make out an expression of understanding in his face. With that, he reached for a cup near him, to do the same thing. It was a yellow plastic cup he had been drinking from. It lit up his sweaty, moon shaped face for anyone on the shore to see. I rolled around on the deck, laughing my ass off!*

*"Alex," Dennis Alexander, is our radioman. He is a little younger than I. He's married. He is of medium height and build. Of all of the crew, he and I have the most similar outlooks on life, dispositions, and general interests. He is different from me in some ways, too. He is very ambitious. Always busy. He's inventive, and kind of an "intellect." He has a terrific sense of humor. He's had three years of electronics and joined the Navy for the schooling. I never see him idle. He's always doing something. That's where we differ. I have about as much get-up and go as a bear…in hibernation.*

*There's two more of the crew to describe, "Willie" and Gould. I'll get to them, soon.*

**Letter from Mom, Monday, July 1st**

*Dear Terry,*

*I finally got some air mail paper. I felt like writing tonight, because, for one thing, I'm worried about you! Judi hasn't gotten a letter from you since Wednesday, and us for a week, now! I just can't understand why we're not hearing. The first of last week, the Navy Boat Patrol and America sailors were mentioned in action, so now I wonder if you were in that action. Well, that's about all the news, so guess I'll close.*

*Love you, Always,*

*Mom*

*P.S. I forgot to tell you on the 6:00 p.m. News, they mentioned and showed the Mobile Riverine Force coming down river at that bridge at Saigon the V.C. blew up.*

**Diary, Tuesday, July 2, 1968**

*We're on the op, today, with the rest of Task Group Bravo. It's a two day reconnaissance operation, with two companies of the 5/12th Infantry Battalion of the 199th Light Infantry Brigade, between Saigon and Nha Be, in Bien Hoa Province. We beached the troops along the Rach Ong Chuoc and Rach Muong Loi. The troops swept to the Song Nha Be.*

*It's a calm operation, so far. I've just finished putting calamine lotion on the rashes on my ankles and my knee. This climate and the way we have to wear dirty clothes often make the conditions for ringworm, athlete's feet and other skin disorders terrible. Wearing boots makes it hard on the ankles.*

*Alex went to the ramp and started giving some kids c-rations and cigarettes. I got a picture of them. It's fun speaking with them, in broken English and Vietnamese with the kids. They love to have their pictures taken. It tears me up when I see some of the kids missing feet, legs, or arms, because of this war. Sometimes, they have crude crutches, made from rough wood. They are like kids anywhere else in the world, though.*

*During a stop in one village, Alex and I tossed C-Rations to the villagers. They started pushing and shoving to get to the canned food. It got out of hand and turned into a riot. I saw a very small girl, maybe four or five years old, get pushed into a roll of concertina wire along one side of the crowd. I grabbed our first aid kit and jumped off the boat, running to the girl. It was a very basic kit. I put some salve on her cuts and scratches, along with some bandages. Within moments, mothers started bringing me babies, toddlers and little kids who were either sick, or had open wounds, or sores. I was in shock and sickened by my inability to take care of them all, the way they needed it. People overuse the expression of being "humbled" by an experience. Actors say they are "humbled" when they are given an "Oscar." Politicians say they are "humbled" to be nominated for high office. No. You are humbled when people think you can work miracles, and you can't. I did the best I could, with what I had, and got back to the boat feeling terribly inadequate, disgusted and saddened.*

*Last night Thom set up a rat trap for our little ugly houseguest in the Coxn's flat. The \*#@#\*\*^ thing ate the cheese without tripping the trap! We have several of the pointy-nosed monsters on the boat. If we don't get rid of them soon, we might as well recruit them! They know their way around the boat better than I do!*

*This morning, Thom got the rodent crewmember. We refer to ourselves as "River Rats," but he was actually the only authentic river rat, on the boat! Mike Thom emptied the metal pellets from a 12 gauge shotgun shell and packed it with crushed malaria tablets. The rat was hiding under our storage of ammunition, several thousand rounds of machine gun ammo. Thom stuck the barrel of the shotgun under the ammunition and blasted it to pieces. At least it didn't die a slow painful death with malaria!*

I don't know if the poverty I saw in Vietnam, and earlier in the Philippines and Hong Kong ignited my cynicism of exaggerated poverty in America, or simply exacerbated it. My family was poor. We had an *"out house."* For a while, my mother and father, and three kids lived in a one room building that later became our "shed." It had a coal oil heater in the middle of the room. We had chickens. Still, we were clothed and well fed. I didn't know we were poor. The poverty I saw in my Navy travels made me grateful for what I had. Obesity is a much bigger problem in America, than starvation. We don't have food riots in America, and although some children may go to bed hungry, we don't have children dying of malnutrition, like many other countries. In Vietnam, children died from infection from small cuts, or medical issues that would never threaten the life of an American child. Americans don't know how good they have it.

Early on Wednesday morning, July 3rd, the boats of Riv Div 131 left the Nha Be area and returned to Dong Tam, via the Cho Gao Canal. The same day, Commodore Salzer presented one Bronze Star, five Navy Commendation Medals, one Navy Achievement Medal and eighteen Purple Hearts to Flotilla personnel. The Bronze Star was awarded to Fireman Daniel Haapala who was assigned to T-91-8.

The Colleton and Benewah both fired into the V.C. base area east of the MRB. Benewah fired a total of ninety-five rounds. The Colleton fired sixty-nine, including one 81MM white phosphorus mortar.

**Diary, July 4, 1968**

*Happy 4th of July, I guess! It is different, over here. We have "fireworks," every day! At the same time, I think we have more appreciation for what the holiday is about than many people watching "the rocket's red glare," at home. Most people at home don't really value what they have. We do. I always will.*

*Yesterday we pulled into Dong Tam, coming from Nha Be. I'm glad we're here. I hope we stay. The MRB isn't here, though. Today was "Holiday Routine," but the well deck was filthy, so Alex and I had to clean it up. I decided my ".50" needed cleaning, too. I put Judi's name on my splinter shield. "Tiny" and I man the two .30 caliber machine guns and the two .50 caliber machine guns that are on each side of the boat, in between the .30 caliber machine guns.*

*I guess it's about time to talk about Willie and Gould, now. I am writing about both of them together, because in Navy slang, they are "brothers." Close buddies. "Willie," real name, Mike Williams is 6', or so, stocky, muscle bound. He has curly brown hair. He is our Mark 19 grenade launcher gunner, a real nice guy. He could probably lick his weight in wild cats, or my weight in Terry Saters, but he has a very sunny disposition and always ready for a good time, in place of a fight. Mike Thom says Willie likes a good fight, too. He is from New Orleans and it is noticeable in his speech. He calls me "Clark," because he says I look like "Clark Kent," with my glasses on. I'll add more after I know him better.*

*Max Gould is a Boatswain's Mate. He is married, and has children. He's twenty-three. He's about 5'10" and has dark hair. He's slim. He is our starboard "20" gunner. He has a happy disposition but gets depressed and looks for fights when he's drunk. He saw some drunks fighting about a week ago and he's taking it easy on the juice now. He's a good guy. Just not himself when he's drunk. I saw him today at the beer blast and he called me over, gave me a beer and was happy as hell. He's impatient to get home to his family.*

*Right now, I'd say it's a good crew, better than average. Everybody is friends, even with a few arguments. We work pretty well together. I feel like part of the crew now, even though I came on the boat late.*

**Gunners Mate Mike Thom eating in the well deck of Tango 6. Note the seats on springs, designed to absorb the blast of underwater mines. Most were taken out. We left a couple. If you look carefully, you can see our "racks," on the bulkheads. The two on either side of Mike Thom are folded up. There are two behind him that are down, in the sleeping position. We eventually threw all of the seats with springs into the river.**

While filming the 1994 movie, *"Forest Gump,"* Gary Sinise, played an officer in the 9th Infantry Division. He wore a rosary with a St. Christopher medal inscribed *"Protect Us In Combat."* The dog tags belonged to his brother-in-law, Jack Treese. Treese served as a Vietnam combat medic, in the late 60's. I gave the rosary I wore in this picture, to my daughter, Dina, although I had to replace the crucifix. While it may be sacrilegious to wear a rosary, or for some, superstitious, I had a feeling it protected me.

**Letter Home, Sunday, July 7, 1968**
*Dear Mom, Dad, Grandma, Judy, Pat, Mike, Sharon, and Tim,*

*Hi! I got a whole bunch of letters yesterday, and enjoyed them all. We're at Dong Tam now, and will probably be here quite a while. I'll try to answer all the letters, starting with the oldest ones.*

*Mom, you wanted to know how I got my helmet back. When I was assigned to "Tango 6," I got a brand new helmet and flak jacket. My old helmet had "sentimental" value, since it was with me on about nine operations, so I traded my brand new one for my old, beat up helmet.*

*I haven't heard from Corky. I'll write him again, soon. He will send it. He may keep putting it off, but out of laziness, not greed!*

*Pat, if you go water skiing, don't let pride get the best of you. Les isn't on the ball that much and even though you are a strong swimmer, the river is stronger. Nobody swims in this river, or even in the harbor. Everybody has some kind of float. These aren't "sissies," either! I don't even go in the water with a life preserver on, since my best buddy drowned. Be careful. Race car drivers have accidents. Champion Swimmers drown.*

*That's too bad about Grandpa. I'll have to write them, sometime.*

*Mom, our boat is well armored. It's the heaviest armored boat of the different types of boats in the Mobile Riverine Force. We have bar armor all around the boat that is designed to stop grenades and rockets. In a way, it would be better if Charlie started a new offensive. Every time he exposes himself, he gets beat. If the whole war were a big offensive, it would end quicker, instead of dragging on. To give you an idea how guys feel over here, on one op, a Commando heard on the radio about a .50 cal machine gun nest that Charlie had, so he asked us to beach his handful of men, so they could get it. The sooner things like that are done, the sooner all of us will be home!*

*I really enjoyed Timmy and Sharon's letters. I would like more letters from them and the older kids. Sharon's getting to be a big girl, now. Her report card was really good. Getting the certificate award for spelling was terrific! I'd like to hear more from Sharon and Tim.*

On July 8th, the 3/60th Infantry killed two V.C. in Kien Hoa Province and took two prisoners. Two infantrymen were wounded by a booby trap and two of the crew of Grif's boat received minor wounds when a round cooked off in the 20MM gun mount. A sailor on A-112-4 was wounded by a sniper when his unit was supporting an artillery fire support base, on the north side of Thoi Son Island.

On July 9th, the assault boats of River Division 131 beached the 4/39th Infantry Battalion on the Gao Stream, three miles west of Dong Tam. The infantrymen swept the area but were unsuccessful in their search for the Viet Cong that have been harassing Dong Tam with rockets and mortars. After destroying eighteen enemy bunkers, the troops returned to the LST, USS Windham County, which was the *flagship* of Group Bravo.

**The Battle of Khe Sanh in northwestern Quảng Trị Province, lasted from January 21st, to July 9th, 1968. Pinned to a bulletin board in Khe Sanh was a note that read,**

## *"For those who fight for it, life has a flavour the sheltered never know."*

**Letter from Mom Wednesday, July 10th**
*Dear Terry*

*Well, it's now been over two weeks since we've heard directly from you, but thank Heaven, I do get news of you. Judi came by, last night, after bowling and showed us the latest pictures you made on the 4th. From what she tells me, you are not getting her letters very promptly, so you probably haven't even gotten the one Dad wrote. Also, I wrote asking you to give me some ideas on what you need, or want, especially for your birthday. As slow as your mail is, I'd better mail something pretty quick, or it won't get there in time for the 5th of August.*

*They sure have been having the U.S. Mobile Riverine Force on the front page a lot, lately. It was in the St. Louis Post-Dispatch, yesterday evening, and the Morning Globe Democrat, Tuesday morning.*

*Judi says you are in Dong Tam, again. I was sure surprised and thought you were around Saigon.*

*Well, I just can't think of anything else worth mentioning, so will close for now. Sure miss you.*

*Love Always,*

*Mom*

On July 10th, our boats set up a water blockade around the area of operations and conducted patrols.

Three crewmen of one of the boats were wounded by shrapnel from their own boat's Mark 19 grenade launcher, while prepping the beach with 40MM grenades, before landing troops. The Mark 19 grenade launcher was a formidable weapon, but when it was used on narrow streams and canals, there was always a chance we'd take some of our own shrapnel.

The 4/39th reconnoitered along the Be Rai Stream and captured a prisoner who had been wounded and claimed to be a member of the Viet Cong 514th Main Force Battalion.

**I took these photos of B Company, of the 4/39th, when T-131-6 was picking them up, on July 11th, or 12th. As primitive as life was on our boats, I felt sorry for these guys and the hardships they lived with. They slept in the mud. They were wet, all the time. They faced the enemy in open rice paddies, and unseen booby traps in any step they took. They suffered greatly, but I never heard one of them complain.**

# Chapter 10
## *"Snoopy's Nose"*

**Diary, Saturday, July 13th, 1968.**

*We're on an op at "Snoopy's Nose," on the Rach Ba Rai, one of the worst spots in the Delta. On the tenth, we had BID patrol and the next morning, we left on this op. The crew volunteered for this one. Last night, the boats took sniper fire. This is a popular ambush site for the VC because of its shape. With the boats in a "U" shaped column, it is difficult to fire into the banks without the risk of hitting our own boats on the other side.*

*At one time, the boats would go through in one long column. The V.C. would start a firefight and we had trouble returning fire, without hitting our own boats on the other side of the bend. We learned our lesson and started sending the boats through a few at a time, so we wouldn't risk hitting others, across the bend. After that, we started beaching boats at the exit of Snoopy's Nose, as a spot to provide cover fire, in the event of an ambush. Charlie learned from each tactic.*

*This morning, at 0810, it "hit the fan." We were on our way out of "Snoopy's Nose," carrying the 4/39th Infantry, and started to relax, as we always did. We thought we had made it through, unscathed. When we started taking off our helmets and flak jackets, we began taking fire. I saw a defective, RPG come out from the river bank, directly abeam of us, in a wild, "corkscrew" spiral. It made some wild maneuvers, then took off, above and behind our boat. At the time, I was standing on our helo pad, fully exposed.*

*We had the monitor and two Alpha boats ahead of us. Tango 8 was the lead boat, "sweeping" for mines. As T-131-8 was beaching at the exit point of Snoopy's Nose to provide cover fire to the boats behind it, it was holed by an explosion which opened up a nine inch gash, below the waterline, next to the engine compartment. The crew immediately put pumps to work to counter the flooding.*

*Rockets (RPG-7's) started flying. One fell just short of our stern and we took heavy shrapnel. I was on the port .50 caliber machine gun. The end of the .30-cal machine gun next to me had its barrel shot off. Five straight legs took shrapnel here, in the well deck. One guy had the .30 right next to me and fell from getting it in the ear. Tango 5 is operating on half their crew. They took two rockets, one at the water line and one in their Mark 19 grenade launcher mount. You can't recognize the Mark 19 gunner; he got it in the face so bad. A heat round went through the starboard side, under his 20mm mount. The 20MM gunner in the mount next to him, received shrapnel in the leg and side.*

*The ambush was about 1500 meters long. That's almost a mile. Imagine going down a two or three lane road, at our top speed of eight knots (about nine miles an hour) with people firing rocket propelled grenades, rifles, and machine guns at you.*

*T-131-13 was sent to assist in off-loading Tango 8 and hit a mine, off the port side of Tango 8. Everything was then off-loaded both boats.*

*After the boats fought through the fusillade, helo gunships and Air Force planes hit the area. After the air strikes, troops were inserted below the ambush site and swept through the area, finding seven dead Viet Cong.*

**I took this photo, after the firing died down on *"Snoopy's Nose,"* July 13th!**

*Two divers from the Sphinx were airlifted to the scene, along with the combat salvage boat and two ASPB escorts to assist in repairs.*

*Nine of the boat crewmen and seven straight legs from the 4/39th were wounded.*

*We are back at the ship, now. We are refueled and are getting our port engine, our port 20 and Mark 19 repaired. Sailors from the ship came down in their blue dungarees to see the damage done to the boats and take pictures. When they came to Tango 5 to take pictures of Tex Frank's gun mount, BM1 Wise, the heavy set captain, screamed at them to get the Hell away from his boat! He was angry and distraught. He was also wounded. I don't think anyone blamed him for being upset.*

*This is a while later. We are back on the line, on the operation. I remember seeing the Mark 19 gunner on Tango 5, now. He is a tall blond guy. Good looking. He has a girl, stateside. Now they say he's not expected to live. Cooper, who is on the same boat, went into shock, but he's OK, now.*

*The 4/39th infantry swept the beach and adjacent areas and established a defense perimeter around the two damaged boats. Several boats beached in the vicinity of Tango 8 and Tango 13. The boats remained inside the perimeter throughout the night while salvage operations continued.*

*Everybody is on edge, unnerved. Everybody knows it could be his turn next time. A colored guy on Tango 5 refused to go out on the boats again. He just stood next to his boat, on the pontoon, shaking, and looking down. "The Rock" Martel was standing near him. He said the guy just kept repeating; "Ain't gettin' back on that fuckin' boat! Ain't getting' back on that fuckin' boat!" A rocket hit in the boat's coxn's flat, burned through the plating until it entered the interior of the coxswain's flat, hit the opposite bulkhead, then dropped through the hatch and hit the guy on the top of his helmet, before dropping onto the deck at his feet, a dud. He felt like he used up all of his luck and wouldn't go out again. Our Lt. "J.G." begged him to go back out, because if he didn't, he would face court martial. He steadfastly refused to get back on the boat and was taken away.*

*The sky is gray, overcast. There is a cool wind blowing. It fits the mood after a battle. Charlie knew we were coming. We got hit just as we were getting to the exit. He had two days to get ready for us. I can still remember it like seconds ago, the sound of Charlie's AK-47 Chicom rifle.*
*July 13th…… a bleak day for Riv Ron 13.*

**Tex Frank's Mark 19 Grenade Launcher gun mount and his flak jacket.**

**Diary, Sunday, July 14th.**
*Riv Ron 13 is mending their wounds. Tex Frank, the Mark 19 gunner is going to be OK. We were sure he was going to be missing one eye, but now he's not. Tango 3 took 50-cal fire, but no injuries.*

*BM3 Bobby Dawson and MM3 Ralph Bigelow, of Tango 8 were given shotguns, M-16's and grenades. The boats were stripped of their heavier weapons, in order to avoid them falling into enemy hands. During the night, Bigelow and Dawson heard movement near their bow. Dawson covered the port side of the bow ramp and Bigelow took the starboard side. They hollered out, asking for a password and received fire as their answer. Dawson and Bigelow opened up. The next morning, the troops did a sweep of the area and found blood trails and a bloody nap sack with clothing in it.*

**Ralph Bigelow, in his Mark 19 gun mount, with his beret, and with his AK-47.**

*We had beer call and I got two letters from Judi. That's all I needed. When I heard about Tex Frank and it sounded like he was going to be blind, I thought of the life he would lead, how I would take it. I would have to find the courage to break with Judi.*

All Riv Ron 13 boats returned to Dong Tam Sunday, July 14th, including T-131-8, which was damaged by a small water mine. Divers flown to the scene from the Sphinx and those on the combat salvage boat completed temporary repairs on the ATC, Sunday morning, permitting it to make the transit from the mouth of Snoopy's Nose to the YRBM-17 at Dong Tam.

Group Bravo results against the Viet Cong for the period of July 11th through 14th was seven Viet Cong KIA, forty-one suspects detained, 75 bunkers destroyed and three RPG-7 rocket launchers captured. Group Bravo casualties included nine sailors and seven soldiers of the 4/39th, wounded. Tom Bohl, one of the guys on T-131-3, with me, was one of the wounded.

The first four ATC's of the new River Division 132 joined Task Group Bravo at Dong Tam Sunday afternoon. The boats completed the two-day transit from Vung Tau at 1445, bringing the total number of Armored Troop Carriers in Task Group Bravo up to seventeen.

Group Alpha achieved the first sustained contact in several weeks, Monday, July 15th, wiping out forty-seven Viet Cong and capturing two, in fighting in the Cang Long District of Vinh Binh Province.

Four infantrymen were wounded by sniper fire or booby traps and one helo crewman was injured by hostile fire while on a *"people sniffer"* mission. One U.S. infantryman was killed and four wounded by friendly fire from a helicopter gunship.

*("People sniffer"* was the nickname for U.S. Army personnel detectors used during the Vietnam War, which picked up the scent of certain chemicals in human sweat, or urine. The purpose was to detect enemy soldiers in hidden positions. The XM-3 airborne personnel detector was a helicopter mounted personnel detector.)

River Division 112 boats, along the Cai Hap river, took sniper fire after beaching the 4/47th Infantry. Monitor 112-1 sustained a 12-inch crack in the port bow when it was hit at 0805 with a rifle grenade. Later, the 20MM gunner on ASPB 112-1 took out one VC who was fleeing from a bunker along the river.

At approximately 1105, two assault boat crewmen received minor wounds when hit with small arms fire during a brief attack on Riv Div 112 boats.

Tuesday, July 16th, the 3/60th Infantry, helicopter gunships and artillery killed thirteen more Viet Cong, in the second day of operations in Vinh Binh Province, which raised the two-day total to sixty.

At 1730, River Division 112 boats were attacked from both banks of the Dua Bo River with rockets, recoilless rifles and automatic weapons, after reloading Echo Company, the 41/47th Infantry. Monitor 112-1 took two rockets, but escaped casualties.

**Diary, Wednesday, July 17th, 1968.**
*We're on BID again. As it turns out, Frank will be losing one eye and the 20MM gunner will be a cripple. Our starboard 20 gunner left for Saigon this morning for a hernia operation. I'll take his place on the 20.*

*The 15th I got paid $517. I only have $340 left to send home. Duenaze, from Grif's boat, is in Japan, recovering from leg wounds.*

Following the ambush on July 13th and the rocket propelled grenade that zeroed in on Tex Frank's *"skull and crossbones"* painted on his gun mount, we were ordered to paint over anything that could provide an aiming point for the Viet Cong. *"The Animal"* motif on the side of Tango 6 had to go, along with Judi's name on the splinter shield of a .50 caliber machine gun and any other personalization on any of the boats.

The Second Brigade returned to the MRB, Wednesday, July 17th, after a sweep through Vinh Binh Province. Troops of the 3/60th Infantry were backloaded in the Area of Operations by boats of River Division 91, while the 4/47th was Infantry was airlifted to a fire support base for pickup by Riv Div 112 ATC's. All troops were back aboard the ships of the MRB at 1745. The wounded were being cared for. The tired, sore and dirty were getting hot showers and rest. The hungry, thirsty and shaken were enjoying hot food and beer. The dead were being attended to and prayed for.

The results of the three-day operation were sixty-two Viet Cong killed and two captured. Army losses were seven killed and twenty-five wounded, including six dead and eighteen wounded as a result of heartbreaking friendly helicopter fire. Every war has friendly fire incidents. Vietnam was no exception. Friendly fire incidents happened far more often than most civilians could possibly imagine.

Boats of River Division 92 spent Tuesday searching for an Army helicopter that crashed Monday night near Fire Support Base Renegade. The body of a door gunner who had been missing in the crash was recovered by the boats, Wednesday morning.

It was a common occurrence, especially during the monsoon season, to wake up in the morning to find a water buffalo, or a pig washed up between boats. One morning, as we were crossing from one boat to another, on our way to breakfast on a ship, we looked down between the boats and stared into the face of a helicopter crewman, wedged between the boats. When he was pulled out, he was in a *"spread eagle"* position, as if he was sky diving. Out of respect for him and his family, I won't describe what I saw, but the image of that poor soul, along with the imagined scene of the headless body Grif and Freddie's boat found, merged into one nightmare scenario that played and replayed in my sleep, for most of my life.

Every day on the Mekong was, in some ways, like every day, everywhere. There was life, and there was death. The *"Circle of Life"* goes on, and on. Mike Thom, our Gunner's Mate, remembered two Vietnamese women who paddled up to the MRB in a sampan, screaming for help. One of the women was pregnant, and on the verge of delivering her baby. The two women tied up to the outboard Tango boat. The mother to be, delivered her new baby on my boat, T-131-6. Mike Thom was there to witness one of the miracles that happened during our year on the Mekong. There were so many memories that gave us nightmares, it was wonderful that there could be moments that brought us the fresh, sweet smell of a new life that could overcome the pervasive stench of death, if only briefly.

Mike comically detailed the time I saw he and Willie at the *"Windjammer Club,"* in Dong Tam. I expressed my concern that I had just bought an engagement ring at the Base Exchange, paying a princely sum of $120.00. I was worried I might have had too much to drink and could lose it on the way back to the boat. I saw Mike as one of the *"responsible"* and serious members of our crew. Willie was more like me. Mike seemed to me to be the calm in the storm. I gave Mike the ring I had just invested a month's pay into, and asked him if he could get it back to our boat for me. I stumbled back to the boat, comfortable in the knowledge that my investment would be safe and rejoin me on our boat. Mike and Willie eventually found their zig zag way back to the boat, spending some time in a muddy ditch, between the Windjammer and the boat. Mike had my ring in his shirt pocket, and dependably delivered it to my grateful hands.

Thursday, July 18th, the Ninth Infantry Division celebrated its 50th Anniversary. The division was organized July 18th, 1918 at Camp Sheridan, Alabama. It distinguished itself in fighting in World War I and World War II. The division arrived in Vietnam on December 19th, 1966. Major General George S. Eckhardt, now the Senior Advisor, IV Corps Tactical Zone, led the first increments of 5,000 infantrymen ashore at Vung Tau.

The six ships of MRB Alfa joined Windham County and Whitfield County at Dong Tam, Thursday afternoon, July 18th. The fifty-seven mile transit took about six and one-half hours.

Friday, July 19th, four ATC's of River Division 131 continued their support of one company of the 6/31st Infantry in the Nha Be area.

**Diary, Saturday, July 20th, 1968**
*We are on our way to My Tho. We'll be there by 1730, or 5:30 p.m., civilian time! We have an op tomorrow and we are getting near the "A.O." I saw Grif yesterday, the first time since we left for Vung Tau, to get the boats.*

Friday, July 19th, was the last time I would ever see my friend, *"Grif."*

One Viet Cong was killed and thirty Vietnamese suspects were detained, Sunday, July 21st, as Task Groups Alpha and Bravo teamed in a search operation that encircled Thoi Son Island, across from Dong Tam and My Tho. Thirty-one boats from Riv Rons 9 and 11 established a blockade around the entire island, at 0420.

Later in the morning, assault boats of River Divisions 91 and 131 beached units of the 3/60th Infantry and Vietnamese Regional Force/Popular Force troops from My Tho, on the north side of the island. River Divisions 91 and 131 then served as chase boats in case sampans tried to escape the island and slip through the blockade. There were several exchanges of fire during the long, hot day, but only one enemy body was found in subsequent sweeps through the areas.

I'm sure experiences with the Vietnamese Regional Force/Popular Force militias varied throughout Vietnam. We referred to them as *"Ruff Puffs."* My impression of them is probably stained by one experience. When we were ambushed, the "Ruff Puffs" hugged the deck, while Tiny and I fired the machine guns in our well deck. One "Ruff Puff" was sitting on the deck, at my feet, his knees up to his chest, in a fetal position, holding his hands over his helmet, crying. I kicked him and made him get up and load the machine guns.

In a separate operation, men of the 4/47th Infantry were backloaded Sunday afternoon from the south bank of the Song My Tho opposite Thoi Son Island and began sweeping toward the 3/60th Infantry. The blockade was continued Sunday night as the infantry set up night positions on the island.

During the July 21st through 22nd operations, a detachment of River Division 131 boats were providing support to the 6/31st Infantry Battalion, four miles southeast of Nha Be. Boats of River Division 131 backloaded the Vietnamese troops in the early evening and returned them to the My Tho area.

MRB Bravo, consisting of Windham County and Satyr (pronounced the same as my last name), had shifted to the My Tho anchorage Sunday morning, but returned to Dong Tam in the evening. I had to pick up something on the repair ship, USS Satyr, one day. After being on board for a period of time, our boat was called to leave and asked the bridge to call for me over their speaker system. When Seaman Sater reported to the bridge, the officer of the watch confided that he thought somebody was pulling a joke on him.

Sunday night, around 2300, July 21st, Monitor 91-1 was hit by an underwater explosion which lifted its stern out of the water. It was remarkable that there were no casualties. It happened while the Monitor was patrolling off the western tip of Thoi Son Island.

Four River Division 91 personnel were presented Navy Commendation Medals by Commodore Salzer Monday, July 22nd, in ceremonies on the Benewah. Lt. (J.G.) James Eldridge, CSO Riv Div 91, was presented both an NCM and a Gold Star in lieu of a second award. BMC Wendol Wasson was presented a Gold Star in Lieu of a second medal, while EN2 J.W. Walton and FN J.H. Greene were presented their first NCM's."

**Diary, Monday, July 22nd, 1968.**

*We are getting our engines repaired right now. On the op yesterday, we set up blocking stations, while Ruff Puffs were on a sweep operation.*

*I got $320 worth of money orders today. I should have a lot more than that.*

*On blocking stations, yesterday, a guy on one of the other boats, shot a girl in a sampan crossing the river. Over the radio I heard one of the Honchos send a boat to investigate the "incident." She was hailed to stop and she didn't.*

*I believe in this cause. I only wish there were a different way. I know there isn't, though. I doubt now if anything will happen to me. I am more afraid of how Judi or the folks would take it, than of actually dying.*

Two sailors were killed and ten wounded, Tuesday, July 23rd, in an ambush of River Division 91, ten kilometers, or a little over six miles southeast of Ben Tre. The two lead ASPB's, Monitor 91-2 and ATC 91-12 were hit hardest in the barrage of fire from both banks of the Rach Ben Tre at 0640.

Killed in the attack were the boat captain, BM1 John Bobb, and a crewman, FN David Pearson, of A-91-4, which was hit hard with recoilless rifle fire and in danger of sinking before the quick thinking surviving crewmen beached it. Two other crewmen aboard A-91-4, and two on A-91-2, required medevac from the area. Less seriously injured were five of the seven crewmen on T-91-12 and one aboard Monitor 91-2. The devastating ambush was sprung where the Rach Ong Huong splits off from the Rach Ben Tre.

The boats of Riv Div 112 were involved in a more substantial ambush farther down the Rach Ben Tre at 1400. Miraculously, there were no U.S. casualties in the assault with rockets, recoilless rifles, and automatic weapons. The Mekong River claimed another life, as EN2 C.O. Roy, the Engineman aboard CCB 111-1, was lost overboard Tuesday morning while his boat was alongside the repair ship, USS Sphinx. The boat was undergoing last minute repairs before getting underway for the AO. Roy was last seen going back aboard the ship to get some oil. A search of the area by assault boats and PBR's turned up only the oilcan, which the missing man was carrying when he left the CCB.

**Letter Home. Tuesday, July 23, 1968.**

*Hi Folks!*

*It's about 8:00 p.m., right now. I'm sitting in the chow hall on the LST we're tied up to. The movie for the night will start in a few minutes.*

*We had BID patrol today. I'm getting a lot of experience on the helm! I didn't like (to say the least!) these orders when I got them, but this duty is so entirely different from being on the Enterprise, I feel it's an invaluable experience, even though I am disgusted and depressed, occasionally.*

*There is <u>no</u> spit & polish on our boat. My boat captain is a 1st Class Petty Officer. He's just "one of the guys." At the same time, he commands respect and we give it to him. He is 31, married and has six kids. We just call him "Mac". His name is Don McGriff.*

*I'm a good shot with an M-16. We just use them for target practice. We toss cans and boxes into the water and fire at them. I'm getting good at blowing them out of the water. As far as I know a Viet Cong has never been directly in my sights, though. I'm kind'a glad of it.* (I continued to hide the fact that I was in action.)

*On the last operation we just set up blocking stations, something like the Highway Patrol sets up "road blocks." We searched sampans, or should I say a "sampan." Only one sampan came into our sector, and it only had a couple <u>kids</u> in it!*

*Judy, I'm enclosing a letter from a buddy of mine on the boat, Jack Elrod. He's a real cool head and he would like a whole bunch of mail! I would appreciate it if you and all your girlfriends wrote him. He used to be engaged. On his last tour over here, he got a "Dear John." It gets pretty dull over here when a guy doesn't get much mail. I'm not complaining, but I know how it would be. He's got blond hair, blue eyes and he won't say it, but he's got a pretty solid build. He is our boat "cox'n." He "drives" the boat, and that's a risky job (If you were a cop and you were trying to stop a car-load of bank robbers, which one would you try to get? The driver!). He volunteered for this duty for a personal reason that I don't want brought up. It's nothing to make conversation about. He has guts, though. He is a big morale booster on our boat and keeps everybody laughing. If he gets a chance to stop in St. Louis when he goes home, you'll see what I mean.*

*Show this and his letter to Judy "Si" and ask her for me to get her girl friends to write him if she can. I know he'll answer every letter he gets. I'll send a picture of him and me together, soon. He's kind of shy (I would imagine), but after you get to know him, he's a real nut. From the way he acts when a good song comes on the radio, I would bet he's a good dancer. He says he forgot to mention his hobbies. They are swimming, surfing, water skiing, (any water sports) and roller-skating. Oh yeah, I forgot, horseback riding. He's from South Carolina, up around Georgia. You can find out more about him from him!*

*Oh, Judy, Happy Birthday! I can't get you a present right now, but if you'll be patient, I'll make it up to ya. You're really getting to be an old lady! These past few months, I've almost been expecting gray hairs myself!*

*Next Day*

*Well, it's a good thing I started this last night. I just found out a few hours ago we'll be leaving for an operation in a couple of hours and we'll be gone for six to ten days, so I just wanted to tell you not to expect any mail for that time. It's just a patrol operation like the last one, so it will be a dull one. We won't be carrying troops. We won't be with a ship, so we won't be able to send or receive mail.*

*In case we don't get back in time, I'll wish you Happy Birthday now and I'll send you something when we get back. So Happy Birthday! That means have a good time, and don't worry about me! I'll tell you all about the op when we get back.*

*Terry*

Light Lift Craft-5 completed extensive salvage operations Wednesday, July 24th, on ASPB 91-4, which was partially sunk during Tuesday morning's savage ambush on the Rach Ben Tre. The salvage boat departed Dong Tam Wednesday afternoon with the badly damaged ASPB in tow.

**Diary, Wednesday, July 24th, 1968.**
*We started this op, late yesterday and did a night transit to an area just north of Ben Luc, in Long An Province. We are to be out six to ten days. On the way here, we encountered small arms fire, occasionally and Tango 7 took heavy automatic weapons fire. He called Mr. Vaught, radio code name "Mariner India," and asked permission to fire back. Vaught told him not to fire back, because there were "friendlies" in the area. Tango 7 came back on the radio and said, "These aren't friendly god-damn shells going over us!" When he asked if he could fire just one M-79 grenade, Vaught said, "Negative! Just keep your heads down!"*

**Diary, Saturday, July 27th, 1968**
*On Thursday, July 25th, we received small arms fire, about 0830, as we were beaching to offload troops of the 4/39th Infantry, above the Ben Luc Bridge.*

*We are in Long An Province, south of Saigon. We had a pretty quiet day up until about forty-five minutes ago, at about 1800. I just finished getting dressed, after taking a bucket shower with river water, when I heard small arms fire off to our port. We were beached starboard of an Alpha boat and several Tangos. I saw everybody* *dive into and behind gun mounts or anyplace else that would offer cover.  Naturally, <u>while</u> I was watching, <u>I</u> was doing a graceful jackknife into the well deck.*

*I found out over the radio that Tango 1 was getting fired at.  Vaught (our C.O.) sent the Zippo and Tango 2 over.  The Zippo let loose on the beach and got return fire, so both boats let loose with the 20's, but still got return fire.  Then, artillery came in on them, then helos, with their mini-guns.  We just finished inserting troops of the 4/39<sup>th</sup> Infantry.  Now I hear they are coming from the other side.*

*I understand that the total for the three day operation, which started on Thursday, we helped fifteen Viet Cong depart life in this tropical Hell Hole, and apprehended four.*

*They have called in air strikes on the nearby enemy positions, by Army helicopters and Air Force planes*

*We were supposed to go back tonight for repairs, but now, I don't know if we will.*

**Letter from Mom, Saturday, July 27<sup>th</sup>**
*Dear Terry,*

*I mailed your birthday present, Thursday.  Sure hope it gets there in time.  I just didn't know what to get you, so when Judi suggested Polaroid film, I was relieved, so I got two color film for it and one slide film for your other camera.  I hope this is O.K.  I also sent Mavrakos candy and three paperbacks.  It cost $2.75 to mail it, including insurance. Judi got hers off days before I did.  I think you'll really appreciate hers.  She's such a nut. You too, so you make a good pair.  She read your funny letter to me and I laughed uproariously.  You were complaining she didn't love you anymore because the mail was slow and you sure were carrying on.*

*Well, Darling, wish we were together here to celebrate our birthdays, but guess I can't and you can't make it, this time.  (Our birthdays were one day apart.)*

*Remember, when I went out to the Scout Camp with our cake?  Well, you are a little too far this time!*

*Dad helped Mrs. Simon move some things of Fran's into their new house and he just got back a few minutes ago.  Judi gave Dad five $20 bills from you.  I sure want to thank you.  We sure needed it and this will sure help a lot, but now, Sweet, don't send us anymore.  Send it all to Judi from now on.  You have to think of your future. Judi will feel good when you start saving and I know she'd get a kick out of taking care of it for you.*

*Boy, Terry, think of how much you could have in the bank if you saved $200 a month until Christmas.  I don't mean to spend.  I mean to save for when you get out.  A good down payment on a house, or a car.  Well, Sweet, I have to close and get busy here, so write soon.*

*Love,*

*Mom*

*P.S.  Grandma sends $1 for your birthday, to have a glass of beer, or something.*

**Diary, Sunday, July 28<sup>th</sup>, 1968.**
*Last night we were beached in a place that was so thick and overgrown, we couldn't see a foot into the jungle.  I had the bow ramp watch, in the middle of the night, I had an M-16, with two clips.  Each clip holds about fifteen rounds.  I heard noises in the jungle, the entire time.  There was only a sliver of a crescent moon, offering little ambient light.  I fought to reign in my imagination.  The jungle foliage kept changing shapes.  One tree took the shape of a hooded banshee.  I was looking through mosquito netting, over my helmet.  They were so thick, I'd be choking on them, without it.  At times, I could feel my heart pounding in my chest.  .*

**(This is similar to where I was standing and how I looked the night a grenade was thrown at me, while I was on watch on the bow of T-131-6. The only differences are, we were beached, I was on the bow, next to the ramp, and I had mosquito netting over my helmet.)**

*Suddenly, a grenade exploded, off our port bow. I heard people running. I was standing on the walkway on the starboard side of the bow. The heavy, armored bow ramp absorbed the blast. If the grenade had landed a few feet towards my side of the bow, I would have been dead. It woke Alex up. I yelled to him; "Back off! Back off!" We couldn't shoot into the jungle, because we could easily hit our own troops, who were out there, somewhere, on a perimeter. Alex immediately threw the engines in reverse and roared us off the bank. We will never know exactly what happened. It was either Charlie thinking he could get a grenade to us, or one of our troops throwing a grenade at Charlie. Either way, it was a close one, for me.*

*Today is peaceful. We killed a snake alongside us that had black and gray rings around it. It may have been a Krait. Tango One, right next to us, had a Bamboo Viper on their boat. They call them "Two Steppers." That's how many steps you can take after you've been bitten, before you die. They threw it off with a piece of wire. They are usually only as big around as a pencil, and not much longer. This one was pretty long. Its jaws were open all the way. They are small, so they have to bite in a spot they can get their jaws around, like a finger.*

*The 4/49th Infantry found an underground hospital and an underground chow hall of Charlie's, yesterday. I saw the bodies of five Viet Cong lying in the mud on the beach. The V.C. had been drug out of their bunkers and holes. The troops tossed them onto the banks, in a casual, haphazard manner. It struck me that the bodies were in positions that only the dead could find comfortable.*

*We had two of our troops wounded. We also captured ten large enemy sampans loaded with ammunition, clothing and a large amount of medical supplies. The seizure indicated that MRG Bravo had located a Viet Cong crossing point.*

We were visited in the field, by the Secretary of the Army, Stanley R. Resor. Commander Peveril Blundell, Commander River Assault Squadron 13, and the Commanding Officer of the 4/49th Infantry Battalion, briefed the Secretary on the MRF Operations during his visit.

**Letter Home. July 30, 1968**
*Dear Mom & Dad,*

*This will be short. The first thing you notice when you opened the envelope is the enclosed picture. The guy on my left is Mike "Willie" Williams, our Mark 19 gunner. He's from Louisiana. He and I are holding "Stations of the Cross," from an old bombed out church not far from here, near Nha Be. A few days ago, the boats beached their troops and one of the boats was in front of this church. It was deserted and bombed–out. The*

*Viet Cong desecrated and destroyed everything, up to the altar. They stopped there, because they are very superstitious. Only two of the stations have Christ intact on them. Only six of the stations are not completely destroyed. In front of this church hangs a bell, shipped from France, as indicated in the engraving. The church is a French mission, built in 1887. Most of the fittings, including the stations are believed to be French. They are badly damaged. In the upper right hand corner of the station I am holding, there is a hole that goes all the way through. They are made of a base layer of cement, then baked red clay. I imagine they were made in the time period of the foundation of the mission. The one I am holding, the seventh station of the cross will be on its way to you and could possibly arrive for your anniversary, as soon as I get it safely crated. It is possible it won't get through customs, but don't sweat it. I picked the cobwebs off of it and sat it in the rain last night. I don't dare try to clean it, though. The writing is in Vietnamese, on the smooth surface at the bottom.*

*I was pretty excited about getting it and I'm not even an antique buff. I hope you like it. One guy has pictures of the church. When I get copies, I'll send them.*

*We'll probably go on an operation tomorrow, so better close and get a letter off to Judi. I haven't had much time to write in the past few days.*

*Love,*

*Terry*

Monday night, July 29th, at 2150, the boats of Riv Div 131 were under a brief mortar attack. The closest round hit 150 yards from the boats. They say *"close"* only counts in *"horse shoes and hand grenades,"* but I think it is fair to say that it also applies to mortars. We were only a "7 iron" away from death and injury.

Tuesday, July 30th, Group Alfa marked the MRF's first day of operations in Kien Thien District of Chuong Thien Province, about thirty-seven miles southwest of Can Tho. Between the 5th Battalion, Vietnamese Marine Corps, Army helo gunships, and the boats of River Division 91, forty-nine Viet Cong were killed.

They captured thirty-two communist Chinese rifles, six .30 caliber U.S. carbines, twelve semi-automatic SKS rifles, three M-60 machine guns, one 120MM mortar, one 75MM howitzer, four mortar sights, one-hundred 81MM mortar rounds, two-hundred-seventy-five 75MM mortar rounds, forty-eight 82MM mortar rounds, 220 grenades, 12,500 CKC machine gun rounds, and thirteen Claymore Rounds.

While River Assault Squadron 13 and Mobile Riverine Group Bravo was operating in Long An Province, that day, the Commanding Officer of the 4/39th Infantry Battalion was killed by a command detonated mine. The 4/39th had been operating with Group Bravo for the past week, south of Saigon. The results of the July 25th to 30th Group operation was nineteen Viet Cong killed, six weapons and ten sampans captured. A total of 340 bunkers and twenty sampans were destroyed. One soldier was killed and two were wounded during the operation.

On Wednesday, July 31st, the body count of Viet Cong wiped out by Army helicopter gunships, Vietnamese Marines and the 3/60th Infantry rose to 102, in the Chuong Thien Province.

Also on that day, River Division 131 boats were hammered with rocket propelled grenades, three miles west of the town of Ben Luc, along the Vam Co Dong River, eighteen miles west of Saigon. ASPB 91-6 took one hit in the exchange of fire. T-131-3 was hit twice, but there was no significant damage and no personnel casualties.

**Navy Historical Summary**

***"During the month of July, the assault forces of the MRF killed 214 Viet Cong and captured 32 prisoners-of-war. Friendly casualties totaled nine killed and 81 wounded; two of the dead and 22 of the wounded were Navymen."***

# Chapter 11
## Tragedy on Tango 9

Thursday, August 1st, Task Group Alfa fought a third straight day, in Chuong Thien Province. Helicopter gunships took out nineteen V.C., bringing the three day total enemy dead to 121, with only three allied wounded. Soldiers of the 4/47th found two large arms and ammunition caches. They also achieved the southernmost penetration of the operation when they were beached by River Assault Division 111, far down the Nga Ba Cai Tau River. The troops seized fifty-one assorted rifles and carbines, two pistols, a shotgun, and an M-60 machine gun. They also confiscated grenades, mortars, twenty-four mines and nine rocket rounds.

The same day, Riv Div 111 assault boats hit an evading sampan with M-79 grenades. The boats fired when the sampan ignored two warning shots, beached, and began offloading material into bushes along the bank.


On Friday, August 2nd, most of River Assault Squadron 13 was operating in the area of Ben Luc, southwest of Saigon. It was a hot, dangerous area, but not the hottest, most dangerous area, that day. It was routine for boats to be *"chopped,"* or transferred, from one squadron, or division, to another, depending on the needs of the various MRF units and the missions they were facing at any given time. At this particular time, Task Group Alfa and River Assault Squadron 9 needed four ATC's from Riv Ron 13, so T-131-9, along with three others, were *chopped* to Riv Ron 9, for an operation in Chuong Thien Province.

The crew of Tango 9 trained together and had arrived *in country* together, in May of 1968. Frank *"Little One"* Springer was their Mark 19 gunner. EN3 Jim Bowen was known as *"Papa-san,"* because although he was only in his mid-twenties, he had a receding hair line of thin blond hair, making him appear older. GM3 Bill *"Hodge"* Hodges was the boat's Gunner's Mate. He manned one of the boats 20MM cannons. Terry Robertson manned the other 20MM cannon. Thomas *"Bird Man"* Bird was the coxswain. RM3 Glenn Ledford was the radioman, who also manned automatic weapons, in the well deck. Bill Taylor was a Boatswain's Mate 2nd Class and manned the .30 caliber and .50 caliber machine guns, in the well deck.

That morning, Tango 9 was preparing to join the boats of Riv Div 9 and Task Group Alfa, near the intersection of the Cai Tu and Cai Nhut Rivers, seven miles southwest of the little town of Vi Thanh. At that time, I was far northeast of there, near Ben Luc.

Map courtesy weather-forecast.com

A friend of Bill Taylor's walked with him to his boat that morning, and told him he would see him when he got back from the operation. Taylor replied; *"No. I'm not coming back from this one."*

As the column of boats moved towards the banks of the Cia Lon River, to offload ARVN soldiers, they were suddenly hit at 0750, with a ruthless barrage of rocket, recoilless rifle, automatic weapons and small arms fire. The crew jumped to suppress the enemy fire. Taylor cranked a round into the chamber of his starboard .50 caliber machine gun. Instantly, a rocket propelled grenade burned through the bulkhead of the boat at Taylor's side, wounding him and killing two Vietnamese soldiers standing behind him. The explosion sent molten shrapnel across the well deck into numerous ARVN soldiers and two of the other boat crewmen. James *"Papa-san"* Bowen received serious wounds to his back and was medevacked. Glenn Ledford, manning the port .50 caliber machine gun, was hit up and down his back and legs with the hot metal, but remained at his guns. Seconds later, another rocket hit the underside of the helicopter deck, raining shrapnel over the men in the well deck. Chunks of shrapnel dealt the fatal blow to BM2 Taylor, striking him in the head and neck. Tango 9 also absorbed five recoilless rifle hits.

An explosion hit the port side of the coxswain's flat, knocking Terry Robertson from his position at the helm. Dazed, confused, and bleeding, Robertson regained his footing, as well as control of the boat. For his actions, and his wounds, Robertson was awarded the Navy Commendation Medal, and the Purple Heart.

As the boat was being rocked from multiple rocket and recoilless rifle hits, the boat captain was knocked from his captain's chair, behind the coxswain. He disappeared from the coxswain's flat and sought refuge near the hatch to the engine room and the commode, abandoning his leadership responsibility in the heat of battle.

Also heavily hit in the ambush were ATC's 91-1, 91-4, and 91-5  Three of the crewmen of T-91-5 were wounded, along with two crewmen of T-91-4 and three UDT-12, who were riding T-91-1

GM3 Hodges jumped into the horror of the well deck, ankle deep in blood. Flesh and blood clogged the bilge strainer and had to be cleared by hand, so that it could be pumped out. Hodges yelled to *Little One* to stay in the Mark 19 mount and keep his eyes on the banks and to be on the look-out for continued enemy threats.

Radioman Third Class Glenn H. Ledford, of Houston, Texas, received the Navy Achievement Medal, the Navy Commendation Medal and the Purple Heart. His citation described his performance;
*"While serving with the River Assault Squadron Nine, Petty Officer Ledford's boat was attacked with rockets and automatic weapons fire. Although knocked from his firing position twice by direct rocket hits and bleeding and dazed from shrapnel wounds, "Petty Officer Ledford courageously re-manned his gun and returned the enemy fire until he was finally overcome by his wounds."*

**Glenn Ledford**

Frank *Little One* Springer received the Purple Heart and the Navy Achievement Medal.  His citation read;
*"Fireman Springer participated in operations involving numerous combat missions which struck deep into the enemy infested waters of the Mekong Delta and inflicted heavy losses to the enemy.  In each instance, he reacted quickly and courageously.  Despite exceedingly long operational periods, he unfailingly met the requirements of the combat situation with enthusiasm and determination."*

**William R. Taylor and Frank *Little One* Springer, next to Frank's Mark 19 grenade launcher gun mount, named *"The Grim Reaper."*  *Little One* may not have been the biggest guy in the River Assault Group, but he took a back seat to no man in courage and performance.**

The next day, Saturday, August 3rd, one sailor was killed and two wounded, when Riv Div 92 and 112 were ambushed while moving west of Can Tho River on their way to the MRF base at Vi Thanh.  Killed in the firefight was SN Charles Dellinger, a 20MM gunner of T-92-8 who sustained fatal head wounds when a jammed 20MM round *"cooked off"* and exploded in his mount.  Neither of the other two wounded were seriously injured.  One was a member of UDT-12 riding T-92-1 and the other was a crewman of Monitor 92-1, which was hit with a 57MM recoilless rifle round.  After the boats suppressed the enemy fire, Army helo gunships attacked the enemy positions.  The assault craft continued their transit down to Vi Thanh without incident.

Gunships flying cover for the 4/47th Infantry Battalion accounted for twenty-six Viet Cong KIA.  That raised to 147 the total enemy killed during the five day operation in Chuong Thien Province.

The Mobile Riverine Force extended operations into the notorious U Minh Forest, the *"Forest of Darkness,"* on Sunday, August 4th.  It was the first allied force in more than a decade to launch major ground action in this Viet Cong sanctuary.  It was regarded as an "R&R," supply, and training area for the enemy.  During the French war against the Vietminh, 500 paratroops dropped into the U Minh in 1952, and were never seen again.

Thirty-four Viet Cong were killed Sunday, the 4th, as the 3/60th Infantry and the Vietnamese Marines swept through an area of the Forest that had been hit with three early morning B-52 strikes.  Gunships of the 7-1 Air Cavalry accounted for eighteen of the enemy dead.  Vietnamese Marines added ten, during a late afternoon firefight with the Viet Cong.  Four VC dead were credited to artillery fire and two were shot by gunners on the Second Brigade Command & Communications ship.  The thirty-four enemy KIA boosted the total for the six-day operation to 181.  A Vietnamese Marine who was killed in the afternoon fighting was the only friendly casualty of the day.  The U.S. Infantrymen and the Vietnamese Marines were airlifted into the Forest after being carried forty-five kilometers, or about twenty-eight miles, down the Xa No Canal and Cai Lon River to a nearby pickup zone.  Boats of River Divisions 92, 111 and 112 remained at a fire support base near the pick-up zone after dropping off the troops.

River Division 91 returned to the MRB about 0825 Sunday, August 4th, from the MRF forward base at Vi Thanh. Before daybreak, at about 0445 the boats at the rear of the column of twenty boats received two rounds of recoilless rifle fire. The rounds landed close, but there were no personnel or material casualties.

The body count in the MRF's week-long operations in Chuong Thien and Kien Giang Provinces rose to over two-hundred, Monday, August 5th, as Army gunships and an Air Force spotter plane blasted seventeen more Viet Cong, hiking the seven day total to 206, the most enemy killed in a single operation since the historic battle of December 4th-6th, when two-hundred-sixty-six VC were killed on the Rach Ruong Canal.

Fourteen enemy were taken out Monday, by the gunships of the 7-1 Air Cavalry, while the other three were claimed by the USAF forward air controller. Alpha Company, of the 3/60th Infantry, found a small arms and ammunition cache in the afternoon, which included six carbines, one grease gun and a machine gun.

Both Vietnamese Marines and the 3/67th Infantry stayed in the field, overnight as the 4/47th Infantry remained at the MRF forward base at Vi Thanh. Boats of River Divisions 92, 111, and 112 spent the day anchored in the Cai Lon River near Fire Support Base Winchester, in support of the troops.

There was an unspoken bond between the sailors of the River Assault Group and the troops we carried into battle. We knew we were a team and would go through hell to help each other, whenever help was needed.

**Letter from my six year old brother, Tim**
*Dear Terry,*

*Terry, I hear that you like to hear from me and Sharon. Sharon is helping me write this. Happy Birthday. Your friendly neighborhood Tim*

**Diary, Monday, August 5th.**
*We began this operation July 24th, and just finished it, today. We're back with the ships of MRB Bravo, at the intersection of the Song Vam Co and Cua Soi Rap. River Assault Squadrons 13 and 15 supported the 4/39th Battalion of the 3rd Brigade, 9th Infantry Division, in Long An, and Hau Mghia Provinces, primarily in the Ben Luc District, along the Rach Vam Co Dong River.*

*This was the longest combat operation by any Mobile Riverine Force unit, to date. During this period, we were ambushed three times and mortared, once. Today, just as we neared the Ben Luc Bridge to refuel, we were ambushed with automatic weapons, recoilless rifles and rockets. I used to be in the well deck of the boat, on the .50's and .30's, but I've been moved to the 20MM cannon mount and still getting used to it. I was asleep under the 20 mount with my glasses off. When I heard everything break loose, I was so panicky, trying to find my glasses; I forgot to turn on the power on my mount! I kept trying to jack a round into the chamber to fire, but nothing happened. No wonder! I still didn't have my flak jacket and helmet on, so between trying to fire, find my glasses, see where the fire was coming from, get into battle dress, I was moving quick and accomplishing nothing. I even quit and grabbed an M-16, but it didn't have any clips! I felt low and disgusted, like I really let down the crew, since I didn't even get one round out. If we had been hit on my side of the boat, I never would have forgiven myself. The boats were able to suppress the enemy fire, however and artillery was called in on the Viet Cong positions. Two boat crewmen, one Army infantryman and one Vietnamese policeman were wounded, but their wounds were minor and they were all returned to duty, after being treated.*

*Late tonight, I remembered it is my 21st birthday. It was a good birthday, though, because we were on our way back and I knew I'd have mail waiting for me. I did! I got one package and a bunch of happy letters!*

I loved getting packages from home, and I received many. My mother frequently sent packages of fudge and cookies. She often sent newspapers, paperback books and magazines.

Judi also sent packages. For my 21st birthday, she sent me a bottle of bourbon in a plastic bottle that originally contained Listerine mouth wash. That was before Listerine had all of the fancy, relatively *"tasty"* flavors, they have today. Judi's father was upset because it was illegal to send liquor through the mail and he was a mail carrier. Unfortunately, the medicinal, pharmaceutical taste of the mouthwash leeched into the bourbon. That didn't deter me, or the crew from enjoying it, of course. As a matter of fact, we were confident that the booze provided us with zesty, clean breath that masked the scent of the bourbon. I savored it and kept it in the metal box in my gun mount that normally held my sound powered phones.

My girlfriend, Judi and my sister, Judy also got together and sent me the July, 1968 "Playboy" magazine. Prior to sending it, however, they spent a fun evening putting "Magic Marker" bikinis on every single picture of a naked, or topless woman. They even did it to the cartoons. I appreciated the humor in it, but my crewmates weren't nearly as understanding. They were genuinely angry at ME for receiving such a frustrating gift.

Thirty-three Viet Cong were slain by the MRF forces Tuesday, August 6th, raising the total enemy eliminated in the eight-day operation to 239. Twenty-five of the Viet Cong were drilled by gunships of the 3-5 Air Cavalry, which was diverted to assist a unit of regional force/popular force troops ("Ruff/Puffs") in heavy fighting, fifteen kilometers, or nine miles, northeast of the Mobile River Force forward base at Vi Thanh. Seven other Viet Cong were destroyed by the 7-1 Air Cavalry gunships. One was credited to the Vietnamese Marines in an MRF operation along the Cai Lon River, three miles from the edge of the U Minh Forest.

Wednesday, August 7th, MRF Group Alfa was concluding eight days of operation in Chuong Thien and Kien Giang Provinces, when they discovered an arms and ammunitions cache which included eighteen rifles and automatic weapons, forty-nine assorted mines, and sixteen 60MM mortar rounds.

River Division 111 was ambushed twice, while returning from the Area of Operations to the MRB. One sailor was wounded in the exchanges of fire on the Xa No Canal and Can Tho River.

Over the eight-day operation, allied casualties were five killed in action and thirty-five wounded, including two sailors killed in action and thirteen wounded. A total of 160 weapons were seized as well as 13,700 rounds of ammunition, 358 mortars and recoilless rifle rounds, 87 miscellaneous mines and 563 hand grenades.

**Letter Home, August 7, 1968.**
*Dear Mom, Dad, Grandma, Brothers and Sisters*

*Hi!*

*Sorry I haven't written lately, but there's a war on, I hear! No. Seriously, I have been pretty busy. We just got off of a sixteen day operation, a couple days ago. I hear tomorrow we leave for Nha Be for a three day operation. I don't guess I'd be telling you anything new by the fact that a new enemy offensive is expected. We are just taking the offensive from them. Riv Rons 9 & 11 are experienced and well seated in the Delta, Riv Ron 13 has her two divisions of ATCs and is becoming a good squadron. River Assault Squadron 15 is getting its first boats, now. U.S. control of the Mekong Delta is becoming stronger every week. The Delta has rivers, canals and streams like New York has streets and alleys. With Riv Ron 9 & 11 in one sector, 13 & 15 in the other, we are keeping Charlie from moving freely. We are accomplishing something!*

*That's too bad about Pat's knee. He better stay off his feet. As for giving Pat advice on what school he should go to, Pat, go to Pattonville if you think it's a better school. You are probably signed up for one school or the other by now, but what I have to say isn't just about school. You probably already heard stuff about "going along with the gang." Don't worry about going to a school just because your friends are going. You might lose some friends by going to a different school, but you would make new ones wherever you went. I think it's important for a guy to make his own decisions. Don't go along with the gang's decisions just because they did it. That goes for anything, not just what school to go to. I'm no "goody-goody" (by a long shot!), but so far, I have a clean record in the Navy. I have never had a "Captain's Mast," for doing something wrong. If I went along with the gang every time, I would have. You have a head on your shoulders, Pat. Use it to make your own decisions, but accept advice. And don't think that as you get taller, you don't have to listen to Mom, Dad, or anybody who is in a position of authority. High School is a ball. Have all the fun you can, but don't let your grades come below what they have been. That's enough advice from your "C-Track" brother.*

*Mom, you asked me to call home. I have to do it from Dong Tam and we aren't there too often. When we are, they can't always get through to the states. I have tried several times. I think the calls are limited to three minutes, because there are so many guys wanting to make them. I'll call as soon as I get a chance, though.*

*As for your idea of the stereo, Mom, I've been way ahead of you on the idea of a stereo for Judi. I always seem to have a coin shortage, though. I have plenty of time for it, though, and I want to save money first.*

*As for the picture of me and the monkey ("monkey and I?"), it was given to my boat as a mascot, but the Commodore saw it when it scampered across our roof and told us to get rid of it! It was a "her," and she was just like a woman... always playing with a mirror! On top of that, she gave crabs to one of the guys on the boat! He had to get some salve to get rid of them!*

*The Navy won't send me back here. I could get a ship. I am requesting shore duty in the south or mid-west. Whether I get it or not is another question! I could stay in the "gator," or amphib Navy and stay just on the coast all the time. I don't really know.*

*I had to laugh about what you said about how our boats looked too close to the beach in one picture. How do you think we drop off our "playmates" (army troops) on an operation? Push them out in the middle of the river? I'm afraid we do get kind of close to the beach, occasionally!*

*Have to close right now. We're leaving for Nha Be!*

*Love, Terry*

### Diary, August 8, 1968.

*I have skipped a few days, haven't I? Well, the last op lasted sixteen days, along the Son Vam Co Dong. We took sniper fire, often. Tango 3 (my first boat) with Lt. JG Robert Conaty on it, took a rocket, so did Alpha 6. Somehow, nobody was hurt.*

*In a different op with our boats, Riv Ron 13 had its first "KIA," while operating with Riv Div 91. BM2 William Taylor, a guy on a ".50" in the well deck of a Tango. Two B-40 rockets hit the well deck of his boat. Two ARVN soldiers were KIA also. Eighteen ARVN's were wounded. Three Navy guys were WIA.*

*Harris, a colored guy from my class, was killed by a rocket in his gun mount. That makes three from my class that have died. I quit counting the wounded.*

*Today, MRB Bravo shifted anchorage from the intersection of the Song Vam Co and the Cua Soi Rap, to just opposite Nha Be. We've been spending the day loading and unloading the 4/39th Infantry.*

*I got paid $233, the other day. I bought a $75 watch for $35.*

*We are getting one engine changed, right now.*

On Friday, August 9th, the four Riv Ron 13 ATC's that had been chopped to Riv Ron 9, including T-131-9, returned to the Group Bravo MRB and River Assault Squadron 13.

St. Louis Post Dispatch, August 9, 1968
**U.S. BOATS AMBUSHED IN DELTA….**
**American Return Fire Hits Village----16 Killed, 120 Hurt**

*"Saigon, South Viet Nam, (UPI)—Viet Cong guerrillas ambushed United States river boats twice at the same Mekong Delta site, yesterday. Both times the American gunners accidentally fired into a nearby village. Sixteen Vietnamese were killed and 120 were wounded, military spokesmen said today.*

*A communiqué said 200 Viet Cong opened fire on the convoys traveling the Can Tho River nine hours apart at a site 80 miles southwest of Saigon. The U.S. Navy boats overshot their targets and hit Cai Rang village. No communist casualties were reported as the boat convoys raced through the half-mile long ambush. Seven American crewmen were wounded and one boat was damaged, spokesmen said.*

***Civilians Killed****. U.S. headquarters said the first volley killed nine Vietnamese civilians and wounded 23. The second, shortly after nightfall, killed six civilians and a soldier and wounded 82 civilians and 15 soldiers.*

*Both incidents are under investigation, the command said. The river craft were carrying U.S. soldiers of the Riverine Assault Force into an Allied operation."*

The primary cause for the civilian deaths in the above incident was that armor piercing rounds, which accounted for every fifth round in a 20MM cannon ammo belt, traveled very far through the jungle. After this incident, we took every armor piercing round out of each ammo belt. It was a labor intensive, time consuming, and tedious job. The article seems to match the time and place where Group Bravo and my boats were operating. I do not recall anything about the incident. I hope and pray that rounds from my gun never killed innocents, but I have no way of knowing.

**Hodges (L), Bird (R), and an unidentified sailor taking armor piercing rounds out of one of our 20MM ammunition belts. The ammo belt also consisted of tracer rounds and high explosive rounds. The 20MM cannon was a deadly weapon. The jungle disappeared in front of a steady stream of fire from the 20.**

**This shot provides a good representation of the size of the 20MM rounds. In this photo, I was removing the armor piercing rounds from the ammo belts, and throwing them in the river.**

**August 9, 1968. Letter to Judi's Mom and Dad**
*Hi, Mom and Dad "Si"*

*I just wanted to thank you for the birthday card and gift. I got it late the night of 5th, or early morning the 6th, just coming off of an operation. The gift came in pretty handy. I hadn't been paid for about a month, so I used it to buy this stationary for one thing!*

*It is 12:25 a.m. We are on "B.I.D. Patrol", until 7:00 a.m. I just finished my turn on the wheel. Our boats are operating with the First and Third Brigade of the 9th Infantry Division, in the Nha Be area. It's been raining, all evening. We are into the middle of the monsoon season, now. I think half of it is landing on this paper.*

*The boats are on "Standby.". Part of them, anyway. Some are on an operation. They expect a V.C. push on Saigon, so everybody is trying to find "Charlie," before he can move. Actually, it seems relatively quiet. Not much action.*

*It still stands that I hope to be seeing you around December 15th. I'll try to make it before 1:30 a.m., this time!*

*Yours,*

*Terry*

**Letter Home, August 11, 1968. U.S.S. Satyr, ARL 23 Letterhead.**
*Hi Folks!*

*Well, I've got some pictures and slides for you. The pictures will probably be stuck together from humidity. This will be short. I have several letters to write. I just wanted to thank you for the birthday present. The whole package was <u>really</u> appreciated. I'm enclosing a letter about something I was going to send, but the Commodore saw it, and several other ones my boat had, and told us to throw them away. Instead, I gave mine to another boat. It made me sick to do it. Later, the church was booby trapped to get some V.C...*

*I got a tape from you today, but I still haven't got the tape recorder! I'll write Corky again.*

*Well, thanks again. I'll write a long letter in the next couple of days.*

*Love,*

*Terry*

The *"something I was going to send,"* was the seventh *"Station of the Cross"* from the old, French church that I had written them about, on July 30th. The church had been destroyed years before and was partially overtaken by jungle growth. Several members of the boat planned on sending the individual stations they had claimed, home. Unfortunately, the Commodore saw them and was concerned that we could be accused of stealing war treasure. Several of the guys tossed their stations of the cross into the Mekong.

On Monday, August 12th, the Third Brigade, supported by my unit, River Division 131, killed eighteen Viet Cong and captured four, seven kilometers northwest of the intersection of the Song Vam Co and Cua Soirap. Six AK-50 rifles were seized.

**Letter from Mom, Monday, August 12, 1968**
*Dear, Dear Terry,*

*I haven't written for a week, but I'm working on a tape. Hope to send it in two or three days. You are always in my thoughts. The first thing I do in the morning is to go out and get the paper to see if there is news of the Riverine Force. Then, watch anxiously for the newscast on the 5:15 news. Thursday night, I thought I saw you and I just screamed! It turned out to be the 199th on the River Boat Patrol. It showed some close ups and I got pretty scared. They were firing at the banks, at VC and just as we watched, the one I thought was you raised his rifle and fired. In a second, the boat apparently took a hit and I didn't know what happened to him and it scared me to death. Then it showed some wounded crew members crawling around the deck. Then, the next morning (Friday), I had just gotten home from my rounds, when Aunt Louise called and when I didn't say anything, she said; "Then you're not worried about the news, huh?" I said, with my heart in my mouth, "What are you talking about?" She proceeded to tell me about one being killed and several wounded in the Delta, among the PBRs. I said "Oh well, that's not what Terry's in." She and I were relieved, but then Dad called me and read the news to me and I realized it could be you and your group and I got all upset. I'm sending the article. Now don't shield me. Were you in this action? Tell me the truth. Anyway, I just bawled and got all choked up and was in very low spirits all day. Dad was pretty upset, too. Mrs. Simon called to tell me about Judi getting a letter and expecting to cheer me up, but I knew this operation could have come after you wrote the letter, so it didn't help much. So, I'm still waiting anxiously to hear that you are okay. They sure have been having the Riverine Force in the news a lot, lately.*

*I was telling Judi how worried I was Friday and mentioned the article, which I had cut out, and she said "Mom didn't tell me about this." I said "Well, dear, she probably didn't want to upset you." Well, Mrs. Simon called me the next morning to tell me Judi got another letter, today. She told me, "Judi was mad at me, for not telling her about the action of the Riverine Force and I told her, "Well, Judi, I didn't want you to be upset, as you were going to Springfield. I was afraid you would be in a bad mood if you knew about it." I'm going to pick up Mrs. Simon and take her over to Fran's, so I can see Fran's baby.*

*I sure hope all this action slows down and you can be safe for a change. I'm also planning on having the basement all cleaned up for your homecoming. In fact, it's uppermost in my mind, now. I'm hoping if Dad ever gets his vacation, we can take this time to take a couple of truck loads of stuff to auction to get rid of it. I just plan on having an antique shop in the garage and not in the basement. I want to fix the fireplace pretty, so I have the incentive to get it done for you, because I love you very much and we are hoping to have a new car for you to drive, too. I was surprised Judi said she's planning on getting one, too. I asked her if you are going to get R&R, and when. Well, darling, keep your head down. Keep safe and healthy and write soon.*

*Love you, always, xoxoxo*

*Mom and family*

The 4/39th Infantry, supported by River Division 131, greased seven Viet Cong, Tuesday, August 13th, raising the four day total to forty. The fighting occurred with a V.C. force northwest of the intersection of the Song Vam Co and Cua Soi Rap. Twenty-one weapons and nine prisoners were taken. The arms captured included nineteen rifles and carbines, a .32 caliber pistol and an RPG rocket launcher. Army losses in the two-day battle were four killed and six wounded.

Bravo and Charley Companies of the 4/47th Infantry returned to the Nueces, late Tuesday afternoon after a costly and heart breaking battle with the Viet Cong near the northeastern end of the Cho Gao canal, in which ten men of the 4/47th died. These two companies had been airlifted to the area to support First Brigade, who ran into heavy fighting with the enemy on Monday morning.

Boats of River Assault Squadron 13 and troops of the 4/39th Infantry returned to Mobile Riverine Base Bravo Wednesday, August 14th, after sweeping through Than Duc District of Long An Province. Four VC bodies were found during the sweep, raising the total body count for the three day operation to forty-four.

Seventeen River Division 91 crewmembers were wounded, early afternoon, Thursday, August 15th, in a firefight on the Rach Ben Tre, ten kilometers southeast of Ben Tre. Three required immediate evacuation. The boats were moving south on the river to pick up troops of the 3/60th Infantry. Monitor 91-3 was the most seriously hit, with ten men wounded by four enemy 57MM recoilless rifle rounds. The injured included the Division's Chief Staff Officer, Lt. JG James Eldridge. Four other sailors were wounded on ASPB 91-3, which took two recoilless rifle hits, including one in the coxswain's flat. Monitor 91-2, A-91-2 and Zippo 91-11 each had one man wounded in the action. The boats took fire for about thirty-five minutes along a ferocious, two-kilometer (1.24 miles) gauntlet, but were able to overcome the attack with fierce return fire. Less than four hours later, the boats were again attacked nearby, with recoilless rifles and automatic weapons. ASPB 91-2 and 91-5 both took rocket or recoilless rifle hits, but escaped casualties.

River Division 112 was hit on the same river, as they moved to beach the 4/47th Infantry. One recoilless rifle round was fired at the River Assault boats, but it exploded harmlessly in the river.

Army Infantry killed four Viet Cong, also on Thursday. Two infantry were injured by sniper fire. Both 3/60th and 4/47th Infantry and boats of Division 91 and 112 remained in the Area of Operations, overnight. Assault craft of Division 92 were supporting barges of the 3/34th Artillery at a fire support base near the intersection of the Rach Ben Tre and the Kinh Giao Hoa.

The 3/39th Infantry, of Task Group Bravo, took out seven Viet Cong, Thursday night near the intersection of the Song Vam Co and Cua Soi Rap. River Division 131 rushed the 4/39th Infantry into the area late Thursday evening to support the fighting. All boats and the infantrymen returned to MRB Bravo Friday afternoon after sweeping through the area. The LST USS Windham County departed MRB Bravo Friday after being relieved by the USS Vernon County.

Task Group Bravo was visited Thursday afternoon by the Master Chief Petty Officer of the Navy, GMCM D.D. Black. Chief Black met with enlisted personnel serving in Vietnam. He visited Task Group Alfa, the next day.

Nine sailors of Riv Div 91 and five infantry were wounded Friday, August 16th, in enemy attacks on the Ben Tre River's *"Ambush Alley."* Wounded in the attack at 0815, by rocket, recoilless rifle and automatic weapons, were six crewmen of ATC 91-4 and two on ATC 91-1. Two of the crewmen had to be evacuated from the area. The boats, which had backloaded the 3/60th infantry and were returning to a fire support base, were able to suppress the hostile fire after a ten-minute battle. An army helicopter fire team placed a strike on the enemy positions. One Viet Cong KIA was credited to the boats during the firefight.

Boats of River Division 112 saw action about 1715 when they were attacked near the same area after loading the 4/47th Infantry. Tango 112-1 took two recoilless rifle hits and reported one crewman and five of the infantry wounded. Less than fifteen minutes later, the boats were attacked again, near the intersection of the Rach Ben Tre and the Giao Hoa Canal. There were no casualties in the final assault. All the assault boats, both infantry battalions and the artillery barges returned to MRB Alfa via the Ham Luong River, Friday night. Two Viet Cong were killed by the infantry and one by army gunships.

**Letter from my Mom, Wednesday, August 17th**

*My dear, dear Boy,*

*I got your letter, yesterday and boy, we all sure enjoyed it! It was the first word from you in three and a half weeks, so we really did appreciate it.*

*I'm glad you got so many letters, all at once, but we will have to get busy so this will happen more often.*

*Now, to answer your letter. I sure got a big kick out of your paragraph on snakes. I sure raised a sarcastic bunch of kids. So Okay, laugh at me, but watch where you step!*

*I felt lot's better since you described your boat and how well armored it is. Yes, I hear your morale of all you servicemen over there is very good.*

*Mrs. Simon and I sure got a kick out of your pictures you sent Judi. Judi called while I was there, and told her Mom, "You can open the letter and take out the pictures, and show them to Mrs. Sater" (Not the letter, of course!) Ha-ha! I did know which one was you in the picture. Where did you get the monkey? Pretty cute!*

*There is one thing I worry about. Is it possible they could send you back for another tour like this? If not, what duty do you think you'll draw? Will you stay in the M.R.F., or will they send you to other duty?*

*I don't care if John Wayne approves or not. I'm glad to hear you're keeping your head down. I'd rather have a live coward, than a dead hero. I love your sunset picture. In that one picture, your boat looked too close to the jungle, to suit me! It looks like the V.C. could throw a grenade on you guys!*

*So stay safe, well, and write!*

*Love, Always,*

*Mom*

# Chapter 12
## Friends Who Die

On Sunday, August 18th, Grif's boat, A-112-2, along with other boats of River Division 112 and Group Alpha was transiting the Hai Muoi Tam Canal, about seventeen kilometers, or ten and half miles, from Cai Be. The ATC's were carrying troops of the 4/47th Infantry.

With Group Alfa operating in one area and Group Bravo, with my squadron operating in other areas, it was difficult to stay in touch with my friends. I hadn't seen "Grif," with Group Alfa, since July 19th.

One of the first boats hit was A-112-2. Two of the men I trained with, and knew well, BM3 Stephen C. Brunton, and GMG3 Edward R. Darville III, GMG3, were killed in the initial moments of the onslaught.

As the radioman, Grif normally would have been in the coxswain's flat, but he had been urging the boat captain to put him on a gun. The captain relented, so Grif was in the forward gun turret of his ASPB. At 1225, the boats were hit with withering rocket, recoilless rifle and automatic weapons fire. Almost immediately, Grif's gun mount was hit with an incendiary rocket propelled grenade, killing my friend, RM3 Patrick J. Griffin.

**This is a photo of me, during River Warfare School, in the forward gun turret of an ASPB (minus the gun), similar to the one Grif was killed in.**

The operations report of the battle noted that *"Missing in action was a boat crewman of ASPB 112-1 who disappeared during the ambush and who had not been located as of sundown."* That was BM3 Billy D. Roy, who was part of my training class.

Fifteen boat crewmen were wounded seriously enough to require medical evacuation. Twelve soldiers were also wounded, as the Tango boats beached the troops. Dust-off helicopters and gunships drew continuous automatic weapons fire. One dust off helo was shot down, but the crew escaped injury.

A sweep through the area failed to reveal the estimated main force V.C. battalion of four hundred to one-thousand men. As a result, the ground forces were back-loaded to the boats and moved several kilometers up river, where fifteen to twenty-two Viet Cong had been spotted earlier in the day.

The Riv Div 112 boats continued to receive sporadic fire as they moved up the canal and at 1700 in the afternoon, there were hit again with a vicious barrage from enemy bunkers, well hidden in the jungle covered riverbanks. Although no one was killed in this attack, fourteen sailors had to be medevacked for treatment to the USS Colleton, or Dong Tam, including Lt. Jim Nelson, the Commander of Riv Div 112, who was wounded in the first attack, but remained in command of his boats throughout the afternoon.

Many boats were damaged during the two attacks. CCB-112-1, the *Command and Communications* boat, as well as T-112-1, had fires that had to be put out in the face of heavy enemy fire. Also badly damaged was A-91-7, which came into the fight as a replacement for one of the Riv Div 112 ASPB's, which had to be towed from the battle.

The 4/47th Infantry was beached near the scene of the attacks and attempted to encircle the enemy, but achieved only moderate contact.

Army artillery and helicopter gunships savagely pounded the Viet Cong positions. Air Force planes saturated their positions with thousands of pounds of bombs. Well into the evening, at 2100, only nine Viet Cong had been confirmed dead. The bulk of the enemy's main force battalion fled the encirclement and bombing.

Four Americans were killed. Eighty-two were wounded, not including many of the less serious injuries from the two ambushes of the assault craft of River Division 112 and River Division 91.

The six ships of MRB Alfa relocated from Dong Tam to Vinh Long Sunday morning, arriving at the new anchorage around 1030.

**Diary, Sunday, August 18, 1968.**
*It's been ten days since I've added anything. I just didn't feel like it. Nothing earth shaking has happened. Yesterday, they had an awards ceremony, giving out Purple Hearts. They presented nine of them.*

*I've been so lonesome for Judi, lately. I hate to think of the months ahead. I hear we won't go home until March, instead of December.*

When I made my diary entry, I didn't know about the battles Group Alfa had been engaged in, or that Grif had been killed.

On Monday, August 19th, Group Alpha slew sixteen V.C., along the Hai Muoi Tam Canal, northwest of Cai Be.

Four Army personnel were killed Monday, in the crash of a *"people-sniffer"* helicopter. The pilot and co-pilot survived the crash and were evacuated to Dong Tam, but the crew chief, a door gunner and both personnel manning the electronics equipment were killed. The only other friendly casualties of the day were four infantrymen wounded by booby traps and sniper fire.

**Diary, August 20, 1968**
*I've been in Nam for five months, now. I think I know the ropes. We left at four this morning on this op. We are operating in eastern Long An Province, after two days of operations near the northeast end of the Cho Gao/Song Tra Canal. This morning, our boats, of Riv Div 131, loaded the 4/36th Infantry. Riv Div 132 is carrying the 3/39th. They've spotted a lot of the enemy converging on the Saigon area. We'll probably be pretty busy for quite a while, now. They are expecting a big "third wave" offensive. Another Tet offensive. I am going to put in for R&R as soon as I can. I think I'll try to get Hawaii.*

*Riv Div 112 was hit hard, a few days ago. There were three dead, and seventeen or twenty injured. This op has been quiet (knock on wood).*

(I couldn't accept the possibility that anyone <u>I knew</u> had been killed. I blocked that possibility from my mind.)

Three V.C. were killed by the 3/60<sup>th</sup> Infantry, Tuesday, August 20<sup>th</sup>, when they engaged a sampan, about 1025. Two AK-47's and a pair of .45 caliber pistols were captured. This incident highlighted the inherent danger that was always present when we stopped a sampan, either in blocking stations, or doing routine searches. Each sampan could either carry women, children and rice, or battle hardened Viet Cong, ready to kill you.

By the end of the three day operation near Cai Be, Tuesday, the assault boats and army units annihilated forty-four Viet Cong and bagged thirteen weapons. Nine U.S. warriors died. Eighty-six were wounded.

MRB Alfa relocated from Vinh Long to Dong Tam, Tuesday morning, while MRB Bravo shifted from the intersection of the Song Vam Co, and Cua Soi rap, to Nha Be.

**On August 20, 1968, the Soviet Union and other Warsaw pact countries invaded Czechoslovakia with over 200,000 troops, ending the much-celebrated *"Prague Spring."***

The entire Mobile Riverine Force was put on maximum alert status Wednesday, August 21<sup>st</sup>, in the face of widespread enemy attacks, interpreted as the beginning of the long predicted third offensive. More than fifty coordinated attacks were launched early Wednesday morning against IV Corps cities, towns, airfields and military installations.

Dong Tam received a total of forty-four mortar rounds in two predawn strikes and five more at 1122 in an unusual daylight attack. Remarkably, there were no casualties and no significant damage as a result of the three mortar attacks. It is difficult to comprehend a total of forty-nine mortar rounds raining in on the Dong Tam base and all of them missing critical equipment and all of the personnel.

During this action, River Assault Squadron 13 supported the 4/39<sup>th</sup> Infantry Battalion in eastern Long An province and two companies of 6/31<sup>st</sup> Infantry Battalion in operations east of Saigon.

The boat captain of ATC 111-10, BM1 R.D. Sullivan, fell from an assault boat in Dong Tam harbor, just before midnight Wednesday. His body was not found.

On August 21<sup>st</sup>, River Assault Squadron 13's two *Zippo* flame thrower Monitors arrived *"in country."*

**Diary, Thursday, August 22, 1968**
*I just came off an op, fifteen or sixteen miles south of Saigon. Found out three guys from my class in Riv Ron 11 were killed. That makes six. God. I'm in a daze. The snipe on Freddie's boat was blown off the boat. They haven't found his body.*

*Today, we carried the 4/39<sup>th</sup> Infantry. They airlifted in some of the 3/39<sup>th</sup>, to help out. Charley fired five mortar rounds at us. There were no boat crew casualties, but two of the straight legs were wounded...*

**Letter home. Friday, August 23, 1968.**
*HI Folks!*

*It's me, your "River Rat" kid. We just left on an operation about a half an hour ago. I'm lying here in my rack with a fan on me, drinking a cold Pepsi. Like the saying goes, "War is <u>hell</u>," ain't it?*

*I got your letter a couple of days ago and the tape a few days before that. As for the clipping you saw about the MRF, we haven't seen <u>any</u> action around here, at Nha Be. The clipping you saw must have been Riv Ron 9 & 11 at Can Tho. My squadron misses out on <u>all</u> the fun! We are on ops near Saigon, but even though I hear about Saigon catching it, we haven't seen any action. I guess Charlie knows I'm with 13, so he figures he better stand clear! He don't <u>even</u> want to "cross my bow," as the old salts say. No, really, we have had it pretty quiet. If we ever do see action, I think I'll hide in the engine room! It seems funny to me that first I get on the "Big E," which is always in the news and now, the Riverine Force. You couldn't keep track of me better if you had a* *crystal ball! It's <u>silly</u> to worry about me. I enjoyed your tape. I had to borrow a tape recorder. I still haven't gotten mine yet.*

*We are going to be taken "off the line" for three or four weeks, in the next day or two. That means no operations unless we're really needed. It's kind of a resting period.*

*I'm going to put in my request for R&R as soon as I can. It takes eight weeks to get it after I request it, though. I don't know where I'll go. I don't really care. I'm not as hot to trot on "seeing new Lands" as I used to be. The states are better than anyplace in the world. I'll be glad to get five days away from this land of grass huts, muddy rivers, and gooks trying to kill me.*

*I don't know when I'll be home. I hear all kinds of stories. I hear December 15th. I also heard that the bunch that came in a month or two after us will be leaving in March, so we would leave <u>sometime</u> before them. I don't know <u>when</u> it will be! I figure between December 15th & February. That's all right. It's that much more combat pay!*

### Diary, Friday, August 23, 1968
*I heard last night that we were being taken off the line for three or four weeks, but bright and early this morning, we left on this operation. You can't believe anything you hear. Rumors on every subject under the sun are passed around, every day. Most of the time, they are bull.*

*They had payday. I had $147 on the books. I let it ride, though.*

*I found out more about the KIA's from my class. Roy got it. Shellhammer and Brunton got it, too. From seventy-two, six down, sixty-six to go.*

*Men of the 3/39th and 4/39th Infantry Battalions found twelve Viet Cong bodies, while sweeping the area where they fought a V.C. platoon, yesterday. They also took two Viet Cong prisoners and two AK-47's. The V.C. look just like the other Vietnamese. We had one soldier killed and eight wounded. Boats of River Assault Squadron 13 loaded the troops in the early afternoon and returned to the MRB by 1500. Nha Be was mortared, last night.*

### August 24th, 1968.  <u>News letter of the U.S.S. Vernon County (LST 1161) "The T"</u>
*"There was considerable enemy activity throughout the night. RAD 131 units in the area of operations received two mortar attacks at 2310H and 0110H. The projectiles hit about 200 yards from the boats, but there were no personnel casualties.*

*Nha Be also received a mortar attack last night. RAD 131 continued support of 4/39 Infantry Battalion. About 1330H the troops of 4/39 Infantry Battalion made contact with estimated one platoon of Viet Cong troops, and RAD movements will depend on development of this contact.*

*In rapid movements reminiscent of the Tet Offensive last February, 2nd Brigade elements bounced from Cai Be to the Xang Canal, back to an area 20 kilometers north of Cai Be, Saturday, August 24th, to establish contact with a significant sized Viet Cong force. There were no official casualty reports for either side as of 2100, but companies of 4/47 Infantry had been in contact since being airlifted into the area late in the afternoon. Both 3/60 and 4/47 Infantry Battalions were rushed to the assistance of an ARVN Battalion, which had been attacked by the enemy forces while sweeping along the Tong Doc Loc Canal, site of a B-52 strike earlier in the day.*

*The U.S. troops had been backloaded between 0300 and 0400 for relocation from the Cai Be area to Dong Tam. Boats of River Division 91 landed 3/60 Infantry on the supper Kinh Xang about 1230, while 4/47 Infantry was transported to Dong Tam for an airmobile assault into the AO. The highlight of the abbreviated sweep was the detention of a Viet Cong who led 3/60 Infantrymen to a cache of 50 B-40 rockets. No contact was achieved along the Kinh Xang before the troops began their airlift back to the area north of Cai Be.*

*In ceremonies at Dong Tam Saturday afternoon, numerous TF 117 personnel were presented Vietnamese Crosses of Gallantry for Heroism during the Tet Offensive. Among the recipients was Commodore Salzer, Group Alfa Commander, who was awarded a Cross of Gallantry with Gold Star."*

### Diary, Sunday, August 25, 1968
*We're on an op again. We're carrying the 3/39th and 4/39th around and beaching them in different areas. We are in eastern Long An Province, ten miles south of Saigon. It seems we're hardly <u>ever</u> on the ships anymore!*

*Today, Bravo Company, of the 439th found a cache of ammunition, including twenty-three B-40 rockets. That's that many LESS that can be fired at us.*

*One of the straight legs was wounded by sniper fire.*

*Last night, we were on the LST and saw a flick with Raquel Welsh in it… Chee! She is unbelievable!*

*I've been in a pretty good mood, lately, daydreaming about having Judi with me at my next duty station. When I think about Freddie, Carrol, Roy, Harris, Brunton, and Shellhammer, before we came to Nam, it really depresses me. Nobody <u>really</u> thinks he'll get it. It's always "the other guy." Taylor left a twenty year-old wife and two little kids. When I leave here, I never want to think about Vietnam.*

### Operations Report. Sunday, August 25, 1968.
*"The Second Brigade troops killed seven Viet Cong Sunday, August 25th, while sweeping through the area of Saturday nights fierce fighting along the Tong Doc Luc Canal. Four of the VC were killed by infantrymen. The other three were taken out of action by gunships of the 6/5 Air Cavalry. Sadly, nine U.S. soldiers were killed and twenty-eight were wounded in the pitched battle with a VC battalion. Alpha and Bravo Companies of the 4/47th Infantry suffered all of the casualties. They were the first U.S. forces airlifted into the area of operations, Saturday afternoon to reinforce an ARVN battalion that was in the thick of it. The area of the fighting couldn't be reached by the River Assault craft. The only boats involved in the operation were six boats providing communications relay at the Long Dinh Bridge, on the Xang canal.*

*Task Group Alfa and Bravo were visited Sunday by Admiral John J. Hyland, Commander In Chief, U.S. Pacific Fleet. The admiral presented seven awards in an afternoon ceremony on the Benewah. Lt. John Collins, Chief Staff Officer, River Assault Division 92, was presented a Silver Star for his heroic actions on the Ba Lai River on April 4, and Captain Raymond W. Allen was awarded a Legion of Merit for exceptionally meritorious service as Chief of Staff, River Assault Flotilla One and Commander, Task Group Alfa.*

*The admiral presented Bronze Stars for heroism to Lt. George A Kitchen, former Commander of River Division 92 and now assigned to the RivFlot One Staff, EN3 Norman W. Moreno, EN3 Thomas J. Etheridge, SN Christopher R. Knabe, all of Riv Div 92, and SN Andrew J. Twist of River Division 91."*

Eight V.C. were killed by the 4/39th Infantry in a clash, Sunday afternoon. The 4/39th lost three men, killed in action, and one wounded.

Ten Viet Cong were dispatched by Task Group Bravo, Sunday, August 25th, and Monday, August 26th, eighteen miles south of Saigon.

On Monday, August 26th, Charley Company, of the 4/39th killed two Viet Cong by detonating a claymore mine.

Three VC were taken out by the 4/47th Infantry, Monday, August 26, as the Second Brigade wrapped up search and destroy operations along the Tong Doc Loc Canal, 20 kilometers, or 12.5 miles, north of Cai Be. The 3/60th and the 4/47th Infantry were airlifted from the A.O. to Dong Tam, Monday morning for return to the MRB.

Two River Assault sailors were injured, one seriously, at 0900 Monday when River Division 92, was returning from a fire support base near the Long Dinh Bridge on the Xang Canal, and was hit with two Rocket Propelled Grenades. ASPB 92-8 took a hit on the port side, aft of the 20MM cannon mount, wounding two crewmen. The ASPB continued at flank speed to the USS Colleton, where the two wounded personnel were treated.

Eight soldiers were wounded Monday as Dong Tam was hit with a barrage of twenty-seven mortar rounds and five recoilless rifle rounds during three early morning attacks. In response, two companies of the 3/60th Infantry were inserted on the south bank of the Song My Tho, opposite Dong Tam, at 1800 Monday, to set up ambush positions to eliminate the Viet Cong mortar teams.

Three sailors were wounded, Tuesday, August 27th, when their boat was brutally ambushed on the Cho Gao Canal while returning from MRB Bravo, at the intersection of the Song Vam Co and Cua Soi Rap, to MRB Alpha, at Dong Tam. Wounded in the rocket and recoilless rifle attack at 1555 were the boat captain and two crewman of A-92-6, which was operating with M-111-3 and ASPB's 111-4 and 92-5. The boats suppressed the fire and moved down the canal to a secure area where an Army helo picked up and evacuated two of the wounded. The third man was treated on board. The Monitor and three ASPB's were returning to MRB Alpha after having completed about six weeks of operations with my boats, as part of Task Group Bravo. The boats were relieved by M-112-2 and ASPB's 112-8, 91-6 and 92-4. Those boats had completed transit between the two MRB's earlier in the morning.

Both Task Groups Alfa and Bravo supported dangerous night ambush operations Monday, but the only contact was reported by Alfa Company, of the 4/39th Infantry, which killed one guerilla in eastern Long An Province.

MRB Bravo moved Thursday from Nha Be to the intersection of the Song Vam Co and Cua Soirap, while MRB Alfa shifted from My Tho, back to Dong Tam.

**Diary, Tuesday, August 27, 1968**
*I found out Grif was killed on August 18th. For the first time, he took the ".50," instead of the radio. It's ironic. 500 V.C. lives weren't worth Grif's. This whole country can rot for all I care. Somehow, I could believe it, when some of the other guys died, but Grif just seemed like it just couldn't happen to him. He was so full of life. I can't remember seeing him angry with anybody. He was a serious guy under the surface, but to everybody around him, he was a clown. Nothing was too crazy, or wild for him to do. It's odd. He was one of my closest friends over here, and I can't think of his first name. He was just known as "Grif," for Griffin.*

*Shellhammer didn't get it, but Darvil did. Now seven young men from my training class have died. Guys like me. They had loved ones. Had plans. Had things they believed in. It could happen to any of us, at any time. If my time comes Judi has to know it's no more "unfair" than any of the other guys dying. For me, the worst thing is in leaving her.*

**From left to right, Duenaze, Bill Roy, "Grif" (on top), Harris. Grif is sitting on the gun mount he died in.**

Two V.C. were finished off by Group Alpha, Wednesday, August 28th, in operations west of Dong Tam. One of the V.C. was killed by infantry. The second was shot by a Riv Div 91 gunner, when the Viet Cong tried to swim out to the boat. A third was wounded later in the day and ultimately, captured by the infantry.

Another milestone was reached on Wednesday, August 28th, with the debut of the new, River Assault Squadron 15. Several of the newly arrived Riv Div 151 units joined River Assault Squadron 13 and Task Group Bravo, in supporting a one-company operation in eastern Long An Province.

On Thursday, August 29th, Task Group Bravo split into three detachments. Lt. Alexander took some boats to Can Giuoc, in support of ARVN elements and the 3/39th Battalion, 3rd Brigade, 9th Infantry Division.

Lt. Vaught took charge of *"TF Starlight,"* an interdiction operation with some of the 4/39th Battalion, 3rd Brigade, 9th Infantry, in southern Gia Dinh and northern Long An Provinces.

The remainder of the Task Group Bravo boats continued to support the remaining 4/39th infantrymen in Gia Dinh and Long An Provinces.

Task Group Alpha boats were ambushed twice, Thursday, August 29th, while operating north of Snoopy's Nose, on the Rach Ba Rai. The first attack occurred at about 1630, as boats of Riv Div 91 were moving back to the Song My Tho, after loading the 3/47th Infantry. Six men were wounded in the small arms and automatic weapons attack, including LCDR "Scott" McCauley, the acting River Assault Squadron 9 Commander.

Less than four hours later, Riv Div 112 took even heavier fire, at 1820, as they were moving north on the Rach Ba Rai, to pick up the 4/47th Infantry. Despite the fact that Tango 112-9 took a B-40 rocket propelled grenade hit and several boats were sprayed with automatic weapons fire, none of the boats took casualties. The boats reported no contact, or resistance when they moved back through the same area about an hour and half later.

A Viet Cong hiding in a *"spider hole"* was killed when an infantryman tossed a grenade into it.

All of the assault craft and the troops they carried returned to the MRB late Thursday night. The only Army casualty of the day was an artilleryman who was wounded by small arms fire at Fire Support Base Alamo.

Task Group Bravo assault boats had no contact while conducting operations in eastern Long An Province. Commander, River Division 131 and eight of his assault boats set up *"aquabushes,"* or ambushes on rivers, south of Saigon with two Army Air Cushion vehicles (PACV's), National Police, MP's, and one platoon of the 4/39th Infantry. Nine boats of River Division 132 relocated to Can Giouc Thursday, to begin operations with Third Brigade forces in that area.

Task Group Alfa was in heated contact with the enemy for much of the day, Friday, August 30th, near the Rach Ruong Canal. The 4/47th Infantry sent eleven Viet Cong to meet their Commie Maker, in that fighting. The 4/47th suffered three troopers killed by enemy fire. Four others were wounded. Captured in a sweep through the area, were one RPG-7 rocket launcher and nine B-40 rockets. The 3/47th Infantry had a relatively quiet day although they did discover a weapons repair factory that morning, and eliminated it.

Assault boats of River Division 112 were ambushed twice, Friday, on the Cung Canal, which is just east of, and parallel to the Rach Ruong. At 1215, the boats were moving north on the canal to pick up one company of the 4/47th Infantry when they were hit with rocket and automatic weapons fire, wounding two men. The boats were attacked in the same area about two hours later, but there were no casualties and no significant damage. The fire was returned and suppressed in both attacks.

Task Group Bravo elements reported no contact in their operations Friday. Riv Div 131 supported men of the 3/39th Infantry while Division 132 worked with a battalion of the ARVN 46th Regiment.

MRB Alfa shifted from Vinh Long to the Sa Dec anchorage Friday afternoon.

The body count in Task Group Alfa operations along the Rach Ruong Canal rose to thirty-three Saturday, August 31st, as the Second Brigade forces stayed in contact with the Viet Cong and found several V.C. bodies that were killed in Friday's fighting. Saturday's total of fifteen VC KIA included nine by gunships, four by the 4/47th Infantry and two by artillery. Five U.S. Army personnel were wounded Saturday, raising the total allied casualties to three killed and thirty wounded, for the two-day old operation. Six AK-47's, were seized by Bravo and Charley Companies of the 4/47th Infantry. Other arms and supplies captured included twenty-four grenades, twelve Bangalore torpedoes, five rocket rounds, four claymore mines and four gas masks.

Boats of Riv Div 112 with the 4/47th Infantry and Riv Div 91 and the 3/47th Battalion returned to the MRB Saturday night. MRB Alfa shifted from Sa Dec to Vinh Long, Saturday night.

**Diary, Saturday, August 31, 1968**
*During the night of the 27th, Alpha 6 was going to Dong Tam to rejoin Riv Rons 9 and 11, with the Monitor, and they were ambushed. Alpha 6 took a couple of rockets. Three are injured, one critical.*

**During 1968, "The Army Reporter" published this editorial about the men I served with;**

*Vietnam is still a pop art oddity 12,000 miles away.*

*The public worries more about living with a possible tax increase.*

*Officials worry about living with world opinion. The GI worries about living.*

*His world there is nightly blackouts and mortars.*

*It's alive with booby traps that can blow his legs, or his life to shreds.*

*It's occupied with an enemy and an ally that look exactly alike.*

*He would give a month's pay for a sound sleep.*

*And ten years of his life for a night at home.*

*He is not a bit-player in a comic opera conflict, not the trump in an international card game and not 12,000 miles away but as near as the muddy and bloody pictures in the newspapers.*

*Moreover, he is usually a very young American citizen, in a hell of a fix.*

*The average age of a combat GI in Vietnam is eighteen and a half.*

*But what a man he is!*

*A pink-cheeked, tousled-haired, tight-muscled fellow, who, under normal circumstances, would be considered by society as a half-man, half-boy, not yet dry behind the ears, a pain in the employment chart.*

*But right now, he is the beardless hope of free men.*

*He is, for the most part, unmarried and without material possessions, except for possibly an old car at home and a transistor radio here.*

*He listens to rock'n roll and the 105mm howitzers.*

*He has learned to like beer by now because it is cold and because it is the thing to do.*

*He smokes because he gets free cigarettes in his C-ration package and it is also the thing to do.*

*He still has trouble spelling, and writing letters home is a painful process. But, he can break down a rifle in 30 seconds, and put it back together in 29.*

*He can describe the nomenclature of a fragmentation grenade, explain how a machine gun operates and of course, utilize either if the need arises.*

*He obeys now, without hesitation. But he is not broken.*

*He has seen more suffering than he should have in his short life.*

*He has stood among hills of bodies and he has helped to construct those hills.*

*He has wept in public and in private and he is not ashamed in either place, because his pals have fallen in battle and he has come close to joining them.*

*He has become self-sufficient. He has two pairs of fatigues. He washes one and wears the other.*

*He sometimes forgets to brush his teeth, but not his rifle.*

*He keeps his socks dry and canteen full.*

*He can cook his own meal, fix his own hurts and mend his own rips… material or mental.*

*He will share his water with you if you thirst, break his rations in half if you hunger, split his ammunition if you are fighting for your life.*

*He can do the work of two civilians, draw half the pay of one and find ironic humor in it all.*

*He has learned to use his hands as a weapon and his weapon as his hands.*

*He can save a life, or most assuredly, take one.*

*Eighteen-and-a half-years old.*

*What a man he is…. Already.*

# Chapter 13
## *Loneliness and Heartache*

**Letter from Commander, River Assault Flotilla One, Captain R.S. Salzer, Captain, U.S. Navy.**
**September 1, 1968**

*Dear Family, Friends of River Assault Flotilla One:*

*Several significant events have occurred since my last newsletter in June.*

*Many of the boats and most of the men from River Assault Squadrons Thirteen and Fifteen have now arrived in country. And by the time you receive this letter we expect that the last of our eleven ships will have joined the flotilla.*

*Due to the size of our expanded force, we have divided our ships and boats into two separate task groups which will normally operate independently of each other.*

*Mobile Riverine Group Alfa consists of River Assault Squadrons Nine and Eleven and seven ships – USS Benewah, USS Colleton, USS Nueces, USS Mercer, USS Askari, USS Sphinx, and an LST supplied by the Commander Seventh Fleet on a two to three month rotational basis. Three battalions of infantrymen from the 2nd Brigade, 9th Infantry Division, will be embarked in the ships and comprise the Army ground force elements of this task group. Captain R.W. Allen presently commands Task Group Alfa; however, he completes his year of duty in Vietnam in September and will be relieved by Captain Thomas F. Boeker early in the month.*

*Mobile Riverine Group Bravo includes River Assault Squadrons Thirteen and Fifteen and four ships – USS Satyr, APL-26, APL-30, and another LST provided on a rotational basis by the Commander Seventh Fleet. Task Group Bravo will support Army elements of the 3rd Brigade, 9th Infantry Division, which will live ashore at Dong Tam Base, about five miles west of the city of My Tho, Captain John G. Now commands Task Group Bravo.*

*The formation of the two separate task groups permits us more flexibility than we have had before. For a ten-day period in late July and early August the two groups were operating on the opposite extremities of the Delta, more than 100 miles apart. Task Group Bravo was conducting missions against Viet Cong elements in the area around Nha Be only a few miles south of Saigon. Meanwhile, Task Group Alfa was making the southernmost penetration of the war into the Delta when it launched ops in and around the U Minh Forest which has been a Communist base area for at least a decade and perhaps for as long as 25 years.*

*More than 250 Viet Cong soldiers were killed and huge weapons caches were captured in this operation south of Can Tho, making it a most successful endeavor. The boats, with their arsenal of heavy weapons, played a significant role as did the Vietnamese 5th Marine Battalion which was operating with the Mobile Riverine Force for this nine-day period. I understand these operations received good play in the stateside press, so you may have read about them.*

*Sincerely,*

*R.S. Salzer*
*Captain, U.S. Navy*
*Commander, River Assault Flotilla One*

Three V.C. were killed Sunday, September 1st, by gunships flying cover for the 4/47th Infantry in Dinh Tuong Province. The infantry also captured a fourth V.C. who was wounded by the gunships. Sadly, a 3/47th Infantryman who had been reported missing in action Saturday night, was found shot on Sunday afternoon.

Task Group Bravo continued operations southeast of Can Giouc in Long An Province. Riv Ron 13 units conducted interdiction and search operations on the Ba Lao and Rach Cac Rivers. They inspected 288 sampans, 77 junks and 10 water taxis with negative results, Sunday.

APL-30 arrived at Vung Tau Sunday, from Subic Bay and began its outfitting prior to joining Task Group Bravo. APL-26, which will also join MRB Bravo, is in the final stages of its overhaul in the Vung Tau area.

**During the Democratic National Convention in Chicago, demonstrations against the war in Vietnam exploded into a riot, resulting in 175 arrests and at least 100 injuries.**

My boat captain on Tango 6, Boatswain's Mate 1st Class Don *"Mac"* McGriff, came to me after a staff meeting and told me that it was discussed at the meeting that Tango 9 was hurt badly, and needed a replacement. Mac told me the boat captains were asked to volunteer a good man to go to Tango 9. I didn't want to go to a third boat, after making friends on Tango 6, but I knew I had to. I know I should have taken Mac's gesture as a compliment, but it was difficult. I had been taken off Tango 3 when they split up that crew, right after Freddie died and I became comfortable with a whole new crew. Now, after *"Grif"* and other guys I knew were killed, I was being uprooted again. I had gotten to know and like *"Willie"* Williams, Mike Thom, Jack Elrod, *"Mac"* McGriff and *"Alex"* for three months, knowing we could depend on each other when it *"hit the fan."* In Vietnam, there was no consistency. Each day brought life changing, or life ending developments.

### Diary, Monday, September 2, 1968
*We are on an op. They have put me on Tango 9, which had only a five-man crew. This is the boat Bill Taylor was on, when he was killed. I'm taking his place. Another guy is in the hospital. I man both 20s, right now. It's going to be interesting in a fire fight. The crew seems to be OK.*

My diary entry of September 2nd was my last. Loneliness and heartache had just taken its toll on me. It wasn't because I was being sent to Tango 9. I had just reached the point that I was dead tired, and tired of death. For months, I couldn't tell Judi and my family what I was going through. Now, I couldn't even tell myself. The despair was too great. I wish I had continued. I had been in Vietnam less than six months. I had been shifted around on three different boats, with three different crews. I lost friends to combat, drowning, relocation, and wounds. I had lost any vestige of naïve perspective, or innocent illusions I had about the war, or, for that matter, life. I just wanted to go home, whole, and vertical.

APL-26 relocated from Vung Tau to MRB Bravo Monday, September 2nd, arriving at 1835, in Long An Province. MRB Alfa shifted from Vinh Long to Dong Tam, on Monday.

River Division 131 and soldiers of the 4/39th Infantry had two encounters with the cunning enemy, Monday night, September 2nd, while conducting aquabushes on the Rach Giang, east of An Giouc. The first incident occurred at 2040 when the boats hailed a sampan and its frightened occupant beached the boat and ran into the jungle. A sailor on M-131-1 fired several M-79 grenade rounds at the panicked enemy. Inspection of the sampan turned up a grenade, two AK-47 clips and a medical kit. Hours later, at 0115, infantry ambushed four V.C. with a Claymore mine and M-79 rounds. A search of the area turned up no sign of enemy bodies.

Meanwhile, the LST, USS Vernon County anchored with MRB Bravo at the intersection of the Song Vam Co and the Cua Soi Rap, and observed four figures moving on the beach, at 2315. Tango 132-1, on Bid Patrol, fired several M-79 rounds into the area, with unknown results.

Tuesday night, September 3rd, and Wednesday morning, during night ambushes in eastern Long An Province, a Long Range Reconnaissance Patrol (LRRP) team, supported by Task Group Bravo, ambushed a V.C., at around

2300, three miles southwest of Nha Be. A search of the area in the morning, yielded no traces of the body. Viet Cong typically removed the bodies of their fallen, whenever possible. Riv Div 131 boats supported two companies of the 4/39th Infantry in a night operation on the Rach Vang four miles southeast of Can Giouc.

On Wednesday, September 4th, Riv Ron 13 carried the 3/39th Infantry, in the Can Giouc area. It was a night of a nearly full moon. The boats doing B.I.D. patrol spotted dark figures on the bank, digging, under a shielded light. The assault boats strafed the bank with one-hundred rounds of 20MM cannon fire. After the cannon fire, no further activity, or movement was observed.

Task Group Bravo units running night ambush, six kilometers southeast of Can Giouc had no contact with the enemy, Thursday night. However, M-131-1 observed two secondary explosions Friday morning while using fourteen 105MM rounds to destroy VC flags and posters along the banks of the Xom Cau River. MRB Bravo moved from the intersection of the Song Vam Co and the Cua Soirap to Nha Be, on Friday morning.

Eleven Navy men were wounded, six seriously, Friday night, September 6th, during a vicious ambush of three Task Group Bravo assault boats of Riv Ron 13, 15, and 9, on the Ong Vien Canal, five kilometers, or about three miles, east of Can Giouc in Long An Province. They were two miles from where my boat was operating with Bravo and Charlie companies of the 4/39th Infantry, off the Song Nha Be.

The boats were engaged in night ambush *"Starlight Operations,"* when they were hit with automatic weapons and RPG's, at about 2230. The boats had just landed a platoon of the 4/39th Infantry and were moving to night positions when they were attacked.

Among those wounded in the attack was Capt. J.G. Now, Commander of Task Group Bravo, and Lt. C.T. Vaught, my Commander of River Assault Division 131. The boats involved in the ambush, ASPB 92-4, Monitor 131-1 and ATC 151-11 returned fire with all weapons and quickly silenced the enemy. Each boat was hit with rockets. The Monitor took one rocket in the coxswain flat and one at their waterline. After moving out of the area, all six of the seriously wounded were medevaced to a nearby hospital by an Army dustoff helicopter. One of those seriously wounded lost his leg, above the knee. The boats placed H & I fire on the ambush positions for the remainder of the night. The next morning, Army troops were landed in the area, but the only result of sweep was the discovery of one B-40 rocket round.

**Letter Home, on USS Vernon County letterhead. Saturday, September 7, 1968**
*Hi Folks!*

*First of all, I'm sorry I haven't written for a while. We haven't been on operations that much, but they have been sending us out on one or two day ops. That keeps us awfully busy, because after an op, it takes us about two days to square away the boat, cleaning the mud out, and cleaning the guns.*

*I'm sorry I didn't write you for your anniversary. I kept meaning to, but I kept getting sidetracked. Anyway, I hope you did have a very happy anniversary, and I hope you like the gift from Judi & I. She told me how you had to bring up the old radio from downstairs every time you wanted to hear it.*

*I just came off an op early this morning. We left yesterday evening and dropped troops late last night. We are switching tactics. Charlie has been hitting only at night, so instead of cruising down the river during the day with our radios barking commands, we transit at night, keeping radio silence, dropping off troops and sneaking back. That's not for our safety. We don't want Charlie to know troops are in the area, so that the army can ambush them, or maybe be close enough to stop them if they try something. .*

*I found out something a few days ago, that may please you. If another big offensive comes up, the 9th Infantry are to set up positions around Saigon, to guard it, so after we take them to their positions, we are no longer needed. If an offensive would come up, Riv Ron 13 would be out of any action, is what I'm saying.*

*It's an experience to work with the army. We get to know them like shipmates. There is a respect for each other. There isn't any inter-service rivalry. No fights between Army and Navy, or anything. That's because we work together so much. I guess the idea is that we figure instead of saying "You are Army and I am Navy," it is "We are Riverine Forces," It really gets to be comical, sometimes, with the difference in slang, or Navy expressions. On an op with troops aboard, there are a lot of funny situations. Picture a soldier asking where the "latrine" is, and he gets an answer like, "The head is on the starboard side, aft, below the coxn's flat." Unless he's been over here a while, he winds up sitting back down, with his legs crossed and a puzzled look on his face. We can't help laughing when they call the fantail "the back of the boat," or a hatch, a "door." Besides that, they have to get used to hearing "topside" and "below," instead of "upstairs" and "downstairs." After being here a while, though, they talk like sailors. I don't mean using dirty words. We understand what they mean when they talk about an operation in the field.*

*I am on Tango 9 now, instead of Tango 6. They have one guy on R&R and another guy went home on emergency leave. They don't expect him to come back. Anyway, I am probably the only guy in the squadron that mans two 20MM cannons, now. Tango 9 is different from Tango 6. It has a helo pad on it. It's ironic. After serving on the largest warship and aircraft carrier in the world, the USS Enterprise. This type of boat is the <u>smallest</u> aircraft carrier in the world!*

*I don't know when I'll be home. Every week I hear a different story. Some guys act like they've got a "hot line" with LBJ, and they are sure we'll be home Dec. 15th. Other guys are just <u>positive</u> we will be here until March. Myself, I just don't know. I would guess at somewhere between the two!*

*My boat captain on this boat is a colored guy. He doesn't seem too bad. When I was taken off Tango 6, everybody told me how my old boat captain tried to get them to take our engineman, "Tiny," a 3rd Class P.O., instead of me. That was pretty nice of him. He and I got along pretty great.*

*I can't wait to drive the new car. I'll be looking for a picture of it, too!*

*Well, this a pretty short letter, but there's nothing here to talk about. I'll sign off now. I should be getting the tape recorder back within a month. I'll try to write again <u>soon</u>.*

*Love,*

*Terry*

In the above letter, I told the family that I was transferred from Tango 6 to Tango 9 because *"They have one guy on R&R and another guy went home on emergency leave."* Actually, it was because Taylor was killed, one of the crew was in the hospital, and another was wounded, but still in action. I also lied when I told them that if there was an attack on Saigon, Riv Ron 13 wouldn't be involved in the action.

Troops of both the 3/39th and 4/39th, moved into eastern Long An Province, south of Can Giouc Monday, September 9th, in an effort to find Viet Cong that had been hit by gunships of 7-1 Air Cavalry. They were being lifted into the area by helicopters and River Assault Squadron 13 and 15 boats.

In other Group Bravo operations, seventy sampans and six junks were searched Sunday night by Task Unit Starlight boats conducting interdiction operations along the Kinh Dong Dien and Rach Doi.

Task Group Bravo units conducted several routine insertions and extractions without incident Tuesday, September 10th, in eastern Long An Province. The ships of MRG Bravo shifted anchorage from Nha Be to the intersection of the Song Vam Co and Cua Soirap.

On Friday, September 13th, both task groups supported the 9th Infantry's Second and Third Brigades. Second Brigade infantrymen reported six of their men wounded in action, as a result of booby traps, before wrapping up operations in central Dinh Tuong Province and in the northwestern section of Kien Hoa Province.

River Division 132 supported the 3/39<sup>th</sup> Infantry near Can Giouc in Long An Province. Five members of the Navy's UDT (Underwater Demolition Team) 11's Hotel Detachment, returned to MRB Bravo, after completing thirteen days of operations with the 51<sup>st</sup> Infantry Division of Cu Chi. The team had been conducting searches for arms and document caches along the Tho Mo River.

The boats of Riv Div 131 moved from the junction of the Song Vam Co and the Cua Soirap arriving in Dong Tam, Friday, the 13<sup>th</sup>, about 1800, after passage through the Cho Gao canal. Three weeks prior, three Alpha boats and a monitor were ambushed while making the same trip and a week prior, a PBR was hit. Intelligence sources informed us that the local V.C. Chief put out the word that any boats transiting the canal between now and October 20<sup>th</sup> would be sunk.

MRB Alfa moved from My Tho to Dong Tam Friday morning.

### Saturday, September 14, 1968. Audio tape to Judi
*Hi Babe!*

*I'm on the stern of Tango 9, my new boat. We're in Dong Tam harbor. We got here yesterday evening. The transit took us about six or eight hours, from Nha Be. On the way here, I saw the ships of the Mobile Riverine Base for River Assault Squadrons 9 and 11. I was excited. I thought I was finally going to get my camera and tape recorder back, from Corky, on the Askari. I tried to call him on the radio, but couldn't reach him. This morning, I tried again. Then, I looked out, into the harbor and saw all the ships pulling out. A guy from Riv Ron 9 told me they are going on an operation and won't be back until the first of October. "Curses! Foiled again!" It's a big joke with all the guys around here that I can't get my camera and tape recorder back! Every time we go near the Askari and Riv Ron 9 and 11, they move!*

*I have liberty, tonight. I don't know if I'll take it. I need to send my folks a tape. I only have about $2.00. I can only buy a few beers with that. Beers at the E.M. Club are fifteen cents.*

*I've got something to tell you. I don't know if you're going to like it. I feel kind of stupid about it. I told you I'm trying to quit smoking. I've switched from Pall Mall's to Winston's, or Marlboro's. I'll smoke either one. They're both filter tip. This guy on Tango 9, "Ledford," is going to quit, too, so we decided to put a bet on it. I wanted to put about $25 on it, but he said $25 didn't mean anything to him, so we're going to bet $50! If we go until I leave here, then the bet is just off, but by that time, I think I'll kick the habit. I don't like smoking, but…Over here, there are a lot of things that just make you…. um… nervous …sometimes. You can't carry booze on the boat. You want to smoke, or drink, or something.*

*My old boat, Tango 6, had barbells made that won't roll around if the river gets rough. They are 90 pounds. So, besides quitting smoking, I'm going over there and start lifting weights with Ledford and the guys on Tango 6. I'm trying to get myself in shape before I come home, for ya. I'm weight lifting, eating every meal and quitting smoking! I don't want to be your "bean pole" when I come home!*

*Dong Tam has changed a lot since we got here. They're always building it up. When we first got here, there were a lot of tents. It's getting to be a pretty big base!*

*When we got in, last night, I saw Freddy and Grif's old boat. I went over and talked to the guys on it. They were pretty nice guys. One of the guys, I thought "got it," but he didn't………*

*We were nervous coming down the river, yesterday. I don't know if I should tell you this or not. It's about the Soi Rap Vam Co that runs between Nha Be and Dong Tam. We don't always cross it, but we did this time. I don't know why. Anyway, a V.C. chief put out the word to sink any boat that comes through. It's a heavily populated VC area, and yesterday was Friday the 13<sup>th</sup>,* (nervous laugh) *so everybody was kind of… nervous!*

*I was working on my guns all day, both 20MM cannons. They told me I had BOTH 20's and I'm going to be covering both sides of the boat, so I was working on them, like mad. I had an M-16 in the gun mount, with five clips. There's about twenty rounds in each clip. I was all ready to get them! We passed through and nothing happened. I guess he just chickened out. Maybe it was because there was a whole division of boats. I don't know. It's nothing to sweat. Riv Ron 13… we never get into anything. I'm not complaining either. We're lucky. I guess Charlie thinks that "13" is bad luck for him, or something.*

*We carried a protestant chaplain and a medic, on our boat, yesterday, since it is a "flattop" and they use it for medical evacuation. I was wondering if the chaplain was going to man a gun, if we got into it. I wondered if he would take one of the guns. There were three guys in the well deck, counting him and we have six machine guns. He couldn't very well say there wasn't any room. I think he would take it, though. They kind of sanction our actions, over here, just by volunteering for it.*

*I just played that part back. I hate talking about that kind of stuff, Honey. It just kind of comes out, sometimes.*

*I'll send home some Polaroid pictures, every once in a while, so you can tell if the weight lifting is doing any good or not. I'm not doing it just to put on muscle, but to put on some weight. I don't care if it's fat! I just want to put on some weight!*

*I don't know what time it is. My watch rusted up and stopped, so I took it off and stomped on it. Sometimes, my nerves get the best of me.*

*I always think about what we're going to talk about the first night I come home. I know what you're thinking, right now, that I'm not going to want to talk, but I will! At least for five minutes! No…. We have an awful lot to talk about when I come home. I think you can play a lot of this tape for your folks and my folks, if you want. The tape's for you. Do what you want. Lock it up in your closet, if you want.*

*I'm anxious to hear what you're going to do about a car. It doesn't matter to me if you get one now, or wait for me. Either way has its advantages. If you get it now, maybe you'll get used to driving it and we can get the bills paid off. I'd like to help you pick it out, but it's up to you. Your dad or your brother can go with you.*

*It's getting close to sunset, now. You'd be surprised how beautiful it is here, along the river. Guys are always taking pictures. A lot of places here, are pretty. When we were on operations up in Nha Be, there was real thick jungle on both sides of the river and the water was real dark green, but it was clear. You could watch something you threw in go all the way to the bottom. When I was sitting up on the "con" one time with "Mac," my boat captain on Tango 6, I said; "Isn't it beautiful, Mac?" He said "No!" He just doesn't like the country.*

*I don't imagine we'll be getting any mail while we're down here. I don't know how long we'll be here, either. We are going on an operation the 16<sup>th</sup>. Today is the 14<sup>th</sup>. I think the operation is supposed to last four days. I don't mind being here at Dong Tam. It's better than being at Nha Be. Nha Be is a PBR base. They don't like the RAG (River Assault Group) sailors to even come in there because we're "ruffians!" The last time our boats went there, somebody swiped two M-60 machine guns, two grenade launchers and a whole bunch of other stuff.*

*It made them kind of mad. Besides that, in the enlisted men's club when everybody's drinking, the rivalry between the PBR sailors and the RAG sailors can get nasty.*

*There's a PBR coming in the harbor, right now. I think I told you about what happened on Tango 6. There was a PBR tied up behind it and one of its 50 cal. machine guns went off. It put a hole right through the "head" (bathroom) hanging off the stern of Tango 6 and It went through the head and into the C-Rations stacked around the gun mounts. Fortunately, nobody was sitting in it!*

*I think the monsoon season is about over. It hasn't been raining that much, maybe once every couple days. In August, it was raining just about every day. August was cloudy, 35% of the month. It didn't rain as much as I was expecting, from what people were telling me.*

*I'm tempted to go get a beer, now. Maybe if I get a beer, I can get a buddy, to help me talk. I think I'll do that.*

I came back to the tape recorder with Jerry Ranson. He and I were in the same training class. His bunk was across from mine. On the plane to Saigon, I sat in the window seat and Jerry sat next to me. We were both assigned to River Assault Squadron 13. Jerry was a devout Catholic boy, from Chicago. He always seemed to use an economy of words, using one word answers, when other guys would use ten. He liked to get to the point.

I asked Jerry if he heard about my bet with Glenn Ledford.

> *Your bet? No. What is it?*

> *We bet $50 on who starts smoking first.*

> *I've got $90 bet on the election.*

I asked *"Who you voting for?"*

> *Humphrey.*

> *I don't know. I don't like Humphrey. I don't like Nixon, either.*

> Changing the subject to something more urgent, Jerry asked: *"Did you hear where we're going, tomorrow?"*

> *Where?*

> *"Route 66!"*

My anxiety immediately shot up. *"Route 66"* was a dangerous spot. It was straight and narrow. It meant an almost certain ambush. I tried to hide it from Judi when I simply responded with a nervous laugh and replied:

> *Oh, yeah?*

(*"Route 66"* is one of the most famous highways in American History. It is known as *"The Mother Road,"* or *"The Main Street of America."* It ran from Chicago, Illinois, through Missouri, Kansas, Oklahoma, Texas, New Mexico, and Arizona before ending at Santa Monica, California, covering a total of 2,448 miles. It passes through, near my home, and I have traveled it, often. With the development of our interstate highway system, much of what used to be Route 66, has become circumvented. It has been featured in movies, songs, and TV shows. It was a popular TV show, from 1960, to 1964, featuring Martin Milner, George Maharis, Glenn Corbett, as two young guys, traveling Route 66 in a Chevy Corvette. Glenn Corbett played the role of a Vietnam veteran. The real name of *"Route 66"* was the Kinh Xang. It was a canal, built by the French. It came out, near Dong Tam, at the Song My Tho.)

Jerry added to the tension when he said, *"All the way down to the bridge."*

*I didn't know we had an operation, tomorrow.*

*First thing! Six o'clock!*

*Who we carryin'? ARVN?*

*I don't know.*

*All boats?*

*Yeah. Everybody. We're going to be up front.*

Jerry's boat, at the time, was our flame thrower, which we referred to as a *"Zippo,"* after the iconic cigarette lighter. *"You, on the Zippo?"*

*Roger.*

*What's the other Zippo gonna be doing?*

Jerry's voice was almost drowned out by the sound of chopper flying overhead.

*I don't know where they're going to put it.*

*Have you seen the formation, already?*

*Yeah*

With tension in my voice, I asked Jerry where my boat was, in the formation;

*Where's 9?*

He hesitated for an uncomfortably long time, then with his head down, murmured,

*I think you're "sweepin'," to tell you the truth!*

I laughed, nervously, afraid to communicate my concern in the tape to Judi. It meant our boat would be in the front of the column, doing mine sweep duty. Our boat would be the first to enter an ambush zone and the first one to cruise over a mine, before our mine sweep gear could catch the wires to a detonator hidden on the bank. We could prevent a mine from exploding under a boat behind us, but we couldn't stop a mine from blowing us out of the water. It was the Navy equivalent of an Army infantryman taking *"point."*

*BREAK*

*I had to leave, because they started shifting the boats around, getting them ready to go on the op, tomorrow. I didn't know we had one. We were supposed to get some rest for about four days. It's not working out that way, though. I think I ought'a go up and get some beers right now, Honey. So, I'll close for now, O.K.? I love you.*

### Continuing tape, in a very inebriated voice.

*I don't know if the tape is going, or not. (Laughing) Judi, this is Terry! I've been over, drinkin.' I've had a whole bunch of beers. Glenn Ledford is supposed to be here in a few minutes to help me finish the tape. I got*

*over there and everybody was drinkin' and they wanted me to catch up. I had to drink two beers, "chug-a-lug" and then just for grins, I drank a third beer, chug-a-lug. Then we just started gulping them down the rest of the time. It was a lot of fun. I had a hard time getting back to the boat. It's bad trying to cross from one boat to another, when you're drunk.*

(With that, I yelled to a group of guys on the bank.)

*Hey guys, when you see Ledford, tell me, will ya? He's plowed under! He's going to help me finish a tape to my girl! He's kind'a drunk! He can't handle it! He was talking to Elrod, just a few minutes ago, up by the office!! Old Elrod's "sweating it."*

*I think I have sand on my hands. I don't know WHY I have sand on my hands! One guy fell in a ditch, on the way over here and I helped pull him up out of the ditch. Then I fell down. He told me to get up or the shore patrol would get me. I told him I didn't care about the Shore Patrol.*

*(Laughing) I got it on, now. I'm playing it back! I noticed I called it a record player! It's not a record player! It's a tape recorder! Not a record player!*

Dennis Alexander, *"Alex,"* from my old boat, Tango 6, joined me. He had been drinking, also. Both of us laughed, joked, and did our best to make coherent sentences, often failing in the endeavor.

I turned to Alex and slurred,

> *Our boat captain just said to throw away our beers! We had to throw them over the side! (Laughing) Wait! I gotta tell my girl about it, again! Black One came over and said: "Who has beer on the boat?" Then, none of us said anything and he came over and said; "You got beers on the boat! You got beers on the boat! Get rid of these beers on the boat! What are ya' tryin' to do? Ya' tryin' to get hung or somethin'? Ya' tryin' to get hung? Ya tryin' to get locked up?" Tell her what the rules, .... the regulations are, about beer on the boat.*

Summoning as much seriousness as he could muster, Alex spoke, sounding very much like a drunken professor,

> *The regulations are,.... that you shall not have... It's kind'a like a rule.... Thou shall not have beers upon the boat!*

Laughter erupted, over our brilliant and thorough summation of the regulations on alcoholic beverages.

Alex left and Frank *Little One* Springer joined in. I introduced Frank;

> *I'm talking with Little One, right now. His real name is Frank Springer!*

> *Alias, "The Rat."*

> *Yes. Alias "The Rat," or "Little One!" Most of the guys call him "Little One," I think. What do they call you most of the time; "Little One," or "The Rat?"*

> *Little One.*

> *Little One? He looks a lot like Frank Judge! You don't know Frank Judge, though, do you?*

> *No.*

*You look a lot like Frank Judge. I went to school with him since third grade. He's kind of short. I'm kind of "short," too. I've only got four months left! We're drinking Schlitz! Ledford and I had TWO cigarettes!*

Frank was aware of the bet Ledford and I had. He correctly guessed, *"Both at the same time?"*

I continued, *"Yes! I got beer and "Little One" has a beer. Why do we call you "Little One?"*

*I don't know. Taylor named me that.*

*Taylor? We won't talk about Taylor. I want to know what happened to Ledford! I think I ought'a go lookin' for Ledford! You wanna help me go lookin' for Ledford? He was talkin' to Elrod, up by the office, up there on the beach!*

I'm sure I sounded pretty cold to Frank, with the remark concerning Taylor. Again, I couldn't tell Judi, or my family that I had replaced a man who had been killed. It wasn't just Taylor. All of us refrained from much talk of anyone who had died. It's the universal defense mechanism of any war.

Little One offered, *"Ledford's probably lying face down, somewhere!"*

Barely able to form a sentence, I exclaimed,

*Well good grief! We ought'a catch him if he's gonna be laying down, someplace! You're NOT supposed to be layin' in a ditch, in Vietnam! That's unhealthy! Actually, it's healthy! If a mortar attack comes and you're layin' in a ditch, what are the chances you're gonna get hit? Tell her! What are the chances?*

*Umm.. I don't think they shoot at ditches.*

*They don't shoot at ditches! Charlie doesn't aim at ditches! We ought'a go find Ledford. Tell you what, I'm gonna go find Ledford. Will you sit here and watch the tape recorder for me while I go watch for Ledford?*

*Alright.*

*Just make sure it doesn't fall over the side! It's got a habit of getting' up and walkin' ... oops. Spilled my beer!*

## Break

*Well, I don't know how this part is going to come out. This is the next day. I think it is Sunday, the 15th. We're out on the operation. I was pretty drunk, last night. It was pretty wild. When you hear me drunk like that, I don't know what you'll think, but that's how I get when I'm on a happy drunk.*

*Right now we're beached and I'm standing in the Mark 19 mount, the "after" mount. That is, the very back mount, on the boat. I'm keeping an eye on the other bank, in case Charlie wants to come up behind us, while we're beached. I haven't seen it happen, though. The weapon I've got in front of me is a grenade launcher that fires about four hundred grenades a minute. It's pretty mean.*

*Sorry I haven't gotten a letter to you. It's been about three days, I think. I'll finish this, then I should be able to write one, too. Then I have to get one of these things off to my folks.*

*I've got a picture for you. It's me, in my 20MM mount. It was taken just before we left to come down here. I just finished putting two of your pictures in waterproof plastic, up in my mount, giving me something to look at when we're going down the river, besides looking at the banks and all the gooks along the river.*

*When I left, last night, I didn't know it, but I left the tape recorder on, so there's a while that it just goes on. We're still on the op, now. It's going to be an awfully long one. We didn't know it, but the tide has just about gone out and I doubt if there's ten feet of water, outside my gun mount, between the boat and the bank. It's awfully shallow. The boats are made to go in shallow streams, but not THIS shallow. The boat has a three foot draft. The boats are having trouble, today. We're getting stuck, up on sand bars. Well, they're not exactly "sand" bars. They're MUD bars! It's really been a mess, today. I've had to stay at "general quarters" all day and it's really hot in this gun mount. We've been waitin' for the tide to start comin' in, but it hasn't done it! Right now, we're passin' an old hootch that some Vietnamese abandoned, some time ago. The roof has fallen off of it and the walls are leanin,' fallin' off. I don't like goin' down rivers this..... narrow. This isn't really a river. It's more like a "channel."*

*One the guys I know from my old boat got caught sleepin' on watch, the other night. Now, instead of being a Petty Officer 3rd Class, he's been broken to the rank of Seaman Recruit! I better watch myself, closer and make sure I don't fall asleep on watch. I'd sure hate to go back a Seaman Recruit!*

*I think the tides comin' in, now. We just passed a stream and I noticed the water's coming into this channel. You wouldn't believe what a mess this has been, today. We haven't been shot at, or anything, but it is almost impossible to navigate in this water. It's incredibly difficult to turn around in it. We had to beach.... They're revving up the engines, for something. Maybe we're stuck...I don't know. We had to beach, pretty far up on the bank, then back off, to turn around. It's impenetrably thick, dense jungle, in front of me. There is hardly any air moving. It feels good when a little breeze comes through the slit in my gun mount.*

**This is the typical view, looking out, over my 20MM cannon.**

*We've got armored plating all around us, and separating the gun mounts from the coxn's flat. It's really stuffy. Right now, we're beached. We're pickin' up troops. I think we're pickin' up ARVN troops. I think you know what "ARVN" means. It's the Army of the Republic of Vietnam. An awful lot of trees around here. High trees. You don't get that an awful lot, here in the Delta. Maybe high palms, or what they call "Nipa palm." I don't know if you're going to be able to hear me, with the way the engines are racing.*

*Oh. We AREN'T "beached." We ARE stuck in the mud! You wouldn't believe how much this mud stinks, either! Bird is racing the engine, trying to get us off of it. We go in some pretty shallow water, sometimes. Right now, this looks more like a "creek," than anything else! The C.O. of River Division 131 is pretty mad, because somebody "in charge" told him that this river was navigable at all times.*

*I was really messed up, last night. I would say you wouldn't believe it, but I guess you do. You heard me. This is kind of a quiet op, right now. Nothing's happening. You may have heard me when I was talking to Jerry Ranson, and he said we were going down "Route 66," I kind of laughed. Then he said we were "sweeping," then I REALLY laughed. You see, "Route 66" is where squadrons 9 and 11 operate. It's very long and very narrow. Parts of it are populated and parts of it is unpopulated. They nearly always get ambushed when they go up it, or down it. One of the two. I won't say "ALWAYS," but pretty often. That's where we are, right now, see? But you get a feeling when an op starts… whether or not something's going to happen, by the area and other things. I can't explain it. I just KNOW if something's going to happen or not. There's not going to be a shot fired on this operation. When he said we were "sweepin,' I started laughing, because that means mine sweeping, and you're out in the very front of the column, ……going down an……. ambush site,….. as the first boat in the column…….. It's kind of bad. It may sound weird that I laughed about it, but that's the way it is over here. You can't worry about it, or it will drive you crazy, so you laugh about it.*

*When we were drinking last, night, we did away with our bet, for about four cigarettes, but I haven't had any, since then. $50 is a lot of money!*

*They stopped racing the engines. Oh. One of them died. No wonder. Now, they're dropping the ramp.*

(My voice is tense, at this point.)

*I played back an old tape I got back from you and the folks. I guess I got it two or three weeks ago. It's hard to tell time, anymore. It was funny. You were reading that sex education book…*

*Oh… I thought we were off the mud, for a minute. I don't know, now. He's not racing the engines, anyway. Ohhh…. One of them died! No wonder!*

*Now they're dropping the ramp. Getting troops on, now. We're carrying the 6th of the 31st, of the 9th Infantry.*

*Anyway, on that tape, my mom was telling me about their new car. I can't wait to drive it! It sounds terrific!*

*Well, we just finished picking up troops. We'll be trying to head out, if we don't get stuck, again.*

(There was a Vietnamese "Tiger Scout" among the troops of the 9th Infantry Division's 6/31st that we picked up. He advised us to watch for an ambush, ahead.)

*I'll certainly be glad when this operation is over.*

*Uh... oh... Now our engine is dead and our bow is swinging around and going to hit the beach.*

*Now, our bow just hit the beach and we're backing up. I told you it's a mess, Judi!*

*Oh, great. The engines went out, again.*

(At this point, I thought our boat was being left behind, alone and without engines.)

*I see one Tango boat way ahead of us, getting ready to go.*

*Oh, boy. It will be a mess if we lose our engines, here!*

*He gets them started, then they die again. It just died, again.*

*Here we go again..... We just drifted up on the beach........ No engines.*

*He gets it started. Then, when he puts it in gear, pushing the throttle forward, it dies....*

*In the background, Bird, the "Cox'n," is yelling; "I can't! I ain't got no engines!"*

*We're supposed to get four day's rest. Then, we're supposed to go on an operation.*

*Oh, good! Now I can see on the other side! I thought we were the last Tango boat, 'cause I could only see one way, down the river. Now, I see the other Tango boats. There's one... two... three... four...five. There's at least five boats behind us.*

*It's a mess, Judi. You just wouldn't believe it.*

*We still haven't got our engines. We're just BOUNCING from one bank to the other.*

(Speaking to other crewman, over our sound powered phones)

*Oh, no. I can just see em' tyin' us up to another boat! What are they going to do? Tie them on TOP of us? There ain't ROOM on the sides! What? I wouldn't doubt it!*

*Just talking to one of the guys on the sound powered phones. Each of the guns has a phone headset, as well as the captain and the guy in the well deck. Because of our helmets, we only have one earpiece on one ear.*

*It just came over the radio that they're gonna have another boat tied up to us and they're gonna take us out. I don't know how they're gonna do it! The river isn't wide enough to get another boat alongside us! That's how bad it is!*

*You can see now why it's hard to quit smoking, over here.*

*We're in one of the worst spots in the Mekong Delta, and....we.... have..... no.... engines.*

(Laughing, nervously) *It's ridiculous!*

*I guess one of the things bad about it is that the jungle is so thick and the river is so straight and narrow. "Charlie" can see us coming for a long, long time. He may be able to see our engines are out and that we're being towed.*

*He can get set up for us....and he... can ... fire ...down,... from up on the banks....*

*It's a pretty steep bank in some places, and he can fire from the trees. I don't know. It's just a mess.*

*Anyway, like I said; nothing's happened, today and nothing WILL happen!*

*I just got that feeling.*

*If anything was gonna happen, it would have happened before now.*

Break

*I just had to go up and rig a tow li...*

*Like I started to say and got cut off, I had to go up to the bow and rig a tow line. The boat ahead of us is towing us. Our engines are out.*

*We're on our way out of the "Route 66" channel, finally.*

*I'll be glad when this day's over!*

*After that little drinking spree, last night, I was feeling a little bad, today! For one thing, being cooped up in this gun mount, wearing a shirt, flak jacket, helmet, no air, and nothing to eat, I was hurtin'! Bad shape! But, after I got up there to fix up the tow line, I took the lid off my gun mount. There's air coming in, now. I feel pretty good! I know your mom wouldn't like this job, with her claustrophobia.*

*I think you've seen a picture of it. My arms go in between two bars that are in kind of a "U" shape. The trigger's mounted on the right bar. I feel kind'a cramped up, sometimes, especially when..... Oh well.*

*I think I just heard somethin' on the radio about beachin' again. I hope not. I want to just get out of here. It's gettin' old. This whole thing is getting' old.*

*I used to count operations that I've been on. When I got on Tango 6, about four months ago, I had been on nine or ten operations, but since then, we've been goin' out a lot more often. It's been quite a while. I couldn't guess how many I've been on.*

*On one tape, you talked about wanting to wait to give me my Christmas present, when I came home. I think that's a good idea, 'cause it is hard for me to send Christmas presents home, from here. Please tell my folks that if they want to get me anything, to please wait until I come home! You and I will do the same! You CAN send me some cookies, or something!*

*There's a Cobra helicopter flying above me. They are really mean! They carry rockets and mini-guns. The mini-guns fire so fast, it looks like they're firing a laser beam, the tracers are going out, so fast!*

*I've been in this gun mount, all day. I've got a carton of cigarettes in front of me, and I haven't touched one!*

*Passing by these trees and bushes and just the way the weather is, really makes me wish I was home, this time of year, or during the summer.*

*I've only been home during the summer, one time, since I've been in the Navy. Oh well.... Maybe you'll be with me, next summer!*

*Cobra gunships are coming in pretty low, for close support. I wouldn't mind being a gunner on one of them!*

*We've passed a lot of hootches! I've seen several with pigs out in front, but no people. That's a bad sign. If you're goin' down the river and you see a bunch of hootches and there's no people around, it's kind'a spooky. It gives you an idea how the people feel about you. It's the same thing when you see a lot of women and children in sampans, coming in your direction, leaving an area you are heading towards. In other places, all the kids will be on the banks, waving, and asking for "chop chop," which is food.*

*Oh. There's a couple old mama-sans, with their kids, now.*

*There's a couple kids, with their hands out, waiting for "chop chop." That's a relief!*

*Several hootches back there didn't have anybody around them, though.*

*It may be just a rumor, or a "legend," but I've heard that last year, a captured V.C. was tied, "spread eagle," on the bow of a Tango boat. That Tango led a column of boats down the river and into a narrow channel. As the boats got farther into the narrow channel, they encountered women and children flowing out, in the opposite direction.*

*Soon, after the last of the women and children passed the boats, the low rumble of the diesel engines was drowned out by the screams of the V.C. captive, warning to his comrades, ahead.*

*The story goes that the boats opened up with all of their automatic weapons, cannons and grenades launchers, then turned, beaching the boats on alternate sides of the river, dropping their bow ramps into the thick, stinking, mud, disembarking troops to attack the Viet Cong in their bunkers. That's when the screaming of the captured V.C. was silenced, forever.*

*Like I said, I don't know if it's true or not, but that's what I heard!*

*We're going to be out of the canal in a few minutes. Then I have to go up and take off the bow line. I'll probably have to go, so...*

*Just passed a bunch of water buffalo, taking their evening bath. They probably get clean more often than I do.*

*Sometimes we pass by women, bathing on the river banks. As we pass by, at four or five miles an hour, ogling the women at twenty or thirty yards, sometimes with binoculars, the women stare back. They don't understand the intense interest in the simple act of somebody taking a bath.*

*There's a whole bunch of really cute kids out here. I often wonder what they're going to be when they grow up, if you know what I mean. What will Vietnam be, when they grow up?*

*They've got their hands out. They get a kick out of saluting us. If you salute back, they really get a charge out of it. All too often, the children come to see us on primitive stick crutches, missing legs, or feet. Sometimes, it's hands or arms. You can't say for sure if their wounds are war related, or simply the speed of terrible infections, in this hot and humid climate. Whatever the cause, it breaks your heart.*

*A lot of people are out here, now.*

*You hear about Asia, or Southeast Asia having a population explosion. You can see it, over here. Every time you go past a hootch.... Wait a second. Another helo is going over....*

*Every time you go past a hootch, there's either a little sister, or an old grandma, or a mother, holding a new kid. A lot of times, the mother will be working in the field, and you see little girls, maybe seven years old, carrying the kid around.*

*Just passed what I believe was a.... Yeah. Catholic Church. They have a Mass going on. It looked like an old warehouse, at first. There's a lot of people out here, now. We're passing through a busy section.*

*Their homes are still made out of grass. Their major buildings, like the church and, I guess the equivalent of a police station, have plaster walls. A few of the rich people have metal sheets for the roofs of their grass hootches. They are the "well to do," though.*

*There's a big store and a bunch of shops, here. This is the first time I've seen a place like this. It's a regular "trading post!"*

A Cobra helicopter flew over us and climbed, straight up, high into the air. I yelled to Hodge and Ledford to look at it. *Little One* was in the well deck and couldn't see it. Lt. J.G. Conaty later recorded that a helo was taking sniper fire from the ground. That would explain what the Cobra pilot was doing. He was trying to get out of range of the sniper rounds.

I waived and called out *"Chao Anh,"* to a Vietnamese man who waived to us.

*We're going to be going under a bridge, pretty quick. It's going to be very low.*

*Well, I was sitting up, kind of high on my mount. I was exposed from about the shoulders, up. We're out of the populated area, now, and I uh.... Got down.*

*We went under a very low bridge and had to put our aerials down, to get under it. A banner over the bridge promoted the "Chieu Hoi" program, encouraging Viet Cong to turn themselves in "Open Arms" of the South Vietnamese government.*

*People got friendlier as we went along. I guess that's because we got closer to Dong Tam. We haven't got much farther to go. It's going pretty smoothly, now. None of the boats are getting stuck, and we're still under tow. Tomorrow, we'll probably be getting worked on, all day.*

*By the way, Ledford and I got our liberty cancelled by our boat captain, for bringing our half drank beers on the boat, last night. Yesterday was the first day of liberty we've had in a month, because we've been on constant operations.*

*It's dusk, now. The sun's going down and it's cooling off. I can finish this up and send it, tonight. I should work on one for the folks, too. I'll try to send them both, at the same time.*

*Well, Honey, We're back to Dong Tam. It's dark. I don't know what time it is. We got back, without a hitch. No trouble, at all. I took my bath in the harbor. It's going to be weird to get home and take a hot bath, or shower, with soap! All I've been doing is taking showers with a bucket, a hose, or jumping in the river!*

*I think this tape is going to end soon, Honey. I'll sign off, for now. I love you, Judi. I can't wait till I'm home.*

*God, I miss you.*

Task Group Bravo moved from the intersection of the Song Vam Co and Cua Soirap to Dong Tam, Monday, September 16th. The U.S.S. Vernon County, U.S.S. Satyr and APL-26 got underway at 0400 and arrived outside Dong Tam at 1330.

**Letter from Dad. Started, September 16, 1968. Monday**
*Dear Terry,*

*So glad to hear you on the phone. It was Friday night here, one half hour after midnight. Today's paper says fifteen Navy men were injured moving troops, fifteen miles south of Saigon. It sure keeps us on edge, hoping you are not involved, or hurt in the action.*

*Also knowing there is not much we can do from here. (Terry, can you believe it, it is now 9pm, Oct. 1. I'm just finishing this letter! I just wrote out my first payment on the car. And say…. I want to thank you so very much for the two $100 bills that you sent us. It was sure used to good advantage, and more than paid your phone obligation. In fact, I feel guilty about most of it, as it was surely our pleasure to hear you all the time.*

*Terry, I never felt so near to you as when we listened to you on the tapes you sent to Judi "Si" and us. It was sure interesting. When you were describing about the boat's motors failing to start, it seemed like we were right there. Anyway, keep your <u>head</u> down, even it if gets hot in the gun turrets.*

*Yesterday, your mother and I went to a party of old friends we used to know before we were married—about ten couples. Before I forget, you know I want to know about the specs on your boat, and you would like to know the specs on the new car.*

*68 Pontiac 9 Passenger Wagon (Ventura, Extra foam interior)*
*Color-Aleutian Blue*
*8 cylinder*
*Turbo Hydra*
*Radio-Clock*
*Power Steering*
*H.P, 543*
*Power Brakes*
*Luggage Rack*
*Tint Glass-All*
*<u>AIR COND.</u>*
*White Wall Tires*
*Heavy Duty Carb. Air Cleaner*

*Thanks for Keeping in Touch—So Much*

*Dad*

**Monday, September 16<sup>th</sup>, 1968. Audio Tape Home.**
*Hi, Everybody!*

*I'm borrowing somebody's tape recorder for this, because we came down from Na Bhe, here to Dong Tam. We went past the MRB, which had Corky's ship, the Askari in it. Corky still has my tape recorder. The next morning, the MRB pulled out on operations and I hear they won't be back for at least thirty days, or even up to sixty. We'll be down here at Dong Tam for quite a while.*

*I enjoyed talking to you, the other day, although it was quick. It's hard to think of what to say on those "MARS" radio calls, because you haven't got that much time. Saying "Over" all the time kind of makes me nervous, although I do it on the radio here and it doesn't bother me.*

*I'm still sticking to my $50 bet about smoking, with Ledford. The other night we got drunk and we both smoked two cigarettes apiece. When I drink I always want to smoke more. We haven't had a cigarette since that night..*

*Today, I filled out my "dream sheet," for when my tour of duty is up, here. I think you know what my dream sheet is. It's my choices for my next duty station. They told me that I couldn't put down sea duty, because I'm not eligible. My choices are pretty good, though, I think. I put down home ports of New Orleans, or Jacksonville, Florida. My choices for types of ships are auxiliary tug, submarine tender, or CVA (aircraft carrier). A lot of guys put down "a fighting man's ship," like a cruiser, or destroyer, I guess, but I don't really care about that. I put down tug and submarine tender because they hardly ever leave port. That will keep me from making any cruises. If I make a Mediterranean cruise, that would be O.K. That would be on a CVA. A guy told me that if I didn't put down something a little less desirable, than a ship that stays in port all the time, the Navy could just give me anything. I thought that if I had to put down a ship that does go out, I'd put down a carrier, since I'm used to carriers. I don't know what I'd do on any of these ships.*

*I keep meaning to get busy on my E.T. course, here, but I just haven't got the time for it. It's not the kind of course to work on, here.*

*We had an operation yesterday. Last night, we cleaned up the boat. Today, our boat is out of the water. We got our screws messed up. We had a whole bunch of wires and stuff in them and our rudder is messed up. They're supposed to finish fixing it between nine o'clock and midnight, tonight. We have an operation, tomorrow. A schedule like this just doesn't let me work on my course.*

*As for when I come home, the way it stands, I'm to be relieved in January, but still not go home until March, because they plan on our relief crews taking over on the boats and then just putting us in Dong Tam and letting us wait here until we are supposed to go back. It doesn't make any sense to me. I don't know why they'd just want to keep a bunch of guys over here, when they just finished putting in tour on the boats.*

*Seems like the Navy likes to compromise on everything you want. I wanted shore duty when I got back, but they told me I couldn't put that down. I could be down a home port, and a type of ship that would stay in port a lot.*

*Today, another guy and I went over to the base ship fitters shop, and we checked into having a set of square barbells made up. We would trade C-Rations or something like that, for them. My old boat, Tango 6 has a set. They are sixty pounders, I think. It does you a lot of good to work out with them on these boats. Do Pat and Mike work out with the set I got them at Christmas time?*

(There is a break in the tape at this point, followed by me bringing in one of the crewmen of my boat, Glenn Ledford. I started out trying to decide how to start the conversation.

*We could start out like they do on the radio, every morning! Do you know how they start out on "The Dawn Buster Show?" You hear everybody saying it on the boats, all the time! When they start "The Dawn Buster Show," they say, "Gooooood Morning, Vietnam!"*

Ledford asked, *"What are you going to say after that?"*

> *After "Good Morning, Vietnam?" I don't know. What's the date, today?*

Ledford jokingly wondered if I was going to be talking about our bet, concerning who could go the longest without smoking;

> *I don't know. Are you trying to figure out how long since we quit smokin'?*

> *No. I'm just wondering what the date is, so they know when we taped the letter!*

> *It's ten after three. Today is the 17th of September, 1968.*

*Yeah. I knew the YEAR! Oh great! We're going to have to work. It's ten after three and we're sitting underneath our boat, since it's up on blocks and our boat captain just woke up which means we're probably going to have to go to work, right?*

*Right! I'll roger that!*

*Every time he wakes up, we have to go to work.*

*Tell them what our boat captain did the other night, when we came back off liberty.*

*Well, when we came back off liberty, we were finishing up the last of our can of beer. Our boat captain came jumping out of his coxswain's flat, and pounced upon us for having beer on the boat! Then, he canceled our liberty and screamed and hollered and panicked! But, on the plus side, he gave us our liberty back, today. He had a change of heart. He figured we'd kill him. He knew we'd kill him if he didn't, anyway.*

*I told Judi about it, on a tape I sent to her last night.*

*Our boat captain is up there, screaming and yelling and ranting and jumping up and down, right now.*

*We had engine trouble on our last operation. Like I told you on the beginning of the tape. Our screws got all messed up. We had to be towed in. The well deck was full of mud. Who'd we carry? ARVN'S?*

*No. Regular army. The 6/31ˢᵗ of the 9th Infantry Division.*

*Regular army? I never even saw them. I was never in the well deck. Anyway, we got in last night. We cleaned out most of the mud in the well deck. Then we took a bath in the harbor. We got up this morning and looked out and saw all the grease and wood and trash and dead fish floating on it. It made us kind of sick, so we got up this morning and took a shower on the base.*

Ledford and I started talking about the Command and Communications Boat of our River Assault Squadron. I explained to those at home,

*A "Charley boat" is a CCB, a Command and Communications Boat. It hast a 20MM cannon, up forward, one on both sides, aft, and a Mark 19 grenade launcher. It has a crew of eleven, compared to our seven. I wonder why they have so many.*

As a radioman, Glenn Ledford explained,

*They need more guys to man the radios. That's what that boat is all about! It's for communications. They have more than two or three radios! They have to coordinate with all the Army units, the different ships, air support, all KINDS of things that would be on different frequencies. You know, Commodore Blundell, who goes by the radio call sign, "Snow Whirl," would be on there!*

I agreed, adding, *"Yeah. Then there's Vaught, the Commanding Officer of Riv Div 131. He's "Mariner India."*

Ledford laughed, *"Should we tell them about Clarence and Peveril?*

*Yes! First you tell them who Peveril is!*

Ledford explained, *"Commander Perevil Blundell is the Commodore of River Assault Squadron 13!"*

I jumped in, adding, *"And then there is Lt. Clarence Vaught, the Commanding Officer of River Assault Division 131. We just refer to them as "Clarence and Peveril." If you say it like "Perevil Clarence," it sounds like some kind of medical condition, or disease! You have to understand, though, we like and respect both of them. They are real leaders. We just like to joke about their names!"*

*I roger that!*

*We always like to imitate Clarence. Whenever somebody tells him something on the radio, he says, "I roger that!"*

Ledford started laughing. *"You can tell by his tone, how pleased he is, by how he says it! "I'll roger THAT!" or, "I'll ROGER that!"*

*He's a real comedian! Lt. Meeks is kind of funny on the radio, too! I think he's pretty cool. I've talked to him a lot! He's O.K.! One time, he came over the radio and told one of the boats to move over from where it was beached on the river, to let some Army guys on the stern of another boat. The boat asked; "Why do you want us to do that?" He simply said; "Because they can't walk on water." It was funny! An officer usually just doesn't SAY stuff like that on the radio! "Mr. C" is cool, too!*

Looking for clarification, Ledford asked, *"Conaty?"*

I confirmed. *"Yeah. Mr. Conaty."* What is he? *"Mariner India One?"*

Ledford threw his hands up. *"I don't know! I don't care, really!"*

*O.K. We can tell them the code names of all the officers. Then, they can send them in to "Hanoi Hannah."*

*She's probably got all of them, anyway!*

I changed the subject. *"Who are you gonna vote for? Nixon?"*

Ledford laughed. *"I'm not overly ambitious about either one of them!"*

*"That's about the way I am. Who are your folks gonna vote for?*

*Humphrey, I think. They're thinking about not even voting!*

Proudly, I announced, *"I've got my absentee ballot! I haven't sent it in, yet, I think I'll vote for Nixon."*

Ledford agreed. *"I ought to get one, since this is my first time of being able to vote."*

I pushed Ledford a little more. *"So who would you vote for?"*

*Humphrey. To tell you the truth, I don't know why! It's just that Nixon..... He's lost so many times...... He just ought'a lose! That's all!*

*He probably feels that way, too. He probably has a complex! Here I am, cuttin' him down, but I think I'd vote for him, just for a change in policy.*

*I almost feel sorry for him. I'd almost like to see him win, just to bolster his ego, a little.*

BREAK

202

Returning to the conversation after a couple hours, I began, *"We went to chow and the PX. I went to the "Acey Ducey Club" to get our boat captain and he told me to have a beer with him, then come back to the boat to work on it, with the rest of the crew, while he has a few more drinks. Not much later, Little One went to the Acey Ducey club to get our boat captain. Black One told him to stay with him for a little while and have a couple rum and Cokes, then sent Little One back to the boat, without him.*

End of the tape.

War has often been described as *"months of boredom punctuated by moments of extreme terror."* Vietnam was no exception. One afternoon, the crew of Tango 9 was sitting around on the helo deck of the boat. We spied a duck, lazily floating down the river. Without a word between us, we looked at the duck, then looked at the box of concussion grenades, used to ward off enemy divers, then looked at the duck, then looked back at the box of grenades. Without saying a word, each of us grabbed the concussion grenades and started tossing them at the duck, which was perhaps forty, or fifty yards away. As the grenades splashed all around the duck, sending up high plumes of muddy water, the duck, looking somewhat alarmed, continued to float down the river. Since the duck wasn't under the water, the grenades probably did no harm, but they did provide us with some momentary relief from the boredom.

On another occasion, the Mobile Riverine Base was anchored in unusually clear water. Most of the time, it was anchored in a main channel that was very muddy. That night, I occupied my time by sitting on the edge of the pontoon, next to a ship, with a case of primer caps, pulling the pins and dropping them in the water. The primer caps were small metal cylinders that screwed into the concussion grenades. There was a ring on the end of them. Once you pulled the ring, you had a few seconds before the primer cap would go off. I sat, mesmerized, as they swirled down and provided the light and sound of mini-explosions, several meters down. They weren't much bigger than a firecracker, but they were mildly amusing. We were always on the lookout for distractions from where we were and what we were doing.

On Tuesday, September 17th, River Assault Division 131 boats supported the 6/30th Infantry, along the Rach Cam River, west of Dong Tam. One soldier tragically drowned Tuesday afternoon as troops of the 6/31st Infantry were loading aboard boats of Riv Div 131 west of Dong Tam. The man was wading toward an ATC when he suddenly fell in an underwater hole and disappeared from sight. A search of the area produced no trace of the missing man. I saw the soldier disappear, out of the corner of my eye. We searched for him with grappling hooks, hoping to at least retrieve his body. We didn't find him. It greatly troubled me when we left the area without being able to bring him home. I only found out recently that he was PFC Lionel Maldonado-Torres (A Co.), from Puerto Rico. My heart goes out to his family.

In Can Giouc, the 3/39th Infantry, with boats of Riv Div 132, captured one Viet Cong Tuesday and discovered a cache that included 4,200 small arms rounds and several 75MM casings.

The Second Brigade ran into fierce opposition, Wednesday, September 18th, during operations twelve kilometers (about 7.4 miles) southwest of Ben Tre. Troops of the 4/47th Infantry clashed with a V.C. force of unknown size about 1115 in the morning. Fighting continued until well after dark. Troops being airlifted in to support the action encountered hot landing zones, resulting in six helicopters being shot up and forced down. As of 2130, twenty-five Viet Cong were permanently dispatched in the action. Four Second Brigade Companies were attempting to surround the enemy force. Helicopter gunships took out fourteen of the dead Viet Cong and also destroyed a machine gun emplacement. The Army suffered two killed and twelve wounded. Both of the brave troopers killed, and eight of the wounded, were members of the 4/47th Infantry. The other four WIA were attached to Delta Company, 3/5th Air Cavalry.

River Assault Squadron 9 saw action early in the evening when they rushed to the aid of ambushed PBR's, five miles downriver from the MRB anchorage. The assault boats got underway instantly, from both the MRB and a nearby fire support base. Upon arriving at the ambush site, they saturated the banks with cannon, machine gun and grenade fire. The Viet Cong, hidden in the jungle canopy, returned fire with small arms, automatic weapons and at least one rocket, or recoilless rifle round, but the only casualty was a 40MM gunner on the Riv Div 91 CCB (Command and Communications Boat) who was wounded when a shell cooked off and exploded in his gun mount. One of the PBR crewmen was killed and three were injured in the battle.

Also operating in the Ben Tre area Wednesday, were boats of Riv Div 132 and 151, with Vietnamese regional force troops from Ben Tre. The boats beached the troops about 0930, on the south bank of the Ham Luong River, eighteen kilometers, or about eleven miles, south of Ben Tre. The *"Ruff Puffs"* had sporadic action, killing two V.C. and capturing a Chicom rifle.

MRB Alfa moved back up the Ham Luong River to the Ben Tre anchorage, Wednesday morning, and MRB Bravo shifted from Dong Tam to My Tho, Wednesday night.

Six more V.C. bodies were found Thursday, September 19th, by 2nd Brigade infantrymen, as they swept through the area of yesterday's fighting. A seventh Viet Cong was killed by troops of the 4/47th Infantry Battalion in a skirmish, about 1800, Thursday afternoon, Southeast of Ben Tre. Sixty-five bunkers were destroyed during the day. For the total four day, successful operation, eighty-four Viet Cong were eliminated.

Light Salvage Lift Craft, YLLC-2, transited from Dong Tam to Ben Tre Thursday, to join MRB Alfa.

*"Route 66"*

# Chapter 14
## Never Quite the Same

Friday, September 20th, we got word at 2200 that we were going to be headed up the Rach Bai Rai and hitting the dreaded and infamous *"Snoopy's Nose."* At 0500, we loaded the 6/31st onto some of the boats. We didn't have any of the troops on our boat. *Little One* was in the well deck, all alone, except for four .30 caliber and two .50 caliber machine guns to choose from, if they were needed. At 0630, we saddled up and headed west. We ALWAYS expected trouble at Snoopy's Nose. Whenever we went there, we had a *"high pucker factor,"* as our Lt. Conaty referred to it. The first day was eerily quiet, for the boat crews. The *grunts*, of the 6/31st had some excitement. They nabbed three Viet Cong and killed five of their buddies. We stayed overnight, just north of Snoopy's Nose. At about 0800, the next morning, we started moving south.

At 0900, we turned and beached our twenty-six boats on alternating sides of the river, to offload two companies of the 6/31st. Coincidently, it was the exact same spot *Charley* was sitting and waiting to ambush us.

It's hard to say who was more surprised, us, or them. One of our Monitors, with a 105 Howitzer mounted on its bow, beached about ten yards from a V.C. preparing to fire a rocket propelled grenade. One ATC was four feet from a Viet Cong bunker. The enemy opened up with rockets and automatic weapons from both banks. They were waiting for us. They were on top of us. We were surrounded. Too bad for them.

Our boats opened up with all weapons, including the Zippo flamethrower. My 20MM cannon couldn't swing forward enough to fire into the bank in front of our boat. The only option was to train my gun across the river, forty or fifty yards, and fire between the boats across from us. I tried to get as close to their boats as I could, without hitting them. As expected, the Viet Cong bunkers were well hidden. You couldn't differentiate the smoke of where a round just hit, or where a round, or rocket was just fired from. I didn't want them to get off a shot.

In the well deck, *Little One* was also frustrated. The .30 caliber and .50 caliber machine guns wouldn't swivel forward enough to hit the V.C. emplacements on the banks, so he grabbed an M-16 and tried to fire through a small port in the front of our bow ramp, but the M-16 kept jamming.

Above the deafening roar and smoke, I heard loud laughter. It took a couple seconds for me to realize it was coming from me. My boat captain screamed back at me; *"Sater! You O.K.? Sater! You O.K.?"* I laughed hard, and yelled back at him, *"This is fun! This is fun!"* It was an out of body experience. I felt like I was standing outside my own body, looking at a madman, wondering who he was. Obviously, it WASN'T fun, or funny. I was scared to death! When you go through a crucible of fire like that, the typical human response is *"fight, flight, or freeze."* Flight or freeze weren't really options and fight just didn't seem to be an adequate response. Laughing was just my body's way of handling the extreme stress of the situation. I wanted to utterly destroy anybody, or anything that wanted to harm me, or my friends. Anyone who has not been in combat may not fully appreciate the emotional impact the heat of battle carries. The only thing I can tell you is that it is far different from anything you may encounter playing *"Call of Duty."*

I ran out of ammo. If your return fire stops for seconds, it is enough time for the enemy to pop up and fire rockets, recoilless rifle rounds, or automatic weapons at you and your friends. As fast as I could move, I grabbed another can of 20MM ammo, ripped it open and pulled the heavy belt of ammo into the chute that channeled the rounds into my cannon. I grabbed the wrench that was used to put the proper tension on the ammo fed into the chamber of the gun. I was moving as fast as my body allowed. I didn't notice that in the process of wrenching the belt into my gun, I scrapped all of the flesh off of my knuckles. By the end of the firefight, my right hand was bleeding and the bone and cartilage of my knuckles were exposed. I didn't feel it. When I finished reloading, I continued firing.

It seemed like an eternity, but I have no idea how long the firefight actually lasted.

As the last shot was fired, I turned to sit on the base of my starboard 20MM gun mount. Our gun tubs circled us, down to around our waist, or hips. As I was doing that, Ledford was doing the same thing, behind me, in his port 20MM gun mount. Each of us sat on the base of our gun mounts, at the exact same time. Our faces were one or two feet apart. We still had our $50 bet riding on who would be the first to light up a cigarette. Our eyes locked. Without a word being spoken, and in slow motion, we mirrored each other's movements. Each of us reached into our flak jackets and pulled out a pack of cigarettes. Completely synchronized, each of us took out a cigarette. With one mind, we put the cigarettes to our lips. Watching each other carefully, each took out a lighter and lit it, at the exact same moment. No discussion was necessary

We offloaded the troops. They swept the area. We had eleven wounded men. Three of them were medevacked. Miraculously, none were killed.

After all was calm, a guy across the river from me, told me that if I had gotten one foot closer to his boat, he was going to turn his 20MM cannon on me. I told him that I knew what I was I was doing and had every intention of getting as close to his boat as I could, without hitting it. I would still do the same thing, today.

Cobra and Huey helicopter gunships provided close air support, buzzing over our heads, firing rockets in between our boats, spraying shrapnel, everywhere. They were doing the same thing from above that we were doing on the banks of the river. Thank God for them.

That night, I fell asleep, exhausted, on the helo deck of our boat. When I awoke, my right hand had swollen to twice its normal thickness. It looked like a cartoon hand. It was engorged with infection. I got to a medic as soon as I could. He cleaned the open wounds of my exposed knuckles and gave me antibiotics to kill the infection. The high heat and humidity of Vietnam served as a perfect incubator for incredibly invasive infection. I was a lucky man, in more ways than I could count. The medic told me that if I had gotten to him an hour later, I may have lost my hand.


The 6/31st Infantry Battalion took three Viet Cong prisoners and discovered a water mine, Saturday, September 21st, during a sweep, east of Snoopy's Nose. The troops were landed in mid-morning by boats of Riv Div 131. The mine, which was discovered just after the landing, was inspected and destroyed by Task Group Bravo EOD (Explosive Ordinance Disposal) personnel. Later, infantry personnel found four batteries in a bunker, believed to have been a power source for the mine.

On Saturday, September 21st, the LST, U.S.S. Westchester County joined MRB Alfa and began preparations to relieve the Whitfield County as the support LST.

As darkness fell, three infantrymen were killed and forty-three wounded in a sudden mortar attack on the Second Brigade fire support base, east of Ben Tre. Nineteen mortar rounds rained in, killing three men of the 3/47th Infantry and wounding thirty-five of the soldiers. Other soldiers wounded included four from the 15th Engineers, two from 9th S&T, one from the 9th Military Intelligence and one LRRP soldier. In addition to these casualties, the 3/47th reported seven more personnel wounded during the day, by booby traps.


At 0900, Sunday, September 22nd, River Assault Division 131 was ambushed while landing the 6/31st Infantry Division troops on the Ba Rai Stream, three miles east of Cai Be. The Viet Cong fired automatic weapons and rockets from both banks. Riverine assault craft fired all weapons, including the *Zippo's* flame throwers, suppressing the enemy fire. My 20MM cannon was out of action. A round had *cooked off* in the chamber.

With my "20" out of action, I was in the well deck, with *Little One,* and the grunts of the 6th of the 31st Infantry. There was never any doubt that when it *"hit the fan,"* our Army buddies weren't shy. They jumped on our automatic weapons, along with *Little One.*

Standing in the middle of the well deck, I grabbed an M-79 Grenade Launcher and began firing grenades into the banks of the Ba Rai Stream. One of the grunts jumped next to me. Whenever I fired a round and popped the breach open, he slammed another grenade into the breach. I probably didn't add much to the overall effort. Hodge was on the Mark 19 mount, firing out more grenades in one minute, than I could do in two hours. Still, I HAD to do whatever I could to add to the effort. If I couldn't do anything else, I would have thrown C-Rations. My loader and I were firing as fast as we could, hitting tree tops, jungle foliage, the river bank, and hopefully, the V.C. In hindsight, I was firing TOO fast.

**Tango 131-9, with curtains hanging from the helicopter pad.**

Our Tango boat had a heavy plastic sheet that hung down from the helo deck, to the walkway deck. On this particular day, it was folded up, so that it hung half-way down. With each shot, I was firing between the bottom of the curtain and the well deck. In one shot, I slapped the M-79 grenade launcher breach shut and fired off a grenade, relying too much on over-active adrenaline.

Like a slow motion scene in a war movie, I watched as the grenade left the barrel of the launcher and hit the bottom of the heavy, folded plastic curtain. There, it seemed to pause, unsure as to whether it wanted to proceed on to kill a Viet Cong, or simply fall back into the well deck, killing us. It seemed like frame by frame movie footage, as the bullet shaped grenade lifted the curtain in agonizingly slow, drawn out fractions of a second, until it flew away from the boat and continued on its way to the intended target. Once again, I don't know WHY God spared me, but he did.

Nine assault boat crewmen were wounded, including Jack Elrod, my old crewmate from T-131-6, and Wayne *"Scooter Pie"* Nash, from T-131-1, one of the guys from my training class.

Later, my 20MM cannon was replaced. I took a photo of it next to an M-16, to provide a better idea of its formidable size.

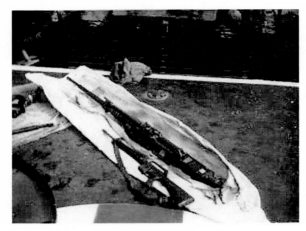

Boats often carried the state, or city flags of their boat captain, or other members of the crew. I asked Judi if she could get me a flag from the city of St. Louis, for our boat. She sent a letter to the mayor of St. Louis, requesting a flag. She received a letter from his office, dated September 23rd, stating that the law prohibited such an expenditure, but, in the hope that it may be of use to me, he sent me the small flag from his desk.

Five soldiers and sailors were wounded Tuesday, September 24th, in an ambush of a supply convoy on the Ben Tre River, just west of Fire Support Base David. Two of the wounded were crewmen of T-111-9, which took a recoilless rifle hit in the attack. The other three WIA were Army troops hit by shrapnel while embarked on an LCU, which had just unloaded supplies at the fire support base and was returning to the Ham Luong River with the river assault boat escorts. The mortar, recoilless rifle and automatic weapons attack was launched at 1305 from the same spot where a similar ambush had been sprung on the convoy at 0810.

A Viet Cong was killed Tuesday, by Second Brigade infantry, continuing their operations in the Giong Trom and Thanh Phu Districts of Kien Hoa Province. The boats of River Division 92, operating with the 4/47th Infantry, conducted several extractions and insertions in the Thanh Phu District on the Vietnam coast.

Danger in Vietnam came from all directions, including friend and foe. At about 1030 in the morning, on September 24th, a crewmen of Riv Ron 13 was hit by shrapnel from a .30 caliber machine gun, in the stomach, arms and head. It was accidentally fired by one of our guns, while a crewman was cleaning it. Friendly fire has been part of war since the first day of the first battle of the first war. The wounded man was medevacked out. We were told he would be O.K., with time.

MRB Bravo, which moved to My Tho, Monday evening, returned to Dong Tam Tuesday night.

**Letter from my sister, Judy. Tuesday, September 24, 1968**
*Dear Rip,*

*How are you? Original way to start a letter, ain't it? Since it's been quite a while since I've written, I thought I'd write you. It's about 11:00 p.m. I'm watching the Joey Bishop Show. I knew you'd be thrilled. I really enjoyed your letter. It's such an honor, for me, a mere potential beautician, to receive a few words of kindness from a "trained killer." I listened to part of your tape. It was really funny.*

*I'm fixing up your room. The bed is fixed, by the way. I'm redecorating it, while Granny is gone. I've got another bed in there, but I'm going to make it look like a couch. I'm getting a big throw rug and I'm putting posters on the walls. I've got one of New York and for your benefit, I'm getting a big one of San Francisco, with the Golden Gate Bridge. Also, just while you're home, to make your stay more enjoyable, I've got a poster of*

*Raquel Welch, to cover up my poster of Paul Newman. Just remember, if you bring somebody home, there's plenty of room, with two beds. Well, enough is enough. I sound like a columnist for "Home Beautiful."*

*Listen, tell your friend, Elrod that I really enjoy hearing from him. Just tell him that if I don't hear from him in a couple of weeks, the whole affair is off!*

*Well, I hate to start closing so soon, but I don't have anything else to say. Oh! The lovebirds; Frank and Karen, stopped by, last Saturday. John Bailey was here, but I was gone. Mom said he's really changed!*

*Also, I wanted to tell you Dodie, Ann, Mary and I went to Forest Park, dressed as hippies, so we could watch the rest of them. I think I got sick. I don't see how those guys can dress so grubby and hairy. I think I'll take a clean cut sailor, anytime! Yeah! Yeah! O.K. I'll get off my soap box, long enough to say Goodbye!*

*Your sweet, beautiful, humorous, trustworthy, loyal, clean sister,*

~~*Sharon*~~ *Judy*

Twenty-four Viet Cong were eliminated, and two were captured, Wednesday, September 25th, in the final day of Second Brigade operations, forty kilometers, or twenty-five miles, southeast of Ben Tre.

Charley and Delta Companies of the 4/47th Infantry took out thirteen Viet Cong, while helicopter gunships smoked nine. Air Force strikes evaporated two. Two U.S. Army soldiers received wounds. The troops were loaded and returned to the MRB early Wednesday evening, by boats of Riv Div 92, to enjoy steaks and beer.

No incidents were reported Wednesday by two groups of Task Group Bravo boats transiting the Cho Gao Canal. Making the trip from the Song Vam Co to Dong Tam were eight boats which had been supporting operations in eastern Long An Province for several weeks and ten newly arrived assault craft, which had completed outfitting at Cat Lo. The second group of boats, which made the transit, were moving from Dong Tam to Nha Be to assume the responsibility for the Long An operations.

Three artillerymen were killed, and eight wounded, early Thursday morning, September 26th, when the enemy mined an artillery barge at a fire support base near the intersection of the Giao Hoa Canal, and the Ben Tre River. The explosion occurred about 0410 and opened a gaping hole in the personnel berthing spaces of the artillery barge. All eight of the wounded were evacuated by Army helicopter.

Earlier in the evening of the same day, an Army infantryman with Alfa Company, 3/47th, operating southeast of Ben Tre, was killed when he stepped on one of the ever-present booby traps.

Boats of Riv Div 131 supported three companies of *"Ruff Puffs,"* Thursday, September 26th, in a search and sweep operation near the crossroads of the Song Ba Lai and Giao Hoa Canal. The Vietnamese troops were beached at 0910 and killed one Viet Cong. They also captured one V.C., and seized an enemy carbine in the sweep. Mobile Riverine Base Bravo reached full strength Thursday evening when the barracks ship, APL-30 joined APL-26, the repair ship, USS Satyr and the LST, Vernon County at the Dong Tam anchorage.

At 2130, Thursday, two V.C. were spotted planting booby traps south of Fire Support Base David. They were taken under fire, dispatching one of the Viet Cong to that *"Great Rice Paddy in the Sky."*

The Second Brigade Command and Communications helicopter crashed and burned in the My Tho River, three "clicks," or a little under two miles, east of MRB Alfa, Friday, September 27th. Sadly, the two pilots and two gunners died in the crash. The helicopter was circling the MRB, waiting to land on the Nueces when it suddenly plunged into the river and exploded into flames. A BID patrol boat, three PBR's and a "Loach," LOH helicopter rushed to the scene, but could not locate any survivors. A UDT team was later taken to the area in an effort to locate the helicopter and extract the bodies.

The MRF was visited Saturday, September 28th, by Commodore Tran Van Chon, who is the highest ranking officer in the Vietnamese Navy and is equivalent to the American Chief of Naval Operations. The Commodore was briefed on MRF operations by Commodore Salzer, visited assault craft alongside the Benewah and presented Vietnamese Crosses of Gallantry to eight TF 117 personnel.

Commander Louis Hamel, former C.O., River Squadron Nine and now ops officer for Task Group Bravo, was awarded the Cross of Gallantry with Palm, the highest award conferred on Americans by the Vietnamese government. Receiving the Cross of Gallantry with Gold Star, were Lt. Lex Boswell, Chief Staff Officer of Riv Ron 11, GMG1 Ernest Bennett and GMG1 john Guthrie, both of Riv Ron 11. Lt. David Miller CSO of Riv Div 112, received the Cross with Silver Star, while Lt. Ralph Hanson, Commander of Riv Div 91, BMC Merrill Pronto of Division 112, and SN Donald Griffin of Division 111 received the Cross with Bronze Star.

On September 29th, Riv Ron 13 and Group Bravo shifted anchorage from Dong Tam to Vinh Long, a distance of about twenty-eight miles.

The MRF was visited Sunday, September 29th, by the legendary Admiral Elmo R. Zumwalt, prospective Commander of all Naval Forces in Vietnam. The Admiral received a two-hour briefing on MRF operations from Commodore Salzer.

**The 900th U.S. aircraft was shot down over North Vietnam, on Monday, September 30th.**

River Assault Squadron 13 and 15 river assault boats returned to the MRB at Vinh Long about 0110 Tuesday, October 1st, after completing two days of operations with regional force and ARVN troops along the Mang Thit River. Eleven enemy bunkers were wiped out, during the operation. Eight V.C. were captured. Twelve Vietnamese were detained. Nine small arms and numerous documents were seized

Riv Ron 13 and River Division 152 joined forces on Wednesday, October 2nd, getting underway before dawn. They moved thirty miles southeast, on the Co Chien River, beaching 932 ARVN soldiers, in Vinh Binh Province, nine miles northwest of Tra Vinh. We maintained overnight blocking stations, along with six PBR's, on the Song Co Chien, just east of the ARVN operations. Seventeen Viet Cong were destroyed by the ARVN troops, most of them, early Thursday morning, by the 9th ARVN Division's 2/14th Battalion.

The ARVN forces also captured three prisoners and took five detainees into custody. Allied losses were one ARVN soldier killed in action and eight wounded. The troops were loaded Thursday evening, with the boats returning to the MRB anchorage at Vinh Long. The return transit took seven hours. APL-30 and YLLC-4, which shifted to the lower Co Chien anchorage Wednesday morning to support the operation, and rejoined the rest of the MRB at Vinh Long, on Thursday.

A detachment of Riv Div 132 boats continued to support U.S. 9th Infantry Division and Vietnamese operations in the Nha Be, Can Giouc area.

Vietnamese forces, supported by boats of Riv Div 132 killed five Viet Cong and took thirteen as prisoners of war, during an operation Friday, October 4th, fifteen kilometers, or nine miles, north of Go Cong. Ground units involved were Charley Company, of the 3/39th Infantry, Regional Force/Popular Force troops ("Ruff Puffs") and Can Giouc District National Police. One AK-47, one M-1, one M-16, two grenade launchers, two pistols and numerous documents were seized in the operation.

One infantryman was killed and fifteen Army and Navy personnel were wounded in an ambush of Riv Div 132 boats Friday, October 4th, in eastern Long An Province, five or six miles east of Can Giouc. The boats were hit with everything the enemy had, including B-40 rockets, recoilless rifle and automatic weapons. T-132-11 bore the brunt of the attack, sustaining multiple rocket hits, including one that passed completely through the 20MM mount. Miraculously, the gunner in the mount was bending down to pick up ammunition at the time and received only minor shrapnel wounds. It was indeed, the sailor's *"Lucky Day."* Nine soldiers of A Company, of the 3/39th Infantry, were wounded when a rocket blew an eighteen inch hole in the flight deck of the ATC and rained shrapnel down on them. Monitor 132-2 and ATC 132-2 was also hit. Six sailors were wounded, including Lt. J.G. Stevens, SF3 A.W. Beaver, SN J.M. Reeves, FN J.L. Barbitta, EM3 R.S. Batten, FN M.L. Olin, and SN J.R. Perry.

Saturday, October 5th, Riv Div 151 supported four regional force companies in operations along the Song Mang Thit. The *"Ruff Puffs"* were landed on the Mang Thit, Saturday morning, twelve miles south of Vinh Long.

Between September 29th and October 6th, River Assault Squadron 13 conducted combat operations in and around Vinh Binh Province, supporting the 14th ARVN Regiment. The boats were supported by the USS Vernon County (LST-1161), USS Satyr (ARL-23), APL-26, and APL-30, in the vicinity of Vinh Long.

River Division 151 returned to MRB Bravo, at Vinh Long, at 0200 Monday, October 7th, after two days of operations with Vietnamese Regional Force troops along the Mang Thit Canal. They destroyed eleven large bunkers, including several near mortar positions, surrounded by lethal Viet Cong booby traps. The boats fired sixty-eight rounds of 105MM Harassment and Interdiction fire along the river banks.

MRB Alfa shifted from Dong Tam to My Tho, Monday. MRB Bravo shifted from Vinh Long to Dong Tam.

Thirty-eight assault boats of Task Group Bravo supported a massive ARVN operation in the Mouse Ears area of Long An Province Thursday, October 10th. The boats of River Squadron 13 and 15 worked in conjunction with Vietnamese RAG (River Assault Group) units, which also were supporting ARVN units in the area.

During our operations with the Vietnamese River Assault Group, something pretty amazing happened, however, I have not been able to find a single official operations report, or historical record that details it. I fully understand why. Several former sailors of River Assault Squadron 13 have verified my memory of the day.

River Assault Squadron 13 was operating with some of our assault craft leading a column of boats from a main channel, into a narrow tributary. The South Vietnamese navy assault craft were in the middle of the column. They had a reputation of being more "cautious" than their American counterparts. To be fair, we were there for one year. They were spending their entire lives, however short, or long, there. The rest of Riv Ron 13 boats were in the rear of the column. My boat, Tango 9, was in the rear group of boats.

As our lead boats entered the narrower channel, they were hit with a vicious barrage. The Vietnamese boats stopped, dead in the water, refusing to follow our boats into the melee. Standing at my 20MM gun mount, next to our coxswain's flat, I heard the radio bark with the voice of our C.O., Lt. Clarence T. Vaught, yelling at the Vietnamese boats to enter the narrow stream and join the fight, to aid our boats. They balked. They sat there, not going in, and blocking our boats, in the rear of the column, from coming to the aid of the lead boats. Our C.O., whose call sign was *"Mariner India,"* continued to scream at the Vietnamese boats to join the fight. They didn't respond. They didn't answer. They didn't move. They sat there, frozen at the entrance to the battle. Finally, I was stunned to hear *"Mariner India"* scream over the radio;

***"If those boats don't either go in, or get out of the way, blow them out of the water!"***

Our commanding officer was telling us that if our ally didn't come to the aid of our friends and countrymen, or move out of the way so that the rear of the column could come to their aid, we were to turn our guns on our South Vietnamese allies! Immediately, the South Vietnamese Navy boats entered the narrow channel, joining in the fight. I was so proud of our commanding officer that if my hands weren't busy with my 20MM cannon, I would have been pumping my fist in the air! These are the kinds of leaders men will follow into Hell!

The operation started at 2200 Wednesday, October 9th, when the U.S. boats loaded a 7th ARVN recon company at the My Tho PBR base. The boats conducted a night transit up the Cho Gao Canal to a ferry landing on the Song Vam Co, nine miles north of Go Cong, where they loaded the 2/11th and the 3/12th ARVN Battalions at about 0300. Continuing west of the Song Vam Co and Vam Co Tay, the boats beached the ARVN units at about 0715. Meanwhile, Vietnamese Navy boats landed other ARVN troops along the Cho Gao Canal, south of the beaching points of the U.S. boats. The Task Group Bravo units were scheduled to extract the ARVN troops after they completed their sweep, Thursday afternoon.

Meanwhile, a detachment of Riv Div 132 boats in the Can Giouc-Nha Be area, completed operations with U.S. troops of the 3/39th Infantry. The 132 boats were relieved Thursday afternoon by Riv Div 151 assault craft and returned to MRB Bravo with the River Assault Squadron 13 and River Assault Squadron 15 boats, which supported Thursday's ARVN operation.

Two assault boat crewmen and a straight leg were wounded during a rocket attack on River Division 111 boats on the Ben Tre River, Thursday, October 10th. The attack was launched at 1355, just after the boats loaded two companies of the 4/47th Infantry. ATC 111-8 sustained two rocket hits in the attack. The boats fiercely returned and suppressed the fire.

Three V.C. were taken out, and two were taken in, by two ARVN battalions and one recon company operating with boats of Task Group Bravo, in eastern Long An Province, near the *"Mouse Ears."* The ARVN's also seized an AK-47, one-hundred grenades and 1,100 detonators. The ARVN were returned to their bases by Vietnamese RAG units and boats of Task Group Bravo, which joined the ships of MRB Bravo at My Tho, by 1930. Also making the return transit down the Cho Gao Canal were a detachment of boats from River Division 132, which had been operating with the First Brigade troops in the Can Giouc - Nha Be area for several weeks and a group of newly arrived Riv Ron 15 assault craft which had completed outfitting at Cat Lo.

In other action, two V.C. were slain, and another was listed as *probably* killed, in brief contact Thursday afternoon by Bravo Company, of the 3/39th Infantry, southwest of Nha Be. Supporting Bravo Company was a group of assault craft from Riv Div 151, which relieved the Riv Div 132 detachment Thursday afternoon. The troops were landed near a nipa palm grove where a *"Loach"* (Light Observation Helicopter) had drawn automatic weapons fire earlier in the afternoon. A sweep of the area after an artillery strike yielded two dead V.C., two B-40 rocket launchers, seven B-40 rockets, an AK-47, and assorted enemy documents.

Light Lift Craft - 4 and UDT personnel were scheduled to return to MRB Bravo and Alfa, respectively, after the search was called off for the NAVSUPPACT helo, which crashed in the Ham Luong River, west of Ben Tre Wednesday morning, October 9th.

On October 10th, one CCB and four ASPB's arrived at our My Tho anchorage, for River Division 131, bringing the total number of boats in the division up to twenty-two. We were scheduled to get two more Alpha boats from MRG Alpha.

**October 12, 1968.** During Summer Olympic Games medals ceremony in Mexico City, Americans Tommie Smith and John Carlos gain attention by displaying black power salutes during the *"Star Spangled Banner."*

On October 13, 1968, River Assault Division 131, moved from the APL-30 to the USS Mercer and APB-39. We learned that our group, Group Bravo, would become the more mobile group, and Group Alpha, would be semi-mobile. Group Bravo would include the Mercer, Nueces (APB-40), Satyr (ARL-23), and an LST.

The 3/47th Infantry Battalion made contact in the Binh Dai District of Kien Hoa Province, on October 13th, about nineteen miles east of Ben Tre. As River Assault Division 111 set up river blockade, River Assault Squadron 13 embarked the 3/60th troops and inserted them near the 3/47th area of contact. In the ensuing action, twenty-four Viet Cong were annihilated. Two soldiers of the 3/47th were wounded. The next day, October 14th, C Company, of the 4/47th, operating in the same district, came upon a Viet Cong rest area and eradicated twenty-three Viet Cong. Twenty-one suspects were detained. Thankfully, there were no friendly casualties.

Twenty-two Viet Cong were exterminated by the Second Brigade Monday, October 14th as troops of Charley Company, 4/47th Infantry discovered a V.C. rest area in the southeast corner of Go Cong Province. In an operation supported by Army Air Cushioned Vehicles (ACV's), the troops clashed with the V.C., about 1610. Infantry killed fifteen Viet Cong. Gunships accounted for another seven. In addition, the infantry seized five weapons and detained twenty Vietnamese for questioning. All of the 4/47th troops were withdrawn from the Go Cong-Binh Dai area, early Monday afternoon, by boats of River Division 92, for return to the MRB.

Meanwhile, one additional body was found Monday in a sweep through the area of Sunday night's contact by Bravo Company, 3/47th Infantry, 20 kilometers, or about twelve miles, east of Ben Tre. A total of twenty-six Viet Cong were sent to *Uncle Ho's Heaven,* in the battle with an estimated reinforced company.

Assault boats of River Division 152 supported the 6/31st Infantry Battalion and a regional force company in a search and sweep operation in western Dinh Tuong Province, five miles northwest of Vinh Long. While in route to the beaches, the boats took small arms and automatic weapons fire, which was quickly stifled with overpowering 20MM cannon fire.

In order to obtain maximum effectiveness of the Mobile Riverine Force in pacifying Kien Hoa, Dinh Tuong and Long An Provinces, the MRF was reorganized on October 15th. Mobile Riverine Group Alfa, supporting the U.S. 9th Infantry Division operations, was assigned the USS Benewah, USS Askari, USS Sphinx, USS Westchester County, APL-26, APL-30, and YLLC-4.

River Assault Division 131, moved from the APL-30 to the USS Mercer and APB-39. We learned Group Bravo would become the more mobile group, ranging throughout the western delta, and Group Alpha would be semi-mobile. Group Bravo would include the USS Mercer, USS Nueces (APB-40), USS Satyr (ARL-23), and an LST, USS Caroline County. Five river divisions were assigned to MRG Alpa, three to MRG Bravo. Although River Division 131 was officially moved to the Mercer, we didn't spend much time on the ships.

With River Divisions 91 and 112 returning to the line, River Division 92 moved to the USS Benewah and assumed responsibility for MRB Alfa defense. River Division 111 went to the USS Westchester County to begin supporting the 3/34th artillery.

# Chapter 15
## Operation Sea Lords

During the period of the Mobile Riverine Force realignment, the Commander of U.S. Naval Forces, Vietnam announced *"Operation Sea Lords,"* a new, offensive effort designed to interdict the enemy and secure delta waterways, pacifying large segments of the delta region. The goal of Sea Lords was to coordinate all naval commands and assets in the delta to stop the flow of enemy supplies their ability to fight.

The forces involved in Operation Sea Lords included just about anybody operating in the Mekong Delta, including Task Force 117 (the Mobile Riverine Force), Task Force 115 ("Swift Boats"), Task Force 116 (PBR's), the U.S. Army, Vietnamese Army and Vietnamese Marine units. Quick, agile and effective reaction to any situation was one of the primary goals of Sea Lords. By the end of October, TF 117 had conducted liaison and training with the 21st ARVN Division and conducted operations as well with the VNMC 4th Battalion in connection with planned Sea Lords operations. Extensive surveys of the western delta canals were also accomplished in anticipation of future operation in that area. If you sloshed through, floated on, or flew over the mud, or the water of the Mekong River, or any of its tributaries, you were involved in Operation Sea Lords.

In keeping with the emphasis on mobility assigned to my group, *"MRG Bravo,"* that group, operating with various U.S. and Vietnamese ground forces, operated in the first days of October along the Nicolai Canal/Mang Thit River in Vinh Long Province, with the ARVN 9th Division and Regional Force troops. In addition, a detachment of River Assault Division 132 operated throughout the month in support of operations in Long An Province near Can Giuoc. Operations during the time also included sweeps into Vinh Binh and Vinh Long with ARVN 14th Regiment troops.

River Assault Boats of River Division 132 supported a battalion of the 9th ARVN Division's 15th Regiment in an operation Wednesday, October 16th, about five miles northwest of Sa Dec. The boats got underway at 1730 Tuesday, and proceeded to the district town of Duc Ton to load troops, then loaded additional ARVN's in Sa Dec and beached the battalion on the Rach Sa Dec, about 0800. There were no known enemy casualties. Unseen enemy snipers killed three ARVN soldiers, and wounded two others.

Two V.C. were killed and one Chieu Hoi rallied to the government side, on Wednesday during Riv Div 151 operations with the 3/39th Infantry in the Can Giuoc-Nha Be area.
.

Task Group Bravo relocated to Vinh Long, Thursday, October 18th. On Friday, they moved further west on the Song Tien Giang, to the vicinity of the Vam Nao crossover.

Saturday morning, October 19th, Task Group Bravo boats supported encircle and sweep operations on Cu Lao May Island, ten miles southeast of Can Tho, after transiting the Mang Thit canal system. The boats of Riv Div 152 landed troops of the Vietnamese Vinh Long Regional Force Battalion and the 4/37th ARVN Battalion.

River Assault Squadron 13 and twelve PBR's established a water blockade, surrounding the island. They stopped and searched a total of 77 sampans and detained one Vietnamese. Later, the boats fired 29 rounds of

105MM Howitzer Harassment & Interdiction fire at the island. Three Viet Cong were killed and one V.C. captured, in the action. Ten detainees were taken into custody and three weapons were captured.

Infantry units working with Riv Div 151 river assault boats in eastern Long An Province took out two Viet Cong, captured two and detained nine suspects, on Friday and Saturday. On Friday, troops of the 3/39th Infantry smoked two Viet Cong and snatched two more, nine miles southwest of Can Giouc.

Saturday, Riv Div 151 supported the 764th RF/PF (*regional force/popular force*) troops, a provincial reconnaissance unit (PRU), and the 3/39th Infantry, six miles south of Can Giouc. Total results of the operation were two V.C, killed and seven detained, including three possible V.C. POW's.

Mobile Riverine Group Bravo was visited Sunday by Brigadier General Nguyen Vinh Nghi, Commanding General of the 21st ARVN Division, and members of his staff. The General was briefed by Commodore Now and was given a tour of the USS Mercer and the River Assault craft of the Mobile Riverine Force.

We had a checker game on Tango 9, but we didn't have chess pieces. So, in the tradition of American fighting men throughout history, we improvised. We overcame. We adapted. We broke open a Claymore mine and extracted the C-4 plastic explosive. It had the comforting feel and texture of *"Playdough."* In one inch cubes, it's great for cooking cans of C-Rations. With only slightly more, you can create chess pieces. The only thing you have to remember is that if a lit cigarette lights a piece on fire, don't HIT it! If you do, it's *"checkmate!"*

Monday, October 21st was "C" Day. We had to turn in any *MPC*, or *"Military Police Certificates,"* which represented our "cash," so that it could be replaced with new and different MPC.

Lt. JG Stephens fell on an ASPB the other night during a transit and was medevacked to an Army hospital. The medivac chopper delivered him to the hospital and within a minute, caught fire and crashed into the river. There were no survivors.

Task Group Bravo conducted training exercises with units of the 4th Vietnamese Marine Battalion in the vicinity of the Ci Rang Bridge, on Tuesday, October 22nd, preparing for a future joint operation.

River Division 151, operating in the Can Giouc-Nha Be area, reported two possible V.C. KIA or WIA in a clash Monday evening, while supporting the 3/39th Infantry. About 1800, the boats spotted two Vietnamese males beach their sampan and scramble ashore. The boats fired on them and later found a Chicom grenade and a satchel charge in the sampan.

Wednesday, October 23rd, Group Alfa fought an estimated reinforced Viet Cong platoon, about seven miles southeast of Ben Tre. Both U.S. Army and Vietnamese Marines were still in contact after darkness. Nine Viet Cong were killed and one AK-47 was captured. Fighting broke out at 1020 when helicopters carrying Alpha Company, 3/60th Infantry hit a hot "LZ", landing zone. One infantryman was killed and a helicopter pilot was injured in this first attack, as the slicks (helicopters) landed the troops in the area. Choppers continued to draw fire during the day. Three Huey's and one LOH (Light Observation Helicopter) were shot down. U.S. ground forces were the target of two enemy mortar attacks during the afternoon and the troops were frequently pinned down by V.C. automatic weapons and rocket fire. As the fighting intensified, Delta Company, of the 3/47th Infantry was airlifted into a Landing Zone south of the enemy. At the same time, River Division 91 brought two companies of Vietnamese Marines into the battle via the Ben Tre River, through one ambush of rocket and automatic weapons fire which wounded one assault boat crewman, slightly. The Marines were beached one kilometer north of the fighting and achieved almost immediate contact as they swept south.

On the same day, River Assault Squadrons 13 and 15 were supporting Vietnamese Marines and ARVN's in the Can Tho area. During the day, boats of Riv Div 152 were beaching the troops on the Cai Con Canal, about twelve miles southeast of Can Tho, when a grenade was suddenly hurled from the east bank. It landed on T-152-11, slightly wounding two crewman and blowing a ten-inch hole in the helo deck, next to the coxswain's flat. The boats immediately fired back with 20MM cannon and small arms fire. By mid-afternoon, the Marines had rounded up ten Viet Cong and the boats had inspected twelve sampans.

Two Viet Cong bodies were found Thursday, October 24th, by MRF forces sweeping through the area where contact had been achieved the day before, with an estimated reinforced platoon.

In other action Thursday, two infantrymen were killed in the early morning hours in a V.C. rocket attack on Delta Company, of the 3/47th Infantry. Six Navy assault boat sailors were wounded in another ambush on the Ben Tre River, five miles southeast of Ben Tre. The attack on the boats of Riv Div 91 occurred at 0940 as they were moving up the Rach Ben Tre carrying two companies of Vietnamese Marines. ATC 91-7 took one B-40 rocket hit and had four of the six wounded. Two men had to be dusted off by chopper, for immediate medical attention. The boats returned and suppressed the fire. Over the course of the two days of operation, ten Viet Cong were killed in action. Allied casualties were four killed and twenty-two wounded.

Boats of Riv Div 152, Thursday, continued one of our primary functions of water blockade operations on the Saintenoy Canal, eleven miles southeast of Can Tho. The blockade resulted in the apprehension of six detainees, during a search of 148 sampans.

During a two-day operation which ended Thursday, four V.C. were killed and six captured, by the 4th VNMC, working with boats of River Division 152 southeast of Can Tho. The assault craft played an active role in the operation, searching 206 sampans and apprehending six detainees while conducting waterborne blockades with two PBR's from Binh Thuy. Friendly casualties were five Vietnamese Marines and two Navy men.

That night, three members of Charley Battery, of the 3/34th Artillery were wounded when their fire support base was attacked with three B-40 rockets.

On Friday, October 25th, an infantryman of the 3/47th, disappeared from sight while crossing a stream.

Saturday, October 26th, our boat, along with the rest of Task Group Bravo, was getting ready for operations with the 4th Vietnamese Marines, near Can Tho. Eleven Purple Hearts were presented to Task Group Bravo sailors, on the USS Mercer, by Commodore Now.

Task Group Alfa forces killed six Viet Cong, on the same day, in Kien Hoa Province. Three were killed by Delta Company, 3/60th Infantry, which was supported by Riv Div 152. Two were killed by 3/47th Infantry and one was taken out by Vietnamese Marines, operating along the Ba Lai River, supported by boats of Riv Div 91.

On Sunday, October 27th, helicopters of Delta Company, 3/5th Air Cavalry, spotted fifteen Viet Cong near a large hootch on the south bank of the Song My Tho, only two and half miles south of our base at Dong Tam. When the gunships fired on the group and the hootch, it set off a large secondary explosion. Two companies of the 3/60th Infantry was airlifted in, and immediately began receiving heavy automatic weapons fire, which killed two of the troops and wounded seven others. Vietnamese Marines who were operating nearby, moved in to assist and reported five of their men wounded in the action.

Also, Sunday October 27th and Monday, the 28th, boats of River Squadron 13 supported several Vietnamese units on the Xa No Canal, twenty-eight kilometers, or seventeen miles, southwest of Can Tho. The force included four companies of the 4th Vietnamese Marine Corps, the 21st ARVN Headquarters Company, one company of Phong Dinh Regional Force troops and four National Police teams. The Vietnamese ground forces cut down fourteen Viet Cong, and took in, two. They seized seven thousand pounds of explosives, three AK-47's, medical supplies, rice, and a large quantity of ammunition and V.C. documents.

During the ground operations, Task Group Bravo ASPB's initiated blocking stations, inspecting 168 sampans and detaining nine Vietnamese. One U.S. Marine advisor was wounded in the action. Allied casualties were three Vietnamese killed and six wounded.

River Division 151 assault boats were ambushed on Thursday, October 31st, four kilometers south of Can Giouc, in eastern Long An Province. Tango 151-13 took four rocket hits, wounding two of the boat's crew and twelve soldiers of Charley Company, 3/39th Infantry, who were in the well deck.

Three Viet Cong were killed by infantry of the 3/60th, operating with Task Group Alfa, Thursday, Two V.C. KIA were credited to Air Force strikes, in northern Kien Hoa Province. Vietnamese Marines sweeping along the south bank of the Song My Tho, twenty kilometers, or twelve and half miles east of Ben Tre, found thirty-two grenade type booby traps and destroyed two Bangalore torpedoes.

**On October 31st, in a televised address to the nation five days before the presidential election, President Lyndon Johnson announced that in light of the Paris peace negotiations, he ordered the complete halt of *"all air, naval, and artillery bombardment of North Vietnam."* Accordingly, effective November 1, the U.S. Air Force called a halt to the air raids on North Vietnam known as *"Operation Rolling Thunder."***

Between October 18th and November 1st, River Assault Squadron 13 conducted combat operations round Vinh Long, Vinh Binh, and Phuong Dinh Provinces, supporting the 9th ARVN, Vietnamese Regional Forces and the 4th Vietnamese Marine Battalion. The support ships of Task Group Bravo included the USS Mercer (APB-39), USS Neuces (APB-40), USS Satyr (ARL-23), and the USS Caroline County (LST-525), near Can Tho.

**Most of the crew of T-131-9 *("Tango 9").***

# Chapter 16
## USS Westchester County

**Letter home, November 1st**
*Dear Mom, Dad, Family*

*We're going out on long op, in less than 45 minutes. I don't have time to write. I just wanted to let you know. Don't worry! It's no special deal. Just a <u>long</u> operation! I should be able to get mail out, but I can't be sure if, or when. Give everybody my love. I'll get out some mail to you, as soon as possible.*

*Love,*

*Terry*

As I wrote my note to the family, the LST Westchester County was sitting at anchor, with Group Alfa, about a hundred miles away, forty miles from the coastal resort town of Vung Tao. At 0322 in the morning, the ship was hit with hellish explosions on their starboard side, amidships, between the ship and the attached pontoons. The attack was a rare, successful mining by Viet Cong saboteurs. The blasts opened two holes at the waterline, both more than twenty feet in diameter. The explosion killed twenty-six and injured twenty-two. The U.S. Navy suffered its greatest loss of life in a single incident due to enemy action, for the entire Vietnam War.

**The USS Westchester County**

**Navy historical records from <u>April, 1968</u> highlighted V.C. attempts to mine the Tom Green County. The entry gave a dire and prophetic warning to what the Viet Cong saboteurs had in mind;**

*"According to captured enemy documents, the Viet Cong sapper squads normally practiced at "dry runs," to probe the target's defense, prior to an actual mining attempt. **It proved interesting to note that both sightings were near the MRF support LST; suggesting that she was the priority target within the MRB, presumably because of the large ammunition supply on board."***

<u>**Operations Report. November 1, 1968.**</u>
*"Sixteen were known dead and nine others were still missing Friday, November 1st, night as a result of the early morning explosion between the pontoons and hull of Westchester County. Another 22 were wounded in the suspected mining in what ranks among the most costly naval casualties of the war. The explosions at 3:22 A.M. opened two holes in the starboard side at the waterline – both more than 20 feet in diameter. A First Class Petty Officer's compartment and an Army bunkroom were the hardest hit, but there were also casualties on the pontoon and on Riv Div 111 boats tied up alongside. Although the ship began taking on water, the rapid reaction of damage control parties quickly controlled the flooding and the ship was never in danger of sinking. The wounded were rushed by assault boat to the Benewah during the early morning hours and the more seriously injured were flown to the Army surgical hospital at Dong Tam. Two Navy men were trapped in a flooded compartment for four hours after the incident. Damage control men cut their way through the wreckage to free the trapped men, and both were later reported in good condition. Many other water-filled spaces had still not been inspected by Friday evening, however, and several of the missing were presumed to be trapped inside. Of the 16 personnel killed, 15 were members of the Westchester County's crew and the twelfth was a Vietnamese sailor who was training aboard the TF 117 boats. Wounded in the explosion were 19 other Navy men and three Army troops. According to Lieutenant Commander John Branin, the Westchester County C.O., every First Class Petty Officer aboard the ship was either killed or wounded. All members of the ship's office died in the explosion. The damage on Westchester County was surveyed Friday morning by Vice Admiral Elmo R. Zumwalt, Commander, Naval Forces, Vietnam, who flew to the MRB from Saigon."*

After beaching for temporary repairs at Dong Tam, the Westchester County went to Yokosuka, Japan for repairs, returning to Vietnam in March of 1969. Two weeks later a salvage barge was sunk by a mine, with the loss of two men.

On November 1st, Group Bravo loaded the 4th Vietnamese Marine Battalion. They were a step above the ARVN forces we had operated with, and two steps above the "Ruff Puff's" we operated with, from time to time. We noticed that each of the Vietnamese Marines that we were loading on our boat, had tattoos on their arms. We were told that each member of the 4th Vietnamese Marine Battalion had at least one family member who had been killed by the Viet Cong.

**The best translation of this Vietnamese Marine tattoo that I have been able to obtain, is "Lonely Marine."**

Our boat, T-131-9, carried seven of them. We had their supply officer, 1st Lt. Phan Ute and six enlisted men.

On Saturday, November 2nd, three new ASPB's, A-132-2, A-132-3, and A-132-4, joined River Assault Squadron 13, giving our squadron its full complement of assault boats.

November 2nd was Judi's twentieth birthday. I wished I was home, with her.

Loading the Vietnamese Marines aboard our boat was surreal. They brought a menagerie of animals on board, as livestock, to be eaten during the long operation. Our coxswain, Tom *"Bird Man"* Bird, let them load most of the animals on the boat, with one notable exception.

*Bird Man* explained to us; *"They had a sampan alongside our boat. They had him in a burlap bag. He was going; "Oink! Oink!" I couldn't see him, but I could hear him. I pointed at the bag and he (the Vietnamese Marine) looked at me with kind of a sad face and I said to him; "That's a no no!"* Keeping a pig on our boat was going one animal too far.

Bird let them load a black goose with funny red growth around its beak. It constantly harassed us, whenever we got near it. It hissed at me, so I gave it wide berth. It loved to be squirted with our shower hose, which was a hose attached to a pump that cleaned us with dirty, *"agent orange"* infused river water.

Hodge explained, *"We got a hose, Frankie rigged up that runs off the engine. It pumps river water. Anyhow, me and this goose, we're "tight." I'd go back there and take a shower, spray the goose down. He'd shake, then he'd charge into the river. Then he'd come back and I'd spray him down, some more."*

They brought two chickens, a rooster and a hen, which we referred to as *"Mama-san"* and *"Papa-san."* Our boat captain welcomed them, thinking he, and only he, could have fresh eggs. The plan was for the rooster was to eventually become dinner. The chickens loved to roost on our six machine guns, in the well deck. They crapped all over them, making more work for us. If we got into a firefight and the guns didn't work, it would have been…. Well… *chicken shit.*

**"Mama-San" and "Papa-San"**

In an audio tape sent to my family, Bird Man described another part of our temporary zoo.

> *The Vietnamese brought a python on board, about seven or eight feet long. We were pretty well hep on keeping it on board. They had the snake on the forward part of the boat and Black One was back on the fantail, the stern of the boat. They were going to take the snake down in the well deck and Black One said: "NO! NO!" You can't take that snake on this boat! We don't want that snake, here!"*

Bird Man moaned, *"We didn't get to keep the snake."*

Hodge angrily declared; *"We should have held an election on that!"*

I wanted Bird Man to calm my anti-snake mother's fears;

> *"My mom is some kind of fanatic about snakes, Bird Man. Tell them how "dangerous" it was!"*

Bird Man played along.

> *"It was six to eight feet long. He just laid around and didn't do nothin'! Just stick his tongue out at ya' now an' then! They eat snakes, over here. It's a delicacy, like frog legs, or somethin' like that! They don't hurt ya' a bit! We saw one in our refuelin' village that was ten or twelve feet long. It was hanging over a little boy's neck. They don't even hurt ya'! Of course, the ones that get up to thirty feet long, they'll hurt ya.'"*

We took on one-hundred cases of C-Rations, much of it left over from WWII. At the time, they cost American taxpayers about $35.00 per case. Each case contained twelve complete meals, of varying degrees of edibility. The C-Rations served several purposes. Some of the food in it was actually pretty good. We ate what we liked, and used the rest to trade with ship crews and villagers. The C-Rations were stacked inside the bar armor, around our gun mounts and the coxswain's flat. Sometimes, the rocket propelled grenades would hit the bar armor and explode into the C-Rations, rather than in our gun mounts, or coxswains flat. It happened to my gun mount, once. I like to say that beans and franks saved my life!

Before the operation, we traded a few cases of C-Rations to Vietnamese for seven cases of Vietnamese *"Tiger Beer,"* or *"Biere Larue,"* and ten cases of soda, or *"pop."* In September, our boat captain screamed at Ledford and I for bringing a half can of beer to our boat when it was in the dock, being overhauled. He cancelled our liberty privileges. Now, he was an ardent partner in smuggling seven cases of beer on a combat operation.

We had one case on ice, in a 20MM ammo can, between the two 20MM cannons, close to Hodge's Mark 19 grenade launcher. When we couldn't get ice, we would use the boat's $CO_2$ fire extinguisher to chill the beer, or soda, with a cold blast. We didn't overindulge in the beer. We shared it with the Vietnamese Marines.

We were going into the U Minh Forest, *"The Forest of Darkness,"* a Viet Cong bastion that Americans rarely entered. We stood at our gun mounts, at *"General Quarters,"* for over twenty-four hours, straight. We weren't supposed to sleep, but at one point, I leaned against my gun, shoved my helmet over my eyes, and closed my eyes. I was somewhere between sleep and rest. If we were ambushed, I would have hit the trigger in an instant.

During the evening hours of November 1st, we linked up with some PBR's and Swift Boats, for the first combined operation in the Mekong Delta, under the operational control of Task Group 154.0, *"First Sea Lord."* We headed for Kien Giang Province. Our mission was to stop the flow of enemy men and material across the Cambodian border, southeastward, into the Mekong Delta.

The boats of Task Group 117.2, which included River Assault Squadron 13 and River Division 152, carried the Fourth Battalion of the Vietnamese Marine Corps, while conducting riverine strike operations, and also conducted interdiction operations to prevent the flow of Viet Cong supplies throughout the Mekong Delta area.

The support ships of Task Group Bravo relocated to Long Xuyen area, on November 2nd.

Saturday night, November 2nd, three assault boat crewmen and six Vietnamese Marines were wounded when a RARE *("Riverine Armored Reconnaissance Element")* was ambushed. Two platoons of troops were beached. They eliminated four Viet Cong during the night. They also captured seventy-two B-40 rockets and three 105MM booby traps.

The boats were hit again in the same area, Sunday morning, after landing additional troops of the ARVN 31st Recon Company. There were no friendly casualties, although the flamethrower, Zippo 151-1, was hit by a recoilless rifle round. During the sweep, the Recon unit seized another cache which included fifty B-40 rockets, 830 grenades, ten anti-tank mines, fifty 57MM and 75MM recoilless rifle rounds, one-hundred-twenty-five 60MM and 82MM mortar rounds, one AK-50 and 3000 meters of communications wire.

Four more Navy *"River Rats"* were wounded at 1325 Sunday, November 2nd, when Monitor 152-1, Zippo 151-1 and ATC 151-7 were ambushed with small arms and rockets. The troops were landed at the point of the ambush and immediately clashed with the enemy, wiping out nine V.C. and capturing the fourth weapons cache of the two-day operation. Included in the captured booty were fifty anti-tank mines, six 82MM mortar rounds, six SKS rifles, one complete 82MM mortar, and 25,000 rounds of small arms ammunition.

Sunday, November 3rd, Captain Dale V. Schermerhorn relieved Captain Robert S. Salzer as Commander of the Mobile Riverine Force. The featured speaker for the ceremony was Vice Admiral Elmo R. Zumwalt, Commander of all Naval Forces in Vietnam. Captain Salzer stayed in Vietnam for weeks afterward, as Commander of Operation Delta Lords, an offensive campaign in the southern Mekong Delta, utilizing the PBR's of Task Force 116, the Swift Boats of Task Force 115, and the River Assault boats of Task Force 117.

We had fun getting to know our VNMC guests. With Phan Ute and his men helping us drink the beer, we ran out of it in three days. With seven of them and our seven man crew, that only came out to about four beers a man. We didn't have a bottle opener on the boat, and this was before twist off caps. Sitting on our helo pad, we'd set the bottle cap on the metal edge of the deck and pop the cap off with a strike of our hand. Sometimes the neck of the bottle would break off. That wouldn't stop us. We had to be careful to not lift the end of the bottle all the way up. We used our lips and teeth to strain out any stray glass shards.

We learned early on, that 1st Lt. Phan Ute was a real *"officer and a gentleman,"* with a good sense of humor. He told us that it was improper for us to call him *"Phan."* Only family members could call him by his first name. We were to address him as *"Phan Ute."*

In describing Phan Ute, in an audio tape home, I explained;

> *"He was a 1st Lieutenant, Supply Officer, in charge of all the Vietnamese Marine on our boat, and he knew quite a bit of English. He taught us enough Vietnamese to get by in a general conversation. He taught us how to count to ten, one hundred, or maybe all the way to one thousand."*

Ledford then counted from one to ten, in Vietnamese;

> *Mot, hai, ba, bon, nam, sau, bai, tam, chin, moui." "Twenty" would be "hai-moui," which is "two-ten." You just keep going like that, in case you ever need it!*

**Me, with Phan Ute (in the white shirt) and his men.**

I reminded Ledford of a funny incident with Phan Ute in the first day or two;

*He was a cool head, though. Remember when he came up on the helo deck wearing his .45 automatic and he had his handcuffs?*

Ledford very sheepishly answered: *"Yeah.... I remember! I got "cuffed!"*

*Tell them what he did!*

Reliving his embarrassment, Ledford said; *"He was showing me how to use the cuffs and he CUFFED me!"*

*Then you asked him for the keys!*

Ledford laughed, then imitated Phan Ute; *"No have key! No have key!"*

*He pulled the keys out, after about five minutes of playing with you.*

With some bravado, Ledford added;

*Yeah. He knew it! He knew by the look in my eyes that he better give me the keys!*

I referred to an earlier operation, in which we carried two Vietnamese police, during a search of river traffic.

*Weeks back, when we were carrying a couple Vietnamese Police on our boat, Ledford and I were in our gun mounts. He told me he heard there was a Vietnamese curse word, a slur, but he didn't really know the meaning of it. He told me it was "Du Ma May," but he pronounced it more like "Do Mammy." We were curious if we had the word right, so I yelled it down, into our well deck, where the Vietnamese cops were. They busted up, laughing, loud and hard, repeating the phrase, several times. They didn't speak English, so we still couldn't learn the meaning, from them. I was able to teach the Vietnamese Police a little English. He could only repeat it back to me. I'm not proud of what I taught him to say. Let's just say that if he ever repeated it to anyone who spoke English, he probably only did it, once...*

*Anyway, when Phan Ute came onto the boat, we could tell he was intelligent and articulate. We asked him what "Du Ma May" meant. The only thing we could get out of him was; "Oh! Nevah say! Nevah SAY Du Ma May!" NEVAH say!*

On Monday, November 4th, the Vietnamese Marines operating with our boats seized another large weapons cache, including; one-hundred-twenty B-40 rockets, one-thousand kilograms of rice, sixteen 82-MM mortar rounds, two 120MM-mortar rounds, sixty 60MM mortar rounds, two-hundred-forty grenades, and forty-eight B-

50 rockets. It was music to our ears when we heard about weapons and ammo like that being captured. It meant they couldn't be used to kill us.

The river assault boats were joined at Long Xuyen by four LCM-6's and one Vietnamese River Assault Group commandment. The powerful task force proceeded down the luminescent green Rach Gia River toward the Gulf of Thailand. The boats completed the thirteen hour, 125-kilometer (78 mile) trip to their objective beaches at 0745. The Marines encountered light resistance during the day, suffering two killed and ten wounded.

They captured six boxes of 60MM mortar rounds, three 120MM-mortar rounds, two 155MM artillery shells, three 82MM mortar rounds and one rocket launcher.

Our boats conducted a *"RARE,"* ambush operation, along the Long Xuyen Canal on Sunday night and Monday morning. While transiting to Rach Gia for refueling, the boats were ambushed with B-40 rocket fire from the east bank of the Long Xuyen Canal. Monitor 131-1 took a direct B-40 hit, but there were no casualties.

In a tape home, I asked Ledford to tell my family more about the humor that would someday become embarrassing to me and a funny thing that happened at the refueling station. As usual, we didn't talk about the ambush on the way to the refueling station.

*Tell them what we called Black One, along with the Vietnamese Marines!*

*Oh yeah, "Snow White and the Seven Dwarfs!" Of course, we didn't let him hear us say it!*

*He doesn't even know we CALL him Black One. Who thought of calling him that? You?*

*Yeah. I don't know where we got Black One. I guess because we called Frank, "Little One." A lot of guys get nicknames they may not be crazy about. It's just what we do!"*

*And we call Tom Bird, "Bird Man." We always call Bill Hodges "Hodge." Black One isn't here, right now. We're using his tape recorder.*

*It's also black.*

*It's a "soul" tape recorder.*

*It's a good tape recorder, but it is a little low on batteries, now, so if it seems a little slow, or it is cutting out....*

*If they have good batteries when they play this, it will play too fast. They need to put old batteries in when they play it.*

*Should we tell them about when we beached and had beer in that little hooch at the refueling station with all the kids and that little old mama-san who said we didn't pay her for the beer a couple days before?*

Ledford nodded; *"O.K. Go ahead."*

*O.K. All the little kids in the village swarmed us. They wanted "chop chop." I gave them some American coins, which they marveled at. They didn't know what they were. One of them was a real fat kid. I told him; "Ten ban la "Chubby!" "Your name is "Chubby!" All of the kids started calling him "Chubby." I guess they knew what it meant, because they kept patting his stomach.*

Monitor 152-1 and four ATC's were ambushed Monday, November 4th, on the Kinh Rach Gia/Long Xuyen. Two sailors were wounded. On the same day, the Vietnamese Marines eradicated seven *"Victor Charles"* and captured a 75MM recoilless rifle.

The first few days of the operation were successful, operating on the Rach Gia Canal, seventy-two kilometers, or forty-five miles west of Can Tho. By Monday, November 4th, thirteen Viet Cong had been wiped out and four large weapons caches seized.

The boats encountered several ambushes along the Rach Gia – Long Xuyen Canal, during the first few days of the operation. Our boat often had the *"sweep"* duty, in the front of the column. It may have been because we only had seven of the Vietnamese Marines on board. Some of the boats had many more than that, so we would have less casualties if we were hit. One day, we were leading the column on the starboard side of the river. Another Tango boat was doing the same thing directly across the river from us.

We had been standing at our battle stations for a long time, when we were directed to crank in our mine sweep gear, on our stern. It was a large chain, with hooks welded to it, to catch the wires of command detonated mines that could blow a boat behind ours, out of the water.

Over the sound powered phones, Black One barked, *"Sater, crank in the mine sweep gear!"* I've always believed that he called on me, because as far as he was concerned, on his boat, I was the *"FNG,"* (the *"NG"* stands for *"New Guy"*) even though I'd been *"in country"* longer than he had been. The rest of the boat crew went through hell, the day Taylor was killed. I understood that. The only thing that bothered me was the feeling that our boat captain would have sacrificed every man on the boat, to save himself from the slightest injury.

I climbed out of the top of my gun mount, scrambled down to the deck and began cranking the wench. Suddenly, a rocket was fired from the jungle covered river bank, twenty or thirty yards away, aimed directly at me. Miraculously, it hit the water, just below my feet. There is no rational explanation how he missed me. I should have been dead. We had a Monitor, directly behind us, probably the one pictured, below. Its 105MM gun turret was pointed directly at the spot the rocket came from. It immediately fired on the enemy.

**Photo courtesy of Harry Hahn**

The rocket fired at me was the opening salvo. The Viet Cong were firing all up and down our column, with rockets, recoilless rifles and automatic weapons. Climbing back up to my gun mount the way I came down, would have exposed me, too much. I lunged for our well deck. In my haste, I tripped and fell to the deck. My helmet and glasses flew off, skittering across the metal deck. I hugged the deck on my belly and retrieved them.

Pushing forward, I slithered into the well deck. Once into the shelter of the boat, I climbed the ladder into the coxswains flat and joined the rest of the crew in returning fire with my 20MM cannon.

I don't know how long the firefight lasted. It was probably between fifteen minutes and twenty-five minutes. It's hard to judge time during a firefight. Time slows. When the fire died down, the boat captain yelled to me, telling me again, to go out and finish bringing in the mine sweep gear.

My nerves were shot, but I repeated my earlier steps, crawling out of the top of my gun mount, climbing down the rebar that protected our gun mounts, went to the exposed stern of the boat, and began to crank in the gear. Like a bad horror movie, a rocket once more fired out of the shoreline, just yards away, and inexplicably, again hit the water, just below my feet. If the V.C. had raised his rocket launcher only slightly, it would have hit me, directly. I don't know how they missed, TWICE! Once again, I scrambled for the well deck, climbed into my gun mount, and engaged the enemy, along with every man on my boat and all the boats behind us.

When the firing trailed off and it was quiet once again, I heard Black One's voice.

*O.K., Sater, go crank it in.*

Something in me snapped. I looked up, through my open gun mount and screamed at the top of my lungs, not at my boat captain, but at God. I cursed him with everything in me. I called him every terrible name I could think of. I screamed an angry, frustrated challenge at him;

**"If you're gonna kill me, just fucking KILL me, and quit FUCKING with me!"**

I have always been a man of faith, sometimes more than others. At this particular moment, I was being tested more than I could bear. I was angry at God. At that moment, I sincerely wanted him to either kill me, or make the Viet Cong stop trying to kill me. I was beside myself with rage. Part of me wondered who this madman was. This couldn't be ME! Quickly, I regained composure and again climbed out through the top of my gun mount and went to the mine sweep gear. I thought I might die, but at least it would be over. As I began cranking the wench, I waited for the next rocket. It didn't come.

When I returned to my gun mount, Ledford looked as drained and sickened, as I felt. He seemed to need to share with me that if I had been hit, he didn't think he could have gone out to get me. I thought of what he went through the day Taylor was killed and he was injured. I told him,

*Hell, Glenn, if I had been hit, **I** wouldn't have gone out to get me!*

General James *"Mad Dog"* Mattis was right, when he said,

**"There is nothing better than getting shot at and missed. It's really great."**

Seven crewmen of the assault craft were wounded during the three ambushes we encountered those first several days, but fortunately, none were killed. It was a testament to the bravery, training and dedication of the rag tag, gritty, *"sailorinors"* of the River Assault Group. During sweeps of the area, Troops of the 4th Vietnamese Marine Battalion eviscerated thirteen Viet Cong and bagged four large weapons caches.

Over the days that followed, we traded more of our C-Rations. We bartered for nylon hammocks, kerosene stoves, bananas and pots and pans. We weren't tying up to the ships. We were on our own.

Riv Div 152 boats came under attack again Tuesday, the 5th, with Tango 152-5 taking a B-40 hit in her port side. One crewman was wounded and the boat sustained minor damage.

As part of the same Sea Lord operation, Group Bravo supported *"reconnaissance in force operations"* in the Soc Son area of Kien Giang Province, from November 9th, through 11th, using the Hat Tien- Rach Gia and the Tri Ton Canals, to transport troops into the area of operations from November 12th to 14th, in the *"Three Sisters"* area, about ten miles northwest of Rach Gia. During the operation, nine rounds of 105MM Howitzer rounds were fired from a Monitor, at a range of about 3 ½ miles. The rounds were spotted by an Army artillery officer and achieved an accuracy of about 30- 40 yards, after the initial spotting round. The firing was done while the Monitor was beached on the Tri Ton Canal. Lacking a fire-control computer, three reference points were used; a stake on the craft's bow, an aiming stake about 25 feet from the shoreline and an open sight position just forward of the coxswains flat, with the bow as the pivot point, the crew maneuvered the Monitor to keep the reference points in line with the sight. On the 14th, the troops were loaded and returned to Rach Gia.

**Richard M. Nixon was elected President of the United States, November 5th.**

Our *Sea Lords* operation was very successful. Between November 2nd and 6th. Twenty of *Charley's* men were taken out of commission. Captured arms and supplies during those five days included; 145 60MM rounds, Six boxes of 60MM rounds, forty 57MM recoilless rifle rounds, sixty anti-tank mines, 27,000 rounds of small arms ammunition, 240 B-40 rockets, forty-eight B-50 rockets, two 155MM rounds, three 105MM booby traps, 159 82MM rounds, one AK-50, one Chicom carbine, six SKS rifles, one 82MM mortar, one 75MM recoilless rifle, one rocket launcher, and 1,000 kilograms of rice.

The *"assault phase"* of the operation ended Wednesday, November 6th. The *"interdiction phase"* continued.

The author of the official MRF "Operations Report" of November 6th, revealed a sense of humor that was rarely seen in official "After Action" reports when he said of a Group Alfa operation;

> *"Operation Delta Raider continued throughout the day, with units of the Mobile Riverine Force reporting no contact. However, three US infantrymen of the 3/47 were wounded by a booby trap, and* **one VC was killed when his own booby trap boobied him."**

**Letter from sister-in-law, Mary Rose. November 7, 1968**
*Dear Terrence Michael*

*Happy Thanksgiving! Hope you got some turkey dinner. How have you been, lately? Have you been in much action? You haven't written for a while and I've been wondering if anything new had happened.*

*What do you think about the election? I suppose you are very relieved Richard Nixon won. I was for Humphrey and your mother was shocked and surprised. Tom was for Wallace. Tom said after we voted we were going to Reno for a divorce, but he chickened out. He didn't want the three kids. Ha! Ha! The election was very exciting and we stayed up very late watching the returns. Both Humphrey and Wallace lost, so we decided not to get a divorce. We are both happy for Nixon and we know he will make a good president.*

*How do you like the pictures? Aren't they cute? I'm prejudiced. The kids are getting so big. Tommy and Bryan are starting to fight, now, and Bryan always starts it. Yesterday, Bryan bit Tommy in the face and poor Tommy still has the teeth marks. Bryan is small, but mighty. Last month, Tommy got some soap in his eye and he wanted me to put a Band-Aid on his eyeball. They say the cutest things. Marlene rolls over, now and is starting to crawl. She can say "Da Da." Tom is so proud of his daughter. He calls her "Pudding," "Sugar," his "Movie Star," "Princess." It gets rather thick around here. I could pack my bags and leave and he would never notice. It is really quite a thrill to watch him play with his little girl.*

*Tommy had a birthday, Sunday. He is three years old. Your mom gave him a party with the family. She also let Sharon take him to the movie, at St. Jude's School. She said he was good, but I doubt it.*

*Tom went deer hunting with Pat Hutchins and Sherman and Steve. He saw three deer, but it was too dark in the morning, to get a shot off, so he came home, very tired and depressed. I think he is going to go again, at the end of this month. Tom wants me to go quail hunting with him, Sunday morning. I'm going. Love makes one do strange things. I'm sure I'll have fun. Tom makes everything fun. He really does.*

*It's time to make supper, so I better get going. Tom likes supper on time. Just remembered, my sister, Judy has been dating Ken Bauman for about two months. They seem to like each other quite a lot. Ken was in Vietnam, in the Army, for a year. They both belong to the ASYA Club. We are hoping something nice may happen.*

*I have to run now, so be good, Terry. Write when you get a chance.*

*Tom, Mary Rose, Tommy, Bryan and Marlene*

**Letter from my little brother, Tim, written by my Mom, November 7, 1968. Tim's 7th birthday was October 12th.**

*Dear Terry,*

*I am writing this letter to you for Timmy. I will write as he dictates.*

*"I am in 1st grade, and I am 7. Terry, one time I called my girlfriend up and she was in the bathtub, he-he-he. Her name is Laura. She's pretty.*

*I had a birthday party and I had ten presents. I had ten kids, and my best one, from Mom and Dad was a High Chaparral gun. (He just told me, this sure feels good, writing to Terry)*

*I was a skeleton, me and my friend, Robert Stokes, for Halloween, and we got lots of candy. Mom took us all over, and I got so tired. My feet were sure aching, and when I got home, I had to just sit down.*

*Some kids are in my class that were in kindergarten with me. I like it very much and my teacher is very nice, and her voice is nice, too. Her name is Mrs. Rathky (She's very pretty). All the kids at school have stood in the corner, all except me. I'm the only one left, and she's very pretty (He doesn't know I said that, already.). There's a boy named Ricky, and she thinks he's very cute and laughs at him. Sometimes I make mistakes. I leave my coat in the cafeteria, by accident. We are supposed to raise our hand before we go outside, and we have very much fun in gym. Some things are very hard in gym, but some things are fun. I told Mrs. Rathky that before you went in the Navy, you played the flute. I showed her one of your pictures, and she said, "Wow, he's handsome," and we have to wake up real early in the morning for school, and sometimes I'm early. That's because Mom takes me.*

*We have reading, mostly like we had in kindergarten, and on the days I don't go to this school, we go to St. Jude's for religious instructions, and we learn about God and Brandy, our dog, is grown up more.*

*All the kids are funny in my room, and one day Mrs. Rathky was telling us to read a story and she said, "You read it," and it said, "Go Dick, go, and he said "Giddy-up". She laughed and Mrs. Cooper, our music teacher, today played the record, "Peter and the Wolf", and we acted it out. One boy was a Grandfather, one boy was a duck, one a wolf and one was gate that Grandfather shuts. There is also a girl named Cindy Redmond and she was the bird and three other boys were the hunters, and I was Peter (He just said, I had a lot to say, when Sharon commented that he's writing a long letter). Tommy 2 is going to be three, November 17th. He just said; "Does Terry know we have another baby—Marlene? Not us—Mary". He said now, "Do you want this to be the end of the letter? Then say, "See you later, alligator. This is your friendly neighborhood Spiderman, saying, "Goodbye for now!"*

*Tim*

**Post Card from Mr. Phil Simon, Judi's father, while on a Jesuit retreat, November 8, 1968**
*Greetings and best wishes from White House. I am remembering you in my Masses and prayers, during my retreat. God bless you, Terry and may he see his way to have you home by Christmas, or soon after.*

*Philip Simon Sr.*

On Saturday, November 9th, Task Group Bravo inserted the 4th Battalion, Vietnamese Marine Corps along the Kinh Tri Ton. The landing was unopposed.

Group Alfa, Riv Div 91 boats were hit in two savage ambushes with rocket and small arms fire, Sunday, November 10th, while supporting two companies of Vietnamese Marines, east of Ben Tre. The first firefight occurred at 1450, shortly after the boats had backloaded the Marines from their morning operations area and were proceeding to new landing sites along the Rach Ben Tre.

One sailor from M-91-2 was tragically killed in the ambush. Three other crewmen were wounded. One Viet Cong was flat lined by the boat crewmen while suppressing the fire. The Vietnamese Marines were landed near the scene of the ambush but were unable to locate and destroy the enemy. The boats again came under attack at 1700, as the marines were being backloaded. There were no casualties in the second attack as the boats returned and suppressed the fire. Zippo 92-11 was one of the boats that took a rocket hit. The Marines were then returned to Base Glenn after which the assault craft returned to the MRB. Four of the Vietnamese Marines were also wounded during their morning operations ashore.

In other MRF Alfa action, Riv Div 112 took one company of the 3/60th Infantry from the MRB to a landing site on the Song Ham Luong, on Sunday morning, November 10th. The troops took one POW and one detainee while conducting operations throughout the day. They were returned to the MRB during the late evening.

Units of the 3/47th Inf. Bn., operating southeast of Ben Tre, reported three Viet Cong KIA and one Chicom carbine taken, during the day. Two soldiers were killed in action. The USAF accounted for ninety-eight bunkers and fourteen structures destroyed with two secondary explosions observed. One Viet Cong was also taken out by the 3/34th Artillery Battalion.

In Task Group Bravo, Riv Div 151 units conducted a *"R.A.R.E."* ambush operation along the Tinh Thi Ton. The 4th Battalion, VNMC, had no strong contact during the day, but received sniper fire. Thirteen Tango Boats were rotated from MRB Bravo with boats in the operations area.

Three men drowned Monday, November 11th, in two incidents at the Dong Tam anchorage. Two sailors fell overboard from A-111-1 about 1900 and could not be found in a search of the area. The two crewmen were FN Eddie M. Adams, and SN Theodore Harrison, Jr. Later in the evening, a soldier reportedly fell off a Tango boat near APL-26 and was still missing at 2200.

Imagine spending one year on a small boat, often with people shooting at you, and not once in that year ever tripping, or losing your footing, during the light of day, or in the dark of night. Imagine a dark, muddy river that sweeps you away before anyone knows you are gone. That was living on the Mekong.

Tuesday, November 12th, Monitor 131-2 was ambushed with a B-40 rocket while supporting *Sea Lords* operations on the Rach Gia Canal, ten kilometers, or six miles, northeast of Rach Gia. One sailor, GMG2 James A. Myers Jr., was sadly killed in the attack. Three sailors and one Vietnamese were wounded.

*"National Turn in Your Draft Card Day"* was observed by sensitive, righteous young men on American college campuses, on November 14th, 1968, protesting John F. Kennedy and Lyndon B. Johnson's war. On that day, Task Group Bravo was conducting patrol and minesweeping duty operations along the Kinh Tu Ha, Tien Den Rach Gia and the Kinh Luvnh Guynh Rivers. I wasn't especially empathetic with the college protesters.

An underwater explosion sank YLLC-4, about 2215, Friday, November 15th, in the Ham Long River, two miles south of Ben Tre. Two of her fourteen crewmen were killed and nine others were wounded. Four sailors aboard refueler R-92-2 alongside the YLLC-4 at the time of the explosion were also wounded.

From November 16th to 21st, River Assault Craft of Riv Rons 13 and 15 shifted their areas of operations to an area about twenty-five miles southeast of Rach Gia. After landing the Fourth Battalion of the Vietnamese Marine Corps, the craft set up interdiction blocking stations in the surrounding waterways.

Late Saturday night, the Vietnamese Marines with Group Bravo deep sixed two Viet Cong in a sampan in the Song Cai Lon. The sampan contained ten grenades, a loudspeaker, VC documents and a Viet Cong flag. The Vietnamese Maries killed four additional Viet Cong during a night firefight and captured one carbine and three AK-50's. One Vietnamese Marine wounded in the ground action was medevacked to the USS Nuesces.

Riv Div 151 boats were ambushed with B-40 rockets and small arms fire from the south bank of the Rach Ong Chuong, Saturday morning, November 16th, two and half miles south of Can Giouc. Two sailors of T-151-1 were wounded when a rocket exploded under the flight deck of their boat.

**Wounded Vietnamese Marine being medevacked off my boat.**

Two men of the 3/47<sup>th</sup> Infantry Battalion, operating with Group Alfa, were wounded Sunday, November 17<sup>th</sup>, on operations in Kien Hoa Province when they tripped a grenade booby trap. Two enemy sampans were destroyed and a Viet Cong recruiting station was discovered.

Group Bravo and the Vietnamese Marines began operations along the Rach Cai Mon on Sunday morning, November 17<sup>th</sup>. One VNMC was killed and two more were wounded during the day's action.

**In a tape home, I talked with our crew about our experiences, while searching sampans.**

I wondered out loud, *"What can we tell them about the operation we just finished?"*

Hodges jumped in, again, sarcastically, *"It was an exciting operation! Steaming up and down the river!"*

I added, *"Blocking Stations! How many sampans did we search?"*

Hodge replied that our boat searched six sampans, further adding, *"Two old women and those kids."*

Joking, I asked, *"Did our captain have us point our 16's at 'em? I can't remember."*

In his natural state of sarcasm, Hodge replied, *"Oh, he wouldn't do that!"*

With underlying mockery, Ledford added, *"Yes. Along with the .30's, .the 50's and the 20MM cannons!"*

I recalled, *"He had everybody train their guns on the old man."*

Shaking his head, Ledford said, *"The "papa-san" couldn't even paddle the boat, he was so old!"*

Imitating our boat captain, I said, *"He kept yelling: "Keep your guns on him! Keep your guns on him!"*

Ledford shook his head, again. *"There was just a little bit of rice in there. You could SEE everything in the boat! It was just a little old sampan, like a dugout canoe!*

I turned to Bird Man. *"Tell them about the sampans that would come out at dark, Bird."*

Bird Man explained,

> *There's not supposed to be any traffic movement of sampans on these small streams, at night, especially down in this place we just came from, call the U Minh Forest, 'cause it's mostly V.C., and there was a sampan out, one night and one of the boats hailed it down for a search and to find out what they were doing, out there. Evidently, these people are scared of us. A lot of these people down there have seen very few Americans, so a boat full of guns scares them, so they ran. The boat opened up on them and shot at them with 20MM cannons.*

I suggested that they should have known better than to be on the river that night. *"There's nothing you can do about that kind of stuff. There's a curfew. What is it? Sundown, or a particular time?"*

Hodge answered, *"2100."*

I continued. *"2100, or, 9:00 P.M., civilian time. They're not supposed to be on the rivers AT ALL, unless they have a white light on the boat, which means it's an emergency. Sometimes, and I don't know why they do it, but they'll go out with NO lights at all, in an area they're not supposed to BE IN, at all!"*

Hodge added *"They try to sneak by!"*

Trying to put some sense to it, I explained to Judi and the family, *"They try to sneak by, and they just don't get by our boats! As a matter of self-defense, the boats logically assume they are V.C. escaping, or trying to get on the other side of us, to put some rounds into us. How many sampans did we sink during the whole thing?"*

Ledford furrowed his brow, thinking about it, then said, *"I don't know. They never gave a count on it, really."*

It seemed to me that we had sunk, or at least shot at, quite a few. *"It was at least six or nine, wasn't it? The first night we had contact, we sunk three of them, didn't we? I saw one of them on fire. I was laying on the flight deck, trying to sleep and I saw one of them, on fire."*

Ledford shrugged. *"They probably actually completely destroyed one sampan."*

I thought back to shooting at one sampan with my M-16.

*I guess we haven't got much proof. We leave that to the brass. That first sampan, the guy said to open up on any sampan we saw. Remember when we all opened up with our M-16's? I took two shots at one, but I couldn't see it very well, so I gave my 16 to a guy who said he could see it. He was looking at it with a "Starlight" scope, though.*

**(In order to avoid a situation in which a Vietnamese could be shot and killed for not stopping when we ordered them to, one of our crew sent home for a pellet gun. Our thought was that if a sampan didn't stop when we ordered them to, possibly because they could not hear us, we would shoot them with a non-lethal pellet gun, first, as a warning. We never encountered that situation. It was only used twice to kill. In one instance, Ledford killed a snake alongside our boat, shooting it in the middle of the head, while standing on our helo deck. Another time, he surprised me with his accuracy, by shooting a bird out of the air. )**

Suddenly excited, Hodge said, *"I wanted to shoot at it with my A.K.!"*

Speaking both to the tape recorder and to Hodge, I said,

*Yeah! Hodges has an AK-47, rifle! It's the prime weapon of the V.C. It is Chinese made, isn't it?*

Hodge nodded. *"Yeah."*

I then gave my opinion on the Kalashnikov

*It's Chinese made, Russian designed, and it is at least as good as the M-16, at least in some respects.*

Hodge was more enthusiastic. *"Better than the 16, at least in maintenance and reliability."*

I further explained to the family,

*The V.C. will ambush American troops, or boats, or something, then, before they can be caught, they'll bury their AK-47, wrapped in a rag. Days later, they can dig it up and fire it, without even cleanin' it! It's a very good weapon. It is not very accurate at long distance though, is it?*

Hodge agreed.

*Nah. Ya' got a leaf sight on it, like the old British rifles. You gotta monkey that leaf sight. Set your leaf sight and it'll shoot straight. You can't hit a target at long range. It's not worth the trouble to mess with. It's just fun to play with, though.*

I supported Hodges evaluation. *"I know V.C. are bad shots with it."*

The overwhelming majority of our casualties on the boats came from RPG's. Some were from recoilless rifle fire, mines, and heavy automatic weapons. It was pretty rare for them to hit anyone on the boats with a rifle round.

Hodge sneered. *"Yeah. Well, they don't even understand leaf sights! If it goes "BANG," it must work!"*

I made a derogatory remark, towards the Vietnamese, but also towards myself.

*As far as mechanical ability, they can't even use a knife, fork and spoon! They gotta use chopsticks! Of course, come to think of it, I can't use chopsticks!*

**Me, preparing to search a sampan.**

The official Operations Report noted that on November 19th and 20th, Task Group Bravo conducted blocking and interdiction operations in central Kien Hoa Province.

Riv Ron 15 was attacked with B-40 and automatic weapons fire from the south bank of the Song Cai Lon on, November 20th. One ASPB was struck in the stern by a rocket. The enemy's fire was returned and suppressed. Following the beach prep, a landing was made at the ambush site by the embarked 4th Battalion of the Vietnamese Marine Corps, which swept the area, destroying six bunkers and snuffing out one Viet Cong.

The official reports indicated that during night action in the same zone, four enemy sampans were sunk and sixty-six sampans were searched.

Thursday night, November 21$^{st}$, Riv Ron 13 was the target of a mortar attack, consisting of six 60MM and 82MM mortar rounds from 500 meters east of our position on the Song Cai Be, in Kien Giang Province. The boats extracted the Vietnamese regional forces we were operating with, and moved to the Song Cai Lon.

On the 22$^{nd}$ of November, A-131-1 and A-132-1 were *chopped* to TF 116 PBR's, for interdiction operations on the Vinh Te Canal, southwest of Chow Duc, on the Cambodian border.

**Audio Tape Home: Saturday, November 23, 1968.**
The tape opens with Ledford softly singing,

> *"Once, there were green fields, kissed by the sun. Once, there were valleys, where rivers used to run.*

> *Once, there were blue skies, with white clouds up above."* That's all.

I broke in, explaining to the family where we were;

> *We're sittin' on the boat, here at Dong Tam!*

Turning to Ledford, I asked,

> *I've got 6:33. What'd you got?*

Ledford replied, "*6:33, right now.*"

Nearby, a *"boatswain's pipe"* blew, three short whistles.

The two of us jumped to our feet. I announced, "*Attention to colors!*"

Ledford and I turned in the direction of the American flag being lowered, and saluted. A few seconds later, the whistle blew three more times, signaling *"At ease."*

(We didn't mind jumping up to salute *"the colors."* It represented our country. It represented home. It represented our loved ones, everything we believed in, everything we cherished and everything Americans died for in all of the wars before the one we were fighting at that moment. We loved our flag. Unfortunately, it doesn't have the universal respect of Americans, today.)

I spoke into the microphone; *"We had to stand for "colors." O.K., Glenn, where's your second hand, since we've got new watches, now and we "set" our watches, today? I'm sure your watch is slow."*

Ledford argued, "*No! Yours is fast! What's the exact minutes you have?*"

> *6:33..... And a half.*

> *Umm... Yeah.*

> *Anyway, it's around 6:30, Saturday, November 23$^{rd}$. We just got back off the op, yesterday, at 1:30. It started the first of the month. I failed to mention it was Ledford singing at the beginning of this tape. He's a Radioman Third Class on our boat. He's O, K., 'cept sometimes he makes me kind'a sick.*

Ledford good naturedly chuckled at that.

I suggested to Ledford that we tell my family about the operation we just completed.

Ledford began, knowing that I didn't want them to hear about firefights, or anything that would worry them,

> *Well, we were out all this month, a very long operation, operating around Rach Gia, a little village on the west coast of Vietnam, facing the Gulf of Thailand. Really not much to it, except sometimes we had to go out at night.*

I told the family what we called it. *"Rat Patrol."*

> *"Rat Patrol," or "Hunt and Kill," as they call it.*

I continued,

> *That's a new area for the Mobile Riverine Force. I doubt if they've been around that area, very much at all. One time, we were all very low on supplies, so they flew out these sundry packs, with candy, soap, shaving kits and stuff like that. We wore dirty clothes, most of the time, wouldn't you say that?*

Ledford confirmed: *"Yes. I would say that!"*

> *We were somewhat unshaven. Ledford was growing a "Van Dyke." He had a goatee and a mustache. I had a... I don't know what you'd call it. What would you call it, Glenn?*

Ledford laughed and said: *"I'd call it an "Uncle Remus."*

> *Oh! Don't give me that! There's no mustache and I didn't grow anything on my neck. It was just down my sideburns and along my jawline.*

Ledford added, *"It was like the old pictures of Abraham Lincoln!"*

> *Yeah, but it wasn't as bushy.*

> *It would have been, after a while!*

I continued; *"We had "Tiger Beer," or "Biere Larue." What do you think of Tiger Beer?*

> *I like Tiger Beer better than "Ba Moui Ba," or "33" beer.*

> *They're O.K. You get hard up for something to drink around here.*

> *Well, they make it out of river water, for one thing....*

> *Do they?*

> *Yeah. They don't have any distributors around here.*

> *We use their ice. It's made from this stupid river water.*

> *Their river water isn't like what you might have in St. Louis; crystal clear river water.*

Ledford hadn't been to St. Louis. I laughed;

> *We don't have "crystal clear" river water in St. Louis! Have you SEEN the Mississippi River?*

> *I've seen it in the Mississippi Delta!*

*Does it look like this?*

*Yeah.*

I answered in the popular expression of American troops and Vietnamese; *"Same same" around St. Louis."*

*"Same same" like Houston*

Perhaps out of exhaustion, I gave more indication of combat operations than I had previously, in letters, or tapes. I had never uttered a word to Judi or the family that I had seen combat.

*We had a little bit of activity. In the letters I get from them, they kept talking about how the war's all stepped up and it sounds like the papers are saying we've really been having a hard time. I haven't noticed much of a change, really.*

Ledford agreed;

*No. It doesn't change much for us, unless they have a big offensive and there's a lot of sampans on the river.*

*The bombing halt hasn't really directly affected us, yet. It might, sometime in the future, but I haven't noticed any increase, or decrease in action.*

*That's because we don't get any "slack!" We're always operating, except for that one month of BID patrol we had, we're always steady operating! No slack! We wouldn't know if there was a lull, or anything!*

After expressing some natural frustration after our long and frequent operations, Ledford and I suddenly realized again that this tape was going home to my family, who we have sheltered from the reality of ambushes, firefights, mortar attacks, sniper fire and other combat experiences. We immediately started to soften the message to my family.

Ledford assured the people at home;

*We're hardly getting any action, anyway.... Occasional fire....Nothin' to worry about.....*

Changing the subject, I quickly threw out;

*We had one hundred cases of C-rations when we started the op. We traded off.... I don't know HOW much!*

Ledford gave his estimate.

*Over three quarters of it!*

(If each case cost the tax payers $35, we either ate, or traded away, $2,625 worth of C-Rations, in 1968 dollars.)

*Yep! For beer and ice!*

*Hammocks.*

*Yeah. Hammocks and bananas.*

Completing the list, Ledford added; *"Cooking pots and pans, kerosene stoves."*

The list of trades naturally brought me to the subject of our new found creativity, regarding C-Rations.

*Should I tell them about our "gourmet delights?*

Ledford laughed and waved his arm at me:

*You go ahead. You're the cook! Terry's the big "cook" on the boat!*

*You cook, too! He comes up with brilliant ideas on how to re-form C-Rations into something edible!*

Proudly, I told Ledford to talk about my culinary combat *"masterpiece."*

*Tell them about our "chicken casserole!"*

*Terry saved up chicken and noodles, boned turkey, turkey loaf, for about three days. What the gooks didn't eat, we saved. Saved it all up for one meal! We just got through trading for pots and pans. We had plenty of cooking utensils and we had our new kerosene stoves that we traded for. So we got it all together and mixed cheese, chicken and noodles, boned turkey, turkey loaf, boned chicken and onions, all in two medium sized pots. They'd be small pots, back home. Then we mixed it all together. It didn't LOOK too good, but it TASTED real good, I'd say!*

*It was the best meal we had, out there!*

*It was definitely the best meal! Black One didn't like it, too much, though.*

*Remember when we told him he could help himself?*

*Yeah. We told him he could eat OUR C-Rations, if he wanted to! Actually, he claims everything on the boat is HIS! We eat HIS C-Rations. We stay on HIS boat.*

*That's the big joke on the boat!*

*We drink <u>HIS</u> water.*

*You're always messin' up <u>HIS</u> radios!*

Ledford's frustration showed: *"I'M the radioman, but they're <u>HIS</u> radios!"*

*"Same same" with the guns. Hodges is the Gunners Mate, but they're all <u>HIS</u> guns!*

Ledford shook his head in agreement: *"He wants all of <u>HIS</u> guns in "good operating order at all times!"*

He's the epitome of courage and, uh... fortitude, on this boat!

Ledford: *"In fact, he's got a new flak jacket that even protects his intestines. Intestinal fortitude!"*

*He wears these new flak pants around his waist and stomach, like a big diaper, plus his flak jacket, then puts another flak jacket over his legs when he sits in the boat captain's chair, behind the cox'n. He's somethin' else!*

*Plus, his helmet. If they had anything else, he'd wear it!*

*I'm surprised he doesn't get "flak sleeves" and "flak gloves!"*

*He's got everything available!*

I described Black One's ritual prior to every operation;

> *Before we go out on an operation, he goes around the coxn's flat, picking up cigarette packages, anything that's white, or anything that may stand out, visually.*

Ledford chuckled;

> *He doesn't want to draw fire, does he? When we were on transit, the night before last, he was in the coxswain's flat. That's when you were on the bow, giving us directions. Black One was kind of creeping his eyes up, so that only his helmet and his eyes were showing. I said: "Hey Dick! You trying to draw fire with that white T-shirt on, under your flak jacket? You can see a "V" of white, under your neck!" He said: "Oh my God! I didn't realize I had that on!" He jumped down into the coxn's flat, tore off his flak jacket and T-shirt, then put his flak jacket back on. He was really worried, there!*

While Black One was having a panic attack because he had a white T-shirt under his flak jacket, I was on the bow of the boat. We were transiting a narrow canal, in the heart of the U Minh Forest, a Viet Cong stronghold, where 500 French paratroopers disappeared, years earlier. The canal was perhaps only slightly wider than a two lane street. From roughly midnight, until early in the morning, Black One told me to stand on the bow, holding a large, yellow, square, battery powered, Navy floodlight. It was my job to yell directions back to him and the coxswain, providing navigation, so that we didn't run aground. On November 20th, 1968, there was no moonlight. For several hours, I stood on the bow of our armored troop carrier, holding a BRIGHT FLOODLIGHT, on a narrow canal, at four or five miles an hour, in Viet Cong territory, YELLING directions to our coxswain and boat captain.

I held the floodlight as far from my body as I could get it. I fully expected the light to be shot at, and that there was a good chance I'd be killed, that night, comforted only by the knowledge that Black One had removed his white T-shirt from under his flak jacket and was safely ensconced, so that only his eyes were exposed to any enemy fire that might miss me.

I really disliked my first boat captain, on T-131-3, as much as I really liked and admired my second boat captain, Don "Mac" McGriff. A boat captain made a literal life or death difference in Vietnam. A bad boat captain could get you killed, or simply make your life miserable. Black One was the second boat captain to be assigned to T-131-9. The crew had so little confidence in their first boat captain, that they expressed it to the division and squadron command, getting him removed from the boat. Later, the crew came to feel that the squadron officers looked upon the complaint as somewhat of a *"mutiny"* and intentionally gave them a boat captain that they would not like. Some may consider the nickname given Black One as evidence that our dislike for him was born of racism, but that wasn't it. It was directly related to how the crew viewed his character, his life or death command decisions, and how he treated us.

I continued making fun of our boat captain, saying;

> *You know, he has that grey flashlight on his flak jacket. I'm going to bring that up, one of these days, just to see how fast he tears it off!*

Ledford laughed hard, saying,

> *He'd do it! He told me about his white shirt, "I didn't realize I had that on! Why didn't you tell me, SOONER?" He ate me out about it, because I didn't tell him about it, SOONER!*

> *We've been kind of cutting him down, here, lately.*

Ledford agreed. *"He deserves every bit of it!"*

*Like when we had the chicken casserole and I told him, "Go ahead! Help yourself! Don't be shy!"*

*He got all upset, because he felt it was all his food, anyway.*

It seemed like we could never run out of stories about our boat captain. Ledford remembered another incident.

*What about the insect repellent? I thought that was pretty funny!*

*Yeah! We were up here, on the helo pad, layin' around and he had a bottle of insect repellant next to him. I picked up the insect repellent and said: "Here, put some of my insect repellent on." He jumped up and said: "What do you mean YOUR insect repellent? That's MY insect repellent! I requisitioned four bottles of it, for the boat! I put three up there, for the six of you and only ONE for me!"*

*He said: "I only kept one bottle for myself! Only one!"*

I laughed; *"I said to him; "Yeah. Three for six of us and one for one of us!"*

Ledford recalled another story:

*Another thing Terry put him down on is when we were in the little gook hootch, when we were drinking beer. Black One told me he wasn't going to let me have any more beer, 'cause I had enough trouble with my radios, as it was.*

*Yeah. He said, "We can receive, but we can't transmit!"*

Laughing, Ledford jumped in:

*Terry said: "You're probably talking into the wrong end of the phone!" That was number one cut!*

I chimed in,

*He called me names for about five minutes! You were laughing, and he was saying; "Yeah! Ledford likes that! Ledford likes that!*

*That WAS "number one!" Why didn't I think of that?*

*I think he really was kind of mad. Not that I really care.*

Ledford laughed,

*He knows that when he talks to you, he usually gets put down.*

*It's not that we're sarcastic, or anything! Let's see…*

I recognized we were living through the most exotic, wild, crazy, days of our lives, and that we were a small part of a tapestry of events that would go down in history. I wanted the family to know any of the details that would not upset them. I pushed for more narrative.

*What are some of the other interesting things we can tell them about? I got a music sheet from one of them. "Moui" was his name.*

Hodge added, *"Tam" had a bunch of that stuff, too!*

Reflecting back on our time with the Vietnamese Marines, I shook my head and replied,

> *This was "Moui," I think. He was a short, nice lookin' guy. He told us about his "lufer" in Saigon. He was a cool head. He had a portfolio of songs. I couldn't read them, but you could tell what they were by the way they were phrased, the stanzas, you know.*

Dealing a pun to the conversation, Hodge threw out,

> *Vietnamese all looks "Greek" to me.*

I was a little dense. I tried to explain, "*You know, like a poem is.....*"

Hodges cut me off: "*Yeah! Yeah! I caught it!*"

Still unaware of my denseness, I pushed on,

> *Anyway, in his portfolio, he had the song, "Greenfields," in Vietnamese and American. We've been tryin' to learn both of them, but not having much luck. Maybe we'll have another go at it, later.*

Here are the lyrics to *"Green Fields,"* in Vietnamese and English

*cánh đồng xanh*
*Green Fields*

*"Một khi đã có các lĩnh vực màu xanh lá cây, hôn bởi ánh nắng mặt trời.*
*Once there were green fields, kissed by the sun.*

*Một khi đã có các thung lũng, nơi con sông được sử dụng để chạy.*
*Once there were valleys, where rivers used to run.*

*Một khi đã có bầu trời xanh với các đám mây trắng ở trên cao.*
*Once there were blue skies, with white clouds high above.*

*Một khi họ đã là một phần của một tình yêu mai.*
*Once they were part of an everlasting love.*

Running out of meaningful conversation, I was grasping at straws, saying,

> *We'll have the chickens say a few words on the tape, before we finish!*

Hodges contributed, *"The chickens are getting fat!"*

I laughed.

> *Yes, they are! We've got a rooster and a hen. We've been feedin' 'em rice that the "Seven Dwarfs" left on board. They used to be scared to death of us. I got a picture of them, today. Judi will probably show it to everybody at home. They're sitting on our .30 caliber machine guns. I said "sitting." They did do something else on them, as well! Dickey Lou (Black One) wants them, so that he can have eggs. We have to clean up after them, so that our Boat Captain can have eggs!*

Ledford jumped in. "*Gunner* (Hodges) *had to clean them! They're his guns!*"

I looked at Hodge and asked,

*We didn't get too much sleep on this operation. I didn't write too many letters. How many hours do you think we spent in our gun mounts?*

Hodge replied:

*On the way down there, it was about sixteen hours. If you counted up each day, I think it averaged out to about sixteen hours a day.*

Trying to give the family back home a broader perspective, I asked Hodge,

*In the whole nineteen or twenty days, how many hours do you think we spent in our gun mounts?*

Sarcastically, Hodge answered, *"Oh, about eighteen days."*

Ledford thought out loud,

*We spent a lot of our time sitting on top of our gun mounts. Black One wanted us to keep our heads up, at all times, so that he could keep his head down.*

Glenn realized he might be giving my family an idea of the real danger of the situation we were in and immediately tried to minimize any concern or worry they could have.

*Not that it was dangerous! It was just "uncomfortable" up there, having to watch where the boat was going, which is HIS job, anyway!*

*The Seven Dwarfs helped themselves to our beer, but of course, they brought us beer, too! As a matter of fact, they wanted us to eat a lot of their meals.*

Ledford shook his head in disgust, thinking of the Vietnamese food. *"We just couldn't hack their chow."*

Hodge joined in, with the expected sarcasm, *"You should try Vietnamese fish! The stuff is great!"*

Remembering our first day with the Vietnamese Marines, I said,

*I smelled it, but that's all I could do! When they first came on our boat, they handed me a small fish, like they were eating. It looked like it was just laid out in the sun, to dry. To be polite, I put it in my mouth and pretended to like it, then I went back on the stern and spit it out.*

Aghast, Hodges added, *"They just burn it over a fire! No salt. No pepper. Just burnt fish!"*

I wanted to warn Judi and the family that they may not be getting letters from me, in the days ahead.

*Before I forget, there's going to be a few days in the future, I won't be able to write. This is Saturday. We're going out again, on Monday.*

Hodges thought I was off by one day. *"No. Tuesday, the 26th."*

I continued.

*Anyway, in the next two or three days. We're going to be going out again for six or ten days. The last time we went out, we were under the supervision of Riv Ron 15. Now, this time, my squadron will be in charge. The commodore and the division officers in charge this time, were pretty good, in most respects, except they kept sticking us with all the rotten jobs, stuff like…*

*Bird Man* was still thinking about the snake.

> *When we go out next time we gotta get a python and get pictures taken with it! I'd like to get one. Tell them what we're gonna get when we get in Dong Tam!*

Hodge was fired up. *"We're gonna get us a pet monkey!"*

I thought back to my time on Tango 6.

> *I had a monkey when I was on Tango 6! Well, I didn't have it. The boat had it! I'm starting to talk like our captain! We had to get rid of it, the same day, because the commodore saw it.*

I continued the tape, alone.

*I'm here by myself, now. We kept talking on the other side of the tape and I didn't know that the tape had run out. There's a quarter moon out.*

*You mentioned in my last letter that I sounded kind of depressed, or something. I just get in moods like that, once in a while. I'm O.K. Most of the time, I'm in a pretty good mood, on the boat. No sweat.*

*One of the things that gets me, lately, is that it's getting closer to the time to come home. I really should be a lot happier.... I don't know...... Now that it's down to two or three months, all I can think about is how much I want to get home! It makes me hate being over here, more, and more anxious to get home! I guess I'll feel better when it gets down to a month. I don't know. And, I guess, on the tape, when you heard about the women getting shot.... Things like that kind'a make me sick. I just get sick of the whole mess, over here.*

*I heard about something in the papers about some boats shooting up some innocent people in Cambodia. It wasn't the Riv Rons. I doubt if it was Riv Ron 9 or 11 and I know it wasn't Riv Ron 13, or 15. I'd say it was probably the Swift Boats that patrolled the coast, or close to the inland waterways, around the coast. Like I said before, those things just happen, and there's nothing you can do about it. It's just like when Marines call in air strikes and get bombed by their own planes. It's going to happen, in war.*

*When the boats are ambushed, the rounds from the machine guns can go a long way. The V.C. decide where and when to ambush us. It is their fault when the rounds fired at them, pass through their ambush and hit civilians. The good thing about my 20MM cannon is that the ammo is "point detonating." When it hits something, it will explode. We have high explosive and incendiary rounds, made to burn, or start fires. There are also armor piercing rounds, but we usually take them out, because they make the guns jam. I'm lucky, because I don't have to worry too much about my rounds going into a village. If there is a risk, they'll give us limits, or tell us to keep our fire on the banks. I was on .30 caliber and .50 caliber machine guns, when I was in the well deck of the boat, on Tango 6. You worry about hitting innocent people, but there's nothing you can do.*

*As far as hating the Viet Cong, I don't really hate them, although there's been moments that I have. It's just a matter of self-defense. We're over here. We're supposed to fight them. They fight us. We fight them back. That's all we can do.*

*I read something once about the serviceman in Vietnam being a "professional fighter." I guess that's true, to an extent. The majority of people over here don't really believe in "the cause." I did, once. It's hard to accept the concept that fighting the Viet Cong is protecting America, but I imagine in the long run, it is. The way we figure it is that the V.C. want to take us on, so we'll take them on. If they fight us, we'll fight them.*

*I've seen V.C., on this operation. The Vietnamese Marines caught quite a few of them. I saw a whole bunch of them, sitting on the stern of our Communications and Command, "CCB" boat. Every time I see them, it surprises me, because I expect them to look "different" somehow, with really mean faces, or sneaky looking*

242

*eyes. But, they look like any peasant, or any "country boy" in Vietnam. Their ages range from the same age as my kid brothers, to very old men.*

*Hodge just stopped by, to borrow my extra glasses, so he can catch a flick, on the base. I've never known anyone else who could see out of my glasses!*

*During this operation, we had to mine sweep, a lot of times, and it messed up our screws and our "port" shaft. We had a large vibration of the boat, due to the shaft being off. They are replacing both screws and the port shaft. It's a pretty big job. I don't really mind. This is like a holiday. We don't have to go on "racetrack," tonight. That's when the ships shift anchor and move, in order to minimize the opportunity for the enemy to attack them during the night, from either bank. When they do that, we circle around like a racetrack, for about an hour and a half, until they anchor.*

*One of the guys from my class that I came over here with, just came over to talk to me. His boat just finished their yard period, in Dong Tam. They had some "skinny," that's Navy for "rumor," that we will be relieved off the boats in January, but not necessarily going home, then. I'm guessing I might have two months, left on the boat. I guess that has good and bad points. If I had some time in Dong Tam, I could get squared away, get a decent uniform and a suitcase. I could rest up a bit. Then again, there's something about the boats. I don't know what it is. I feel like I'm doing a job, over here. I was a pawn, on the Enterprise, with 6,500 men, on it. Sometimes it distressed me that I would be gone for all the time we were in the Tonkin Gulf, but it really wouldn't make any difference if I was there, or not. On the boats, every man is important. With seven men, every man plays a vital part. Every man is needed. We matter.*

*If I was just sitting in Dong Tam, I wouldn't feel useful. On the boat, I do a job, and I think I do it pretty well.*

*Oh yeah! I got that Thanksgiving package! Thank You! I didn't even realize it was Thanksgiving! When you're on an operation, you just forget stuff like that. I'll be at Dong Tam for Christmas, so maybe I'll catch a USO Show, there. I've been thinking about rigging up some kind of Christmas tree and making some decorations to put on the boat, doing something to give it the "Christmas Spirit."*

*Happy Birthday to Timmy! I'm awfully sorry I didn't get a letter to him. It's kind of busy here, sometimes. Anyway, Happy Birthday, Timmy!*

*Mom, you are too worried about me being in danger. I guess anybody in Vietnam is in a certain amount of danger, but I'm not at all worried, so you don't have to. I mean, really! I'm not in any danger. I don't know how to explain it. It's no sweat. I'm O.K.! I'll be O.K.!*

*Since Thanksgiving is coming up, I feel like I have a lot more to be thankful for, being over here, than a lot of people in the states, do. I've had some good things and some bad things happen to me, over here, but, every year, I feel more and more thankful of the blessings that I have. I've had more luck than some of the guys I came over here with, especially the guys that went to Riv Ron 9 and 11. My buddy, Freddie, was the same age as me, and he drowned, in May.*

*You said something about that LST that was mined. That's the LST that was with Riv Ron 9 and 11, the Westchester County. It was with Group Alpha. One of the guys from my class was on the pontoon, next to the Westchester County. He's been sent back to the states. They don't know if he's going to live, or not. Some guys....well,..... I'm thankful for what I've got.*

*Tim and Sharon got good report cards? I'm glad they are both doing very well in school!*

*I'm the only one on the boat, right now. Glenn was supposed to be on watch, but he wanted to catch a flick and I wanted to do this, so I took it.*

*I see you're upset about me being near Cambodia. I think Riv Ron 13 and 15 are probably still going to be in this area when I'm taken off the boat.*

*You said, what if I got captured? That's no sweat! On the last operation, I counted thirty-one boats! We have Cobra gunship support! They have rocket pods and mini-guns! They fire something like 6,000 rounds a minute! We also have artillery and air support, whenever we want it! Besides, these boats are more powerful than they may look in the pictures! They can put an incredible amount of destruction on the beach. There's NO chance of us getting captured!*

*It seems like these little countries get brave when they're facing unarmed, or lightly armed intelligence ships, or when a "not at all armed" launch strays near their territory. That's what Cambodia captured. It was a "Mike 6." At the most, it had just a couple .50 caliber machine guns, with a crew of three or four. It might have even been an "LCU," too. They carry two .50 caliber machine guns. They're a little bigger. I told you what we carry. We carry four thirty caliber machine guns, two .50 caliber machine guns, two 20MM cannons, a Mark 19 grenade launcher that fires four-hundred grenades a minute, plus our crew has personal weapons, such as M-16's, shotguns and M-79 grenade launchers. Anyway, it's "no sweat" about Cambodia. They would NEVER try anything with our boats! As a matter of fact, I got so mad when Korea took the intelligence ship and Cambodia took that LCM, or LCU, I kind'a wanted them to come and take us! They wouldn't take these boats without a fight! The V.C. aren't operating around Cambodia. It's mostly North Vietnamese. In a way, we have an advantage with them. They wear uniforms and can't blend in with the population, as well. Don't worry about me. I'm safe.*

*I'm really lucky as far as letters, go. Some guys go three months without getting a letter. I get all bent out of shape if I don't get one every day!*

*Tim, I read your letter to some of my buddies! They think you're really funny! By the way, do you think it's alright to call that girl, Laura, while she's in the bath tub? I'm glad she's pretty, anyway!*

*That must have been some birthday party, to have ten kids, ten presents, and a "High Chaparral" gun! I think I've seen that show, maybe five times, at the most. It's good, though!*

*I'm standin' watch. It is quarter after nine, now. I'm reading the letters and taping by flashlight. We can't have any lights on the boat, at night.*

*I got a nice post card from Mr. Simon. I want to thank him, for it.*

End.

One or two nights after coming back from the long operation, Ledford and I came back to the boat after having a few beers. The chickens, *"Mamma San"* and *"Pappa San"* annoyed Glenn, because WE had to clean up all of their chicken crap, so he grabbed them, tied a set of sound powered phones, or whatever he could find, to them, and then threw them in the river.

Saturday, November 23rd, M-131-2 and T-131-11 assisted 2 PBR's late Thursday evening in the salvage of one damaged PBR at an ambush site along the Kinh Rach Soi Di Vam. The boats fired 105MM and 20MM rounds into the ambush area, but no return fire was reported.

Allied Forces wiped out thirty-five Viet Cong, as *"Operation Mangrove Serpent II"* continued Sunday, November 24th, in the Mo Cay District of Kien Hoa Province. The 3/47th Infantry Battalion sent one V.C. to his Heavenly Hootch. They also uncovered an enemy first aid station, and detained eight suspects for questioning. Two U.S. soldiers were wounded during the day. The 3/60th Infantry Battalion captured ten pounds of enemy documents, detained thirty-six suspects, and killed nine Viet Cong. One of their own troops was killed by a booby trap, however, and one other injured. Air gunships scored nine V.C. KIA's and sustained three friendly wounded Sunday, while the Air Cavalry ventilated thirteen Viet Cong, and an Army C&C, chopper killed two.

244

The Vietnamese Marines, supported by boats of Riv Div 91, captured twenty-five pounds of medical supplies and destroyed forty Chicom grenades. U.S. Air Force planes destroyed twenty-seven enemy structures and bumped off one Viet Cong. At 1520 Sunday afternoon the Ben Tre Airfield received six rounds of 82MM mortar fire. No casualties were reported,

A Medcap mission was conducted at a village approximately one-kilometer southwest of BenTre, with seventy-five patients treated and four medically evacuated to the Ben Tre Hospital. An assortment of papers, pencils, and various school supplies were also distributed among the children.

Sixteen Viet Cong got their wings, courtesy of the MRF Monday, November 25th, in Kien Hoa Province. Air action accounted for eight of the dead V.C. The 3/34th Artillery Battalion took out five. Meanwhile, the Air Force destroyed twenty-seven structures. The 3/47th Infantry Battalion wasted two Viet Cong, captured one Chinese communist carbine and two pounds of documents. They also destroyed several booby traps. The 3/60th Infantry Battalion scratched one Viet Cong, but also sustained one friendly fatality and eight wounded in action. Most of the casualties were due to an enemy booby trap.

Later, on November 25th, my unit, River Assault Squadron 13, loaded some of the 1/32nd Battalion, 21st ARVN Infantry Division., the 4/14th Battalion, 9th ARVN Infantry Div., two companies of the Ba Xuyen Regional Force, one company of the Ba Xuyen PRU's, and fifteen Ba Xuyen National Police teams, at Can Tho. We then traveled down the Bassac River, to conduct river assault operations on the Dung Island complex. While the troops searched for Viet Cong, ashore, the Vietnamese River Assault boats joined PBR's in blockading the islands. We searched 264 sampans and checked out 410 Vietnamese. The operation ended on November 29th, the same day that River Assault Division 151 concluded its lengthy operations at Nha Be and rejoined Mobile Riverine Group Bravo. One Viet Cong was killed by the ground forces, on the morning of the 25th.

Group Bravo, including Riv Ron 13, searched 257 sampans, checked 352 people and detained fourteen suspects Wednesday, November 27th, as operations continued in the vicinity of the Dung Island complex. ARVN units captured two POW's, one rifle, ten kilos of TNT, fifty grenades, and 1,000 rounds of small arms ammunition. Two Viet Cong operated POW camps, each having a 500-person capacity, were destroyed.

In Group Bravo activity on November 27th, Seawolf helicopters provided spotting assistance for the USS Hunterdon County, which supported riverine-armed reconnaissance along the Kinh Phu Huu and Kinh Sang.

ARVN ground forces continued sweep operations southeastward on the Dung Island complex, and liberated two government of the Republic of Vietnam personnel from a Viet Cong prison camp. They also captured one Viet Cong, three kilos of documents, fifty protective masks, and three Viet Cong flags. River Assault boats of Riv Ron 13 and 15 searched 196 sampans and checked 411 people. Five suspects were detained.

The Group Bravo MRB moved to a Binh Thuy anchorage on Friday, November 29th.

Support and supply for the large operation was provided by the USS Mercer (APB-39) and USS Satyr (ARL-23), anchored in the vicinity of the Area of Operations. The operation was a riverine assault and waterborne blockade of Cu Lao Tron, Cu Lao Dung, and Cu Lao Con Coc. This operation was the first true test of Operation Sea Lords, with the combined forces of TF 115, 116, 117 and Vietnamese Navy units participating in one of the largest waterborne blockades attempted. The blockade was considered 95% effective.

Group Bravo assault boats blockaded the Dung Island complex and searched twenty-nine sampans and almost one-hundred personnel, on Thursday, November 28th. Two V.C. were killed and two carbines captured. On the next day, ground forces on the island cut down four V.C. They also captured four Viet Cong and two rifles.

Over the total November 25th through 29th operation, thirteen Viet Cong bought the rice farm. Eight V.C. were captured, and two Viet Cong suspects were detained for further interrogation. In addition, 1,291 sampans were searched, 2,873 Vietnamese were checked and 65 detainees taken into custody. Captured or destroyed were two Mauser rifles, one Russian rifle, one German rifle, 1,000 rounds small arms ammo, fifty grenades, two 500 person capacity Viet Cong operated POW camps, a ton of white paper, two M-1 rifles, three cook stoves and various other supplies and documents.

**CDR E. J. Sottak relieved CDR P. Blundell as Commander River Assault Squadron 13 on December 4th.**

**Letter home-Undated**
*Dear Mom, Dad, and Everybody,*

*Sorry I haven't written much, lately. I tried to tape a letter last night, but it was so messed up, I decided not to send it. My tape recorder hasn't been working at all, but today, me and a couple guys took it apart, found two broken wires and a bad drive belt, so now it's OK.*

*I'm not exactly sure where we are, right now. It's a relatively new area for the Mobile Riverine Force. We are in deep, DEEP South Vietnam. We (Riv Rons 13 & 15) are Group Bravo, and Riv Rons 9 & 11 are Group Alpha. Anyway, Group Alpha is at Dong Tam. I honestly think that a joint drive by all four River Squadrons could win the war in the Mekong Delta. For this environment, it's the only answer. It's a new phase of naval warfare that will change American military history. That may sound pretty dramatic, but it's the truth.*

*I thought the bombing halt was a good idea, but now, I hear that "Uncle Ho" (Ho Chi Minh) told all Vietnamese to fight even harder despite the bombing halt. I doubt if that is to be considered a gesture of "good will!" Now, I wonder if it was such a good idea. If allied casualties rise, we should go back to bombing North Vietnam, harder than ever before!*

*I'm kind of depressed tonight, and it's hard to write a cheerful letter when it's not in ya'. I've seen some sickening things, over here in the past six months, and when I have all of them on my mind, I get fed up. Oh well, I'll try to snap out of it.*

*Hey Dad, ever hear of a Jim Sater, from North Hollywood? He's a PFC in the Army, and he's over here with the 9th Infantry Division. I saw his name on the barbershop appointment list, and I found out from another soldier what his first name and hometown is. I don't know how, or when I could get in touch with him. I told his buddy what my outfit and hometown is, in case he wants to get in touch. Is he a relative of Uncle Ralph's? I'm awfully curious. His name is spelled S A T E R.*

*Don't let Judi "Si" hear about this, but I plan on getting her a stereo for Christmas. I'll have it sent home, so you can wrap it. Besides, I just wanted to tell you so that nobody else gets her one. It won't get there for at least five or six weeks. I still have to order it.*

*Not much is really new, here. I'll be on the line until the end of this month. It could be a little longer. I am going to be in Dong Tam for at least ten days, from December 21st to 31st, for an overhaul on my boat. I still haven't received word on when my tour is up. I doubt if it will be January, though. Probably February.*

*I'll be going on an op within the next few days. I was supposed to go out a couple days ago, but my boat stayed behind, instead. It's odd, in a way… It makes us glad when our boat has to stay behind, but then again, something makes me wish our boat was out on the op with my buddies.*

*I know I owe a lot of people "Happy Birthdays," and "Happy Anniversaries." I feel horrible about it, too. I'll try to make up for it when I come home. I keep thinking of writing Frank and Karen, and John Brune and Sharon, but I'm always either too busy, or in circumstances that don't give me a chance to.*

*I guess it is cold there, now, huh? It's hard to imagine that, anymore. It was a real scorcher, here, today.*

*Say, if anybody wants a watch there, tell me. I bought a $110 watch for $55, not long ago. It's waterproof to 660 feet, shock resistant, and self-winding. It even tells me the time in St. Louis, as well as here. When I checked it with the radio time, one day, it was only four seconds off. I can't use greenback dollars here, so if you want one, you can give Judi the money for me.*

*By the way, Judy "Sa," thanks for the Halloween candy and mask. All of us thought the mask remarkably resembled our boat captain.*

*I guess I'll close for now. I'll get off a tape as soon as I can. Tell everybody "Hello" for me.*

*Love,*

*Terry*

**The Mobile Riverine Force, along with other naval and Coast Guard units was awarded the Presidential Unit Citation, by President Richard M. Nixon, for action during Operation Sea Lords. The action reads,**

*THE PRESIDENTIAL UNIT CITATION (NAVY)*
*FOR EXTRAORDINARY HEROISM TO*
*COMMANDER TASK GROUP 194.0*
*(Units Participating in Operation SEA LORDS)*

*For extraordinary heroism and outstanding performance of duty from 18 October to 5 December 1968 while engaged in armed conflict against enemy forces in the Republic of Vietnam. Commander Task Group 194.0 initiated and prosecuted the first of several interdiction campaigns to sever enemy lines of communication and resupply and to establish the legal government in areas previously held by the enemy. The naval units engaged in Operation SEA LORDS consistently displayed the striking power and professionalism, which were to mark this and following campaigns. Tasked with routing a myriad of enemy forces from their previous sanctuaries, personnel of Commander Task Group 194.0 ventured courageously into little known canals and backwater areas, fighting valiantly through countless intense enemy rocket and automatic weapons attacks. The naval units, through their persistent and aggressive strikes against enemy strongholds, were eminently successful in their campaign to interdict enemy resupply routes and base areas throughout the lower Mekong Delta region. The courage, professionalism, and dedication displayed by the officers and men of Commander Task Group 194.0 reflected credit upon themselves and were in keeping with the highest traditions of the United States Naval Service.*

*Richard Nixon*

On Friday, December 6th, Group Bravo was working with the 4th Battalion, VNMC, who discovered a Viet Cong prison camp in Chuong Thien Province, and liberated ten Vietnamese prisoners. The VN Marines fought a V.C. squad, which was attempting to escape the area and took it under fire. Two V.C. died with their sandals on, and one VN Marine was wounded by a booby trap. Monitor 151-1 and Zippo 152-1 were dispatched to the area and provided close fire support. Three additional Viet Cong bodies were discovered the following morning, and interrogation of local villagers revealed several other Viet Cong were also killed. The Monitor's 105MM Howitzer fire was credited with all Viet Cong KIA's.

Saturday, the VNMC put one more V.C. belly up, while the Group Bravo assault boats sank eleven enemy sampans and recorded one V.C. killed in the action.

One Day they sent Tango 9 to Dong Tam to pick up a USO singer for a show on a ship in the Mobile Riverine Base. She was a very sweet and friendly girl. She changed from army greens to her dress for the performance, in our well deck. When she came back up on our top deck, I asked her if I could take her picture. She kidded me about being shy and told me to get in the picture.

**Letter from Grandma Bess, December 7, 1968.**
*Dear Terry,*

*Well, will try to write you a few lines. I am still up here in the cold. Right now it's snowing hard, and it is cold out, and I don't like it one bit. I would lots rather be in good old California, where they don't know what cold weather is. I am leaving here, Tuesday, the 10th of December, for New York, if everything goes OK. It will take me just a little over an hour to get there and in February, if I am still here, I'll be 92. How is that for a young gal? Am still going strong. Got new glasses today, and they cost me $80. I had to have them. I talked to your Dad a few nights ago, and Mike has to get glasses. Pat has them, Judy, you, and your Mom and Dad. Don't know any news from around here. When will you get to go home? I hope real soon, and all the other boys, too, as I know they want to.*

*There is a good joke I heard on television the other day. Three old men were sitting on a street bench. A pretty gal comes along, and the first old man got up and kissed her. Soon another pretty girl comes along, and the second old man got up and gave her a big hug and a kiss. Another pretty girl comes along, and the third old man said "Wasn't there something else we used to do?" Now, they were old! Anyhow, I just thought I could make you smile. Did I?*

*I'll be glad to hear from you, but I know it's hard for all you boys to write so many letters. I hear from your Mom all the time. I call them about every two weeks. I get home sick, so just call. So, by the time you get this, I'll be at Uncle Milford's, so write me there. Take care of yourself, and write to Mom as often as you can. I have lost your address, and will send this to St. Louis, for Dale to mail. Bye now. Stay well, and be careful.*

*All my love,*

*Grandma Sater*

(Grandma Bess was born Feb. 7, 1877, in Fort Madison Iowa. She was born in living quarters, above the jail, which still stands, today, next to the town court house. Her father was the sheriff. She was born less than eight months after Custer's Massacre, which occurred on June 25–26, 1876. The month before she was born, the Battle of Wolf Mountain occurred. Crazy Horse and his warriors fought their last battle with the United States Cavalry in Montana. Grandma Bess loved playing poker and watching "Wrestling at the Chase." I will never forget her watching wrestling and yelling at the TV; "Pull his hair! Punch him!" I was told that one night, when she was pregnant, in Fort Madison Iowa, her husband Burt (my grandfather) was going into town with the horse drawn buckboard. She told Burt she wanted to go along. He chastised her; *"You'd do that! You'd go into town, looking like that! Embarrassing me!"* I also recall the story that her brother had a stroke, while he was

248

being chased by Indians. Grandma Bess shifted between the homes of her four sons and one daughter, who lived in New York, Florida, Texas, Missouri and Ohio, or her brother in California. She died on March 25th, 1979, at almost 103.)

On the afternoon of Saturday, December 7th, Monitor 152-1 was hit with a rocket, while Group Bravo was conducting interdiction operations along the Rach Nuoc Trong, in Chouong Thien Province. Fortunately, the rocket was a dud and failed to explode. It was later removed by EOD personnel. The 4th Battalion of the Vietnamese Marine Corp conducted sweep ops in the same area, killing one Viet Cong tax extortionist. For him, taxes may no longer be certain, but death certainly is. They also captured one POW.

On Monday, December 9th, Viet Cong fired two B-40 RPG's at a River Assault Squadron 15 refueler, on the Song Cai Tu, in Chuong Thien Province. Both rounds missed. Two hours later, River Assault Division 152 boats were ambushed, while transiting the Rach Ba Cai Tau, about twenty-five kilometers, or 15.5 miles, SE of Vi Thanh. Fierce return fire by the refueler's automatic weapons caused two secondary explosions. T-152-8 took one B-40 rocket hit in the engine room, but no other material or crew casualties were reported.

On Saturday, December 14th, Lt. P.W. Wolfgang relieved Lt. C.T. Vaught as COMRIVDIV 131. Lt. Vaught assumed command of River Assault Squadron 13.

### St. Louis Post Dispatch, December 15, 1968
*"**Gunboats Attacked.** Near Saigon, Communist troops firing from ambush bombarded six U.S. Navy gunboats with rocket and machine gun fire, apparently in an attempt to break an American blockade of a river infiltration route. The series of attacks along three rivers west and northwest of the capital killed two U.S. sailors and wounded 14, spokesmen said."*

### Letter home, December 15th, 1968
*Dear Mom, Dad, Judy, Pat, Mike, Sharon, and Tim*

*Hi! Merry Christmas!*

*This is my Christmas card to you, since I can't get any real ones. I don't really know what to say, except that I do wish everybody a very Merry Christmas, and New Year season. I know I can't be with you, but that doesn't mean the birth of Christ, and the coming of the New Year should be marked off the calendar. Judi sent me a Christmas tree, so we'll have it to decorate the crew's hootch (barracks) while we are staying at Dong Tam, over Christmas. I'd like to be home for it, certainly, but Christmas is no time for the blues. I'll spend it drinking, laughing, and relaxing with my crew. We may catch the Bob Hope Show, even! It's no time to be sad. 30,000 or more guys have died in Vietnam and well over 100,000 wounded. I've come through without a scratch! I have a wonderful girl, family, and a lot of friends, so there are no complaints. I would have a hard time trying to give presents from here, but when I come home, I can take care of that.*

*Dad and Mom, as a Christmas present I'd like to take you out to dinner and a show, or something, when I come home. My treat. It will be fun to have you "double" with Judi and me. Maybe I'll be home next Christmas!*

*Love, and a Merry Christmas!*

*Terry*

**Letter to Judi's Mom and Dad, on stationary from the USS Mercer, APB-39**

*Dear Mr. and Mrs. Simon,*

*Hello, and Merry Christmas!*

*This is my Christmas card! It's not too funny, or very pretty, but it's the best the store had to offer.*

*I remember sitting in your living room, last Christmas Eve. I can even remember being there Christmas Day, about three years ago, when everybody was playing Bill Cosby albums. I had met the whole family by then and just getting to know Judi, pretty well. I wish I could see you this Christmas, and enjoy the laughing, Christmas carols, whiskey sours, lying on the floor, by the TV, and the general atmosphere of nostalgia and joy. In the back of my feeble mind, I'll be day dreaming of being there. Unfortunately, "Uncle Ho" is a party pooper and I have to stay here little longer. It will be soon, though and as a Christmas present, I'd like to treat you to a night on the town with Judi and me! Until then, I hope you have a Merry Christmas and a very Happy New Year.*

*Mr. Simon, Thanks again for including me in your prayers, on retreat. You'll never know how much I appreciate it and maybe we'll both never realize how very much they have helped me.*

*Yours,*

*Terry*

*P.S. I would appreciate it if you would keep an eye on Judi, around the mistletoe. It's only fair. Vietnam doesn't have mistletoe!*

## THE SECRETARY OF THE NAVY
### WASHINGTON
**The Secretary of the Navy takes pleasure in commending the**
**RACH GIA INTERDICTION GROUP (Task Group 194.6)**
**For service as set forth in the following**

CITATION:

*For exceptionally meritorious service from 7 November to 17 December 1968 while engaged in armed conflict against North Vietnamese and Viet Cong communist aggressor forces in the Republic of Vietnam. During this period, the various elements of the Rach Gia Interdiction Group pressed an extremely daring and effective campaign against the ingression of communist personnel and war materials from Cambodia into the lower Mekong Delta region. Operating under hazardous and austere conditions, the patrol and air-support units of the Rach Gia Interdiction Group stalked the narrow, enemy-infested canals in an unceasing effort to detect and destroy the communist aggressors. Although the toll of American casualties was high during these days of countless engagements, Task Group personnel consistently displayed a determined and aggressive fighting spirit, braving continual heavy enemy fire at point-blank range. Ultimately, the enemy threat was quelled, a major route of communist resupply was severed, and pacification and Vietnamese resettlement commenced. By their valiant professionalism, courageous sacrifice, and inspiring devotion to duty in the face of grave enemy opposition, the officers and men of the Rach Gia Interdiction Group were singularly responsible for the prodigious successes of the campaign, and reflected great credit upon themselves, their units, and the United States Naval Service.*

*All personnel attached to and serving with the Rach Gia Interdiction Group (Task Group 194.6) during the above-designated period, or any part thereof, are hereby authorized to wear the Navy Unit Commendation Ribbon.*

*John W. Warner*

*Secretary of the Navy (Acting)*

# Chapter 17
## A Bob Hope Christmas

My boat had the extreme good fortune of drawing the best possible schedule for boat overhaul. Along with T-131-10, T-132-3 and T-132-4, we spent December 20th through December 31st in Dong Tam. We were able to celebrate Christmas and New Year's Eve on dry land. Judi sent me a one-foot high Christmas tree that I proudly displayed in our *"hootch."* I wish I still had it. It actually DID provide some good cheer.

(During River Warfare Training, we were told we would get five days of "R&R," for every three months we were in Vietnam. I never got one day of it. I'm not aware of anyone who did get it. I have heard that you had to put in for it when your boat was being overhauled, but I don't know if that was the case, or not.)

**December 20, 1968. Audio Tape Home.**
*We're in Dong Tam. It's 11:30 a.m. I'm going to cut out for chow, pretty quick, but I thought I'd bring you up to date, for a few minutes. I'm here with Ledford. He's combing his hair! You want to look pretty for them?*

Ledford explained,

> *I don't want to talk until my hair's combed! It gives me confidence!*

I asked Ledford to start off, telling him,

> *Tell them about coming in! Then, I want to tell them about the news I got!*

Glenn seemed to enjoy the banter and helping with the tape home. He happily jumped in,

> *On the way here, for our yard period and overhaul, they gave us an Alpha boat (ASPB) to tow us, to give us extra speed. There were two Alpha boats and two Tango boats. We started out with a bow to stern tow. The Alpha boat was leading. It was flooding us out, because our ramp gasket was leaking. That's the rubber seal that goes around the ramp that we used to drop off troops. Our boat captain panicked, as usual, so we decided on a side to side tow. We rigged that up and finally got squared away. I had a ten dollar bet with Bird, on time of arrival. Bird said 5:00 in the afternoon. I said 8:00, or 8:30. We got in at 9:00, so I won the bet. It was worth the whole trip! Ten dollars!*

I had to ask Ledford about one of the changes in Dong Tam, that I noticed that morning.

> *It was dark when we got in. Dong Tam has changed a lot. What is that "Old Reliable Academy?" It's on the Navy side. I heard it's a training center for the NCO's, noncommissioned officers.*

> *I don't know. I haven't even hit the dirt, yet!*

> *Really? I walked around last night when I had "channel fever."*

Ledford cautioned me. *"You better tell them what "channel fever" is."*

> *"Channel fever" is the excitement a sailor feels when your ship, or boat approaches land, after being on the water for long time, with the prospect of liberty ashore.*

I added; *"The chow hall has changed completely. You haven't seen the chow hall, yet?"*

> *No. What did they do to it?*

*They've got wooden paneling and a dozen fans and an ice cream machine next to the water fountain.*

*Oh boy! The chow's still "same same," though?*

*Yeah. I had breakfast up there, today. It was O.K. I had pancakes, ham and eggs. I went up there several times for coffee, last night, while I had the watch.*

In a very excited voice, I added,

*I guess I can tell them the news! I was sitting around on the flight deck, last night, after we got in. Somebody ran down and told me I got my orders for when I leave here. That doesn't mean I can go home right away. It just means my orders are ready for when I go home. I went up to check on them, to see what they were. Sure enough. There they were, in black and white! They had a whole list of all the orders for the guys I came here, with. I got a ship, the USS Hunley."*

Ledford joked, *"It's an amphibious ship that lands marines in Cambodia!"*

Laughing, I reassured Judi and the family, *"No! It's a submarine tender!"*

Ledford laughed, *"I don't even know what a "sub tender" is!"*

Explaining to both Glenn Ledford and everybody at home, I said;

*It's a ship that takes care of subs. It supplies them, repairs them and maintains them. The big advantage of a sub tender is that it just sits in port. It may never pull out for the year and a half I have left in the Navy! It will be good duty! The home port is Charleston, South Carolina, about eight hundred miles from home, which is a big difference from being two thousand miles away, on the west coast. I'm pretty happy with the orders. I hope everybody there is. Another advantage is that I get sea pay, for being on a ship. The sub tender just sits in port and the subs come to it! It's like shore duty! I think it's going to be terrific! It would have been nicer if it was in New Orleans, but I won't look a gift horse in the mouth! Well, that's about all I can tell you, about my orders. When I come home, I'll get advanced travel pay for travel to it. St. Louis is a stop-over on the way to Charleston, so it won't cost me anything to fly home. The travel pay is always way more than I need. I think I get $173.00 to fly to Charleston, so I'll be making out like a bandit!*

At that point, we took a break for a few minutes. I started the tape up again, just as Ledford was returning.

*We've got some company here, right now. It's a "she." Her name is "Dien cai dau." Americans usually pronounce it more like "Dinky Dow." It is Vietnamese for "crazy," or "crazy head." She's real cute. She's a guinea pig. Ledford left for a couple minutes, but now he's back with me. Glenn, I think the company was better when I just had Dien cai dau with me!*

*All right! I'll leave!*

*No! Come here! Pull up a chair!*

*Make me feel wanted!*

*Come on! Pull up a chair and sit on the flight deck (our helo pad)! Want me to give you my "friend winning smile?"*

*Yeah. Let's see it. Yeah. That's pretty bad! "Dien cai dau" smiles better than that, and she's got rotten teeth!*

*We put her in our flak jacket pockets when we go to General Quarters!*

*Yeah. She'll be eating flowers in somebody's pocket, while we're shooting our heads off! Did you tell them her full name?*

*No. They may look it up in a Vietnamese dictionary.*
  (Her full name was *"Dien cai dau du ma may."*)

I noticed our pet was suddenly quiet.

*She isn't "talking" much, right now. She's very shy! She's rubbing her stomach.*

*We got some other good news, too. The Bob Hope Show is going to be here, at Dong Tam. They've got bleachers and speakers set up, on the Navy side, instead of the Army side. We've heard different dates for it, the 22nd, the 27th and the 28th. One of those three days. We'll be living in the "hootches," here on the base, while our boat is being overhauled. Right now, I'm sitting on the boat. There won't be anything for us to do. We're talking about going to the "Windjammer" club, tonight. When do you think we'll get a chance to go swimming?*

Ledford responded, *"Hell! We can go anytime we want to! We can go tomorrow, if you want too! Did you see where our hootch is? Our hootch is going to be right next to where the Bob Hope Show is going to be! We'll be able to see the crowd building up and we can jump right in, up front!"*

*Should we take "Dien cai dau?"*

*Yeah! She hardly ever gets a chance to go out!*

*We don't take her out much, do we?*

*She looks rejected! She gets less liberty than WE do!*

*We haven't been treating her right, really.*

*Every time we go to chow on a ship, we bring back lettuce for her.*

Switching back to the topic of the Bob Hope Show, I added, *"I want to camp out there and get good seats!"*

I continued, *"I bought a jacket the other day, at the base at Binh Thuy. I don't even think I can even tell you where that is. Not that it's confidential. I've been to so many places, all over the Delta. I lose track of where the places are, all the towns and cities. I think it is farther south of here. It's a real good jacket. It's made out of quilted material that are used for blankets in the field. I'm thinking of sending it home, after having it double stitched, here."*

*What are you going to do with it back in the states? You're gonna' look funny running around in a camouflaged jacket! Everybody will think you're in the army!*

*I'll be a professional sniper!*

*A mercenary!*

*Oh, "mercenary!" You know what that brings to mind, don't you?*

*Yeah. Cambodian mercenaries.*

*River Assault Squadrons 13 and 15 are on an op, right now. All of them except us, because our boat is getting worked on, are carrying three hundred Cambodian mercenaries, in case they have to travel over, into Cambodia.*

Ledford frowned, slightly. *"I don't know if I agree."*

*Why? What do you think it is? Why wouldn't they carry the Vietnamese Marines?*

*They cannot beach on the Cambodian side, because they could capture our boats. If they do use Cambodian mercenaries, for operations in Cambodia, they can't beach them on the Cambodian side. In other words, the Cambodian mercenaries are going to have to swim!*

*Is the Cambodian and Vietnam border split all the way by the river?*

*I don't know. We'll find out when they get back.*

My good friend, Randy Peat remembers the Cambodian operation well. He was the Mark 19 gunner, on T-132-12. He and the other boats of River Assault Squadron 13 delivered men and supplies to a base of Cambodian mercenaries that included a detachment of U.S. Special Forces. It took the boats twenty-four hours to reach the area. Randy was extremely nervous, and understandably so. It was on this operation that he learned to sleep, standing in his gun mount. His Tango boat was carrying fourteen 55 gallon drums of fuel. His mind was preoccupied with the fact that if ANYTHING hit their boat, it would have gone up in one enormous ball of fire.

Continuing my conversation with Ledford, I changed the subject back to another item I bought at the Vietnamese tailor shop, I added;

*I also bought a one and a half foot by three foot banner we have flown from our boat, between the antennas. It is white silk with red felt lettering that spells out "HO CHI MINH." Below that, is lettering in red, white and blue that spells out; "KISS MY ASS." If "discretion is the better part of valor," we probably shouldn't rub it in the Viet Cong's faces when we are in a dangerous area. Still, it DOES express our sentiment pretty well. Are we going to go get drunk, tonight?*

*Yes. Very drunk! We gotta make up for lost time! We haven't had any liberty for what, two months, or more? We haven't spent any time on the beach for at least three months! All you can do is go to the exchange, anyway, walk around on the base, or just walk around on dry land, which is really great!*

*You know, I spend more time on the water now, than I did when I was on the Enterprise!*

*Far more! You never hit land, except when we go to Dong Tam, or some other big base.*

Hodges yelled up from the well deck; *"Hey anybody going to chow, yet?"*

Ledford and I wanted to let Hodges, Frank Springer and Bird Man know we could stay on watch on the boat until they got back. I yelled,

*Make it! Make it! Go ahead!*

Ledford added, "*We got enough on the boat! Go ahead! We've got Black One, me and Terry.*"

Just then, Black One appeared. Ledford, turned to him and said;

*Aren't you going to stay here? Stand by? Don't you love this boat? It's my home, man!*

Black One invited Ledford to extend his orders to remain with the Mobile Riverine Force and T-131-9.

*I'll tell you what… Why don't you extend on it?*

I jumped in. "*I'm going to do it!*"

Black One replied, skeptically, "*Yeah?*"

Playing it up, I nodded, "*Yeah! Shippin' over for ATC's!* "

(*"Shipping over"* means to re-enlist.)

My boat captain called my bluff. "*I've got some forms I can get for you. You can extend!*"

*There's probably a long line. I hate lines.*

Black One played along.

*We got to have somebody on this doggone boat to keep the old spirit goin.' I think that ole' Terry Sater really will fit the bill. Whoever this tape is going to, this guy really likes this old boat. He talks about it all the time!*

*Yeah. I'd HATE to go home! You KNOW that!*

Black One was getting into it.

*Yeah. He doesn't want to go home! He always tells me how much he likes this river. He loves the river. It's beautiful! The scenery is tremendous. You should see the scenery, here! Lots of vegetation. The people are friendly. There's no sweat! There's no possibility of even getting a scratch! Whatever you heard about Vietnam, just overlook it, because it's not as bad as everyone says it is. It's nice. All Terry does is take pictures all day and make recordings like this. This is a beautiful boat. It has everything you've got at home. It's very clean. The color is green, all over. We've got nice beds. They're very comfortable. Canvas bottoms. If you have a weak back, canvas is very good for you. Canvas is very stimulating! Makes your blood real rich! Terry doesn't sleep in the rack. He sleeps in that… what do you call it? A "slingshot?" Oh, a hammock! He's been here so long, he lives like the Vietnamese! He hunches over when he eat his food. He eat with chopsticks. He puts all this funky stuff on his food, chop soy sauce on everything. He doesn't even eat American food anymore! He likes rice and fish, onions, fish eyes, fish heads…Really, he doesn't want to come home! He told me, he wants to extend for six months! I believe him!*

I deadpanned, "*Yeah, everybody's going to hold their breath until I ship over!*"

Black One laughed and said;

> *Everybody's goin' to hold their breath until he ships over! I feel we're going to live a long,* long time.
> *I'm holding mine right now! That's one of my virtues!*
>
> *That's your ONLY virtue!*

Black One feigned anger.

> *Negative! "Only virtue?" He says that's my ONLY virtue!*

BREAK: I had to tape over Black One cussing me out. He continued.

> *The main thing is, young lady, he's goin' home safe, I think. I imagine that's all that counts. So I figure if he can get off here safe, I figure this is a pretty good old boat. We're the "boots," and he's the old veteran, on here. So he's going to leave us shortly, but we're going to be right behind him, on his heels. We'll be glad to see him leave! We'll be glad to see him go!*

Knowing what he meant, Ledford confirmed; *"Yes, we will!"*

Black One continued.

> *Beautiful! Beautiful! Right! Because when he leaves, that's an open for us. Because we look for the day he leaves. That means we just a little "shorter!" All in all, this is a nasty war and I'm sure all the American fellas know that this is something we can't help! We're here, but we don't wanna be! If I could do it, I'd be a draft dodger! No kiddin'!*

Ledford cocked his head and asked,

> *On what grounds?*

Our boat captain broke from what would normally be expected under the circumstances and said,

> *Grounds of "Hippie!" I like "Flower Power!" I'm one of those old hippies wearin' big glasses and a flower in my ear! I think everything is beautiful! It could be rainin' and snowin' outside, but it's still beautiful! Things of this sort. I still have lunatics to put up with, when Terry leaves. I got Glenn, Hodges, Bird Man and Little One. Well, I've taken up enough of this tape! All I can say is I wish everybody back there a very Merry Christmas and a Happy New Year! Terry will be home very soon! We should be right behind him! But, never the less; "Ya' all...I don't say "YOU all". I'm an old rebel. Ya'all be good! Don't' take no wooden nickels! "World!" "World!" That's the slang for the United States, "the world." That's what's happenin'! Merry Christmas!*

As I took the microphone from Black One, I said, *"Thank you for your commentary."*

Walking away, he yelled back, *"No sweat! Number ten G.I.!"*

In another life, Black One wouldn't have been a bad guy. I think he wanted us to like him, but he was simply too scared and too interested in his own comfort, to really have our respect, or friendship. I felt sorry for him.

With the conversation again back to Glenn Ledford and I, I looked to him to confirm a rumor.

> *I hear Riv Ron 9 and 11 are going to be taken over by the gooks!*
>
> *Do they know what "gooks" are?*

256

*Gooks are Vietnamese.*

Ignoring that line of conversation, Ledford changed the subject to something more urgent.

*You got your stuff ready to go to the club?*

*What "stuff?"*

*Your hat.*

*My hat? THAT'S what you mean by "Do I have my "STUFF" ready to go to the club?" My hat? Yeah! I got all "MY STUFF" ready!*

*Well, you got your boots on? You got your pants on? You got your little broken up sign that you wear around your neck?*

*It's not a "broken up sign!"*

*Yeah it is!*

*No. It's not!*

*It's a.... a..... What do you call it?*

*"Mizpah coin."*

*All right, you got your broken up "mizpah coin!"*

*It's SUPPOSED TO BE BROKEN! I told you what it was, didn't I?*

Rolling his eyes, in a tone dripping with sarcasm, Ledford answered,

*Yeah… It's a "token of lovvve…*

*You don't have to be mushy about it!*

*I try not to be.*

*Put simply, my girlfriend has the other half, see?*

*Still, it's a "token of lovvve." You got the other half!*

*You're a real romanticist, aren't you?*

*Yes. O.K. You got your stuff ready to go to the club?*

*Yeah. I got my "STUFF" ready to go to the club!*

*We gotta go to chow, too!*

*Chow's going to be closing before long!*

On December 23rd, Randy Peat, with T-132-12, was on an operation. There was an ASPB nearby. The boat captain of the ASPB was called *"Papa-San,"* because he had achieved the ripe old age of thirty-two. As he was standing on the bow of the ASPB, a Viet Cong suddenly launched an RPG at the boat, hitting *"Papa-San"* squarely in the chest, going completely through him. Before he fell, Randy and those around him, were scarred by the memory of seeing a man standing upright, with daylight shining through him. That visual image is eerily similar to the nightmare that would plague Randy, for the rest of his life.

The next day, Christmas Eve, Randy and a couple other guys from his Tango boat, joined the crew of the ASPB and went back to the spot of the ambush. They conducted *"recon by fire,"* strafing the banks of the area with automatic weapons fire, in hopes of initiating a firefight with the Viet Cong who killed *"Papa-San."* It was a totally *"off the books,"* unauthorized operation. It was revenge. They did not receive any return fire. They left with their thirst for revenge, unquenched.

### December 26, 1968: Audio Tape Home.

*I'm walking over to where they are going to have the Bob Hope Show, tomorrow. I don't know, for certain. They've got enormous bleachers set up and gigantic speakers. It's near our perimeter. They are extending our normal perimeter out, much farther. They are also adding immense warehouses. They have an army of Vietnamese workers and a helo pad. There are helo's flying over. Tractors are moving stuff in every direction.*

*The speakers are playing Christmas carols. I'm not sure if this tape is going to work very well, with all the noise coming from the tractors, the helos and the speakers. If it doesn't, I'll have to go back to our "hootch." The hootch is filled with dust and mosquitoes. At least we have the small Christmas tree Judi sent me, to give us a little bit of Christmas spirit. It's about a foot and a half tall, with garland and ornaments on it.*

*They have endless rows of benches set up in front of a huge stage. They still haven't officially announced the Bob Hope Show coming here. So far, it's just a rumor. I think they are worried about the security, but they don't build something like this for no reason!*

*I saw a USO show, last night. Hodge, Ledford and "Hank," a guy from another boat, went to the Army side of Dong Tam and watched the "Louie Carroll Show." He's a little midget. He had a Filipino band with him, and a blond that's supposed to be a stripper, in Frisco, I think. She didn't do any strippin' but she wore a pretty small bikini. The show was real funny and kept everybody in stiches! The band was real good and the stripper…… well…., as you can imagine, she kind of pleased the guys, too. Everybody was laughing, clapping and having a GREAT time!*

*The night before last, they had a hillbilly band, the "Lefty Pritchett Show." He wasn't too good, but we appreciate anybody who comes over here to entertain us. We left early. I got kind of homesick and thought it would be better to get the crew together, with Little One and Bird Man, so we went back to the "Windjammer," on the Navy side. It's a good thing we did, too. We found out the next morning that they had to close down the Army's enlisted men's club. There were racial fights and somebody tossed in a couple of smoke grenades.*

*(The sound of a man's voice testing the enormous speakers drowned out my tape recording with "TESTING! ONE! TWO! THREE! FOUR! TESTING! ONE! TWO! THREE! FOUR!)*

*If they're going to have the show, tomorrow, it might be kind of bad for me. I'm supposed to have the watch, on the boat. Our boat is out of the water, but we're supposed to have somebody down there, all the time, to watch it. So, there's a chance that I may not get to see it. You can figure that I'll figure out a way to see it, though.*

*We've had a pretty good time while we've been here, at Dong Tam. I really don't have a good excuse for not writing. I could have written a lot more, lately. We've spent just about every day over at the pool. It feels good to get some healthy exercise. I was pleasantly surprised at how well I've been able to swim, as far as lung power. I thought I'd be a lot worse.*

*I think we're going to be here until at least the 31st. I'm not getting any mail here, but I should have a lot when I get back.*

*I've enjoyed the last tape you sent, very much! I told everybody about Timmy's song and played it for them. They got a big kick out of it!*

*Mom, I was listening to your tape while the guys and I were getting ready to play cards. You were talking and Ledford asked: "Does your mom always talk that fast?" I said; "Ummm. Yeah." He said; "Hmmm. Maybe my mom is just slow witted."*

*I told you about "Dinky Dau," or "Dien cai dau", our pet Guinea Pig, on the first part of this tape. She died, the next morning. We don't know if she ate some of the rat poison that is all over around here, because of all the rats, or if somebody stepped on her when they came back to the boat, drunk.*

*Dong Tam has really developed. They never would have thought of having a show this close to the perimeter, when I first got here. They've extended the perimeter and have the Army out a lot farther. The defenses are much better.*

*They had a mortar attack a few nights ago. It was when I was trying to get a call through the MARS radio station and it was 4:00 a.m. I couldn't get the call through, so I went back to the hootch and hit the rack. The mortar attack hit at 4:30 and ruined the rest of my night's sleep. They hit on the Army side. We didn't even go to the bunkers. We just kind of stood around the outside of the bunker. It was nothing for you to worry about. As a matter of fact, even before they stopped the siren on the Navy side, all of us just went back to bed.*

*I just got a little package from the Red Cross, today. A lot of people in Florida are sending packages over here. I got a package from a Mr. & Mrs. Sage, or something like that. I've got to drop them a line and tell them "Thanks!" By the way, it wasn't addressed to me, specifically. Our boat had to go and pick up a package for each of us. This one just happened to be mine.*

*Riv Ron 13 is operating around Can Tho, right now. They aren't carrying Vietnamese Marines. The Marines had to take up positions around Saigon. I imagine there was an expectation of a "Tet Offensive," or something. I hear they're carrying three hundred Cambodian mercenaries, which is pretty interesting...*

*I can see ships from "Group Alpha," with River Squadrons Nine and Eleven. They're just outside the Dong Tam harbor. I was hoping to see Corky. He's due to be going home, soon. He got here a month before me.*

*I'm going to get a bunch of my stuff together, today, and mail it home. I don't want to bother with carrying a lot of stuff with me, when I come home. I'll send all of the letters I've gotten since I got over here. I keep all of them. I'll send all my notebooks on my electronics courses and a whole bunch of other junk. I'll send my electric razor. The last thing a guy needs on a river assault boat is an electric razor.*

(The audio tape is filled with the sound of a helicopter flying overhead)

*There goes another helo! You wouldn't believe how many choppers they have at this base! In the Riv Ron, we hold quite an affection for the helicopters and their pilots and crews, especially the "Cobra" gunships. Korea was the first time helicopters were used, extensively. Over here, helicopters have a HUGE combat role, as well as medivac and material transport. The "Cobra" has rockets and mini-guns. They usually come with us, on our operations. They scout ahead and give us close air support, flying at tree top level. They are extraordinarily brave and effective!*

*The stadium seating they have set up here looks like just what you would expect from all of the Bob Hope Shows you have seen on T.V.*

*Well, I just found out from a guy here that the show starts tomorrow, at 11:30. It's got Ann Margaret, Roosevelt Grier, Miss Universe and "The Gold Diggers."*

*Our "hootch" is just about the closest barracks to the stands, here. We'll be here bright and early, to catch a seat. We might catch a front row seat! I know we'll be up close!*

*On the beginning of this tape, Ledford and I were talking about getting drunk. I didn't. I got a little plastered, on Christmas Eve. I'm sure you can understand that.*

*Today is the 26th. It's about a quarter after twelve. I have to go to chow, soon. We're lucky that we're all here, at Dong Tam, at Christmas, instead of being on the boats. We've had a lot of free time. It's been like a holiday for us. It's just great!*

*I've got a list of guys in my class that just got their orders. I sent it out on a boat, to the rest of the guys, so they can find out what their orders are, when they leave here. That will be a nice Christmas present for them.*

*I got a new I.D. card. As you know, I lost my wallet before I came here. In the states, or on ships, when a sailor has an I.D. made up, it's made in a studio, from the shoulders up, in black and white and you like a convict, in dress blues. Mine will be in color, against a hootch, and I'm wearing army "greens." I'm going to have some explaining to do, whenever I get paid! They're going to think it is fake!*

*It is 5:00 p.m., now. We're sitting outside, where the show is going to be, tomorrow. We plan on getting here about six, seven, or eight in the morning, to get a good seat! We're even thinking of camping out! We're going to bring some cards and other stuff. They're going to have certain areas roped off, for different 9th Infantry battalions. They don't even have a special place for the Navy, which makes me mad, because they are having it on the Navy side! I just asked a guy working on it to tell me about the seating arrangements. He said; "Who are you with?" I said; "The Riv Ron." He said; "Never heard of it." He must have just gotten here.*

*When I was walking over to the club, last night, one of the guys had his hat off and I wearing my beret and tiger greens. We came up on an officer who looked like he just got "in country." You CAN tell! First, he looked at my buddy and told him to put his hat on. Then, he looked at me and said; "What kind of hat is THAT, soldier?" I just said "Riv Ron," and walked past him. He gave me a very funny look. Wish you could have seen it! This experience has changed how I look and react to officers like that. Once he's seen what I've seen, I'll respect him more. Of course, once he's seen what I've seen, he won't act like that, anymore.*

*They're going to a LOT of trouble, for the show. They've got a parachute umbrella, held up by a crane, over the stage. Before they put up the parachute, they washed the crane and put a new coat of paint on it. They even gave it new tires!*

*They built a couple new bunkers, right next to the stage, just for this occasion. I wouldn't doubt it if we didn't get a couple mortars in.*

*It kind of irks me that on the stage, it says; "9th Infantry Division, Dong Tam," with their insignia. On the front of the stage, they have all of the emblems of all of the different Army units. They don't have ANYTHING representing the Navy units! I would like it to at least be <u>acknowledged</u> that we are over here*

**Our Gunner's Mate, Bill Hodges, in front of the Bob Hope USO Show stage.**

During the period of December 17th through December 26th, 1968, parts of Task Group Bravo conducted combat operations in southern An Xuyen Province, supporting two companies of the 4th Mobile Strike Force Command and UDT/ODD teams from other units. Supply and Support were provided by the USS Mercer, APB-39, USS Satyr, ARL-23, and USS Iredell County, LST-839. The objective of the operation was the destruction of a series of barricades located on the Song Cua Lon. The operation involved over seventy-five miles of open sea transit for the River Assault Craft. It was the deepest penetration by units of the Mobile Riverine Force into the Ca Mau peninsula and the first assault from the sea by the Mobile Riverine Force.

### December 27, 1968. Audio Tape, Continued

*Well, this is the 27th. It is a little past 8:00 p.m. I just saw probably the best live performance I'll ever see in my life. There was Bob Hope, Ann Margaret, Roosevelt Grier, the football player, who is also the guy who tackled Sirhan, after he assassinated Bobby Kennedy. There was also Miss Universe, the Gold Diggers and a real funny trampoline artist.*

*The show started at 12:45. I went out there as soon as I woke up, at 7:15 a.m. There was already a crowd. They had been waiting in the bleachers since 6:00 a.m. We were all told we had to move. They had the seating planned out. We were sent way in the back, in the bleachers. The front line Army troops were in the first rows. The only Navy guys that got to see the show were the guys whose boats were in the yards for overhaul, or repair, like ours, and a few guys that got liberty from the ships. We Navy guys were definitely in the minority, so they put us way in the back. On the ships, the "ship's company," or crew, get preferential seating for movies. Now, for the Bob Hope Show, on the Navy side of Dong Tam, the Army gets the preferred seating and the sailors of the River Assault Force sit in the back. Even though we were way in the back, we really enjoyed it. I am glad the wounded troops were in the front rows. It had to really boost their spirits.*

*The show is going to be on T.V, there, on January 16th, on NBC.*

*Right in the beginning of it, he made a few jokes about the Mobile Riverine Force. They pointed the cameras in our direction.*

*When the troop pulled into the stage area, I was within four feet of Bob Hope, Ann Margaret and all of those that passed through. I believe I got some fabulous pictures. I can't wait to see how they turned out.*

*Bob Hope looked younger than expected him to look and Ann Margaret was really beautiful.*

*In the beginning of the show, Bob Hope came out swinging his golf club, of course. After a minute, he said; "I hear we have the Mobile Riverine Force, here! The "River Rats!" All of our section started applauding and yelling. He said: "You can always spot a River Rat! They're the ones with minnows hanging out of their pockets!" Then he said we were always "up the creek." You won't see a lot of his jokes on T.V. They were a little more off color, or risqué than you might expect, but they were very funny!*

*They really made us feel good, the way they talked. It really made me homesick. It seemed like everybody in the troop was really concerned about the men over here. They said they'd rather spend their Christmas, with us, than at home. That got to me. I don't think it was just a "put on," either. I think they really meant it. Louie Carroll, in the other USO show I saw the other night, said the same thing. At the end, when they sang "Silent Night," you could tell we were all choked with emotion. I don't think I will ever think of that song as just a Christmas song, again. There wasn't a dry eye in the audience.*
.

*There's supposed to be another USO Show on the 29th and then the 31st, but neither one is supposed to be big names, not that we need big names. It's just nice to know someone cares enough to come here.*

*Since you will get this after the 31st, I hope everybody there had a Happy New Year! I hope Judi had a Happy Anniversary of our first date.*

*During the Bob Hope Show, there was some action on the opposite bank, across from Dong Tam. Bob Hope made a couple of cracks about it, but kept on with the show. They sent a couple helos over to rocket the Viet Cong position and fire mini-guns on it.*

*I'm anxious to see how the pictures turn out. I took almost sixty shots! When the show was over and they were pulling out, they had the area roped off, so you couldn't get too close to the jeeps, as they pulled out. I was down to my last picture and Ann Margaret's jeep was coming through, so I just jumped out, right next to her jeep, before the M.P.'s got me. They just told me to get back.*

**Bob Hope in the jeep on the left. Singer and actress Ann Margaret, in the jeep on the right.**

*I'm a little afraid to send the pictures home. Guys told me that last year, a lot of pictures never made it home. Guys stole the pictures, in the mail.*

*It's going to be hard to get used to being back on the boat and on operations. Getting our boat overhauled has been like a vacation. We haven't hardly had any responsibilities since we pulled into the yards, on the 18th, or 19th. It has really been great!*

*I'm considering trying to call home, through the MARS radio station, and seeing what kind of Christmas you had. I'm anxious to hear what Judi thought of her stereo Christmas present*

*I hear we won't get back to the MRB until the 1st or 2nd of January.*

*I guess I'll close for now. Tell everybody "Hello!" for me! Goodbye!*

**I took this photo from our seats in the bleachers.**

**As of December 31st, 1968, the number of Americans killed-in-action in Vietnam totaled 30,568. During 1968, 14,501 Americans died. Some of those were my friends. 1968 was the highest American casualty year of the Vietnam War.**

# Chapter 18
## No Glory in the Fight

During the first week of January, T-131-9, *"Tango 9,"* was back in the fray. With our Christmas break over, we joined River Assault Squadron 13 and conducted an attempted rescue of American P.O.W.'s, after being tipped off by a Viet Cong officer who defected. We didn't find them. It was a very sad and disappointing operation.

We conducted an operation along the Cambodian border. At times, we were on the Cambodian side of the river.

**St. Louis Post Dispatch, January 10, 1969**
*"..other B-52 bombers flew a mission near Ben Tre in the Mekong Delta, 53 miles southwest of Saigon. Their bombs fell less than two miles from where U.S. Ninth Infantry Division troops in armored personnel carriers killed 13 Communists in two separate clashes yesterday. American officers said the U.S. force suffered no casualties."*

We were near B-52 strikes, a couple times. You can feel the concussion from one of their strikes, miles away. A bomb doesn't have to fall on the enemy to kill them. The concussion causes internal hemorrhaging, making them bleed from every orifice of their body.

**"The Stars & Stripes", January 14, 1969**
**ATC's Attacked.** *Eight U.S. Navymen were wounded when three armored troop carriers (ATCs) came under enemy mine and rocket-grenade attack on the Cai Tu River in Chuong Thien Province, 101 and 107 miles southwest of Saigon, January 14th. In the first incident, two ATCs were damaged when they came under enemy rocket-grenade fire from the banks of the river, 107 miles southwest of the capital. Three Navymen were wounded in the encounter. The armored river craft were on their way to a landing area when they came under enemy fire. The fire was immediately returned and suppressed with unknown results. During the 20 minutes firefight, the riverine force received more than 20 rocket-grenade rounds and heavy automatic weapons fire.*

*The second incident took place six miles upriver when the lead boat of a column of river assault craft hit an enemy mine and immediately sank. Five crewmen on the craft were wounded."*

**On January 14, 1969, disaster struck the USS Enterprise, off the coast of Pearl Harbor, Hawaii.** A fire broke out after a MK-32 Zuni rocket attached to an F-4 Phantom, detonated. The calamity spread to other aircraft. Explosions blew holes in the flight deck, allowing burning jet fuel to enter the ship's interior. At one point, during my tour of duty on the Enterprise, my berthing compartment was directly under the flight deck, towards the stern of the ship. I heard every plane land on the deck, stretch the arresting cable and snap back. There were a total of eighteen munition explosions or detonations. Twenty-eight sailors were killed. Over three-hundred were injured. Fifteen aircraft were destroyed. The total cost of aircraft replacement and shipboard repair was over $126 million. The "Big E" was repaired over several months at Pearl Harbor and returned to action later in the year.

**Letter Home, Friday, January 17, 1969**
*Hi Folks!*

*It's 8:45 PM right now, and we are getting some work done on our engines before we head for Ha Tien, which is on the coast, almost on the border of Cambodia and Vietnam. Right now, we are at An Thoi, on Phu Quoc Island about 40 miles off the coast. It's a Swift Boat base. We'll be traveling about five hours once the repair work is finished. I'll have to make this short, so I can catch a couple hours sleep tonight. I just thought I'd let you know everything is fine. I don't know if I told you, or not, but we (just my boat) are operating with the Swift boats. I remember a tape in which Mom was very worried because you heard a couple "Swifts" took sniper fire. Mom, I hate to tell you this, but I cracked up when I heard that! <u>Everybody</u> on the boat got a laugh out of it. Tango boats are the heaviest armored boats in Vietnam, designed to sustain a <u>rocket hit!</u> Sniper fire is something to worry about for the Swifts, but not for us. A couple of weeks ago, we took sniper fire, but it means so little to us, the other 20 gunner and I just sipped a cup of coffee, and played cards while the sniper wasted his ammo. He couldn't even hit the boat! Even if he did, it would be like shooting an elephant with a pea-shooter. We didn't even bother to fire back. The Swift boats are frail. We don't go in any bad spots. Right now, we are 40 miles off the coast! I should be off the rivers entirely in a couple weeks, so you can stop worrying right now. I'm just about finished with operations.*

*It's 1:45 am. I'm on watch until 4am. We decided the sea is too rough to try to make it to Ha Tien, tonight. We'll probably go early in the morning. My boat captain made me "section leader," meaning I'm in charge of a watch section. It's not at all impressive, because a watch section is just me, and another guy. The guy that used to be the section leader is a seven year seaman, but he was always falling asleep on watch, or drinking on watch, so now I've got it.*

From the day I received my orders to the Mobile Riverine Force, to the day I came home, I tried to minimize the true danger we faced, every day. I wish I could have been more successful.

**"...the greatest honor history can bestow is the title of peacemaker. This honor now beckons America...."** President Richard M. Nixon Inauguration speech. He had campaigned on a pledge of *"peace with honor." January 20, 1969*

**The Secretary of the Navy, John W. Warner, awarded River Assault Flotilla One the Navy Unit Commendation. He detailed the reasons, here.**
*"For exceptionally meritorious service from 5 March 1968 through 24 January 1969 while operating with friendly foreign forces engaged in armed conflict against communist aggressor forces in the Mekong Delta region of the Republic of Vietnam. As the naval component of the Army/Navy Mobile Riverine Force (Task Force 117), the ships and assault boats of River Assault Flotilla ONE provided close logistic, communication, and gunfire support to troops of the United States Army's 9th Infantry Division, the 2nd, 3rd, and 4th Vietnamese Marine Corps Battalions, and the 9th and 21st Divisions of the Army of the Republic of Vietnam during riverine assault operations which were part of a concerted offensive campaign into communist-dominated rural areas. Ambushes and fire fights on the rivers and narrow canals were almost daily occurrences; and rocket and mining attacks were frequent and ever-present dangers. The multiple operations of River Assault Flotilla ONE during this period were directly responsible for weakening the hold of the Viet Cong and their North Vietnamese cohorts on the Delta, for depriving them of sole possession of hundreds of waterways, and for ensuring freedom of movement for Vietnamese civilians throughout much of the Delta. In the kind of close combat action which requires exceptional courage, enterprise, and patience, the officers and men of River Assault Flotilla ONE consistently exhibited these qualities. Their gallantry in the face of continuous enemy opposition, and their superlative performance as individuals and as a team, were in keeping with the highest traditions of the United States Naval Service.*

*All personnel attached to and serving with River Assault Flotilla ONE during the above-designated period, or any part thereof, are hereby authorized to wear the Navy Unit Commendation Ribbon."*

**Letter Home, Friday, January 24, 1969**
*Hello, Everybody!*

*I am at An Thoi, on Phu Quoc Island, in the Gulf of Siam. It is a Navy and Coast Guard Base. There is a P.O.W. camp, right next to where we are, housing Viet Cong and North Vietnamese prisoners of war. I saw them unloading a plane load of them, from the mainland of Vietnam. The last prisoner in the column was dragging behind and I saw the guard give him a boot in the ass.*

*My boat is fire support for the Swift boats. So far, all we've done is waste ammo on test firings, or "reconning by fire." It's aggravating. After shooting one belt of my ammo, I have to clean up over 300 spent shells.*

*We've only gotten mail twice, since the 17th of December. The last time was January 2nd. Our mail hasn't caught up. I DID get a lot of Christmas cards. I've been meaning to answer, but I haven't gotten around to it.*

*I have a letter started to you. Oh yeah! Tell Tom and Mary thanks a lot for the care package. I got it the day we pulled out on an op, the beginning of this month. Their Christmas card was beautiful, and very unusual.*

**Continued Letter Home, January 26th, 1969**
*Hello Again!*

*I've been pretty busy since noon, yesterday. Glenn, Hodge, Bird, and I went into the base here for liberty, since my boat will be tied up to the repair ship here, for five or six days. When we got to the base, the other guys went to the club, while I checked at the post office for mail. There wasn't any. I only had a couple beers between 12 and 4:30 because I like beer when I'm thirsty, but I can't stand getting drunk on beer. I prefer mixed drinks. Well, at 4:30, I started drinking "7-7s," and didn't stop until the liberty boat was due, at 9:30.*

*At one point, the captain of a Coast Guard cutter, with the rank of Commander, ordered Ledford and me to drink with him. We obeyed the order, in the spirit of inter-service cooperation. He was an interesting guy. He was a big, hefty, barrel chested guy, with a full, dark beard. If you dressed him up like a pirate, he would look like "Black Beard!" We were getting pretty well lit, and he wanted to have a deep, philosophical discussion on whether or not "altruism" really existed. He argued that it did not. He believed that nobody ever does anything for purely selfless reasons. I suspect being in a war may have something to do with that. We brought up the example of someone rushing into a burning building to save a child. He contended that when someone does that, it is because it makes them feel better about themselves, not because they are selfless. I wish I could have recorded the sight and sound of Ledford and I having such a deep, philosophical, intellectual discussion with a Commander in the United States Coast Guard, while all three of us were sloshed!*

*Glenn and I are pretty good buddies, so we left there, and started out to the pier. We saw four or five of the dogs that are pets of the guys on the base. They are real tame, but playful. We started chasing them all over the beach and wrestling with them, having a <u>wild</u> time. If you had seen us, you would have doubted our sanity! We were laughing and trying to catch this one big, black dog. Glenn was on his hands and knees, trying to catch another dog, and the black dog jumped on his back and pushed his face in the sand. We were covered with sand from head to foot. I decided to take a walk in the surf, so I took my shoes off, and walked in water about up to my knees, then we walked down the pier, to catch the liberty boat, but it wasn't there.*

*A Coast Guard cutter was pulling out, and Glenn got into an argument with one of the guys, and smacked him in the mouth, before they pulled away. On the other side of the pier, there was a gunboat from Thailand, and we thought we'd go over and check it out. We asked if we could come aboard. They were plastered, too, I think, so they waved us on, took us to their chow hall, gave us drinks, and brought out watermelon (booze and watermelon?). We were laughing and talking in broken English and broken Vietnamese. I began to wonder about the guy sitting next to me, who kept putting his hand on my leg, and since they knew broken English, I told Glenn that "I believe we should take absence of the premises, because I believe the person on my immediate right has homosexual tendencies." So, we got up and left quickly.*

*As I crossed the plank from the gunboat to the pier, I fell. I managed to keep from going in the drink, but one of my shoes (I was still carrying them since my walk in the surf!) fell in the drink. One shoe isn't any good, so I threw the other one in, and went barefoot the rest of the night.*

*As we walked down the pier, we came across a bunch of Vietnamese sailors and one American sailor, sitting on the pier, talking. The American asked Glenn to pick up some beers for them (18 to be exact), if we were going to the club, so we went to the club and met our boat captain and Bird, another member of our crew. They looked at us kind of funny (I wonder why?), and then our boat captain pulled out two letters for me! One was from Judi "Si," and one from Judy "Sa." I was real happy about that. They were both postmarked the 10th. That's the first mail we've had since January 2nd. I read them, then we went back to the pier, where Glenn gave the American and all the Vietnamese their beer. I took a couple drinks from a bottle of booze one of the guys on the Thailand gunboat gave me, then kind'a hung over the side of the pier, where I got sick. Glenn kept thinking I was going to fall over, so he kept grabbing my shirt.*

*After a few minutes, a Swift boat came to take guys back to the ship. As it was pulling away, we jumped on it, then this Lt. J.G. came running over, jumped, and almost missed. He was hanging by his hands over the side of the boat. We helped him up, and started talking to him. It was really funny. Glenn and I started cutting down officers, and he was cutting us down. He was a young guy, and the drunkest officer I've ever seen! Then he was cutting down the Tango boat, and we cut down the Swift boats (He was the Captain of a Swift boat).*

*When we pulled alongside the ship, I went to the chow hall where they were showing "The Graduate," but my mind wasn't functioning very well, so I left to go back to the boat. When I went down the ladder into the boat, there was Glenn and this officer, talking, and drinking. I remember telling the officer that I didn't care if he was an officer, I was going to call him by his first name! He said his name was Jerry. I hit the rack. Unfortunately, my rack wouldn't stay still. It kept spinning. I managed to hold on, until I finally fell asleep.*

*I had a hangover all day. It's the drunkest I've been since I've been in Vietnam. It's only about the third or fourth time, though. Most of the guys get drunk every chance they get. It will be a while before I do that again! Well, that's the story of last night. I told you because I knew I could fill a couple of pages with it. It was kind of funny to look back on. I don't want Mom to start worrying about me getting drunk. I take care of myself and stay out of trouble when I'm sober. I do the same thing when I'm drunk. I just blow off steam. I don't smash windows, fight everybody I see, or pass out in a ditch. I never have and I never will.*

*Pretty soon I'm going to send away the film I took of the Bob Hope show, and have the slides sent there, after they are developed. I doubt if I have enough time left over here for them to be developed and sent back to me before I leave. It's nice to have something like that to worry about! Anyway, they probably won't get there for about a month. When they do, a lot of them will need explaining, because they are pictures of the base, and guys I know. Please keep the slides of the Bob Hope show separate from all the others. I'd hate for any to get lost with the others, or on the floor. I guess I'll close for now.*

*When I find out when I'm coming home, I'll let you know. It might be a month, but at the most, seven weeks. I owe a lot of letters. I should be able to get them out in the next few days. Well, until then,*

*Love,*

*Terry*

Our time at An Thoi was fun. At one point, we stopped by a Vietnamese village on the island that had crystal clear water surrounding it. We swam under the boat and removed some line that had gotten fouled up in our screws and wrapped around the shaft. After clearing our screws, we got out of the water and went fishing with concussion grenades. As stunned fish floated to the surface, villagers rushed into the surf with baskets, to retrieve the bounty we provided.

We stocked up on food and water for our boat, in An Thoi. On the ride back to Ha Tien, we enjoyed the rare treat of a three gallon tub of Chocolate ice cream. The seven of us had to eat it at one sitting, on the sun baked ride back to Ha Tien.

On the trip from An Thoi to Ha Tien, we had a swim call, in the Gulf of Siam. We lowered our bow ramp, even with the ocean, then we swam around the boat. We took turns standing watch on our helo deck, with an M-16, looking for sharks. I think each guy who took the watch, in turn, would suddenly yell, *"SHARK!"* We were always 90% sure it was a joke, but that 10% of doubt always made us swim like hell for the boat.

After swimming, we started the engines and continued our return to Ha Tien. We towed a wooden board and shot at it with our M-16's, to keep our skills sharp, even though it was rare for us to use the M-16's in combat, since we had more machine guns, than people to fire them. As I was firing, our boat captain came up behind me and opened up with his M-16, on full automatic. The muzzle was about a foot from my right ear. He could have just as easily blown my head off. I was almost completely deaf, for about twenty-four hours. I would have kicked his ass, if he wasn't my boat captain, out ranked me, bigger than me, and a black belt in Karate.

At one point, Black One told Ledford to go to the well deck and make him lunch. Ledford told him that it was unlawful to use rank for personal services, or favors. Recognizing he was right, Black One responded by telling Ledford to get a scrub brush and start scrubbing the boat from bow to stern, which Ledford did, without complaint. Then, our boat captain turned to me and ordered me to go make his lunch. I said; *"Where's the other brush?"* Ledford and I shook hands and scrubbed the boat. Black One made his own damn lunch.

I had no experience with drugs, in high school. I wasn't aware of anyone who used them. That's not saying nobody used them. I just wasn't aware of it. It wasn't very prevalent when I first arrived, almost a year earlier. Although most of us liked to drink, the guys who smoked pot were, in the minority, at least with my unit. Our coxswain, Bird Man, liked the stuff. We got on him, about it. We didn't want him *"high,"* when we needed him to be 100% effective. He talked me into trying it, late one night, while we were sitting on the helo-deck, at Ha Tien. I took a few drags on it, but I don't think it really affected me, much. It wasn't that I was nervous I'd get in trouble. I was too nervous that something could happen and I wouldn't be able to respond.

**On January 25, 1969, The Paris peace talks commenced.**

**During January, of 1969, River Assault Division 91, the first squadron formed and active, was pulled out of service, and turned over to the South Vietnamese Navy, in February.**

**February 12, 1969 Letter home**
*Hi, Everybody!*

*Well, here I am at Ha Tien. We have been operating out of here since the first of last month. It really doesn't make sense to stay here. If there IS Viet Cong around here, they are a pretty shy bunch, to say the least. It's quiet here, but I hate it, because being out in the boonies makes mail a rarity, good food non-existent, and the last time I was clean was about three days ago, when we went out to an island for "swim call." The water here makes you sick to look at! Now that I've painted a real cheerful picture of the place, I am feeling pretty good, because mail came a couple days ago, and I had plenty. I got a package from you and one from Grandma and Grandpa. I also got your tape. I'll have to play it over before I answer it. My tape recorder is still messed up, and I have to borrow one from one of the guys.*

*We see the kids in Ha Tien, quite a bit. When we first got here, we noticed one real scrappy kid that wasn't big, but could handle himself very well. We told him that if he fought one of the other kids, we'd give him a can of C-rations. He turned around and punched a little kid half his age in the face! We felt terrible and gave them both several cans. His name is "Hom," pronounced "Home." He really is a good kid. Sometimes, in the afternoon, he brings me his homework from school. I can't read it, of course, but he shows me the teacher's markings on it and I compliment him on it.*

*A kid did make me angry, one day. I was in the well deck, cooking some canned sweet potatoes on our kerosene stove. We were tied up to a pier, and a kid maybe ten or twelve kept standing next to our machine guns, along the top of the well deck. I know he couldn't do anything with them, but it made me nervous. I kept telling him to "Di di mau," but he wouldn't leave. Finally, I reached into the frying pan, grabbed a cooking chunk of sweet potato, and hit him in the head with it. I'm sure it didn't hurt him, but it did make him leave.*

*Tonight at 6:30, we have to go on an op in support of a "Seal" team. That's the Navy's "Green Beret." I think we'll just be out overnight. I still haven't heard any news of when I'm going to be taken off the boat, or coming home. I have to leave by March 20th, though. I'm pretty edgy about it, and every op we go out on, I hate more than the one before. These things have a way of getting <u>very</u> old, after so many times out.*

*I hope you like the slides I sent last night. You should get the Bob Hope pictures and slides in a couple of weeks. I meant to send you the slides, and Judi the prints, but I sent all of them there. Would you give Judi the prints? If you want to, you can have duplicates of any, and if Judi wants prints of any slides, could you have them made up? I'll reimburse you when I come home. I just hope the Bob Hope pictures and slides come out OK. The film was old.*

*We stayed out all night, last night. Not much happened. One sampan tried to cross the river at night, and the guys shot it up. Results-unknown. Oh hell! I just got word we have to pull out in two and a-half-hours, at 11pm. You wouldn't believe...*

*February 14*

*Well, "you wouldn't believe" is as far as I got, last night. We pulled out right away, and stayed out the entire night. I still haven't had any sleep. This morning, before dawn, everybody was on edge. If I didn't have anyone who cared what I did, I would have mouthed back at a Commander that got on my nerves. Bill Hodges, "Hodge," is a pretty good buddy of mine, but last night, we got into an argument, and I almost came at him, swinging. My boat captain stopped us. He blamed me for something I didn't do, and apologized afterward, but I still felt bad about the argument. The thing was, intelligence reports said V.C. were dug in up river, waiting for us, so we spent the entire night in heat and bugs and no sleep, looking for them. As usual, nothing happened, but it's not the easiest thing in the world, on our nerves. Well, so much for that junk.*

*Recently, we were beached at Ha Tien, just below the Army and C.I.A. intelligence base. I had the watch in the middle of the night. There is a curfew at night and Vietnamese aren't supposed to be on the river. As I stood on the stern of our boat, I saw what appeared to be a fishing boat, maybe a hundred yards from our boat. There was a quarter moon, so the light was pretty low. Still, I could make out a guy casting a net in the water and bringing it in. As I watched, he kept coming closer and closer to our boat, casting his net. Again, he certainly looked like a fisherman, but that's exactly what a Viet Cong would want us to think if they wanted to attack us, or plant a mine on us. Finally, he just got too close and I hurled a concussion grenade a couple feet from his sampan. Boy, was he mad! He was screaming at me and I imagine calling me everything but a "Great American!" He got the message, though, and took off. He was lucky. I'm sure there are guys that would have just shot him.*

*I just finished reading "Rosemary's Baby," the book you sent in the "care package." Boy, it was weird! Well, at the <u>most</u>, it's about 34 days before I leave for home. That's getting on my nerves, too. The anxiety!*

*We are going swimming, tomorrow, not just for recreation. It's to get clean! The river down here is filthy, so we are pulling out off the coast, into deeper water, to swim there. We throw out a bunch of air mattresses and lower the bow ramp until it is even with the water, then jump in with our clothes on, mainly because after a week of no laundry, they smell kind of ripe, too! I'll have to <u>adjust</u> to clean clothes, when I come home!*

*Well folks, I better close for now, and write Judi a letter. Give everybody my love! Your River Rat Kid,*

*Terry*

**On February 23rd, 1969, Viet Cong attacked 110 targets throughout South Vietnam.**

Ha Tien was an interesting place, located on the Gulf of Siam, on the Cambodian border. It was a communications and intelligence base for the Army and Air America. *"Air America"* was the CIA operation that used a civilian airline as a cover. There were very few Americans in Ha Tien. Tango 9 was the only boat from the Mobile Riverine Force in the town, although "Swift" boats and PBR's came in, now and then.

**"Tiger Greens" described a particular jungle pattern of "camo," during the Vietnam War. They are much different than the camo worn by today's services. I'm wearing the *"tiger greens"* that had belonged to Jim Sater, a distant relative, from Hollywood, California. He was in the Army. One day, we were able to put all of our dirty, raggedy uniforms into a mesh bag that was fastened shut, then sent up to the building at the top of the hill, for a rare wash in something other than river water. When we got the bag back, Jim Sater's uniform was in the bag. He was <u>exactly</u> the same size I was, and had my name, "SATER," over the pocket. What's the chances of something like THAT happening? A Central Intelligence Agency, *"Air America"* chopper sits behind me. The Army communications and C.I.A. base is at the top of the hill. Note the bunker above the chopper.**

I, along with the rest of the crew DID get one other, extra set of tiger greens. The captain of a Coast Guard cutter wanted our boat to tow and guard his personal "Boston Whaler." It was not much bigger than a regular "john boat." Not long after we started taking care of it, a Green Beret officer stopped by boat, asking if he could have it. We told him we couldn't give it to him. It belonged to a Coast Guard cutter captain. He nonchalantly waved his hand and said that it was no problem. He'd just come by and take it, some night, unless of course, we'd be willing to trade for it. Faced with those options, we gave him the Boston Whaler, and each of us got a new set of tiger greens.

During one visit by the Swift Boats, they were tied up a half mile upstream from us, on the other side of Ha Tien. We heard shots, and saw that sailors on the Swifts boat were shooting at someone in the river, half way between their boats and where we were beached. A dugout canoe was picking up the swimmer directly in front of the village. We were a little closer to the swimmer than the Swift boats, so I grabbed an M-16, and ran into the village, expecting to take a V.C. as a prisoner. As I got to the point that the swimmer was being brought ashore, I realized that he was actually a drunken Vietnamese Marine. A few of his friends were holding him up by his arms, when they, and the drunken Marine, suddenly noticed me.

I was the only American in the village, and I was holding an M-16. I was surrounded by maybe a couple hundred Vietnamese. Some probably were either Viet Cong, or Viet Cong sympathizers. The drunk Vietnamese Marine swimmer immediately assumed I was the one shooting at him. He started screaming, and trying to get loose from his friends to attack me.

My mind raced with options. I could shoot him, and be killed by his friends. I could just hit him with the butt of the M-16 and be killed by him and his friends, I could be passive and probably be killed by him and his friends. Under those options, I was a dead man. Suddenly, a Vietnamese civilian was standing before me, pushed me in the chest, and said, **"YOU GO!"** I said, **"YOU GOT IT!"** and ran as fast I could, to the boat.

We used to patronize the town bar, on occasion. It had a dirt floor, but it had cold *"Ba Moui Ba"* beer. Whenever we went to the bar, we went heavily armed, with M-16's, shotguns and grenades, just in case. One night we went on an operation that lasted all night, and into the next day. That evening, we went to the bar. The owner of the bar told us everything there was to tell about our operation. He knew where we went, when we ate, when we left and when we came back. He knew when we were at our guns, with our helmets and flak jackets on, and when we took them off. It was painfully obvious that the Viet Cong also knew our every move, every minute, of every day.

It was in the same bar that we feasted on shrimp, with delicious sweet and sour sauce. Before long, we regretted eating it. All of us came down with terrible dysentery. When we went to one of our ships to get medication, the medics looked us over. Doctors inspected our boat and our cooking utensils. We were cleaning ourselves, our clothes and our eating utensils in the river water, at Ha Tien. In addition to the dysentery, all of us had ringworm and lice. We were given medications and sent on our way. Soon, we were back at Ha Tien and noticed a primitive pier, coming out from the village, with primitive outhouses build on it. Downstream from the pier, we saw village women cleaning shrimp and other food. We never ate in the village, again.

**Months later, Admiral Zumwalt's son, Lt. Elmo Zumwalt III operated in Ha Tien, on his Swift boat. He wrote in his book; "My Father, My Son"**
*"Of all the places I had been in Vietnam, the Ha Tien area was the most primitive. Besides the constant feeling of danger, we had to contend with impoverished conditions. On our patrols, we ate from C-Rations and what food we could buy in the different Vietnamese Villages. We were so far down the supply line that no swift boat base had even been established yet. Supplies like toilet paper and soap were hard to find. When my complaints finally reached Dad, he sent a supply officer to Ha Tien for a couple of days, and the supplies began improving after that. But the living conditions remained miserable.*

*We suffered from dysentery much of the time. Once it got to be so awful we required intravenous fluids because we had become so dehydrated. We almost constantly suffered nausea and diarrhea. This is an intensely hot and humid part of the country, infested with an ungodly number of mosquitoes. We carried huge cans of insect repellent and spread it on like shaving lotion when we went on patrol, but those damn mosquitoes would still be at us like bees on a hive."*

Ha Tien also had a dirt floor barber shop. Not too long before I left, we were walking through the village. On a dare, I went into the barbershop to have my beard shaved off by an old, gray-haired man. I guessed that with my friends there, even if the old man WAS a V.C., or just a V.C. sympathizer, I would be safe. I didn't think things through, nearly enough. The old man splashed cold water on my face and started scraping the beard off with a straight razor. No shaving cream. No soap. No hot water. Tears rolled down my cheeks as the old man scraped away my beard. Out of either pride, stupidity, being stubborn, or a combination of all three, I didn't stop him. I am certain he was either an old Viet Cong, or a V.C. sympathizer.

**On March 4th, President Richard Nixon threatened to resume bombing of North Vietnam in retaliation for Viet Cong attacks in the south.**

# Chapter 19
## Going Home

One sunny day, on March 4th or 5th, a Hughes OH-6 Cayuse chopper landed in the area where the Air America choppers usually came in. They were called *"LOACHES,"* after the military acronym, *"Light Observation Helicopter."* A young guy in brand new greens, Seaman Richard Alves, carrying his *"sea bag,"* got out of the chopper and ran towards Tango 9, calling my name. He was my replacement.

**An OH-6 Cayuse, similar to the one I flew from Ha Tien to the MRB, near Dong Tam.**

The chopper pilot told me I had five minutes to get my things together, and get on the chopper. I was as excited as I could be, but felt bad about having only a few minutes to tell the crew goodbye. It didn't seem fair. After being part of the original crew of Tango 3, then spending three months on Tango 6, I had been a part of the crew of Tango 9 for seven long months. We lived together 24/7. We fought back to back. We fought with each other. We went through the crucible. I had five minutes to tell them all *"Goodbye."* I thought I'd get some kind of notice that I would be leaving in a month, a week, or a few days. I didn't expect to be plucked into the sky, on five minutes notice. I wish I had at least an hour or two to talk with the guys, to exchange home addresses and reminisce. Leaving my buddies made me a little sad. At the same time, I felt like I had just won the lottery. I know my crewmates had mixed emotions. They looked on, happy for me, sad it wasn't them, and feeling perhaps a little jealous. They probably also had anxiety at the prospect of breaking in a new guy, wondering if he would fit in and contribute to the daily chores.

The chopper took me to the Mobile Riverine Base near Dong Tam, landing on the USS Benewah, APB-35, about 125 miles, away. We flew just above the tree tops, for what seemed to be a very long time. It was nerve wracking that we were in such close range for anyone with a gun. When we landed, I asked the pilot why in the world he flew so low. He explained that if we were flying higher, a Viet Cong could see us coming from far away and take their time shooting us. By flying low, he would zip over them before they knew he was coming. I wish he would have told me that when we took off!

**March 6, 1969.** My "Performance Appraisal" was written up, with a copy forwarded to my next ship, the U.S.S. Hunley. I was given a perfect "4.0," with the exception of "Military Appearance." I was downgraded the next level down, described as being *"Smart. Neat and correct in appearance."* I don't think there was one day in Vietnam that I didn't look like a mess. This is how the Performance Appraisal described me;

*"Gunner and Deck Seaman on ATC 131-9, operating in an intense combat environment with the Mobile Riverine Force, engaged in Riverine Assault Operations in the Mekong Delta, RVN. Assists in the maintenance of his boat and its equipment. Man's one of the boats automatic weapons at G.Q. Sater has done an excellent job while attached to this command. He is a capable, conscientious, dependable and hardworking seaman who takes great pride in a job well done. Sater performs coolly and effectively under fire."*

**The chopper ride out of Ha Tien was nerve wracking, but exciting. In the photo on the right, you can see my leg is hanging out of the chopper.**

**I took this photo as our chopper approached the Benewah.**

My last full day in Dong Tam was March 6th. While checking out of River Assault Squadron 13, the personnel clerk handed me a long form to sign. I asked, *"What is it?"*

He matter-of-factly responded *"You requested the east coast on your "dream sheet." This extends you in the Navy for an extra month, to compensate the Navy for your travel to Charleston, South Carolina."*

I blurted out; *"Fuck you! I'm not going to sign that!"*

The clerk shrugged his shoulders and said; *"Fine. You can wait here until new orders come."* Angrily, I reached for the clipboard and said; *"Gimme that fucking thing!"* I signed it. I had enlisted for a four year hitch, which would have been up, fourteen months later, on July 10, 1970. After serving one tour of duty on the USS Enterprise, in the Gulf of Tonkin and one year in the Mekong Delta, the Navy demanded an additional month of service, to cover the $100 it cost them to send me to Charleston, South Carolina for the next fifteen months.

I threw away most of the clothes I wore in Vietnam. They were ragged. I don't think any amount of soap and washing could have saved them. I lost my treasured beret, with my Riv Ron 13 patch and clipped loop.

The day before we flew home, they loaded us on open trucks for a convoy to Saigon. It was a much smaller group than when we arrived, a year earlier. Tommy Snow and Rudy Mahanes, from Tango 3 were there, along with Teddy Underwood, Rich Twigg, Bob Grout, Bill *"Rock"* Martel, Jerry Ranson, and a few of the other guys. At least eight of the guys I arrived with were dead. One or two went home due to nervous breakdowns, or performance issues. I heard that one of our guys snapped and fired a grenade launcher, in the base, at Dong Tam. Another guy, the one who was always getting in fights during River Warfare School and said he couldn't wait to get to Vietnam and *"kill gooks,"* was said to come back to his boat one night, hysterical, and in tears. He kept saying we were *"all going to die."* I have no idea how many went home seriously wounded. I believe the group that got on the trucks that day was probably 25% of the seventy-two that arrived in Vietnam with me.

We stayed in a hotel, our last night in Saigon. I had spent every day over the last twelve months, in Vietnam. I never had one day of the "R&R" they promised us, during training, but I was incredibly lucky, and I can't complain.

One memory stands out. About a dozen of us were spending our last evening together in a cozy banquet room of the hotel. It had a long, dark wood table. We all sat around the table, drinking beer and telling stories about our experiences and remembering the friends we lost. Meanwhile, exotic, beautiful, French-Vietnamese prostitutes, in high heels and satin dresses, with the high mandarin collars, worked the room, hoping for some quick cash.

As I look back on that night, it was a *sacred* time. I'm sure most of the guys felt the same. We had been through so much, together. We went through the legendary, tough, S.E.R.E. training, and River Warfare School, unique in Navy history. We went through battles together. We experienced loss, rage, fear, despair and pride, together. We were brothers in arms, soon to be cast apart. We mourned lost friends. There was a heaviness, a keen awareness of the absence of friends who had fallen. We knew that night was the end of our brotherhood in Vietnam, but we were deliriously happy with the thought of going home, in just hours. Within one day, I would be home with family, and Judi would be in my arms. If you could gage the level of excitement of a kid on Christmas Eve and multiply it by one-thousand, it might get close to how I felt that night.

While we were talking, laughing, and reminiscing, one of the women in the room came up behind me and lifted off my glasses. I didn't even turn around, continuing the conversation with my buddies. I figured she'd give them right back, or put them back on my face. As the evening wore on, we began to turn in for the night. I asked for my glasses. None of the women in the room acknowledged having them and acted like they didn't know what I was talking about. The Vietnamese hotel manager was standing there, in a dark suit and tie. He didn't seem interested in helping. All of a sudden, Tommy Snow, my crewmate from my first boat, stood up, got in the manager's face and screamed;

### *"If he doesn't get his fucking glasses in the next ten fucking seconds, we're going to tear this fucking hotel apart!"*

With that, a petite woman stepped up, lifted the front of her dress, took my glasses out of her panties, and tentatively handed them to me. The explosive situation was diffused. All of us then turned in, facing an early morning flight home. I slept on the top floor of the hotel. The hotel was mortared that night and there was call to evacuate the building. I slept through it, blissfully unaware.

A few of the seventy-two guys from Class 14-R leaving Vietnam for home on a "MACV" (Military Airlift Command, Vietnam) flight out of Saigon on March 7th, 1969, at 0700. We had been through a lot together, including firefights, beers, cheers and tears. During the last twelve months, some of us had been assigned to Riv Ron 13, and some to Riv Ron 11, but we were going home together. Together, except for those who had died, been wounded, or had broken under the mental and emotional stress. Over the course of the war, 1,448 men died on the day they were scheduled to leave Vietnam. In this photo, Tommy Snow is holding his ticket home. Ron Tope is behind him. Bill *"The Rock"* Martel is in the middle, next to me. Green is over Rock's right shoulder. Teddy Underwood has his arm around Rock. Jerry Ranson is behind me, in the blue shirt.

# Chapter 20
## The Nightmare of the Mekong

When the plane touched down at Travis Air Force Base, San Francisco, we stomped our feet, clapped our hands, yelled and celebrated. It felt as though the plane was going to be shaken apart. We were euphoric. Some guys came home in their dress whites. Some went home in their *"greens."* A few, like me, went home in civilian clothes. I didn't have a decent uniform to wear. I'm not sure I would have worn a uniform, even if I had one ready to go. As it was, I was still called a *"baby killer"* when I arrived. It was shouted at me, as I walked through the airport. At the time, it seemed surreal and didn't bother me much. I was too elated at being on American soil, to be hurt by some idiot hippie. It was only with the passage of time and moments of reflection that the incident angered me. From Travis, I caught a TWA flight home. The ticket cost $51.00. Ron Tope lived in Columbia, Illinois, just across the river from St. Louis. He didn't have a ride home from the airport, so my family took Ron to our house for a while. When we sat at the dining room table, Ron began pouring out what the year was like, giving Judi and my family the first true description of what we had been through. I would have told them, eventually, but it was taken out of my hands. Mom cried, hard. I think tears came to my father's eyes, as well. I'm sure they knew things occurred that I hadn't told them about, but they weren't prepared for what they heard, since I had lied, in my letters home...

Being home was wonderful, yet strange. It seemed unreal. There were really only two attitudes about Vietnam vets, aside from immediate family. It was generally either outright hostility or indifference. A stranger at the airport might call you a *"baby killer."* If you ran into a friend you hadn't seen for some time and said *"Hi! I just got back from Vietnam!"* You might have heard *"Hmm cool. Did you see my new car?"* Looking back, I think indifference was harder to take. We were changed. The rest of the world wasn't. For years after I came home, few people were aware of the "Brown Water Navy." The typical reaction of someone who knew I went to Vietnam was, *"Well, at least you were way out to sea!"*

Judi noticed that I had changed. I was no longer the kid the teachers in high school said didn't have *"a serious bone in his body."* I wasn't quite the same.

On March 19th, I asked Judi to marry me. Mom went crazy with joy, of course. She wanted Judi in the family almost as much as I did. Most of the brothers and sisters were mildly amused. Mike was watching TV. When we told him the news, he simply said *"'Bout time,"* without turning his head away from the TV screen. Later, Judi and I went to her house, to tell her Mom and Dad. They were watching TV. When Judi started to tell her, her Mom said, *"Wait until the commercial."* I am sure that on one hand, she knew it was coming, so it was not a huge surprise. I think she may have also wanted a couple of minutes to think about it.

We set the date of September 20th, of 1969, for our wedding. We bought a '64 Chevy Impala, to take with us to Charleston, when I came back for the wedding. After buying the car, I took it to a *"do it yourself"* car wash, on Page Avenue, not far from my parent's home. While I was using the sprayer, a car on the street backfired. Instinctively, I hit the ground, spread eagle, into a big puddle of water. Only a combat vet could understand my emotions at that moment. Immediately, I jumped back up, looking around, to see if anyone was watching. I was embarrassed, humiliated and angry. I couldn't understand why I would do something so stupid. It was my first taste of PTSD, but it would be many years, before I understood it. In those days, we didn't talk much about it. I thought I was the only guy who did stuff like that.

**President Richard M. Nixon awarded the Mobile Riverine Force and other units the Presidential Unit Citation for "Extraordinary Heroism" in our efforts in "Operation Giant Slingshot. His citation read;**

*"For extraordinary heroism and outstanding performance of duty from 6 December 1968 to 31 March 1969 while engaged in armed conflict against enemy forces in the Republic of Vietnam. Commander Task Group 194.9 initiated and prosecuted a determined interdiction offensive against the ingress of enemy personnel and war material from Southeast Cambodia into the upper Mekong Delta region of the Republic of Vietnam. The naval units engaged in Operation GIANT SLINGSHOT, including the Riverine Warfare and River Patrol Forces who supplied support, consistently distinguished themselves by their countless deeds of valiant service while carrying out patrols along the narrow, enemy-infested Vam Co, Vam Co Dong, and Vam Co Tay Rivers. Operating with limited logistic support under austere and dangerous conditions, personnel of Commander Task Group 194.9 countered intense rocket and automatic weapons barrages at point-blank range with unshakable determination. As a result of their intrepidity and resolution, the enemy threat was significantly diminished and vital routes of resupply were severed. The quantity of captured enemy war material reached staggering proportions, and the ever-increasing number of enemy casualties attested to the effectiveness of ingeniously developed individual and group offensive tactics. The selfless dedication and inspiring professional performance of the officers and men of Commander Task Group 194.9 reflected credit upon themselves and were in keeping with the highest traditions of the United States Naval Service."*

April 7th, 1969, I reported for duty to the submarine tender, USS Hunley (AS-31) in Charleston, South Carolina, at 7:06 PM. It was difficult to readjust to the *"Blue Water Navy"* after being in the *"Brown Water"* Navy for almost fifteen months, including the training. The 1st Class Petty Officer on duty in the Deck Department asked me what the round pin above my pocket signified. I told him it was the insignia for River Assault Flotilla One. He told me to take it off. It wasn't an *"authorized"* insignia to wear on my dress blues. He said it with a definite attitude of disdain.

During my remaining months in the Navy, I had the distinct impression that the stateside *"regular"* Navy disliked sailors who were rotating back to the states from the *"Brown Water Navy."*

I was assigned to mess cook duty in the Chief Petty Officer's galley, which didn't sit well with me. I wasn't thrilled with the idea of being kitchen help. I developed an attitude. As far as I was concerned, I had done my duty for my country. I didn't owe the Navy a year of spit and polish while I peeled potatoes for a Chief Petty Officer's lunch. I still remember a short, fat Chief Petty Officer who finished a bowl of ice cream, and instead of turning around, or asking for more, clinked on his ice cream bowl with his spoon, his back turned to me, wanting me to jump like Pavlov's dog to refill his ice cream bowl.

One day, I was slicing a slab of bacon with a large electric slicer. I was listening to some "Motown," and thinking about the upcoming wedding. I wasn't thinking. As I pushed the bacon into the slicer, I sliced the end of my thumb off. I wrapped my thumb in a towel and quickly ran to sickbay. Moments after I arrived, another mess cook came into the room, carrying the end of my thumb, wrapped in a slice of bacon. The doctor sewed it back on. I learned *"first hand"* that there are a lot of nerves in the ends of our fingers.

When I went on liberty the next day, I had to get my *"liberty card"* from a 3rd Class Petty Officer, Rich Patterson, who later became a good friend of mine. Patterson's first reaction, was to tell me that my shoes weren't really shined well enough to go on liberty. I told Patterson, *"Come on. This is my first liberty in the states since getting back from Nam. I'll shine my shoes better tomorrow!"* A voice from behind asked if I thought I was going to get the card. I didn't turn around all the way, but I could see that it was an officer in dress whites. I answered, *"Yeah, I guess."* A young ensign, probably not long out of Annapolis, said *"Not "Yeah, I guess! Yes, Sir! You turn around and salute me, sailor!"* Over the course of the previous fifteen months, I had been trained, conditioned, lived and fought, as a part of a wild, proud and formidable wolf pack. In Vietnam, I served under, fought alongside, and got drunk with Navy Lieutenants, and Coast Guard Commanders who earned and deserved my respect, my loyalty and my salute. Now, I was being treated as an unruly lap dog on a short leash with a tight collar, being brought to heel. I had a hard time accepting the arrogance of a young ensign with a stick up his ass, whose idea of *"action"* was rousting an enlisted man. I gave him the salute he demanded and made it my mission to have enough drinks to forget the indignity of having to salute the untested plebe.

On February 16, 1970. I became certified to operate the missile/cargo crane of the Hunley. It was an enormous crane. The cab was two or three stories off the top deck. The crane was large enough to load the huge Polaris missiles into the missile tubes of the nuclear subs, *"Boomers,"* that tied up alongside the Hunley. My duties did not involve loading or unloading the missiles.

**By April 30th, 1969, U.S. troop strength in Vietnam peaked at 553,400.**

**Letter from Judi. May 7, 1969.**
*Hi, Rip!*

*Well, how are things going in Fun City? Not too much going on, here. I would have written to you last night, but I figured I'd better answer a letter I got from Margie Williams about a month ago, so after I wrote that, Fran and Larry came over and we sat and talked.*

*Last night, after Fran & Larry left, I was looking through some of my stuff and I found some of your letters from when you were on Tango 9. It gives me the creeps, now that I know that worse things happened than what was in the letters. Every time the news about Vietnam comes on, especially when they've had trouble in the Delta, I get that same old sick feeling. I guess that after a year of worrying about it, it's kind of hard to get it out of your system. Looking back at it, the year went by pretty fast, but I'm glad we don't have to go through it again. I don't wish that on anyone. That year was the worst one I've ever spent. Worrying if you were alright, wondering where you were, and how you were. I'm so thankful it's all over, and I thank God you made it home in perfect condition. That's one year out of our lives neither of us will ever forget. Well, that's enough talk on that subject. I'm just glad it's over!*

*We're still waiting for Pat to have her baby. The doctor said she won't go before May 30th. I hope she's back in shape by September.*

*Well Luv, I guess I'd better get back to work now - lunchtime is done past.*

*So until next time-----*

*Love Ya Bunches,*

*Judi*

**Letter from Judi, Sunday, June 2, 1969.**
*Hi Terry!!*

*Guess what? You're almost an uncle again!! Pat & Steve are now the proud parents of a bouncing baby boy, by the name of Daniel Philip Simon!! He arrived at 11:31 p.m. last night, at 7 pounds, 6 ounces and 19 inches long. He has a dark complexion, black hair and dark eyes. I can't wait to see him. I'm all excited!!!!!!!!*

*I think Pat had a pretty rough time. She had a terrible cold and was in labor for almost twelve hours. Finally they had to give her a shot to knock her out, because she was pretty bad off. She's okay this morning, though. She called us at six o'clock to tell us all about it. She says he's just beautiful (not that I doubt it). I'm glad it's all over. I'm sure she is, too. Steve was very calm both times he called us. She said that she thinks she worried him a couple of times when she let out with a scream.*

*I never did get to the hospital to see your grandfather yesterday. After I talked to you, your mom's leg was all swollen up and hurting pretty badly, so we had to take her over to the hospital to get her foot x-rayed. We didn't get home until around 11:00. I will go to see your grandfather this week, though. Maybe I'll go tonight when Mom and Dad go to see Pat. I bought some Polaroid film so Steve can take a couple pictures of the baby so I can see what he looks like.*

*Guess what else I bought today? I got a Tom Jones album! I bet you're all excited about that, aren't you? I decided to write you a letter here at work so that I could tell you about the new baby right away and I don't know what I'll be doing tonight.*

*I forgot to tell you before about Mom. She's okay. She's just got a badly sprained ankle and she's hopping all over. This morning she said she ached from one end to the other. She sure has been falling a lot here lately.*

*I talked to your grandpa, yesterday. Your mom called from the hospital to find out how Mom was so I asked him how he enjoyed your call. He told me that he told you he thought you were getting "a gem" (that's ME sparkle, sparkle). He also told me he thought I was getting one, too.*

*Well, Lover, I can't think of anything else to say, and since I only have an hour left of work I guess I'd better clear off my desk and get ready to go home.*

*Love Ya Bunches,*

*Judi*

On September 20th, I married Judith Ann Simon, at All Souls Church, in Overland, Missouri. It was exactly one year from the day that I laughed, hysterically, as we were ambushed, near *"Snoopy's Nose"* and scrapped the flesh from my knuckles as I reloaded my 20MM cannon. I was twenty-two. Judi was twenty. When I came home, from Vietnam, I weighed about 170 pounds. My mother tried to fatten me up. When I reported to the USS Hunley, they assigned me to "Mess Hall" duty, where I had good, fresh food available to me, all day. After a year of C-Rations being my primary food, I stuffed myself. When I came home for our wedding, I weighed 235 pounds. I gained sixty-five pounds in six months. My ring didn't fit, and had to be quickly resized. Fortunately, I lost the weight before I got out of the Navy.

We spent our wedding night at the nearby Henry VIII Hotel. We spent the next couple days with the family, before heading out for my next duty station at the Navy Base in Charleston, South Carolina, on board the USS Hunley, AS-31, on the Cooper River. It took us three full days to drive from St. Louis, to Charleston. We rented a mobile home in Summerville, South Carolina, right next to the Francis Marion State Park. The rent took $90.00 of my $196.00 monthly pay. To me, it was a castle. I was in Heaven. I even had a genuine *"naugahyde"* recliner! I spent every fourth day and every fourth weekend, on duty, on the ship. Other than that, I was home with Judi.

When Christmas came, I went into the park next door and cut the top off a fir tree. We put it in our trailer and decorated it with lights, and strings of popcorn and cranberries.

**Judi and I at our wedding reception, and our home, in Summerville, South Carolina, 1969.**

I never had a nightmare, while I was in Vietnam. When I laid my head down on a ball of dirty clothes, I escaped to idyllic dreams of home, holding Judi in my arms, or floating in the air, above my home.

Once I was home, the nightmare began. It was as if it had been there, in the undercurrents of my mind, like a body, flowing deep in a river. The nightmare suddenly bobbed to the surface. It was always the same. It was the culmination of everything I had seen, heard, and feared, in Vietnam. In it, I fell from our boat, into the Mekong. The river was thick, swollen with bloated water buffalo carcasses, dead pigs, and the bodies of men. I swam through them, to an island. There, I was chased by dark, relentless Viet Cong, carrying long, gleaming swords, intent on taking my head. Most often, the nightmare consisted only of me running, and running, and running, but never being caught. Once, I was captured, forced to kneel and my head was sliced from my body. That's when I woke up. I had always heard that you couldn't dream your own death. You can.

I spent much of my adult life being startled awake with the sense of falling. I always felt it was something entirely separate from my nightmare of the Mekong. It was only while writing this book, and the regeneration of memories, that I awoke from the feeling of falling, and realized I was falling off my boat and into the Mekong. My lifetime nightmare of the Mekong came often, but sometimes startled me awake before I got into the full length version.

When the nightmares came, Judi patiently endured my body flopping around in spasms. Sometimes I would be moaning, or uttering some expression of fear or pain. She would reach over and soothingly rub my back, or neck, instantly calming me, reassuring me that I was home and safe, at least for a while.

I sent wedding invitations to some of the guys I served with in Vietnam. I didn't expect any of them to make it to the wedding. Many of us were still in the service and had to go to their next duty stations. I also knew that those who were fortunate enough to get out of the service on their return would be working hard at getting their lives together. I just wanted my buddies to know Judi and I were getting married, and that I thought of them.

Shortly after we arrived in Charleston, I received an unexpected letter from Mike *"Willie"* Williams' father, Mr. J.R. Williams. *"Willie"* was a buddy, and crewmate, on Tango 6, my second boat.

**Letter from Mr. J.R. Williams**

*Mr. Terence M. Sater*
*Overland, Mo.*

*Dear Mr. Sater*

*We want to apologize for not acknowledging the invitation to your wedding sent to our son, Michael.*

*Michael's return was a happy occasion, but our joy lasted less than twenty-four hours. He and his twin brother, Joseph, were passengers in an automobile that was involved in an accident, and Michael was killed instantly, and his brother, fatally.*

*Please remember them in your prayers and may God bless you and your wife and grant you happiness and success.*

*Sincerely,*

*J.R. Williams*

I was stunned by the staggering misfortune and at the same time, blown away by the infinite warmth and grace of Willie's father. I wish I could have met him. I'm sure he was a remarkable man and father. As a father, today, I cannot imagine the pain and anguish Mr. Williams went through. I've come to know Willie's family, through social media, and I see Willie, in them. I want them to know that I, as well as others that served with him, will think of him, always.

**Mike ("Willie") Williams (far left), Jack Elrod, Dennis Alexander and I**

On June 1, 1970, I finally achieved the rank of ETR3, Petty Officer Third Class, Electronics Technician, Radar. Most made 3rd Class before I did, but I became singularly focused on survival in Vietnam, not electronics.

August 10, 1970, I received my discharge from the active duty Navy.

On April 30, 1975, Saigon fell to the North Vietnamese and Viet Cong forces. I was working as an outside salesman, at Glasco Electric Company, selling electrical equipment and supplies. My boss, Bob Finley, appreciated the service of Vietnam veterans. He had three of them on his sales force, me, Gary Chastain, and

280

Paul Dunker. Gary and I became best friends. He served with the 173rd Airborne, *"Sky Soldiers,"* as a Sergeant, and Squad Leader. He once told me that he often took *"point,"* leading his men into combat, even though he could have passed the dangerous task down to one of his other men. Gary felt he was better at it, and accepted the risk. Gary was awarded the Air Medal for Meritorious Achievement, the Silver Star, and two Purple Hearts. One of the Purple Hearts was for wounds received during action on September 27th, 1968. Gary was never ashamed, or embarrassed by his service in the unpopular war, nor did he brag or boast. Like many, he only really spoke of it with other Vietnam veterans. He once told me of the time he and a Viet Cong both swung their rifles around and put each other in their gun sights, at the exact same instant. Gary just happened to be quicker on pulling the trigger.

When I came home, that evening, the television news programs were broadcasting the chaotic scenes of the final conquest of Saigon and the total collapse of the South Vietnamese forces. South Vietnamese soldiers were casting off their uniforms, in the streets of Saigon. I stood in our living room, wearing a sport coat and tie, watching the North Vietnamese tanks break down the gates to the Presidential Palace, in Saigon. I stood, frozen in place, holding my briefcase. I was overwhelmed with the sadness of the lives of my friends and over 58,000 other Americans that were sacrificed in that war.

I watched the horrendous and humiliating scene of Americans scrambling to get out of Saigon and taking as many Vietnamese military and civilian allies with them, as they could fit into helicopters, in *"Operation Frequent Wind."* The pain was difficult to bear.

Vietnamese pilots were flying helicopters out to sea, hoping to land on, or near American aircraft carriers, to escape. So many landed on the carriers, their flight decks were filled to overcapacity. Helicopters had to be pushed off, into the sea. Vietnamese pilots even flew their choppers into the sea, near Navy ships, desperate to be picked up and kept safe from the North Vietnamese. I wondered what became of Lt. Phan Ute and the men of the Vietnamese 4th Marine Battalion that we got to know. I still wonder if they were killed, or put into re-education camps.

# Chapter 21
## It Happened Long Ago

I came to appreciate and understand the long term mental and emotional effects of war better after watching interviews with World War II veterans who choked back tears when they spoke of comrades who died at Normandy beach, on June 6th, 1944. I know memories fade with time, but they never really go away. Even now, almost fifty years later, everyday sights or sounds take me back to the Mekong Delta. It is the same for many vets. I usually don't mention it, simply because it happens so often. Memories of Vietnam are stirred by guns, boats, rivers, rice, dark green, helicopters, explosions, fireworks, Memorial Day, Veterans Day, the Fourth of July, mosquitoes, anything in the road, news about any war, or anyone of Asian descent.

War affects every person, differently. If two people went to combat tethered together, and you asked them what it was like when they returned, you would hear two entirely different accounts. Each person filters the experience through their own eyes, their own fears, expectations, or character. One person may have his head turned to see a friend disappear in an explosion, while the other person, looking in a different direction, sees nothing. In every firefight I went through, every man saw it from a different angle. They saw things I didn't see, just as I saw things they didn't see. I hear all the time about vets who never speak of their experience. Others, like me, talk about it, especially with other vets. I am convinced it is better to talk, not just for our own peace of mind, but I because we owe it to our fallen to speak of them, and for them.

I opened up about my Vietnam experiences with Judi, in 1985. My son, Chris, believes that I started talking about it with him, after the movie *"Platoon"* came out, a year later. I don't exactly know why. I didn't like most of the movies that came out during the 70's and 80's. Too often, they portrayed Vietnam veterans in a very poor light, either as suicidal, or homicidal. For me, *"Platoon"* achieved a sense of realism, in some ways. There were three scenes that resonated with me. The first was when the Charlie Scheen character stepped off the plane on his arrival, and was hit with the extreme humidity of Vietnam. The second was the scene in which Charlie Sheen's character, *"Chris,"* had the *"shit detail,"* burning the human waste in the half-barrels that we stored under the latrine seats. It vividly brought to mind the most disgusting job I had, in my entire life. The third scene that rocked me, was the one during the night, when Sheen woke and could hear his heart beating, as he listened for noises by the creeping Viet Cong. It reminded me of the night I stood watch on the starboard side of the bow of our boat and a grenade was lobbed at me, exploding on the port side. Beyond that, I thought the movie did a good job of capturing the emotional dynamics between the men who fought in Vietnam. Friendships were very close, but tempers flared easily, and there were explosive animosities.

For many years, I didn't know I had PTSD. I poured myself into my work, which was typical of many combat veterans. I drank too much. I think that without Judi, I could have easily become an alcoholic.

Vietnam veterans enjoy their simple pleasures in a more visceral way than civilians who did not experience war, firsthand, because we experienced life without them. A hot shower is a luxuriant indulgence. Sitting on a bench with your grandchild is a moment to treasure. Sipping a glass of wine, surrounded by family and friends brings a sense of overwhelming happiness and satisfaction. A hot meal is something to savor, and appreciate. If Americans are guilty of anything, it is that they take the bounty of their lives, or certainly the potential quality of life available to them, for granted.

*"Survivor Guilt"* is a malady that is often attributed to Vietnam veterans, I don't believe it is an accurate description, or the primary factor in PTSD, for my generation. The vast majority of veterans have nothing to feel *"guilty"* about. We did what we could, and did nothing intentionally, to cause harm to our buddies, or to leave them vulnerable to death or injury from the Viet Cong. The demon that torments our dreams is the randomness of fate. When I questioned a psychiatrist at the V.A. about my nightmare, I couldn't understand why my dreams would be dominated by the image of a body that I didn't even <u>SEE</u>! Grif and Freddie described it to me, but it stuck in my head, for decades. The doctor told me that I *"empathized"* with the poor soul who

had been tortured and killed by the V.C. It could have been me. It wasn't guilt, per se. It was the unnerving thought that it could have been me. How did I survive, without a scratch?

After my boat captain ordered me twice to crank in our mine sweep gear and twice, the rockets missed, I cursed God in furious rage. I harbored anger for years. One evening, I was expressing that anger to my brother-in-law, Dave Elder. He pointed out the fact that I came out of the two incidents unscathed, and perhaps my anger at God was misplaced. For years, I overlooked that obvious fact.

All my life, I have wondered why I was so blessed to come home, marry, have children and have a good life. At the same time, it greatly saddens me that so many of those I served with did not have that blessing. They are forever in my thoughts and prayers.

I don't know if I am here today because of fate, serendipity, chance, destiny, fortune, providence, luck, Kismet, Karma, or the Hand of God. I'm just grateful. Today, I think of the story, *"Footprints in the Sand."* I cursed God, because I thought he was toying with me, yet, I came home without any visible wounds. It can't be because I'm any different, or better, than others who died, or suffered injuries. I'm not. Somehow, for some reason, I've been blessed. I've had an angel on my shoulder. I don't know why. I simply drew the "lucky straw" in Vietnam. At one time, I felt I was destined to perform some great deed, like saving a busload of kids from going over a cliff. That never happened. Now, I assume, I was supposed to get married, have children and have grandchildren. Perhaps one of them will save a busload of kids.

On October 8th, 1993, my friend, Gary Chastain, the decorated *"Sky Soldier"* of the 173rd Airborne, suddenly died of a heart attack, while lying on his couch. Gary was a trim, fit, young man of 47. His death shook me to my core. Naturally, anyone who loses a friend is hit by it, but for me, the shock was multiplied because I had assumed that I no longer had to worry about good friends dying too young. I told Judi that I thought Gary and I would enjoy our friendship and grow old together.

A few days later, I gave Gary's eulogy, at Jefferson Barracks National Cemetery, at a ceremonial area, prior to his private burial. Days after that, I went to the cemetery to visit Gary's gravesite. As I looked at the long row of freshly dug graves, continuing into a dozen open graves being dug by an equipment operator, I searched for Gary's name. A worker approached me and asked if he could help. I explained that I was looking for Gary Chastain's grave site. The worker casually explained that it is hard to keep up with the pace of the burials because *"that Agent Orange stuff is really knocking off those Vietnam veterans."* Gary is lying high on a beautiful, peaceful hill, surrounded by good men, not far from my father. Weeks after Gary died, I dreamed that he stood by my bedside and told me not to worry about him, that he was fine.


Every once in a while, when fellow *"River Rat"* veteran friends of mine discuss the war, we wonder out loud whether or not the effort was worth it. I vacillate between hopeful optimism and pessimistic despair on that judgement. There was an incident, several years ago, that gave me a warm glow of gratification that we DID accomplish something. I was grocery shopping, wearing a leather jacket that says *"Vietnam Veteran,"* and has some patches from the Mobile Riverine Force. A voice from behind me said; *"Thank you for your service, sir!"* I turned around to see a young man of Asian descent. His hand was out, to shake mine. I shook his hand and told him that I appreciated it and that he struck me as someone who was either active duty, or a veteran, himself. He smiled and said that yes, he was active duty. He was a sergeant in the U.S. Air Force and he was home on leave from Iraq. He was in the process of helping shut the base down.

He told me his name was Tom and that he always thanked Vietnam vets he met. I'll never forget his reason. He told me his father was in the South Vietnamese Navy, and that when Saigon fell, his father was put into a *"re-education camp."* While his father was in the prison camp, men came to their home and started to take their property. His mother tried to stop them. He said one of the men hit his mother in the mouth with the butt of his AK-47. His voice trailed off as he told me he saw things a boy shouldn't see. I can only imagine. When his father got out of the *"re-education camp,"* he told his family they had to get out of Vietnam, that there was no future for them, in the country of their birth. They made their way out to sea, going from one country to another, until they finally made it to America. He told me that because of Vietnam veterans, tens of thousands of Vietnamese people got *"a taste of freedom."* He told me there are Vietnamese all over the world, living in freedom today, because we gave them that taste. That is why he thanks every Vietnam veteran he sees. He went on to tell me that he told the men and women who worked under his leadership in Iraq, that they were giving the people of Iraq a *"taste of freedom,"* today, and that because of them, future generations of Iraqi people will be free.

When I returned home with the groceries, I tried to tell Judi what I had just heard, but every time I tried to tell the story, my voice broke and I was too overwhelmed to tell the story. It took hours before I could attempt to get the story out without the emotional impact of his message making me break down. Tom's message to me was the most uplifting, reassuring message I had heard since the day I came home from Vietnam. I want all of my Brother's In Arms, and their families to hear it, too. We <u>NEED</u> to know some good came of it.

I was able to attend a reunion of the Mobile Riverine Force Association, in San Diego, in 1998, with Judi. That is the only MRFA reunion Judi has attended. For her, the memories of that year are too painful, and she simply wants to forget them. At the same time, she understands my desire and need to attend them. I was thrilled to see men I had not seen since Vietnam. I was elated to see Tex Frank, who was badly wounded in the July 13th ambush at "Snoopy's Nose," in 1968. Tex lost one eye, but he looked great and had enjoyed a career in teaching and real estate. I was terribly saddened to learn that he died in a motorcycle crash, on August 7th, 1999, just before our reunion at the end of that month.

**From left to right, Frank *"Little One"* Springer, Tex Frank, Ralph Bigelow, and me.**

**My dad, Dale, and I, at a Mobile Riverine Force Association Reunion.**

I attended Mobile Riverine Force Association reunions in 1997, 1999, and 2001, with my Dad, Dale. Dad had not been away from Mom, for sixty years, except for when he was in the Army occupation forces, in Italy, at the end of WWII. On the first night of the first reunion, we went to dinner, with a large group. Dad looked at the menu, then whispered to me, *"Do you think it would be O.K. if I just ordered appetizers and dessert?"* I told him to order whatever he wanted, although I put it a little more colorfully than that. He ordered stuffed mushrooms, followed by a hot fudge sundae. That night, I was playing poker and drinking, with the guys. Around midnight, I told them that I better get my dad off to bed, since he was getting up in his years. I turned from the table and saw him drinking a beer with the guys and having the time of his life! After the first reunion, my mom insisted she wanted to go along, but knowing how it would change the nature of our son/father long weekend, we came up with excuses why that wouldn't work.

My father, Dale, passed away on August 16th, 2003, two weeks before that year's Mobile Riverine Force Association Reunion. My son, Chris, joined me on that reunion, and every one, since.

**Chris and I, at the 2015 Mobile Riverine Force Association Reunion. The father/son MRFA Reunion Weekends continue.**

When I retired in 2009, my mind was no longer occupied with working and career. It drifted more towards my Vietnam memories and the nightmares came more often. Judi encouraged me to go to the Veterans Administration and undergo counseling. I was apprehensive, but agreed that it might be beneficial. I began counseling at the V.A. Hospital at Jefferson Barracks, in St. Louis, Missouri. It was comprised of three elements. We had some *"classroom"* education on PTSD, including its history and the various things it had been called, through different wars, such as *"Soldier's Heart," "Battle Fatigue," "Shell Shock,"* etc. We had *"one on one"* counseling. We also had group sessions, which were emotional and intense. It included men who fought in Vietnam, Iraq, and Afghanistan.

One of the young men in the group was roughly my son's age. He had already tried to kill himself, once. A friend of his died in a helicopter training crash. He came upon his body, shortly after, in a following chopper. He told us his friend looked like he was sleeping, except for a small cut on his lip. He had dreams in which his friend came to him, telling him to join him. I was terribly afraid the young man would kill himself between each session. I worried about him, constantly. I gave him my name and phone number, telling him to call me, should he feel the need.

Another man in the group was an Army Vietnam veteran. His story was riveting. He told us that one day, as the M-60 gunner for his unit, he was riding atop an APC tracked vehicle, as part of a larger column of APC's. He had extra belts of ammo across his chest. He spotted a dog, lying by the side of the dirt road that had been run over by one of the APC's. He said that from its front legs, back, it was *"flat as a pancake."* As his APC passed, the dog suddenly lifted his head and stared into the eyes of the soldier. Twenty minutes later, the APC's were ambushed. The soldier jumped off the top of the APC and began to run, but the weight of his M-60, and the ammo was so great, that his femur snapped into a compound fracture, pushing through his pants leg. He laid in the mud, while bullets splashed all around him. After what seemed an eternity, he heard footsteps coming towards him. He didn't know if they were Viet Cong, or his buddies. They were his buddies. The soldier was medevacked out of the area, for immediate medical attention and ultimately, came home. He never got to say *"Goodbye"* to his buddies that he had spent eleven months with, in combat. Can you guess HIS nightmare? He sees the dog, lifting his head and staring into his eyes.

Oddly enough, I don't recall even one of the men in the group saying their nightmares were of actual combat. Mine were not. Most people would expect that any combat veteran's nightmares would exclusively be a reliving of combat experiences. The mind works in mysterious ways. For whatever reason, the combination of the classroom PTSD education, the group counseling, and the one-on-one talks, helped tremendously.

In meeting with different doctors in the V.A., one disputed my PTSD, saying that I seemed to be *"bright,"* and that I *"smiled a lot."* He also said that there was construction on the floor above us that *"sounded like a machine gun,"* and that I *"didn't jump."* In my appeal, I explained that PTSD doesn't have anything to do with how bright, or intelligent anyone is. It was as if he was saying that he expected only stupid men to have PTSD. I then described the firefight in which I not only smiled, but laughed, hysterically, while firing my 20MM cannon at the enemy. I couldn't believe that a psychiatrist would believe that the act of smiling would imply there was no evidence of PTSD. As for the noise above us. I noted that I had spent an entire year firing .30 caliber machine guns, .50 caliber machine guns and 20MM cannons. I fired many thousands of rounds. I knew the different sounds of various weapons, whether I was firing them or they were being fired at me. I inquired as to how many of those weapons the doctor had experience in firing, and how much did he know about what they sounded like. I explained that I didn't hear anything that sounded like them, coming from the floor above us. I would like to have had his "expert opinion" on the auditory signatures of various automatic weapons.

Many times, over the course of my life, I have wondered if I had it in my power to have changed my fate and not served in Vietnam, would I have chosen to avoid it. I have vacillated back and forth. Initially, I believed that I would have avoided it. Today, I would not. For better, or for worse, it is who I am. I've tried to make this book an *"open kimono"* representation of my experience, with all my faults, frailties and vulnerabilities. One thought stands out. When we came home, we were hated and vilified, for decades. Despite that, most of us stood proud. When Uncle Sam called, we stood up. We fought for our country. We fought for our lives. We fought for each other. We bled. We lived. We died. It always seemed we were supposed to be ashamed of our service, but we never were. We went through the crucible. Nobody can take that from us.

As I get older, I am struck by not only the passing of people in my life, but also things that meant so much in my youth, or during my Navy years. My high school, Mercy High, in University City, Missouri, was vacated in 1985. It was torn down in 1997, to make way for a grocery store.

The USS Enterprise (CVAN-65), was deactivated on December 1, 2012, and decommissioned, on February 3, 2017. Her namesake, the ninth USS Enterprise (CVN-80), is scheduled to be in operation sometime in 2025, to 2027. She will be 10,000 tons heavier than *The Big E."* She will be the third "Supercarrier" in the Gerald R. Ford class.

The USS Hunley (AS-31), was only seven years old when I served aboard her. The Hunley was decommissioned from the regular Navy in 1995 and transferred to the U.S. Maritime Commission. In 2007, she was sold for scrap.

Hard, documented evidence on the disposition of the River Assault Boats of the Mobile Riverine Force is difficult to come by, but it is believed that the government of Vietnam eventually sold the entire fleet of boats to Japan, for scrap. There is only one boat left in the United States. It is a CCB (Command and Communications Boat), which is on display within the U.S. Navy Base, in San Diego, at the Vietnam Unit Memorial Monument. You are invited to visit their website, at http://vummf.org/#.

**Photo courtesy Vietnam Unit Memorial Monument**

My high school, "The Big E," the boats of the Mobile Riverine Force," the USS Hunley, and I have all been decommissioned and retired. I thank God for giving me the wife, family, friends, and life that He gave me. I feel more blessed than I ever deserved. I can't explain how, or why, but I have always felt certain that somehow Judi helped me make it through Vietnam. When I came home, she was my shelter in the storm. I could not have made it, without her.

One of the popular expressions in Vietnam was, *"Once you get back to "the world," it's all gravy!"*

*"The world,"* was *"home,"* in the United States of America. It meant that once you got home, the rest of your life was a bonus. It was a blessing that so many didn't have the opportunity to enjoy. It didn't mean we wouldn't have problems. It meant that compared to what we went through in Vietnam, we would have it made.

There has never been a day in my life that I doubted the truth in it.

Towards the end of my PTSD sessions with the Veterans Administration psychiatrist, I became alarmed at a disturbing change. My nightmare evolved into something different. I began to have nightmares of urban combat, here. I would awake in the morning, with aching forearms, from firing semiautomatic handguns, in my sleep. When I went to the counselor, concerned over the development. He broke into a big smile and said, *"Oh! That's good news!"* Stunned, I asked him why it was good news. He told me, *"You're coming home! You are leaving Vietnam."* He assured me that soon, those nightmares would end. They did. After almost fifty years, I was really, truly home.

# Epilogue
## The Vietnam War and My Band of Brothers

While I was back in the United States, Frank Springer and the rest of the crew of Tango 131-9 was training their replacement crew, in Vietnam. The replacements weren't excited about their boat assignment. Tango 9 was considered a jinxed boat, since it recorded the first KIA for River Assault Squadron 13, when William Taylor was killed and members of the crew were wounded. During the days of training, a replacement Mark 19 gunner was wounded while firing the boats grenade launcher during a practice exercise.

We had a reverence for the flags of our boats. Over time, they became frayed and faded, tattered and torn, just as we did. When it came time to replace the *Stars and Stripes* on Tango 9, as the boat was being turned over to a new crew, my old crew played a hand of *"Show Down,"* for the honor of taking the battered flag home. Frank Springer won the hand with a pair of Jacks. He treasures it to this day.

Randy Peat was a Third Class Gunner's Mate, on T-132-12. He was second in command, to his Boat Captain, a Boatswain's Mate, Petty Officer, First Class. On March 25th, Randy's boat was on B.I.D. patrol, circling the Benewah, outside Dong Tam harbor. They were ordered into Dong Tam, to pick up supplies. On the way into Dong Tam, a sampan approached their boat from a cluster of hootches, just outside Dong Tam. The boat captain decided that while the rest of the crew went into Dong Tam, he would visit the hootches with the "Mama-San" in the sampan, to enjoy some cold beers, or perhaps, some other form of *"entertainment."*

On the return trip out, the boat captain was nowhere to be seen. It put Randy on the spot. If he followed regulations, he would have reported the unauthorized absence of his boat captain, but he just couldn't do that to the guy. He wanted to give him a break, so he kept quiet about his boat captain being "AWOL" (Absent Without Leave). As you will see, the events that followed, made that a tortuous decision.

**March 26, 1969 - St. Louis Post Dispatch front page article.**
**"Big U.S. Base Shelled; Ammunition Explodes, Helicopters Destroyed. Reds Use Biggest Mortars"**
*"Heavy Communist mortar salvos struck the biggest United States base in the Mekong Delta today, demolishing the Ninth Infantry Division's ammunition dump and forcing the evacuation of half of the sprawling complex.*

*U.S. military sources said barrages from the biggest mortars in the guerrilla's Vietnam arsenal damaged or destroyed six helicopters, the copter pad, a mess hall and several other wooden buildings on the U.S. Army-Navy base. These sources said three Americans were killed and 65 wounded in the attack. The U.S. Command said casualties and damage were "light to moderate."*

*Rarely do Communist shelling's, however heavy, cause more than light damage to big U.S. bases. This time, the sources said, hundreds of men fled from the Navy portion of the complex to escape more explosions in fuel stores. The base at Dong Tam, 42 miles southwest of Saigon, is headquarters for the Ninth Division and has an adjacent naval facility where ships of the division's mobile riverine force are repaired."*

As Randy watched the ammo dump blow up, two thoughts came to him. The first, was that they killed his boat captain! The second, was that he would be court marshaled, for not reporting the absence. Still, he kept silent. His boat was sent into Dong Tam to assist in any way possible. After working to patch things up as much as possible, his boat began its return to the relative safety of the MRB, outside Dong Tam harbor. On the way out, the crew spotted their errant, AWOL captain, waving frantically to them from a nearby sampan. Randy told him he was never so glad to see ANYBODY! He asked him how he survived the attack of the night before. His captain explained that when the explosions began and bullets were flying, he saw the Mama-San move to a corner of the hootch and throw back a mat, which covered a hole in the dirt floor hootch. It was a shelter, made for just that sort of emergency.

Randy was there when an ASPB boat captain took a rocket propelled grenade through his chest. In Randy's nightmare, he was standing on a PBR, which he had never set foot on, when someone yelled *"Grenade!"* In his nightmare, two grenades went off, sending shrapnel through the gunnels of the PBR. As he looked down at his body, the same jagged shapes of shrapnel holes that were in the gunnels of the PBR, were in his body. As he looked down, his *"life juices,"* his blood, poured out of him. The worst part of his nightmare was not that he was dying, but that as he fell to the deck, he could not fight back. His nightmare stayed with him his entire life, until seeking help in his retirement.

Upon returning home in April of 1969, Randy, his brother and another partner, built a successful software company. He married his wonderful wife, Madelynn, in 1979, and have three children. Randy is an Agent Orange related cancer survivor. He still has the patched up uniform he wore home from Vietnam.

**Randy Peat, with an M-79 Grenade Launcher, playing with Vietnamese kids, at in his Mark 19 mount.**

On that same day, my old crewmates from Tango 9 had arrived at Dong Tam. *Little One* Springer recalled that he had gone to the Enlisted Men's club with a friend from his home town. Afterwards, he returned to their hootch, and fell asleep in the top bunk. He awoke to the deafening sound of the ammo dump exploding and a truss from the hootch's roof, falling across his legs. He got his legs out from under the truss and jumped out of bed to get to a bunker. The floor of the hootch was covered in broken glass from light fixtures. The first thing he noticed was that many of the hootches had been turned into nothing more than piles of lumber. Exploded ordnance from the ammo dump was lying everywhere. *Flechettes* from exploded *Bee Hive* rounds, littered the dirt, along with live ammo and brass casings. He entered a bunker, but after a few minutes, wanted out. A soldier told him he had to stay, threatening to shoot *Little One*, if he tried to leave. Frank shoved the soldier aside and left the bunker. He commandeered a pickup truck, and took wounded to the Army side of the base, to get first-aid.

Frank Springer and the crew of T-131-9, caught their *Freedom Bird* home, on Easter Sunday, April 9th, 1969. Frank and his lovely wife Mable, were married in 1976 and have three children. Frank worked as a mechanic during his career and is now retired. He has had recurring nightmare visions of "running the Mekong" and seeing Viet Cong hanging on meat hooks, along the bank. Frank's nightmare of the Mekong wasn't based upon anything he had actually seen. Each of us had our own demons that haunted us at night. To this day, many of us wake at night, once again feeling bugs crawling over our face and bodies. Frank confided that he still sleeps with a towel over his face, to keep bugs off of him. When summer arrives, the warm weather puts me back in Vietnam and I toss and turn, wiping imagined insects away from my face and body.

At that time, Harry Hahn served on Monitor 131-1. The last 4 1/2 months, he was on Riv Ron 13 staff as squadron radioman. Harry spent a lot of time in the Communications Shack in Dong Tam, then on a CCB

(Command and Communications Boat) on the Grand Canal, for his last eight weeks. Harry was in over 200 firefights. He gave this account of the mortar attack,

*"The round that hit the ammo dump came in around midnight. This was my first night in country. Because there was an earlier mortar attack, I knew where the bunker was. I ran out the door of the hootch and saw the ammo dump. It was burning bright red, like a road flare. I dove in between a hootch and a bunker as the dump blew. Chunks of shrapnel were flying past me. I ran from the first bunker, through to the other side of the base. As I passed through the army barracks I raided one of them for an M-14 and an M-16 plus ammo. There was a possibility of a ground attack and I did not want to be unarmed."*

**Harry Hahn, loading a 105 round, on his monitor, going for a ride, and sitting on his boat.**

After Harry left the service he used his technical skills in communications and retired from a company after forty years, where he was Sales Manager and Regional Manager. In 1972, Harry married Chris Kieklak. They are still married, after 45 years. Like many of us, the *"Nightmare of the Mekong"* still plagues Harry.

*"I have a reoccurring dream every once in a while, about going through a canal at low tide and the VC shooting down at us from the bank. In the dream, we can't elevate the guns high enough! I have another reoccurring dream of fighting in the delta and then it morphs into a more modern boat where we end up fighting in a bay! Your dreams are your fears played out!"*

Soon after the ammo dump blew, Randy Peat was finishing his tour of duty. His boat crew was turning their boat over to a new crew. Randy believes the Viet Cong knew that, and decided to test them. It would not be difficult for the V.C. to arrive at that appraisal. You could spot a new guy, a mile away. Their uniforms weren't raggedy, like everybody else's. Every day, whenever they went out on operations, whether it was down *Rocket Alley*, or at *The Crossroads*, they were ambushed. That went on for two or three weeks. Randy had a nice set of *"greens"* set aside for his trip home, hanging under the helicopter pad, over their well deck. After one firefight, he was frustrated to find his uniform riddled with shrapnel.

In one ambush, his boat was hit from both banks. The crew quickly returned fire. After the enemy was either killed, or withdrew, the boat captain called out, *"Cease fire!"* A few seconds later, Randy heard an explosion in the port 20MM gun mount, right next to his Mark 19 grenade launcher. Quickly, he jumped out of the top of his gun mount and looked into the port 20MM mount. The gun, ammo belt, and the gunner were all on fire, due to oil lubrication on the ammo. The gunner wasn't quick enough to clear the chamber of his gun, and a round cooked off. After the first round exploded, four more, in succession, ratcheted into the gun, exploding. The port gunner was hit with shrapnel, from his chest to his shoes.

Randy, acting on instinct, ripped off his flak jacket and threw it over the gun, protecting the gunner from any additional injury. In doing so, he left himself completely exposed to enemy fire. At the same moment, their boat captain appeared under the gun mount with a fire extinguisher, and extinguished the fire. Thanks to good training and extraordinary bravery, the fire was out in about three seconds.

Five days later, Randy Peat was on his way home, in his patched up *"greens."* When he landed at San Francisco with two of his buddies, hippie protesters gave them a hard time. A huge brawl was avoided only because a cab driver who was also a veteran, intervened and put a stop to it. Randy and his buddies could have easily ended up in jail. The hippies could have easily ended up in the hospital!

That ugly homecoming was significantly offset when the stewardess on his flight home asked Randy if he was returning from Vietnam. When he replied that he was, she promptly escorted him to a seat in First Class.

Gerald Burleigh went through River Warfare School at the time I was leaving Vietnam. He arrived at Dong Tam in May, of 1969. He was assigned to T-132-13, which became T27 after River Assault Squadrons 13 and 15 were combined. The group of young men that Gerald arrived with relieved Randy Peat and the men with him. During the time of Gerald's tour of duty, the 9th Infantry Division's presence was being drawn down. Gerald's boat carried the 9th Infantry Division until August, of 1969, when they were being transitioned home. After that, his boats carried Vietnamese troops.

Gerald's most vivid combat memory is from a terrible firefight in May, of 1970. His boat was saturated with six B-40 rocket propelled grenades as the Viet Cong tried to take out an 81MM mortar that was mounted on Gerald's boat. He was wounded on June 22nd, 1969, in Tay Ninh, northwest of Saigon. In that firefight, Gerald took shrapnel through his hand.

The nature of operations changed, at least for Gerald's boat, over the course of his tour. At first, his boat hauled Vietnamese troops into combat. As time progressed, however, they spent more time doing night patrols and ambushes, or setting up river blockades. Boats would set up blocking stations, one kilometer apart. Gerald's boat operated in the Chau Duc area, northeast of Vung Tau and far-east of Saigon, an area my boat never operated in. His boats conducted blockading operations on the Grand Canal, from Aug to May with no chow hall hot meals, or showers.

When Gerald came home, he too struggled with PTSD. Due to hypervigilance, he *"could hear an ant walk across a carpet."* When he was on the rivers or lakes in his home state of Texas, he couldn't help being alert for potential ambush spots.

Like many of us, Gerald had nightmares. In his, he was in the Navy reserve, and was repeatedly sent back to Vietnam. Sometimes, he was on his same boat, with the same crew. Sometimes he was on a different boat. In his dreams, he would explain that he had aged and shouldn't be there.

Each of us dealt with our own versions of night terrors. None were alike. Gerald and his wife, Sheila were married eleven months before he left for Vietnam, and they remain together, today. In 2018, they will celebrate Fifty Years, together!

**The Mobile Riverine Force was awarded the Presidential Unit Citation for "Extraordinary Heroism" between January 25th and July 5th, 1969.**

*"For extraordinary heroism and outstanding performance of duty from 25 January through 5 July 1969 while engaged in armed conflict against enemy forces in the Mekong Delta region of the Republic of Vietnam. With enemy forces planning to launch a large-scale, winter-spring offensive against Saigon and other cities of the upper Mekong Delta, the ships and assault craft of Task Force 117 provided waterborne mobile support to United States Army, Vietnamese Army, and Vietnamese Marine Corps troops. By riverine assault operations preempting enemy offensive operations, the Force made a significant contribution to thwarting the threat to Saigon and the Mekong Delta. Surprise attacks and routine fire fights on the narrow streams and canals were an almost daily occurrence, while rocket and mining attacks against the Mobile Riverine Bases were an ever-present danger. The courage and determination of Task Force 117 personnel contributed significantly to the successful completion of each Force objective. The skill, fortitude, perseverance, and sustained outstanding performance of the officers and men of the United States Navy Element of the Mobile Riverine Force reflected great credit upon themselves and were in keeping with the highest traditions of the United States Naval Service."*

**July 8, 1969**. The first U.S. troop withdrawal took place when 800 men from the 9th Infantry Division were sent home from the Mekong Delta.

**August 4**, 1969. Henry Kissinger met with delegates from North Vietnam in Paris in secret.

There is a book titled *"Woodstock."* The subtitle reads; *"The event that defined a generation."* The Woodstock festival took place in **August, of 1969**. It stuns me that this event could be referred to as a defining moment of my generation. Woodstock was a drunken, drugged-out music concert. It took place while young men who answered the calls of President Kennedy and President Johnson were dying.

**September 2, 1969**. Ho Chi Minh died of a heart attack. His successor, Le Duan, publicly read the last will of Ho Chi Minh, which urged the North Vietnamese to continue their fight *"until the last Yankee has gone."*

**September 5, 1969**. Lt. William Calley was charged with the murder of Vietnamese civilians at My Lai.

**September 16, 1969**. Nixon ordered the withdrawal of 35,000 soldiers from Vietnam and a reduction in the draft.

October 23rd, 1969 was a day that RM3 (Radioman 3rd Class) Ralph Bakle will never forget. It was the day his boat captain took him, Boyer, the boat's "snipe," and Ross, their Gunner's Mate 3rd Class, before Lt Commander Connolly, for Captain's Mast, for falling asleep on watch. Each of them were busted one pay grade and forfeited ninety days of pay. That evening, at dusk, their boat headed out as the second boat in a column of ten boats. Ralph was on the stern of his boat, taking down laundry he had washed in the river and hung up to dry. All of a sudden, rockets started flying. The first rocket hit *"Brass Rail Five,"* the code name for the squadron commander, in the lead boat. One rocket hit the water, eighteen inches below Ralph's feet. Ralph jumped to the 20MM mount on top of the boat and started laying down all the fire power he could muster. The enemy fire was so intense, it knocked out both the engines and the transmission of Ralph's ASPB. Ralph lost power to his 20MM, so he jumped to the .50 caliber machine gun on the stern of the boat. He fired so much, it burned up the gun barrel. They were dead in the water and receiving rockets and automatic weapon's fire. A trainee on the boat was hiding, laying over the cover to the boat's engines. All five of the Vietnamese "Ruff Puff's" they carried, were wounded. When they were calling for help over the radio, there was confusion over the identity of the boat needing help. When Ralph called for help, another boat pushed them to the river bank, so they could patch holes in the boat, to keep it from sinking.

Ralph, Ross, and Boyer performed so well, their boat captain put them all in for Silver Stars. In a discussion on the Command and Communications Boat, Lt. Commander Connoly expressed his exasperation that earlier in the day, the three were the *"scourge of the Navy,"* only to be called *"superheroes,"* that evening! The Lt. Commander ripped the Captain's Mast page out of his book, adding that he was *"ripping a page from history!"*

Ralph Bakle doesn't suffer nightmares of combat. He relives his days in Nam, over, and over. He doesn't sleep. He takes naps, normally forty-five minutes at a time. His biggest problem stems from *waterboarding* during his S.E.R.E. training. When he naps, he has to have a fan blowing air over his face. He has a fear of drowning. Ralph was twenty-five years old when he went through S.E.R.E., and admits to being somewhat of a *smart-ass*. His training class size was only about a third of the average size. Ralph believes that gave the instructors more time to spend on each individual. They repeatedly dunked him head first in 55 gallon barrels of water, and poured water over his face while he was lying on a slant board. He is proud that he NEVER BROKE! I suspect the reason Ralph's training class underwent waterboarding and mine did not, is because Ralph's class went through the training in June, and my class went through it during freezing temperatures, in January.

Today, Ralph attends weekly PTSD meetings, and reaches out to help others dealing with the scars of combat. It is not lost on veterans of S.E.R.E. training that average Americans seem to have more concern with the treatment and waterboarding of actual terrorists, than the often WORSE treatment of Americans who go through our own military training.

Ralph and his wife, Peggy, have been married for forty-seven years and have four children, Debbie, Mark, Cathy, and Kim. He also has seven grandchildren. Ralph is retired from management positions in the automotive industry. He continues to serve his country as President and Historian of his local Vietnam Veterans of America, chapter #1027, America Legion Post 303, and Veterans of Foreign Wars, Post 9820.

RM3 Ralph Bullethead To Canal Sep 1969

Ralph at Song Ong Doc on M152-1 1970

**November 22, 1969**. According to a Detroit Free Press reporter, Jane Fonda, whose wealth is estimated at $120 Million, told students at Michigan State University,

### *"I would think that if you understood what Communism was, you would hope…, you would pray on your knees, that we would someday become communists."*

**December 1, 1969**. The first draft lottery since WW II was held. Each day of the year is assigned a number. Birthdays with low numbers are more likely to be drafted.

**December 15, 1969**. Nixon ordered the withdrawal of 50,000 more soldiers out of Vietnam.

**December 31, 1969**. To date, 40,024 American servicemen had lost their lives in Vietnam. The years 1968 and 1969 accounted for approximately 42% of the war's total death casualties.

**April 20, 1970**. Nixon withdrew another 150,000 Americans from Vietnam.

**May 4, 1970**. National Guardsmen shot and killed four students and wounded four at Kent State University in Ohio, during protests.

**June 22, 1970**. The U.S. stopped usage of chemical defoliants, like "Agent Orange," in Vietnam.

**June 24, 1970**. The U.S. Senate repealed the 1964 Gulf of Tonkin Resolution.

**August 11, 1970**. American border defense positions were taken over by South Vietnamese troops.

**November 20, 1970**. American troop levels were reduced to 336,600.

**January 4, 1971**. *"The end is in sight."* President Richard Nixon

**March 1, 1971**. A bomb exploded in the Capitol building in Washington, D.C., causing an estimated $300,000 in damage. The *"Weather Underground,"* a radical leftist group, cofounded by William Ayers, claimed credit for the bombing, which was done in protest of the ongoing U.S. supported Laos invasion. William Ayers, who launched President Obama's political career in his Chicago home, was never prosecuted for his involvement in the Weather Underground and spent his career in academia, promoting his ideology.

**April 19, 1971**.  The Vietnam Veterans Against the War began a week of protests, nationwide.

**April 22, 1971**.  John Kerry testified in front of the Senate Foreign Relations Committee.  Kerry spoke for members of his Vietnam Veterans Against the War, group's *"Winter Soldiers."*  He began,

*"I would like to talk, representing all those veterans, and say that several months ago in Detroit, we had an investigation at which over 150 honorably discharged and many very highly decorated veterans testified to war crimes committed in Southeast Asia, not isolated incidents but crimes committed on a day-to-day basis with the full awareness of officers at all levels of command....*

*They told the stories at times they had personally raped, cut off ears, cut off heads, taped wires from portable telephones to human genitals and turned up the power, cut off limbs, blown up bodies, randomly shot at civilians, razed villages in fashion reminiscent of Ghengis Khan, shot cattle and dogs for fun, poisoned food stocks, and generally ravaged the countryside of South Vietnam in addition to the normal ravage of war and the normal and very particular ravaging which is done by the applied bombing power of this country."*  Further adding, *"These were not isolated incidents but crimes committed on a day-to-day basis with the full awareness of officers at all levels of command."*

One of the great ironies and blatant fabrications of John Kerry's fables is that on one hand, he slandered America, the military, and all Vietnam veterans with the idea that widespread atrocities occurred with *"the full awareness of officers at all levels of command,"* despite the fact that we were specifically taught that we had not only the right, but the responsibility to refuse any order that was unlawful, or unethical.  A shining example of this would be Hugh Clowers Thompson Jr., a U.S. Army Captain, and formerly a Warrant Officer in the 123rd Aviation Battalion, 23rd Infantry Division, who played a critical role in ending the My Lai Massacre, on March 16, 1968.  Thompson and his OH-23 helicopter crew, Glenn Andreotta and Lawrence Colburn, stopped many killings by threatening and blocking soldiers of Company C, 1st Battalion, 20th Infantry Regiment, 11th Brigade, 23rd, Infantry Division.  If the My Lai Massacre was done with the *"full awareness of officers at all levels of command,"* how, and why would these men have stopped it?

Kerry's inconsistency and ignorance is further displayed in Douglas Brinkley and John Kerry's book, *"Tour of Duty."*  On page 298, Kerry refers to *"Operation Sea Lords,"* as *"Captain Hoffman's pet project,"* when it was actually an enormous and pivotal strategy, coming down from "the top," and carried out *with the full awareness of officers at all levels of command."*  In other words, Kerry claimed that a project and strategy that came from the top, with the full awareness and buy-in of all levels of command, was a local *"pet project,"* of his own commanding officer, while every aberration of local atrocity that may have happened, was done with the full knowledge and blessing of the entire chain of command.  His assessments of the two disparate issues lacks any semblance of intelligence, logic, or reason.

*"Stolen Valor"* usually refers to someone who *"falsely represents oneself as having received any U.S. military decoration or medal."*  John Kerry stands alone in the disastrous impact of his *"Stolen Valor."*  John Kerry often drew the parallels between himself, and John F. Kennedy.  It is brought up, ad nauseam, throughout *"Tour of Duty."*  They had the same initials.  Both served on fast Navy boats.  Both liked sailing. John Kerry served in Vietnam and saw combat, so his *"Stolen Valor"* isn't because he lied about that.  He couldn't build his political fortune upon his small part in the Vietnam War.  He wasn't that special.  I served with many men who did more, with more humility and character than John Kerry could ever muster.  In order to set himself apart, he set out to destroy the reputation of the almost three million American fighting men who served in Vietnam.  He decided to stand on the carcass of THEIR honor, in order to inflate his own, and to launch his political career.  It was the most cynical, despicable calculation a would-be president could possibly make.

Reports of the number of suicides committed by Vietnam veterans varies widely.  Some estimates put the total figure at somewhere between 50,000 and 100,000.  Combat, by itself, can cause Post Traumatic Stress, but once you add testimony such as John Kerry's to the mix, vilifying every combat veteran who served in the Vietnam War, can there be any doubt that John Kerry has the blood of many of those men on his hands?

During the month of April, 1971, while John Kerry was smearing the honor of Vietnam veterans and kicking off his own quest for fame and fortune, 230 American fighting men were being killed in combat, in Vietnam.

In 2004, I was shocked and saddened that John Kerry was the Democrat Party's candidate for president of the United States of America. It wasn't his policies that upset me. It was his anti-American, anti-Vietnam veteran smear campaign. His candidacy wasn't just a slap in the face to Vietnam veterans. It was another spit in the face, punch in the gut, and kick in the balls.

Once again, I thought of the admonition of our S.E.R.E instructors, who chastised my class for not reading the communist propaganda on the bulletin board of the "P.O.W." camp. While most of those who were voting for George W. Bush and against John Kerry read "Unfit for Command," by John E. O'Neill and Jerome R. Corsi, my first priority was to read Douglas Brinkley's romantic tome, glorifying John Kerry's time in the Navy, *"Tour of Duty."* More than anything else, the book was a literary *"selfie,"* published for Kerry's presidential ambitions. The only thing missing was a *"duck face"* pose of Kerry, on the cover.

After reading *"Tour of Duty,"* I wrote an e-mail to Michelle Malkin. I picked apart a number of his falsehoods, lies, and distortions, in his book. She published it on her website. It was shared, thousands of times. A search of "John Kerry Terry Sater," will take you to it. It is titled, "A Vietnam Vet Fisks "Tour of Duty."
John Kerry's political career was based entirely on leveraging his anti-war sentiment, demeaning all of his fellow Vietnam veterans, while portraying himself as the one true hero of the war. John Kerry wasn't just against the war. He was against the men sent to fight the war. My comments here have nothing to do with his ideology. It's not politics. It's personal.

John Kerry's story telling didn't begin, or end with his tales of serving on the Swift Boats. Men who served with him the USS Gridley have torn him apart in similar fashion to what I have done, here. A simple search of "John Kerry USS Gridley Phil Carter RD2" will reveal more of the dishonesty of John Kerry.

**April 29, 1971**. Total American deaths in Vietnam passed 45,000.

**June 22, 1971**. The U.S. Senate passes a non-binding resolution urging the removal of all American troops from Vietnam by year-end

**July 1, 1971**. 6,100 American servicemen left Vietnam, a daily record.

**June 17, 1972**. Five burglars were arrested inside the Watergate building in Washington, attempting to plant microphones in the Democratic National Committee offices, in an attempt to spy on political opposition. It was revealed they had ties to the Nixon White House, ultimately bringing down the Nixon presidency.

**July 18, 1972**. Jane Fonda broadcast anti-war, anti-American propaganda over Hanoi Radio.

**January 27, 1973**, The Paris Peace Accords were signed, with the aim of ending American involvement in the war in Vietnam. The accord called for an immediate cease-fire, and the withdrawal of all American forces within sixty days. Two months later, Nixon met with South Vietnamese President Thieu and promised him a *"severe retaliation"* against North Vietnam should they break the cease-fire.

**July 1, 1973**. President Richard M. Nixon signed the Case-Church Amendment into law. The amendment prohibited further U.S. military activity in Vietnam, Laos and Cambodia unless the president secured Congressional approval in advance. The amendment cut off funding for American support of the Thieu government, allowing North Vietnam and the Viet Cong to violate the Paris Accords with complete impunity.

Tom Bohl, a fellow crewmate of mine on my first boat, T-131-3, passed away on January 6, 1992 due to Agent Orange exposure. He was an Engineman and remained on Tango 3, during his full year.

Ralph Bigelow, whose Tango boat was sunk by a Viet Cong mine at Snoopy's Nose, had a great forty year career with Detroit Edison, as a lineman. He has two great children, in Michelle and Ralph. He also has two lovely grandchildren, Natalie and Whitney. Ralph has expressed his pleasure of knowing and have served with the greatest group of sailors and soldiers he's ever had the honor to know.

Captain Peveril Blundell, who served as a Commanding Officer of River Assault Squadron 13, passed away on October 9, 2003.

During 1999 and 2000, I reconnected with two of my buddies from the group of seventy-two that trained with me and fought with, in River Assault Squadron 13. Bob Grout has been happily married and living in California. He retired as a fireman, at Disneyworld. Bob put me in touch with Rudy Mahanes, who was my crewmate on our first boat, Tango 131-3. Rudy was the one who raised hell on *"The Apple,"* because they had preferential seating for ship's company. Rudy got out of the Navy as a Gunner's Mate, 2nd Class. He had a son, and a grandson. He laughed that his son, Justin, looked just like Rudy did in his pictures from Vietnam. He told me he had contacted Bill *"The Rock"* Martel, once, but had lost his address and phone number. When I heard from Rudy, he was living on his own sail boat, 300' from where he worked, in the Cayman Islands. He was happy to hear that I came home and married Judi. He complimented me for picking such a "good one." Rudy passed away due to cancer, on July 18, 2005. His wife Martha, said of Rudy, *"He was a good friend, good father to his son and a decent human being. He will be missed by all who had the honor of knowing him. Rudy's ashes will be dispersed at sea."*

BMCM Richard E. Twigg (USN Ret.) passed away on February 25, 2011. While in Vietnam Rick served with River Assault Squadron 13 – River Assault Division 131. He was Boat Captain on Tango-131-1 from March 1968 to March 1969. I reported to for a while, before my boat arrived, in Vietnam.

Donald D. *"Mac"* McGriff, my boat captain on T-131-6, passed away on February 12th, 2012, in Baxter, Iowa, leaving his wife, Shirley. I spoke to Mac, not long before he died. He told me he had retired from the Navy, as a Chief Petty Officer, and from the police force. He had a picture of the crew of Tango 6, hanging in his garage. I confided in him that the crew looked up to him as a *father figure,* and asked him how old he was, in Vietnam. He was thirty-one. I was surprised when he told me he wanted to send me a box of home movies from his year in Vietnam. I can only guess that he knew when he spoke to me, that he was going to die, soon, but he didn't tell me. I forwarded the movies to Mike Thom, who spent his entire tour of duty on Tango 6, with Mac.

Mike Thom, my crewmate from T-131-6, got out of the Navy, not long after his tour in Vietnam. He made his career as a pipe fitter. He married his wife, Diane, who goes by the nickname "Red," in 1984. Mike is disabled, due to Agent Orange. He and *"Red"* live in Fort Meyers, Florida.

Glenn Ledford, was my friend, audio tape partner, port 20MM gunner and radioman on T-131-9. He put Vietnam behind him when he came home. After Vietnam, Glenn didn't want anything to do with anything connected with Vietnam. He became an accomplished artist, in oil paintings. I purchased one of his paintings, a few years ago. Glenn passed away on April 14th, 2013, at sixty-five.

Robert Gosnell served in an Army artillery unit, in Vietnam, in 1969. During his tour of duty he was wounded in action and was awarded the Bronze Star. In the course of his duties, he was heavily exposed to the chemical defoliant, *"Agent Orange."* Bob passed away due to cancer, on November 3rd, 2013, at the age of 65. He gave the world many gifts. I am most grateful for the gift he and his wife, Cheryl, gave my family. They gave us their daughter, Tessa, who married my son Chris, on June 18th, 2005.

I support *"The Weinberger Doctrine,"* which later morphed into *"The Powell Doctrine."* Secretary of Defense Caspar Weinberger, under Reagan, in 1984, established the conditions under which U.S. ground combat troops should be committed, or the U.S. becomes involved in any foreign conflicts. The primary elements of the Weinberger Doctrine include 1) There should be no commitment of U.S. forces to combat unless there is a threat to the vital interests of the United States, or a close ally. 2) If our forces are committed, there should be total, overwhelming support, including resources and firepower, to complete the mission and achieve victory. 3) Before any commitment is made, there must be unshakeable support of the people and our leaders. 4) There must be clearly defined political and military objectives going into the conflict and getting out of the conflict. History has shown that the lessons of Vietnam have not been learned, and the principles of the Weinberger Doctrine have never been followed.

Lt. Gen. Barry R. McCaffrey, assistant to the Chairman of the Joint Chiefs of Staff, said to Vietnam veterans and visitors gathered at *"The Wall,"* Memorial Day 1993, that one out of every ten Americans who served in Vietnam was a casualty. 58,169 were killed and 304,000 wounded out of 2.59 million who served. Although the percent who died is similar to other wars, amputations or crippling wounds were 300 percent higher than in World War II. 75,000 Vietnam veterans are severely disabled.

During the 1968 calendar year, 14.501 Americans died in Vietnam. It was the highest casualty year of the war. During the 1969 calendar year, 10,096 Americans gave their last full measure of devotion. The total America KIA in either of those years, exceeds all of the fatalities America has experienced in Iraq and Afghanistan, combined, from 2001, to 2017.

Approximately 66,000 men served in the 9th Infantry Division, in Vietnam. 2,558 of them gave their lives.

Twenty-nine Americans who crewed the support ships of the Mobil Riverine Base gave their lives.

It is difficult to achieve an accurate count of casualties on the River Assault Boats. The formation, growth, and eventual disbanding of the Mobile Riverine Force would appear similar to a *"bell curve,"* if the manpower of the Mobile Riverine Force was plotted at its beginning in 1967, to its peak, in 1968, followed by the eventual *"Vietnamization"* and the turnover of the boats to the South Vietnamese Navy. The most accurate total I have been able to arrive at for total fatalities for River Assault Boat crewmen, is 86. I have seen an estimate that approximately 1,400 sailors manned the boats during the operations of the Mobile Riverine Force. While the number of sailors lost their lives may not be dramatic, to some, the casualty rate certainly was.

An article in the "VFW" magazine; "Soviet Communism's Downfall, 20 Years Ago," begins;

**"Startling finding; according to a citizenship test administered by Newsweek and reported in the March 28 & April 4, 2011, edition, a whopping 73% of Americans could not identify communism as the ideology America opposed during the Cold War."**

To young Americans, the words *"communism," "Marxism"* and *"socialism"* have little or no negative impact. They missed *"The Cold War."* They also missed the *"hot"* wars of Korea and Vietnam. They are oblivious to the murder of sixty million under Stalin and Mao. They are unaware of communist V.C. atrocities, the tens of thousands who perished after the fall of Saigon, or the inhumanity of the *"Killing Fields"* of Cambodia. What they think they know, they've learned from leftist professors preaching utopian collectivist ideology.

My disappointment in our leaders and the American involvement in the war in Vietnam does not mean that I view those who protested against the war in a favorable light. The counter culture protests following the Tet Offensive gave encouragement and comfort to the enemy. It became their realistic and achievable goal to outlast the will of the American public to stomach the weeks, months and years of wounded, dead and dying young men on the nightly news. The enemy would have been more likely to negotiate an honorable peace had it not been for the protest movement.

I am enormously proud of the men I served with. I am grateful that I was honored to fight alongside them, and count them as friends, today. I believe our intentions were honorable and we did our jobs well.

This record clearly shows that our units clearly won the battles of the Mekong Delta. The politicians and protestors lost the war, at home. Still, many confuse the war with the warrior. General Frederick C. Weyand famously told his North Vietnamese counterpart, during negotiations in Hanoi, a week before the fall of Saigon, *"You know, you never beat us on the battlefield."* The North Vietnamese general pondered that remark for a moment and then replied, *"That may be so, but it is also irrelevant."* The truth of that can certainly be debated, but I know that even when the enemy inflicted casualties on the Mobile Riverine Force, they left blood trails and their dead, as they ran from the scene of the battle. WE never ran. We stayed until they were either killed, or slipped away in the night. The skill, courage, and sheer firepower of our river assault boats, artillery, infantry and air power was overwhelming. The front line troops who fought in Vietnam still suffer from a bad rap. They fought well. The war was lost in the United States, not in Vietnam.

My daughter, Dina, offered one answer to the question that has haunted me; *"Why did I come back, when so many others didn't?"* She suggested that perhaps I was meant to tell this story, <u>our</u> story, of the young men of the Mobile Riverine Force, who fought, bled, laughed, cried, lived, and died, on *"The River of Nine Dragons."*

Photo courtesy flickr.com

# Acknowledgements

According to the "Word" program, I spent 292,803 minutes, writing this book. That's 4,880 hours. If I worked on it forty hours a week, that would be the equivalent of two and one third years. I imagine there was close to an equal amount of time spent on the project, off the computer. That's a lot of time, but I could not have accomplished this without my family, my friends, and my Vietnam Band of Brothers. They have helped in every way, imaginable. I can't possibly acknowledge every person by name, but I have to say that at the top of the list stands my wife, Judi, my son, Chris, and my daughter Dina. My nephews, Tom Sater, and Matt Elder, have been invaluable in their assistance. I could not have gotten through the completion of this effort, without all of them.

For additional information, please go to;

"The Mobile Riverine Force Association," "MRFA.org."

*"Muddy Jungle Rivers,"* by Wendell Affield

*"Duty Honor Sacrifice"* by Ralph Christopher

*"Unfit For Command,"* by John E. O'Neill and Jerome R. Corsi, PH.D

*"Tour of Duty."* By Douglas Brinkley

*"The Nightmare of the Mekong"* Facebook page.

Witness to War.org website. Search Terry Sater

Contact the author, at terry.s8er@reagan.com

**A lot has been said about the effects of war, and PTSD. I encourage, I BEG, anyone who lives with the symptoms of PTSD to seek counseling, either privately, or at the Veterans Administration. Don't ignore them, or just try to live with them. Seeking help doesn't make you weak. It makes you stronger! Join the American Legion, or Veterans of Foreign Wars. Talk to other men, or women, who have walked in your shoes, or boots.**

**Veterans Crisis Hotline and Online Chat**
**www.veteranscrisisline.net and 1-800-273-8255 then press 1.**
**Professionally trained clinical staff. Can provide referral to other services, such as substance abuse treatment, marital counseling, treatment for depression and PTSD. Run by the VA. Since 2007. Over 18,000 life-saving interventions. Answered 500,000 calls.**

**National Suicide Prevention Lifeline**
**www.suicidepreventionlifeline.org 1-800-273-TALK (also chat on website).**
**Spanish language line 1-888-628-9454.**
**Funded by the U.S. Department of Health and Human Services**